T0305222

Transnational Corporations and International Law

CORPORATIONS, GLOBALISATION AND THE LAW

Series Editor: Janet Dine, Director, Centre for Commercial Law Studies, Queen Mary College, University of London, UK

This uniquely positioned monograph series aims to draw together high quality research work from established and younger scholars on what is an intriguing and under-researched area of the law. The books will offer insights into a variety of legal issues that concern corporations operating on the global stage, including interaction with WTO, international financial institutions and nation states, in both developing and developed countries. Whilst the underlying foundation of the series will be that of company law, broadly-defined, authors are encouraged to take an approach that draws on the work of other social sciences, such as politics, economics and development studies and to offer an international or comparative perspective where appropriate. Specific topics to be considered will include corporate governance, corporate responsibility, taxation and criminal liability, amongst others. The series will undoubtedly offer an important contribution to legal thinking and to the wider globalisation debate.

Titles in the series include:

Corporate Governance and China's H-Share Market
Alice de Jonge

Corporate Rescue Law – An Anglo-American Perspective
Gerard McCormack

Multinational Enterprises and Tort Liabilities
An Interdisciplinary and Comparative Examination
Muzaffer Eroglu

Perspectives on Corporate Social Responsibility
Edited by Nina Boeger, Rachel Murray and Charlotte Villiers

Corporate Governance in the 21st Century
Japan's Gradual Transformation
Edited by Luke Nottage, Leon Wolff and Kent Anderson

National Corporate Law in a Globalised Market
The UK Experience in Perspective
David Milman

Transnational Corporations and International Law
Accountability in the Global Business Environment
Alice de Jonge

Transnational Corporations and International Law

Accountability in the Global Business Environment

Alice de Jonge

Department of Business Law and Taxation, Faculty of Business and Economics, Monash University, Australia

CORPORATIONS, GLOBALISATION AND THE LAW

Edward Elgar
Cheltenham, UK • Northampton, MA, USA

Published by
Edward Elgar Publishing Limited
The Lypiatts
15 Lansdown Road
Cheltenham
Glos GL50 2JA
UK

Edward Elgar Publishing, Inc.
William Pratt House
9 Dewey Court
Northampton
Massachusetts 01060
USA

A catalogue record for this book is available from the British Library

Library of Congress Control Number: 2010934053

ISBN 978 1 84980 368 7

Typeset by Cambrian Typesetters, Camberley, Surrey
Printed and bound by MPG Books Group, UK

To Ian

Contents

Abbreviations

AIB	Association of International Business
ASX	Australian Securities Exchange
ATCA	Alien Tort Claims Act (US)
BIT	bilateral investment treaty
CLCC	Civil Law Convention on Corruption
COP	Communication on Progress
CSR	corporate social responsibility
ECOSOC	UN Economic and Social Council
EITI	Extractive Industries Transparency Initiative
EPFI	Equator Principles Financial Institution
FDI	foreign direct investment
FDIS	Final Draft International Standard
FSIA	Foreign Sovereign Immunities Act (US)
GATT	General Agreement on Tariffs and Trade
GRI	Global Reporting Initiative
IBA WG	International Bar Association Working Group
ICC	International Criminal Court
ICJ	International Court of Justice
ICL	international criminal law
ICSID	International Centre for Settlement of Investment Disputes
ICTR	International Criminal Tribunal for Rwanda
ICTY	International Criminal Tribunal for the former Yugoslavia
IFC	International Finance Corporation
IFI	international financial institution
ILC	International Law Commission
ILO	International Labour Organization
ISO	International Organization for Standardization
ISO WG	ISO Working Group
MAI	Multilateral Agreement on Investment
MIT	multilateral investment treaty
MNE	multinational enterprise
MoU	Memorandum of Understanding
NAFTA	North American Free Trade Agreement
NCP	National Contact Point
NGO	non-governmental organization

NGPF	Norwegian Government Pension Fund Global
NHRI	national human rights institution
OECD	Organisation for Economic Co-operation and Development
PNG	Papua New Guinea
PRI	Principles for Responsible Investment
RICO	Racketeer Influenced and Corrupt Organizations Act (US)
SIF	Social Investment Forum
SR	social responsibility
SRSG	Special Representative of the Secretary-General
TNC	transnational corporation
TVPA	Torture Victim Protection Act (US)
UN	United Nations
UNCLOS	United Nations Convention on the Law of the Sea
UNCTAD	United Nations Conference on Trade and Development
WHO	World Health Organization
WTO	World Trade Organization

1. The corporation: a good tool but a bad master

A. INTRODUCTION

The corporation has been described as 'the most effective structure for capital accumulation', having 'the potential to demonstrate an effective management system' because 'it allows a separation of ownership from management'.[1] In other words, the usefulness of the corporate form – indeed the very basis of its creation and continued existence – stems from the fact that the 'corporate body is not a natural person but has legal personality attributed to it by the law ... Additionally it has a legal *persona* separate from that of its investors'.[2]

But the corporation, particularly the global corporation, is also much more that a legal concept. It is, increasingly, a very significant economic, political and social presence in today's world.[3] According to the 2009 World Investment Report by the United Nations Conference on Trade and Development (UNCTAD), there were, in 2009, an estimated 82,000 transnational corporations (TNCs) worldwide, with 810,000 foreign affiliates.[4] The Report goes on to note that 'these companies play a major and growing role in the world economy. For example, exports by foreign affiliates of TNCs are estimated to account for about a third of total world exports of goods and services, and the number of people employed by them worldwide totalled about 77 million in 2008 – more than double the total labour force of Germany'.[5] It has been estimated that of the top 100 economies in the world, 51 are corporations and only 49 are states.[6]

The fundamental role played by TNCs in global trade and the global economy generally has been acknowledged by the WTO and other international bodies.[7] TNCs also play a major role in, and have a significant impact upon, local economies at all levels, national, provincial and local. Governments everywhere recognize the role of TNCs in economic development, particularly through global direct investment.[8] Governments are also prepared to deal with TNCs on a virtually equal basis under a growing number of bilateral investment treaties (BITs) which allow TNCs the right to initiate international arbitration directly against a host state for alleged breaches of BIT rights.[9]

These facts alone demand much more than a dictionary definition in answer to the question 'what is the *nature* of the corporation as a participant in the global economy, in global and local politics and society?' One answer is provided by those who argue that corporations are, by nature and by law, bound to act selfishly.[10] In the words of one commentator, 'Businesses have no purpose other than reproducing themselves profitably. If *en route* to this project they develop new technologies, ... and generate employment they are all besides the point. Businesses' business is business'.[11]

This book challenges such a view of the corporation, particularly the corporation as a participant in the process known as 'globalization'. A number of writers have reminded us that economic growth should not be valued simply for its own sake. David Kinley, for example, argues that the economy should be seen as a means to an end – an improved quality of human life – rather than an end in itself.[12] This book is similarly based on the belief that the corporation should be seen as a vehicle to an end, rather than an end in itself. In particular, the TNC, as a member of the global community, should be seen as a valuable vehicle for promoting the welfare of global society. The TNC should also be designed and regulated in a way which best promotes the global good and the realization of globally agreed goals, including the Millennium Development Goals[13] and the environmental goals agreed upon in 2009 at Copenhagen and other environmental forums.[14]

Kinley also calls for recognition of the interdependency between global corporate activity and international human rights law. His latest book, *Civilizing Globalisation*, points to this inter-dependency within the broader context of the link between the global economy and human rights.[15] *Civilizing Globalisation* takes a broad look at all three arms of the global economy – trade, aid and global business – and their impact on human rights. In this book, my focus is much more narrow, but deeper. I examine global business, in particular the TNC, in much more detail. This first chapter begins by exploring the nature of the corporation as a legal entity: the nature of its personhood. Non-corporate global entities and organizations, both inter-governmental organizations and non-governmental organizations (NGOs), can certainly have an important influence on human rights; and there are important debates to be had about the role and status of each of these entities under international law. The special focus of this book, however, is upon the TNC – the legally incorporated entity doing business in more than one nation.

This first chapter examines the legal definition, nature and form of the corporation as it currently exists in different legal systems around the world. The focus is on the modern form of the corporation in different common law and civil law systems, the aim being to explore whether one corporate form might be more conducive to good social citizenship than others. Chapter 1 also explores the expanding acceptance of the concept of corporate social responsibility, and the different varieties of codes and other instruments aimed at recognizing and facilitating socially responsible corporate behaviour.

Chapter 2 begins by reiterating both the mammoth capacity of TNCs for great good, and also their ability to perpetuate great harm. The great disparity between the significant impact of TNCs in global business and society, on the one hand, and the virtual refusal of international law to recognize the activities of TNCs as coming within its ambit, on the other, is highlighted. Chapter 2 examines the ways in which TNCs have responded to international criticism and concern by attempting to 'self-regulate' through voluntary codes of conduct. Different approaches to adopting and implementing such codes, some more successful than others, are explored. In Chapter 3, the focus is on the relationship between host states and foreign TNCs under BITs and other international instruments. The ways in which these treaties appear to protect TNC rights, while remaining silent on TNC responsibilities, is illustrated using a number of case examples. The ways in which host states have attempted to overcome this deficit through regulatory measures establishing standards for corporate behaviour are then explored. The limitations of such efforts to regulate corporate behaviour are highlighted.

Chapter 4 examines the way in which some home states have sought to plug existing gaps in international law by enacting extra-territorial legislation allowing TNCs to be held accountable for breaches of international standards. The significant legal problems that need to be overcome by individuals and NGOs making use of such legislation are highlighted by examining a range of cases, mostly unsuccessful, involving litigation against TNCs for human rights and environmental harms. Chapter 5 then examines the theory and practice of corporate criminal liability for extra-territorial harms.

Chapters 6 to 9 present an alternative solution to the problem of holding TNCs accountable for their conduct away from home. Chapter 6 outlines a set of theoretical principles for bringing TNCs under the jurisdiction of international law in respect of their global activities. At United Nations level, a concept of 'sphere of influence' has been used within the context of the Global Compact[16] and the Draft Norms on the Responsibilities of Transnational Corporations and Other Business Enterprises[17] in attempting to define the responsibilities and potential liabilities of TNCs. The problems with this concept have been emphasized on a number of occasions by the Special Representative of the Secretary-General (SRSG), Professor John Ruggie.[18] Professor Ruggie suggests that a more appropriate anchor for defining the international responsibilities of TNCs is the duty to take reasonable measures to avoid complicity in human rights abuses – a concept akin to the common law concept of due diligence. The obligation to exercise due diligence forms an essential element of what Ruggie has identified as the corporate duty to respect human rights. The corporate duty to respect human rights, in turn, is an essential pillar in Ruggie's 'Protect, Respect and Remedy' Framework for business and human rights,[19] about which more will be said.

What is missing from the SRSG's current vision of TNCs' 'responsibility to respect human rights' is the vital element of enforceability. In Chapter 6, I highlight similarities between Ruggie's description of the 'corporate responsibility to respect' on the one hand, and the International Law Commission's Draft Articles on the Responsibility of States for Internationally Wrongful Acts ('Draft Articles')[20] on the other. Chapter 6 then offers the Draft Articles as an appropriate model for building a set of theoretical principles to govern TNC liability for internationally wrongful acts.

Chapter 6 further argues that just as TNCs have already been invited to sign up to the Global Compact (as discussed in Chapter 2), so also should they be invited to sign up to other international standard-setting instruments as well. This process should be just as voluntary as it is for states when deciding whether to sign up to treaties. When a TNC has appropriately indicated its consent to be bound by a treaty, however, that treaty should be just as binding on the TNC as on states parties to the treaty. In addition, just as states are also bound by certain mandatory, fundamental rules of general international law known as *jus cogens*, so should TNCs likewise be subject to those same peremptory norms.

Chapter 7 then explores institutional avenues for holding TNCs accountable for internationally wrongful acts. It is argued that TNCs should also be invited to sign up to one or more voluntary, graduated enforcement mechanisms, ranging from simple reporting obligations (such as currently imposed on Global Compact signatories), to submission to complaints-handling tribunals. In relation to human rights norms, TNCs could be invited to submit to scrutiny by one of the regional or international human rights tribunals that currently supervise compliance by states with human rights obligations. There may even be scope for a new World Court of Human Rights,[21] something proposed as early as 1947 but still stigmatized as utopian.

It is likely to be some time before TNCs will submit to scrutiny, let alone complaints handling, by human rights tribunals. In the meantime, it may be more acceptable for BITs to incorporate some minimal and basic, but important, responsibilities for foreign investor corporations that wish to enjoy the rights bestowed by those BITs. For example, BIT rights could be extended more readily to corporations signing up to the Global Compact minimum standards. Questions and disputes arising under these more modern BITs could then continue to be settled by existing arbitration bodies. This idea is also explored in Chapter 7.

If it is accepted that international law does and should impose responsibilities on TNCs, should there also be criminal liability for corporations under international law? Individuals can already be prosecuted for international crimes before the International Criminal Court (ICC).[22] Should TNCs likewise be invited or obliged to submit to the jurisdiction of the ICC? While the idea may initially be appealing, there are two major problems. First, there are the significant and powerful political interests that would oppose any proposal to expand the ICC's jurisdiction to TNCs. The second major problem with the idea of international criminal liability for TNCs is that imposing such liability would treat TNCs differently to states under international law. The International Law Commission (ILC) took several decades to draw up the Draft Articles, and in so doing it looked long and hard at the question of whether states could or should ever be subjected to criminal liability. The ILC eventually decided that state responsibility should *not* imply or entail criminal responsibility. Likewise and for similar reasons which are explored in Chapter 7, I argue that TNCs should be held accountable, but not criminally liable, when responsible for wrongful acts in their international activities.

Chapter 8 explores the important role of TNCs in the ecological future of the planet. The current state of international environmental law and environmental law enforcement is explored. There is currently a proliferation of environmental courts and tribunals around the world, but little coordination or consistency between them. Nor do they generally have any jurisdiction over TNCs, despite the often significant environmental impacts of TNC activity. At the UN level, despite the establishment of a specialized Environmental Chamber, the International Court of Justice (ICJ) has been hesitant, at best, when it comes to dealing with environmental issues. And while the Security Council has expressly recognized the security implications of global climate change,[23] it, too, has been mostly absent from the debate over the future international environmental obligations of states and other global actors. But these and other UN institutions could potentially play an important role in designing, monitoring and resolving disputes arising under future environmental law treaties. In Chapter 8 I would like to suggest that TNCs have a lot to offer to this process, as well as lot to gain from participating in it.

The final substantive chapter of this book examines the need for an international forum that could act as a final court of appeal in appropriate cases, in order to unify international jurisprudence relating to TNC responsibility. It is argued that an appropriately resourced ICJ would be well placed to accept this role.

The book concludes by stressing the importance of what the SRSG has called 'principled pragmatism' in bringing TNCs out of the accountability vacuum. The need for trust-promoting mechanisms to be in place when building the future of TNC global citizenship is also highlighted.

B.   EXISTING MODELS OF THE CORPORATION: PRIVATE VEHICLE OR SOCIAL ACTOR?

1.   Common Law Models

Many commentators have noted the influence that the principal-agent model of the corporation has had on company law in Anglo-American legal systems.[24] This model is one which assumes that corporations are run well when directors (agents) make decisions 'in the best interests of' shareholders (principals). When directors fail to do this, inefficient 'agency costs' result. In order to overcome these agency costs, Anglo-American legal systems give primacy to the interests of shareholders, and impose obligations on company management to exercise their decision-making powers in 'good faith' and in a manner which furthers the best interests of the company.[25]

The generally accepted common law test defines 'best interests of the company' as essentially equivalent to the interests of the company's shareholders, or where a company is insolvent, its creditors.[26] It remains unclear, however, whether and to what extent directors are permitted to take into account the interests of other 'stakeholders', such as the company's employees, its suppliers, or those in the community affected by the company's activities. A narrow reading of the 'best interests of the corporation' rule could well make it illegal for business leaders to take such stakeholder interests into account – at least when those interests come into conflict with the need to maximize shareholder returns.[27]

The question of whether or not company directors should be permitted, or even required, to take into account the interests of specific stakeholders was examined in some detail during a series of investigations into company law initiated by the United Kingdom government since 1992.[28] The UK government eventually decided that such a requirement was necessary. Section 172 of UK Companies Act 2006 therefore now provides that:

> A director of a company must act in the way he considers, in good faith, would be most likely to promote the success of the company for the benefit of its members as a whole, and in doing so have regard (amongst other matters) to—
> (a) the likely consequences of any decision in the long term,
> (b) the interests of the company's employees,
> (c) the need to foster the company's business relationships with suppliers, customers and others,
> (d) the impact of the company's operations on the community and the environment,
> (e) the desirability of the company maintaining a reputation for high standards of business conduct, ...

The UK government has also confirmed that pension fund trustees are not prohibited from considering social, environmental and ethical issues in their investment decisions, provided they act in the fund's best interests.[29] In both cases, however, it remains clear that promoting the success of the company or fund should remain the primary consideration in corporate decision-making.

The Australian Parliamentary Joint Committee on Corporations and Financial Services (JCCFS)[30] has also considered whether or not the Australian Corporations Act 2001 (Cth) (specifically its provisions dealing with directors' duties) is the right mechanism to address issues of corporate social responsibility (CSR).[31] In its report, released on 21 June 2006, the JCCFS found that:

> the Corporations Act 2001 permits directors to have regard for the interests of stakeholders other than shareholders, and recommend[ed] that amendment to the directors' duties provisions within the Corporations Act is not required.[32]

The Report also noted that ASX listing rules and other provisions in the Corporations Act already encourage various forms of CSR reporting by Australian-listed firms. For example, section 299(1)(f) of the Corporations Act, introduced in 1998, places an obligation upon directors to ensure that the company reports include details of the entity's performance in relation to any 'particular and significant' environmental regulation under a law of the Commonwealth or of a State or Territory. One effect of this requirement has been to encourage an increase in sustainability reporting by Australian-listed firms.

In rejecting an express requirement for directors to take CSR considerations into account, the Australian government reached a different conclusion to that reached in the United Kingdom. What both the UK and Australian governments have agreed upon, however, is that corporate social responsibility should remain essentially voluntary. Government might encourage and promote good corporate behaviour, but the market, rather than legal regulation, should be relied upon to guide business behaviour in socially and economically optimal directions. The committee's reliance on the 'business case' argument in support of CSR is made obvious through its various recommendations, such as its recommendation that:

> the Australian Government, in consultation with relevant sections of the business community, [should] undertake research into quantifying the benefits of corporate responsibility and sustainability reporting.[33]

The JCCFS also recommended the establishment in Australia of a new organization, the Australian Corporate Responsibility Network, modelled on the UK initiative Business in the Community, and charged with the job of publicizing and promoting 'best practice examples across the spectrum of corporate responsible activities and across industry sectors'.[34]

Nearly all of the more ambitious legislative attempts to impose minimum standards on corporate conduct, however, have been notable for their lack of success. Examples include a Corporate Code of Conduct Act referred to the United States House Subcommittee on International Monetary Policy and Trade on 17 July 2000. A Bill was introduced to the First Session of the 107th Congress in 2001, but failed to pass.[35] In Australia, a Corporate Code of Conduct Bill 2000 was rejected by the Commonwealth Parliamentary Joint Standing Committee on Corporations and Securities, and thereafter was very quickly defeated when an attempt was made to introduce it into Parliament.[36] The draft Bill would have imposed environmental, employment, health and safety and human rights standards on the conduct of Australian corporations with large overseas operations.[37] It would not only have required corporations to report on their compliance with these standards, but would also have provided for enforcement through fines. More importantly, it would have provided a right for overseas communities and special interest organizations to take legal action against Australian TNCs to protect human rights. Remedies would have included both compensation and injunctions to prevent further damage.[38] Not surprisingly, the Bill received significant criticism and opposition from TNCs with operations in Australia – firms which exercise significant economic and political lobbying power in that country.

In June 2006, the reluctance of Australian authorities to even recommend, let alone impose, international standards on Australian firms became even more obvious. It was in that month that the Joint Parliamentary Committee investigation into corporate responsibility issued its Report concluding that it was premature even to adopt the Global Reporting Initiative Framework as a *voluntary* Australian sustainability reporting framework.[39] The Committee did not even consider whether or not the broader principles of the *Global Compact* should be incorporated into the Australian Stock Exchange Corporate Governance Council's voluntary Principles of Good Corporate Governance and Best Practice Recommendations.[40]

2.   Civil Law Models

In contrast to the model of the corporation found in the United States, Australia and other Anglo-law jurisdictions, the German and other civil law legal systems ensure that stakeholder interests are expressly recognized in corporate decision-making. This is achieved essentially through two mechanisms: structural transparency of the corporate form, and participation by stakeholder interests in corporate decision-making. The aim is to ensure that the benefits of the corporate form can be fully realized for customers, employees and the community, as well as for the shareholder.

In Germany, structural transparency and cooperation in corporate decision-making are facilitated by two main features: a two-tiered board structure and a system of co-determination. The two-tiered board system consists of the management or executive board and the supervisory board.[41] The members of the executive board manage the company and the supervisory board members control and monitor the management board. The supervisory board may, *inter alia*, examine the business decisions made by the management board and may examine all financial statements and accounts. Independence of the supervisory board is maintained by legislation which provides the two boards with totally separate functions. The system of co-determination operates through the structure and mechanisms of the supervisory board. By requiring that a certain proportion of supervisory board members must be employees, the system ensures that the supervisory board provides a mechanism through which employee representatives can safeguard employee interests.[42]

Another way in which the German system operates to promote a working relationship between management and labour is by requiring consultation and agreement between employer and works council at establishment level with regard to any 'co-determination matter'. Thus, to take action relating to a co-determination matter in terms of the Works Constitution Act 1972, employers must first obtain the consent required to do so from the works council. Any unilateral action on the part of the employer becomes void and unenforceable in the absence of works council consent. When the employer and the works council cannot come to agreement on a co-determination matter, the matter is referred to an arbitration committee (*Einigungsstelle*). Any decision made by the arbitration committee is binding on both sides.[43]

Finally, a mention should also be made of employee share ownership schemes, which have become common in Europe in the 1990s. While it remains true that penetration of employee shares in Germany is much lower than in the United States and Britain, the potential for employees to exert financial as well as supervisory influence in shaping corporate decision-making is one which could well be realized in future.[44]

Within the Asia-Pacific region, the civil law tradition has provided the basis of the Indonesian legal system (inherited from the Dutch) and, to a very large extent, the Chinese legal system as well. As in Germany, the Chinese Company Law 2006 mandates a dual-board structure for listed corporations.[45] There must be both a board of directors and a supervisory board of not fewer than three members. At least one-third of the supervisory board must comprise workers' representatives who must be democratically elected by the company's employees.[46] Employees of large Chinese firms are also increasingly able and willing to exercise a voice through share ownership incentive schemes.[47]

Japanese corporations have also traditionally been characterized by an 'insider system of corporate governance', though of a uniquely Japanese nature. Although no longer a mandatory requirement of Japan's Companies Act,[48] most large corporations in Japan have traditionally had a dual structure: a board of directors, which carries out the functions of strategic decision-making; and the board of auditors, which audits management's execution of business activities.[49] Most large Japanese companies also have unions and joint committees with access to senior management. Thus, employees are important stakeholders and management mediates between the shareholders, employees and other stakeholders.[50]

What is needed now is a closer examination of the relationship between key features of different corporate decision-making structures, on the one hand, and the propensity of the corporation to incorporate social, environmental and human rights concerns into the making of business decisions. To what extent do features like the two-tiered board, employee representation on the board, employee share ownership and other features impact on the social responsibility record of corporations? Do companies with a certain type of governance structure have a better record of 'social responsibility' than other companies? Certainly a quick survey of participants in the Global Compact, perhaps the most ambitious project aimed at promoting 'corporate social responsibility' to date, shows that the number of participating TNCs based in Anglo-American company law systems is roughly the same as the number from European-style company law systems.[51]

C.   TAKING CORPORATE RESPONSIBILITY SERIOUSLY: REGULATORY REQUIREMENTS

The traditional 'shareholder primacy' view of directors' duties in corporate law is largely based on the idea of directors as agents of the shareholders of a company. However, the changing role of corporations in society has caused this view to be questioned with increasing force in recent times. As Bryan Horrigan has pointed out, shareholder primacy thinking is predicated upon a 'zero-sum game' between the interests of shareholders and the interests of other 'non-shareholder stakeholders'. This is far from the reality of the modern corporation, where shareholders often have an extensive commonality of interests with other stakeholder groups.[52] A number of recent measures introduced into the laws and listing regulations of many nations have recognized this reality. Such measures have resulted in the express recognition of non-shareholder interests in the Annual Reports of public companies around the world, and have coincided with increased media coverage of, and academic interest in, issues of corporate responsibility.

1. National Reporting Requirements

Despite the political obstacles that often stand in the way, governments in nearly all modern economies have put in place measures to promote corporate awareness of social responsibility. Reporting requirements have been an important tool in these efforts. To begin with, governments have often found it easier to extend such requirements to their state-owned enterprises.[53] In 2008, for example, China issued guidance to its state-owned enterprises, recommending systems for corporate social responsibility reporting and protecting labour rights.[54] Sweden requires its state enterprises to have a human rights policy and to engage on human rights issues with business partners, customers and suppliers. They must also report on these issues, tracking Global Reporting Initiative indicators.[55] Dutch state-owned enterprises are encouraged to do the same.[56]

Publicly listed firms are subject to reporting requirements everywhere, and in many countries governments and/or stock exchange authorities have expanded the scope of these requirements to include social, environmental and human rights reporting for all listed firms, or for all firms above a certain size. In Denmark, recent legislation requires companies above a certain size to report on their CSR programme, or report that they lack one.[57] In Malaysia, annual reports of listed companies must include a description of their CSR activities (including those of their subsidiaries) or state that they have none.[58] France has required all companies listed on the *premier marche* to report on social issues, including community engagement and labour standards, since January 2002. A more recent Bill, if passed, will extend standardized sustainability reporting requirements beyond listed companies to large, non-listed companies.[59] In India, reporting requirements for publicly listed firms contain a significant focus upon environmental performance issues.[60]

The problem is, however, that the expansion of reporting requirements appears to have done remarkably little to alter company behaviour, or even to greatly improve levels of transparency. Even in those countries where CSR-related reporting is required, reporting obligations mostly remain both minimal and vague. Moreover, reporting methodologies adopted by different industries, and even within industries, are highly variable,[61] making comparisons difficult or impossible. Some governments have therefore recognized that further measures are required.

2. Other Regulatory Measures Aimed at Fostering CSR

Most countries have introduced codes of corporate governance.[62] Yet these codes rarely extend beyond traditional governance issues into the realm of broader human rights or environmental obligations. Where CSR standards are recognized, they are inevitably expressed in voluntary form. In a smaller number of countries, however, governments have gone further than mere reporting requirements or voluntary codes of behaviour in an effort to foster greater awareness of CSR. Sweden's requirements for companies to develop a human rights policy was mentioned above. In South Africa, a new Companies Act allows the government to prescribe social and ethics committees for certain companies.[63]

India also provides an example of a country which has gone beyond reporting requirements in its attempt to foster socially responsible corporate behaviour. A draft Companies Bill currently before the *Lok Sabha* includes a provision requiring publicly listed companies above a certain size to have a broad-level 'stakeholder relations committee' to 'consider and resolve the grievance of stakeholders'.[64] The Indian government has also released new Voluntary Guidelines on Corporate Governance (CGVG)[65] and Corporate Social Responsibility Voluntary Guidelines (CSRVG).[66] The CGVG expand upon the existing provisions in clause 49 of the Securities and Exchange Board of India (SEBI)'s Listing Agreement (popularly known as the corporate governance clause).[67] As with corporate governance provisions in most other major jurisdictions, including the United Kingdom, United States, Australia, Hong Kong and China, the CGVG include calls for a minimum number of independent directors on company boards, separation of the roles of chairman of the board and chief executive officer, executive compensation more closely linked to performance and disclosure of a critical risk management framework that identifies risks, as well as strategies to minimize them.

More interesting are the provisions of the new Indian CSRVG. The CSRVG begin by stating the fundamental premise that 'Each business entity should formulate a CSR policy to guide its strategic planning and provide a roadmap for its CSR initiatives, which should be an integral part of overall business policy and aligned with its business goals'. Six core elements are then identified which 'should normally' be covered by a company's CSR policy:

- care for all stakeholders;
- ethical functioning;
- respect for workers' rights and welfare;
- respect for human rights;
- respect for [the] environment; and
- activities for social and inclusive development.[68]

Express mention of human rights is relatively rare in national provisions relating to CSR; and express mention of 'activities for economic and social development of communities and geographic areas' is even rarer. But what is really interesting about the new Indian CSRVG are its provisions on

'Implementation' of CSR policies. The 'Implementation Guidance' section of
the CSRVG begins by providing that company CSR policies:

> should provide for an implementation strategy which should include identification
> of projects/activities, setting measurable physical targets with timeframe, organiza-
> tional mechanism and responsibilities, time schedules and monitoring. Companies
> may partner with local authorities, business associations and civil society/non-
> government organisations. They may influence the supply chain for CSR initiative
> and motivate employees for voluntary effort for social development. They may
> evolve a system of need assessment and impact assessment while undertaking CSR
> activities in a particular area.[69]

The CSRVG then go on to state that 'Companies should allocate specific
amount in their budgets for CSR activities. This amount may be related to
profits after tax, cost of planned CSR activities or other suitable parameter'.[70]
The express recognition of the desirability (as opposed to permissibility) of a
budgetary allocation for CSR activities is another notable feature of the Indian
CSR Guidelines.

The impact of the new Indian CSRVG on actual company behaviour
remains to be seen. Certainly, the Indian record on CSR, as with other developing countries, indicates a need for improvement. A 2009 report from
Karmayog, a Mumbai-based online organization, found that while 51 per cent
of Indian companies practised CSR in some form, only 2 per cent published a
separate sustainability report, and only 3 per cent reported the amount they
spent on CSR.[71] The conclusions of the Karmayog Report were verified in
December 2009 when the Emerging Markets Disclosure (EMD) Project of the
United States-based Social Investment Forum (SIF) issued its report finding
that Indian companies were amongst those in emerging markets with the
lowest disclosure rates on CSR reporting.[72] In two separate 2009 reports,
commissioned by the International Finance Corporation (IFC), Indian companies were found to be ahead of the field in the quality of sustainability reports
produced when compared with companies from five other emerging market
countries.[73] At the same time, however, Indian equities investment managers
were found to be reluctant to utilize voting or engagement as tools for pursuing actual implementation of social or environmental programmes.[74]

Corporate websites also provide evidence of the way in which corporations
have been careful to make sure that the pursuit of social responsibility is
aligned with the strategic business interests of the company. As John Hall, the
manager of Corporate Relations at Rio Tinto Australia, has acknowledged, the
tendency is to recognize little more than that the company's:

> [l]icence to operate depends on community acceptance of, and support for, its activ-
> ities … The business case is clear: we aim to maximise shareholder value over the
> total life of the resources and assets that we manage, which is typically several

decades. With that time span it obviously makes good business sense to invest in the future by earning the trust and respect of people who could be a part of our community for many years to come. Good community relations provide a surer basis for effective, uninterrupted business operations.[75]

Despite the setbacks faced by its proponents, corporate social responsibility is becoming an increasingly important concept in emerging forms of corporate regulation throughout the world. The following chapters explore the evolving regulatory structure governing the global activities of TNCs. First, however, some of the terminology used throughout the rest of this book requires explanation.

D.   TERMINOLOGY: PARENT, HOME AND HOST STATES

The term 'parent' is used in this book to refer to a corporate legal person that exercises control over other legal-person entities in other parts of the world. Typically, a 'parent' entity will be the controlling centre for the operations of a global group of business operations known as the corporate group. Control is often exercised by means of direct ownership, but not always. For example, control may just as effectively be exercised through means of a minority ownership stake combined with majority voting rights on the board of directors of the controlled entity. The UN Draft Code of Conduct for Transnational Corporations (discussed below) defined 'parent entities' as 'entities which are the main source of influence over others'.[76] This definition is consistent with the definition of TNC adopted in the successor to the Draft Code, the Draft Norms on the Responsibilities of Transnational Corporations and Other Business Enterprises with regard to Human Rights.[77]

The term 'home state' is used in this book to refer to the state where a TNC is based. In the case of a TNC with a single parent controlling the whole operation, the home state will be the state where that parent is incorporated, and where decisions about the TNC's operations are made. The home state is typically a state with a well-developed legal system and well-developed financial and securities markets, providing a haven for the TNC's core property and other legal rights, and a launching pad for its global operations. It may not be easy to identify a single decision-making centre of a TNC's operations, and thus for many TNCs it may not be easy to assign a single home state. In such cases, there may be two or more home states.

The term 'host state' is used for all states where a TNC operates, other than its home state. These definitions of 'home' and 'host' states are consistent with those established in the UN Draft Code of Conduct for TNCs.[78]

NOTES

1. Michael Spisto, 'Stakeholder interests in corporate governance: is a new model of governance a change for the better for South Africa, Part 1' (2005) 18 *Australian Journal of Corporate Law* 129, 129–30, citing D. Bailes, 'Watch your corporation' (1995) 3:1 *Journal of Business Law* 24; P. Jiang and L.F. Fang (eds), *New Corporate Law Textbook* (9th edn, 1998) 48–50, as cited in Y Wei, *Comparative Corporate Governance: A Chinese Perspective*, Global Trade and Finance Series, vol. 3 (Kluwer Law International, 2003) 2.
2. *Ibid.*
3. For an extensive overview of the history of the corporate form as originally an important agent of colonial power structures, to its more modern but equally powerful private form, see Steven R. Ratner, 'Corporations and human rights: a theory of legal responsibility' (2001) 111 *Yale Law Journal* 443, 452–9.
4. United Nations Conference on Trade and Development, *World Investment Report 2009*, vol. 1, *Transnational Corporations, Agricultural Production and Development*, overview, xxi, available at www.unctad.org/en/docs/wir2009_en.pdf.
5. *Ibid.*
6. David Kinley and Justine Nolan, *Trading and Aiding Human Rights: Corporations in the Global Economy*, Sydney Law School Legal Studies Research Paper No. 08/13 (January 2008), 358, available at http://ssrn.com/abstract=1080427, citing Sarah Anderson and John Cavenagh, *Top 200: The Rise of Global Corporate Power* (Institute of Policy Studies, Washington DC, 2000).
7. UCTAD, above n. 4.
8. For discussion see David Kinley, *Civilising Globalisation: Human Rights and the Global Economy* (Cambridge University Press, 2009) 145–201. See also Gillian Triggs, *International Law: Contemporary Principles and Practices* (LexisNexis Butterworths, 2006) paras 8.106–8.109.
9. See e.g. North American Free Trade Agreement (United States, Canada and Mexico), Chapter 11, opened for signature 17 December 1992, 32 ILM 296 and 32 ILM 605 (entered into force 1 January 1994), available at www.nafta-sec-alena.org/en/view.aspx?x=34; Australia–United States Free Trade Agreement, opened for signature 18 May 2004 (entered into force 1 January 2005), available at www.austrade.gov.au/AUSFTA8310/default.aspx and United States–Singapore Free Trade Agreement, opened for signature 6 May 2003 (entered into force 1 January 2004), available at www.ustr.gov/trade-agreements/free-trade-agreements/singapore-fta/final-text.
10. Leo Strine, Lawrence Hamermesh, R. Franklin Balotti and Jeffrey Gorris, *Loyalty's Core Demand: The Defining Role of Good Faith in Corporation Law*, Harvard Joh M. Olin Discussion Paper Series, No. 630, Harvard Law School 3/2009 (26 February 2009), available at http://ssrn.com/abstract=1349971. See also John B. Cobb, Jr, 'What is free about free trade?' (August 1991), available at www.religion-online.org/showarticle.asp?title=102.
11. Anthony P. D'Costa, AIB member, comment during an online debate between members of the Association of International Business (AIB) via AIB-L@LIST.MSU.EDU, September 2005.
12. David Kinley, *Civilising Globalisation: Human Rights and the Global Economy* (CUP, 2009) 1-3.
13. Millennium Declaration, GA Res. 55/2, UN Doc. A/RES/55/2 (8 September 2000).
14. Copenhagen Accord, Draft Decision CP.15, UNFCCC, 15th Session, Copenhagen 7–18 December 2009, Agenda item 9, High-level segment, FCCC/CP/2009/L.7. Noted by the COP. See further Chapter 8.
15. David Kinley, *Civilising Globalisation: Human Rights and the Global Economy* (Cambridge University Press, 2009).
16. United Nations Global Compact (2000, amended June 2004), available at www.globalcompact.org.
17. Draft Norms on the Responsibilities of Transnational Corporations and Other Business Enterprises with Regard to Human Rights, E/CN.4/Sub.2/2003/12 (2003), available at www1.umn.edu/humanrts/links/NormsApril2003.html.

18. John Ruggie, *Interim Report of the Secretary-General's Special Representative on the Issue of Human Rights and Transnational Corporations and Other Business Enterprises*, UN Doc. E/CN.4/2006/97 (22 February 2006), available at www2.ohchr.org/english/issues/ trans_corporations/reports.htm; John Ruggie, 'Business and human rights: the evolving international agenda' (2007) 101:4 *American Journal of International Law* 819; John Ruggie, *Business and Human Rights: Mapping International Standards of Responsibility and Accountability for Corporate Acts*, Report of the Special Representative of the Secretary General on the Issue of Human Rights and Transnational Corporations and Other Business Enterprises, UN Doc. A/HRC/4/035 (9 February 2007), available at www.business-human rights.org/Documents/SRSG-report-Human-Rights-Council-19Feb-2007.pdf; John Ruggie, *Protect, Respect and Remedy: A Framework for Business and Human Rights*, Report of the Special Representative of the Secretary-General on the Issue of Human Rights and Transnational Corporations and Other Business Enterprises, UN Doc. A/HRC/8/5 (7 April 2008).
19. John Ruggie, *Protect, Respect and Remedy: A Framework for Business and Human Rights*, Report of the Special Representative of the Secretary-General on the Issue of Human Rights and Transnational Corporations and Other Business Enterprises, UN Doc. A/HRC/8/5 (7 April 2008).
20. Report of the 53rd Session of the International Law Commission (2001); UN GAOR 56th Sess., Supp. 10.
21. Professor Manfred Nowak, 'A World Court of Human Rights: how would it work?', speech delivered at the Sydney Ideas Series, University of Sydney, 13 May 2010.
22. Rome Statute of the International Criminal Court, art. 25, opened for signature 17 July 1998, UN Doc. A/CONF.183/9, entered into force 1 July 2002 following deposit of the 60th instrument of accession (Russia) pursuant to article 126).
23. The first Security Council debate on climate change and its implications for international security was the Security Council open debate on Energy, Security and Climate Change, a one-date debate convened by the United Kingdom on 17 April 2007: UNSC 5663rd Meeting. See also 'General Assembly, expressing deep concern, invites major United Nations organs to intensify efforts in addressing security implications of climate change', UNGA, 63rd Sess. (Plenary), 85th Meeting (AM), GA/10830 (3 June 2009).
24. See e.g. Lynne Stout, 'On the nature of corporations' (2004) 9:2 *Deakin Law Review* 775; Bryan Horrigan, 'Fault lines in the intersection between corporate governance and social responsibility' (2002) 25:2 *UNSW Law Journal* 515; Lucian Arye Bebchuk and Mark J. Roe, 'A theory of path dependence in corporate ownership and governance' (1999) 52 *Stanford Law Review* 127.
25. In the United States, see e.g., *Grobow v Perot*, 539 A.2d 180 (Del. 1988); *Aronson v Lewis*, 473 A.2d 805, 812 (Del. 1984) and other cases on the business judgment rule as recognized throughout the United States. In Canada, see the Canada Business Corporations Act RSC (1985), c. C-44 (CBCA). Section 122(1)(a) of the CBCA states that directors of a corporation must 'act honestly and in good faith with a view to the best interests of the corporation' when exercising their powers and discharging their duties'. See also *Peoples Department Stores Inc. (Trustee of) v Wise* (2004) 3 SCR 461, 2004 SCC 68. In the United Kingdom see s. 172 of the Companies Act 2006, and in Australia see s. 181(1) of the Australian Corporations Act 2001 which provides that: 'A director or other officer of a corporation must exercise their powers and discharge their duties (a) in good faith in the best interests of the corporation; and (b) for a proper purpose'.
26. Therese Wilson, 'The pursuit of profit at all costs: corporate law as a barrier to corporate social responsibility' (2005) 30:6 *Alternative Law Journal* 278, citing *Greenhalgh v Ardene Cinemas* [1945] 2 All ER 719 and *Kinsela v Russell Kinsela Pty Ltd (In Liq.)* (1986) 4 NSWLR 722.
27. *Ibid.*
28. The Reports emerging from these investigations have typically been named after the high profile individual leading the investigation. Thus, there has been the Cadbury Report (1992), Greenbury Report (1995), Hampel Report (1998), Turnbull Report (1999) and the Higgs Review (2003). The UK government also conducted a long-running investigation associated

with the Company Law Review: Department of Trade and Industry, *Modern Company Law for a Competitive Economy, Final Report* (London, 2001). For further discussion see Igor Filatotchev, Howard Gospel and Gregory Jackson, *Key Drivers of 'Good' Corporate Governance and the Appropriateness of UK Policy Responses, Final Report to the Department of Trade and Industry* (January 2007). Available at SSRN, http://ssrn.com/abstract=961369.

29. Investment and Pensions Europe, 'Lords confirm SRI can be applied in UK pensions' (9 October 2008), available at http://ipe.com/articles/.

30. On 23 June 2005, the Parliamentary Joint Committee on Corporations and Financial Services resolved to inquire into corporate responsibility and triple bottom line reporting for incorporated entities in Australia: the Committee's Report dated and released on 21 June 2006 is titled *Corporate Responsibility: Managing Risk and Creating Value* and is available atwww.aph.gov.au/Senate/committee/corporations_ctte/corporate_responsibility/report/index.htm.

31. Peter Henley, 'Were corporate tsunami donations made legally?' (2005) 30:4 *Alternative Law Journal* 154.

32. Joint Committee on Corporations and Financial Services (Parliament of Australia), *Corporate Responsibility: Managing Risk and Creating Value* (2006) ('JCCFS 2006 Corporate Responsibility Report'), Recommendation 1.

33. Parenthesis added. JCCFS 2006 Corporate Responsibility Report, above n. 32, Recommendation 13.

34. *Ibid.* Recommendation 17.

35. Corporate Code of Conduct Act, HR 2782, 107th Cong. (1st Sess. 2001), see also Washington College of Law, Center for Human Rights and Humanitarian Law, Human Rights Brief (2000), available at www.wcl.american.edu/hrbrief/08/1 watch.cfm.

36. Corporate Code of Conduct Bill 2000, Parliament of Australia, Senate, Senator Bourne (first reading), available at www.austlii.edu.au/au/legis/cth/bill/ccob2000248/.

37. The Bill, tabled by Australian Democrats Senator Vicki Bourne in September 2000, would have applied to all Australian corporations employing more than 100 persons in a foreign country.

38. Igor O'Neill, 'Long arm of the law may get longer for companies' (2000) 5:4 *Mining Monitor* (November) 4.

39. JCCFS 2006 Corporate Responsibility Report, above n. 32.

40. The Council's Principles of Good Corporate Governance and Best Practice Recommendations were released on 31 March 2003. A revised version of the Principles of Good Corporate Governance and Good Practice Recommendations was released by the ASX Corporate Governance Council on 2 August 2007. The Principles and Recommendations are 'not prescriptive' but are 'designed to produce an efficiency, quality and integrity outcome'.
     So far as the Global Compact is concerned, the only reference to it in the JCCFS Corporate Responsibility Report Recommendations is in Recommendation 25, which recommends that 'the Australian Government develop educational material to promote the UN Global Compact and to encourage Australian companies to become signatories where it is appropriate for them'.

41. In German, the *Vorstand* and the *Aufsichtsrat*: Michael Spisto, 'Stakeholder interests in corporate governance: is a new model of governance a change for the better for South Africa?, Part 1' (2005) 18 *Australian Journal of Corporate Law* 129, 140.

42. Spisto, *ibid.*

43. *Ibid.*

44. *Ibid.* 141.

45. PRC Company Law (Amended) (2330/05.10.27) PRC President's Order No. 42, art. 118, promulgated on 27 October 2005 and effective on 1 January 2006, translated in (2005/2006) 19:10 *China Law and Practice* (December/January) 21. See also arts 54-5 outlining the powers of the supervisory board.

46. *Ibid.* art. 118.

47. William Booth, 'Fortune cookies' (2007) *Chartered Secretary Focus* (Supplement to *ICSA Magazine* 7–9, available at www.charteredsecretary.net/uploads/supplements/20.pdf.

48. 'New Japan Corporations Law: Summary', available at www.japanlaw.info/japan commercialcode/NEWCOMPANIESLAW.html. Every company that is defined as being both a large company and a public company, however, must use either a board of company auditors or the committee system which involves the establishment of three compulsory committees – audit committee, nominating committee and compensation committee – with outside (independent) directors forming the core of managerial supervision: Kenichi Osugi, 'Companies Act, Overview', Transparency of Japanese Law Project, Group for International Corporate Law. available at www.tomeika.jur.kyushu-u.ac.jp/corporate/index.html. The Japanese Companies Act was enacted in 2005 and came into effect on 1 May 2006. Translation available at Attorney Roderick H. Seeman's 'Japan Corporations Law', www.japanlaw.info/law/contents.htm.

49. Corporate Governance Committee, Corporate Governance Forum of Japan, *Corporate Governance Principles, A Japanese View (Interim Report)* (30 October 1997) para. 2-6. Further noting, however, that the traditional board of auditors 'does only *ex post facto* auditing, and tends to be remote from the decision-making process'. See further Kanji Tanimoto, 'Structural change in corporate society and CSR in Japan' in Kyoko Fukukawa (ed.), *Corporate Social Responsibility in Asia* (Routledge, 2010) 45–66.

50. Michael Spisto, 'Unitary board or two tiered board for the new South Africa?' (2005) 1:2 *International Review of Business Research Papers* (October/November) 84, 88–9.

51. See Chapter 2, n. 86 and accompanying text.

52. Wayne Gumley, 'Can corporations law reform save the planet: seeking a missing link between environmental and economic policies' in Gerald Acquaah-Gaisie and Val Clulow (eds), *Enhancing Corporate Accountability: Prospects and Challenges Conference Proceedings, 8–9 February 2006, Melbourne* (Monash University, 2006) 239, 243–4, citing Bryan Horrigan 'Fault lines in the intersection between corporate governance and social responsibility' (2002) 25:2 *UNSW Law Journal* 515, 531.

53. John Ruggie, *Business and Human Rights: Further Steps Towards the Operationalization of the 'Protect, Respect and Remedy' Framework*, Report of the Special Representative of the Secretary-General on the Issue of Human Rights and Transnational Corporations and other Business Enterprises, GA HRC 14th Sess., UN Doc. A/HRC/14/27 (9 April 2010), para. 27, noting that States 'find it easier to promote respect for rights by State-owned enterprises. Senior management typically is appointed by and reports to State agencies. Associated government departments have greater scope for scrutiny'.

54. Instructing Opinions about Central State-owned Enterprises Fulfilling Social Responsibility, issued by the Chinese State-owned Asset Supervision and Administration Commission of the State Council, 4 January 2008.

55. Ministry of Enterprise, Energy and Communications, *Annual Report State-owned Companies 2008* (Sweden Regeringkansliet 2009) 17–27, available at http://www.regeringen.se/content/1/c6/13/43/68/906181f3.pdf. See also Ministry of Enterprise, Energy and Communications, Guidelines for External Reporting by State-owned Companies, 11 December 2007, available at www.sweden.gov.se/sb/d/2025/a/94125.

56. See Minister of Finance, Wouter Bos, Letter to the Chairman of the House of Representatives, 'Public interests and state holdings', Netherlands, 24 April 2009, available at http://www.minfin.nl/Actueel/Kamerstukken/2009/04/Brief_publieke_belangen_en_staatsdeelnemingen.

57. Act amending the Danish Financial Statements Act, 2008, cited in John Ruggie, A/HRC/14/27 (9 April 2010) para. 37, n. 20.

58. Bursa Malaysia listing requirements (appendix 9c, part A (291), available at http://www.klse.com.my/website/bm/regulation/rules/listing_requirements/downloads/bm_mainchapter9.pdf. See further Roszaini Haniffa and Mohammad Hudaib, 'A multilevel assessment of corporate social responsibility disclosure in Malaysia' in Kyoko Fukukawa (ed.), *Corporate Social Responsibility in Asia* (2010) 95–120.

59. John Ruggie, *Business and Human Rights: Further Steps Toward the Operationalization of the 'Protect, Respect and Remedy' Framework*, UN Doc. A/HRC/14/27 (9 April 2010), para. 37.

60. For example, clause 2(A)(d) of the Companies (Disclosure of Particulars in the Report of

Board of Directors) Rules 1988 requires, *inter alia*, reporting by manufacturing companies of energy conservation measures undertaken during the reporting period. For discussion see A. Sahay, 'Environmental reporting by Indian corporations' (2004) 11:1 *Corporate Social Responsibility and Environmental Management* 12; P. Malarvizhi and Sangeeta Yadav, 'Corporate environmental reporting on the Internet: an insight into Indian practices', paper presented to the 'Environmental Strategy' track, 11th Annual Convention of the Strategic Management Forum, 8–10 May 2008, Indian Institute of Technology, Kanpur, India, available at www.iitk.ac.in/infocell/announce/convention/papers/Industrial%20Economics, %20Environment,%20CSR-10-P%20Mlarvizhi,%20Sangeeta%20Yadav.pdf.

61. Gumley, above n. 52, 261–2.
62. For an extensive index list of codes of corporate governance in countries throughout the world, see 'Index of codes' published by the European Corporate Governance Institute, available at www.ecgi.org/codes/all_codes.php.
63. Companies listed on the Johannesburg Stock Exchange must also disclose compliance with a national corporate governance code that recommends integrated financial and non-financial reporting: John Ruggie, A/HRC/14/27 (9 April 2010), above n. 53, para. 37, n. 22, citing http://business-humanrights.org.
64. The Companies Bill 2009 (Bill No. 59 of 2009) introduced into the Lok Sabha by Corporate Affairs Minister Shri Salman Khurshid on 3 August 2009, available at http://164.100.24.219/BillsTexts/LSBillTexts/asintroduced/Companies%2059%20of%2020 09.pdf. Clause 158(12)–(13) of the Bill requires the establishment of a stakeholders relationship committee by the board of directors of any company with a membership of more than 1,000 security holders.
65. Ministry of Corporate Affairs, Government of India, *C*orporate Governance Voluntary Guidelines, available at www.mca.gov.in/Ministry/latestnews/CG_Voluntary_Guidelines_ 2009_24dec2009.pdf.
66. Ministry of Corporate Affairs, Government of India, Corporate Social Responsibility Voluntary Guidelines 2009, available at www.mca.gov.in/Ministry/latestnews/CSR_ Voluntary_Guidelines_24dec2009.pdf.
67. SEBI Circular dated 21 February 2000 specified principles of corporate governance and introduced a new clause 49 in the Listing Agreement of the Stock Exchanges. These principles of corporate governance were made applicable in a phased manner and all listed companies with paid up capital of Rs 3 crores and having a net worth of Rs 25 crores or more were covered as of 31 March 2003. For details of subsequent circulars on the subject of corporate governance see SEBI Circular dated 26 August 2003 (SEBI/MRD/SE/31/2003/26/08), available at www.sebi.gov.in/circulars/2003/cir2803.html.
68. Corporate Social Responsibility Voluntary Guidelines 2009, above n. 66, 11–12.
69. *Ibid.* 13.
70. *Ibid.*
71. Robert Kropp, 'Indian government issues voluntary guidelines for corporate governance and corporate social responsibility', *Sustainability Investment News*, 5 January 2010, available at www.socialfunds.com/news/article.cgi?sfArticleId=2857. See further 'Karmayog CSR Rating 2009 of the 500 largest Indian companies', available at www.karmayog.org/csr2009/.
72. Kropp, above n. 71. See further Social Investment Forum, *The Emerging Markets Disclosure Project (EMD Project) Fact Sheet*, available at http://socialinvest.org/projects/iwg/documents/EMDPfactsheet.pdf; and Social Investment Forum, *Sustainability Reporting in Emerging Markets: An Analysis of the Sustainability Reporting in Selected Sectors of Seven Emerging Market Countries* (January 2008), available at www.socialinvest.org/ resources/research/documents/SIF-SIRAN-KLDReportforEMTransparency2008.pdf.
73. International Finance Corporation and World Resources Institute, *Undisclosed Risk: Corporate Environmental and Social Responsibility in Emerging Asia* (April 2009) 3,, available at www.ifc.org/ifcext/sustainability.nsf/Content/Publications_Report_Undisclosed Risk.
74. Kropp, above n. 71. See also International Finance Corporation, *Gaining Ground: Sustainability Investment Rising in Emerging Markets* (March 2009) 5, 27–30, available at www.ifc.org/ifcext/sustainability.nsf/AttachmentsByTitle/p_SI_GainingGround_Mercer/$F

ILE/270309MIC9080_IFC+Report_WEB+secured.pdf. Report compares policies and prac-
tices of emerging market equities managers from four different countries: Brazil, China,
India and South Korea. See further International Finance Corporation, *Sustainable
Investment in India 2009* (May 2009), available at www.ifc.org/ifcext/sustainability.nsf/
Content/Publications_Report_SIinIndia; and International Finance Corporation, *Sustainable
Investing in Emerging Markets: Unscathed by the Financial Crisis* (July 2009), available at
/www.ifc.org/ifcext/sustainability.nsf/Content/Publications_Report_SIEmergingMarkets.

75. Wilson, above n. 26, 280, citing John Hall, 'The social responsibility of corporations' (2002)
     27 *Alternative Law Journal* 12, 13–14. Wilson also refers to the example of Australian bank-
     ing corporation efforts at operating in a 'socially responsible' manner, such as Westpac's
     work in enhancing financial literacy, and its involvement in the No Interest Loans Scheme
     (NILS) in Tasmania: citing Westpac, *2003 Social Impact Report 10*, 34–5.

76. Draft United Nations Code of Conduct for Transnational Corporations, UN Doc. E/1990/94
     (1990 draft) ('Draft UN TNC Code')..

77. E/CN.4/Sub.2/2003/12 (2003). 'Transnational corporation', for the purposes of the Draft
     Norms, is defined as 'an economic entity operating in more than one country or a cluster of
     economic entities operating in two or more countries – whatever their legal form, whether
     in their home country or country of activity, and whether taken individually or collectively'.
     The Norms are also presumed to apply to non-corporate business enterprises 'if the business
     enterprise has any relation with a transnational corporation.

78. The 1983 version of the Draft UN TNC Code, in para. 1(d), that 'The term "home country"
     means the country in which the parent entity is located. The term "host country" means the
     country in which an entity other than the parent entity is located'.

2. Corporations behaving well: voluntary strategies

The idea that corporations should act in accordance with standards of good citizenship and social responsibility is not a new one. As Peter Henley points out, even in states where corporate governance remains shareholder focussed, 'The question "what is the social responsibility of companies?" has been asked since the time of *Salomon v Salomon & Co Ltd*.[1] The association of familiar company names such as Bhopal,[2] James Hardie[3] and British Petroleum[4] with large-scale breaches of environmental and work-safety standards has brought to public attention the need for corporations to behave responsibly beyond the financial bottom line. In addition, the proliferation of numerous NGO Internet websites calling attention to corporate misconduct has generated greater awareness of corporate social responsibility (CSR) issues.[5] NGOs and investment managers have also begun to publish 'corporate responsibility indices' and 'ethical investment rankings' to inform shareholders and potential shareholders with concerns about the ethical standards of behaviour demonstrated by companies they invest in.[6]

Many global corporations have themselves become concerned to persuade both themselves and others that they are serious about behaving responsibly both at home and abroad. An example of TNCs demonstrating good international citizenship was seen when numerous TNCs committed to making substantial donations to support relief work for areas affected by the 2004 Boxing Day tsunami in Southeast Asia.[7] Assistance, both financial and in-kind, was also provided by Australia's largest corporations following the October 2005 bomb attacks on nightclubs in the Indonesian province of Bali.[8] Corporations from around the world announced record donations following the 11 September 2001 terrorist attacks in New York, and again following the Cyclone Katrina disaster in late 2005.[9] In nearly all cases, company managers appear to have recognized that the value of maintaining a reputation for ethical behaviour would more than outweigh the cost of providing the promised assistance.[10]

A.   CORPORATE CODES OF CONDUCT

Particularly following the economic excesses of the 1980s, the publication of
individual corporate codes of conduct became a particularly noticeable feature
of corporate reporting throughout the 1990s and into the twenty-first century.
By the end of the 1990s, Mendes and Clark were able to identify five generations of corporate codes.[11] The first generation dealt primarily with conflicts
of interest between management and the firm and were primarily designed to
address the agency risks arising from the corporate form. The second generation broadened their scope to deal with issues of ethical business conduct, such
as the bribing of foreign officials. Examples include the Boeing Company
Code of Ethical Business Conduct, the Halliburton and Subsidiary Companies
Code of Business Conduct, and the Lockheed Martin Corporation Code of
Ethics and Business Conduct.[12]

The third generation of corporate codes of conduct turned their attention to
ensuring respect for stakeholder rights, especially employee rights, but also
recognizing the interests of creditors, suppliers and customers. Examples
include TOTAL General Policy regarding the Management of its Human
Resources, and the WMC Code of Conduct.[13] Such codes were often justified
as being in the long-term interest of the firm by promoting improved corporate relations, a motivated workforce, and satisfied customers. The fourth
generation of codes of conduct focus on wider social issues such as protection
of the environment and respect for the community. Examples include the
Exxon Environment, Health and Safety Policies and the WMC Indigenous
Peoples Policy.[14]

The fifth generation of corporate codes of conduct emanated from concerns
around investment in countries where the rule of law lacks proper government
support and where human rights abuses occur. Early versions of such 'extra-
territorial' codes focussed upon the working conditions of suppliers based
overseas in countries with low standards of labour protection. Examples
include the Reebok and Adidas-Salomon voluntary codes for suppliers in the
textile and footwear industries. Other 'extra-territorial' codes of conduct have
been designed to address the perception that foreign investors are implicated
in or at best fail to adequately address or even express concern about the
human rights abuses occurring around them. Examples include Royal Dutch/
Shell's Use of Force Guidelines, the Reebok International Human Rights
Production Standards, and Wal-Mart Stores, Inc. Standards for Vendor
Partners. Another example is Nestle's Corporate Business Principles which
specifically address the health issues arising from its controversial marketing
practices for breast milk substitute in the Third World in the 1970s and 1980s.
The point here is that multilateral enterprises are themselves recognizing the
limits of confining human rights duties to nation states. Unocal, for example,

has stated publicly that 'human rights are not just a matter for governments'.[15] This recognition is reflected in the fact that voluntary human rights initiatives have expanded rapidly in recent years. While uptake of rights-related company codes of conduct is concentrated among European, North American and, to a lesser extent, Japanese firms, it remains unclear whether this reflects a difference in approach in these countries, or is simply a matter of timing.[16]

B. INDUSTRY-WIDE CODES OF CONDUCT

In addition to individual company policies and codes, there are also various industry-wide voluntary codes of conduct, an example being the Australian Minerals Industry Framework for Sustainable Development.[17] But the Minerals Industry's Framework remains entirely voluntary, has not even been signed by a number of Australia's largest global mining companies,[18] and lacks sanctions for those companies which have become signatories then fail to comply. More effective are those sector-wide codes that have the added contribution of backing from governments and/or NGOs. Two prominent examples of such cooperative sector codes are the Voluntary Principles on Security and Human Rights involving extractive industries,[19] and the Equator Principles, focussing on the investment banking sector.

1. Voluntary Principles on Security and Human Rights

The Voluntary Principles on Security and Human Rights (VPs) were concluded in December 2000 after dialogue facilitated by the UK and US governments between six TNCs in the oil and mining industries, trade union groups, human rights NGOs and business representatives. The VPs aim to counter both the incidence and perception of complicity by the extractive industries in human rights abuses committed by security forces in developing countries. Other government, NGO and TNC participants joined the process established by the VPs after their commencement. By early 2010, the VPs could claim 17 TNCs, seven states,[20] and nine NGOs as participants. The International Committee of the Red Cross, the International Council on Mining and Metals and the International Petroleum Industry Environmental Conservation Association have observer status in relation to the VPs.[21]

The VPs set out a series of broad principles relating to the proper use of security forces and their potential impact on human rights. These include the need for human rights and security concerns to form an integral part of a thorough risk assessment process, consultation with local communities and governments, vetting of security contractors, and receipt of and response to allegations of human rights violations. While there is a reporting process and an attempt to establish the basis of procedures for handling allegations of human rights abuses, the voluntary nature of the instrument means that there is no binding sanction for non-compliance.[22]

The VPs have generated a greater awareness of human rights issues in the extractive industries, particularly in relation to the use of external security forces, and a greater practical integration of human rights concerns into the industry's day-to-day operations. Some participating TNCs have incorporated the VPs into their contracts with security forces, giving the VPs binding force; albeit only in the context of the contractual relationship, and not in a form enforceable by victims. When codes of conduct are incorporated into contractual relations, this only partly overcomes the major deficiency of nearly all voluntary corporate codes of conduct: a failure to include provisions relating to implementation, reporting, verification or enforcement.

Complementing the VPs are the Kimberley Process Certification Scheme[23] to stem the flow of conflict diamonds; and the Extractive Industries Transparency Initiative (the EITI),[24] establishing a degree of revenue transparency in the sums companies pay to host governments. Each seeks to enhance the responsibility and accountability of states and TNCs alike by means of operational standards and procedures for firms, often together with regulatory action by governments. Kimberley, for example, involves a global certification scheme implemented through domestic law, whereby states seek to ensure that the diamonds they trade are from Kimberley-compliant countries by requiring detailed packaging protocols and certification, coupled with a chain of custody warranties by companies. While the EITI is voluntary for states, once a state does sign up, TNCs are legally required to make public their payments to that state's government.

2. Equator Principles

The finance industry's Equator Principles are possibly the most effective attempt to date to bring as many enterprises as possible within the terms of a contractually-binding code of conduct. Directed towards private financial institutions engaged in development finance, they were developed by ten leading banks from seven countries, in consultation with NGOs. The Principles proclaim themselves to be 'a financial industry benchmark for determining, assessing and managing social and environmental risk in project financing'.[25] They were modelled on the policies and guidelines of the World Bank group and the International Finance Corporation (IFC) (further discussed in Chapter 7). By the end of January 2010, 70 large financial institutions were listed as having adopted the Equator Principles.[26] These institutions are known as Equator Principles Financial Institutions (EPFIs). In all funding applications for new projects finance involving a total capital cost of US$10 million or more, or to fund expansion of existing projects, EPFIs commit to provide loans only to projects that conform to ten specified principles.

The Equator Principles use a screening process for projects based on the IFC's environmental and social screening process. Projects are categorized as A, B or C (high, medium or low environmental or social risk). For A and B projects (high and medium risk), the borrower completes a social and environmental assessment addressing the environmental and social issues identified in the categorization process. After appropriate consultation with affected local stakeholders, category A projects and, when located in a non-OECD country or OECD country 'not designated as High-Income', category B projects, must prepare an action plan which addresses mitigation and monitoring of environmental and social risks.[27]

The Equator Principles were revised in July 2006, in line with revisions to the IFC Performance Standards, and to accommodate lessons from the first three years of experience with the Equator Principles. While the 2003 version only applied to direct project loans of US$50 million or more,[28] the 2006 revised version applies not only to direct project financing of US$10 million or more, but also to project finance advisory activities. In the case of project finance advisory activities, 'EPFIs commit to making the client aware of the content, application and benefits of applying the Principles to the anticipated project, and request that the client communicate to the EPFI its intention to adhere to the requirements of the Principles when subsequently seeking financing'.[29] The Equator Principles still do not, however, apply to project finance deals where a bank may be an underwriter, arranger, manager, etc. and not just a creditor.[30]

The 2006 revised version of the Principles also differentiates between 'High-Income OECD countries' on the one hand, and 'non-OECD countries and OECD countries not designated as High-Income' on the other, when applying standards that go beyond host country laws and regulations. For projects in the latter category, compliance with the IFC's Performance Standards, as well as compliance with relevant industry-specific environmental, health and safety guidelines, is required.[31]

As regards enforceability, the Equator Principles currently contain a 'disclaimer' clause making clear that EPFIs view the Principles as a non-binding benchmark for development of individual internal social and environmental policies, procedures and practices. They are not binding, and 'do not create rights in, or liability to, any person, public or private'.[32] The teeth in the process envisaged by the Equator Principles lies in the incorporation of covenants in financing documentation designed to ensure compliance with the Principles.[33] 'Where a borrower is not in compliance with its social and environmental covenants, EPFIs will work with the borrower to bring it back into compliance to the extent feasible, and if the borrower fails to re-establish compliance within an agreed grace period, EPFIs reserve the right to exercise remedies, as they consider appropriate.'[34]

The other strength in the Equator Principles lies in its attempt to ensure ongoing monitoring and reporting over the life of project loans. Under Principles 9 and 10 of the Equator Principles:

> EPFIs will, for all Category A projects, and as appropriate, for Category B projects, require appointment of an independent environmental and/or social expert, or require that the borrower retain qualified and experienced external experts to verify its monitoring information which would be shared with EPFIs.

In addition:

> Each EPFI ... commits to report publicly at least annually about its Equator Principles implementation processes and experience, taking into account appropriate confidentiality considerations.

A further review of the IFC Performance Standards was launched in September 2009, with a new updated framework to be released by January 2011.[35] The IFC Performance Standards Review Process is extremely important for the Equator Principles and all EPFIs, as it will define the standards they undertake to apply in coming years. It remains to be seen whether the review process will lead to an expansion of the scope of the Equator Principles outside the context of advisory services and direct project loans. The review process also may or may not enable the IFC to respond to criticisms that its Performance Standards (and the Equator Principles) do not take the human rights impacts of funded projects adequately into account, nor do they facilitate consideration of the human rights impacts of activities surrounding and/or arising from funded projects.[36]

C.   ON THE GROUND: DO VOLUNTARY CODES OF CONDUCT HAVE A PRACTICAL IMPACT?

Do corporate codes of conduct, whether at the individual company level or more broadly based, actually have an impact on corporate decision-making and behaviour? This question is one which has been asked by a number of researchers who have set out to investigate the effectiveness or otherwise of such codes. Michael Posner and Justine Nolan, for example, have asked 'Can codes of conduct play a role in promoting workers' rights?'[37] They conclude, not surprisingly, that such codes cannot bring about meaningful results unless they establish standards that are measurable, and are supported by effective systems of monitoring and enforcement.[38]

At the moment, a variety of monitoring, reporting and enforcement mechanisms exist at the local, national and international levels. Voluntary codes are clearly most effective when independent bodies are involved in some observer or monitoring capacity, such as is the case with the VPs and the Equator Principles. Least effective are those single company codes which rely on self-monitoring. Many of the shortcomings of self-monitoring have, however, been mitigated by the emergence of a large number of 'self-appointed' independent monitors at local, national and international levels, including NGOs, union bodies and specific-issue groups, as well as independent media organizations.[39] The involvement of such independent bodies has generated an often admirable degree of transparency in relation to corporate behaviour, with information reaching an ever-broadening audience through modern avenues of communication.[40]

It remains the case, however, that tensions which arise between making a profit, on the one hand, and social responsibility, on the other, are still primarily left to be resolved through free markets. But free markets can and do fail. International ground rules are needed to promote the benefits of corporate activity, as a form of cooperative enterprise, while at the same time restraining and mitigating the worst effects of unhindered consumerism and corporate greed. The market alone demonstrably cannot achieve this. As Raj Patel has noted, subject to market forces alone, 'Corporations are *Homo economicus*. Quite rationally and without malice, they try to increase their profits by any means, legal and occasionally illegal. Corporations that don't follow this cardinal law of the jungle will go out of business, which means that whatever else a corporation makes, it'll invariably produce externalities'.[41] Regulation is needed to overcome and minimize the negative externalities that corporate activity produces because corporations cannot be expected to minimize their own negative externalities.[42] It also stands to reason that to the extent that the negative externalities of corporate activity are global in nature, then the laws aimed at minimizing them need to be global in nature as well.

D.   GLOBAL STANDARDS FOR CORPORATE RESPONSIBILITY

To be effective, international ground rules for corporate activity require at least three things that are lacking in existing industry codes of conduct: a minimum degree of consensus on the content of uniform global standards; reliable and consistent reporting practices that are globally standardized, and independent verification and monitoring mechanisms that also meet minimum standards agreed upon at a global level. At the moment, such standards simply cannot be found in existing 'voluntary' codes of behaviour at the individual company or industry-wide level. There are, however, a growing number of UN and multinational instruments and guidelines for TNC behaviour which together are creating the foundation for a more broadly accepted set of principles in relation to corporate responsibility in a variety of areas, including human rights, labour standards, the environment, socially responsible investment and anti-corruption.

1.   Global Reporting Initiative

The lack of globally standardized reporting practices remains a problem. Amongst the increasing number of companies taking up social and environmental reporting initiatives, each has adopted its own unique position on the coverage and extent of such reports, the nature and kind of the material included and the methodologies used. This makes comparisons between companies, industries, countries and regions impossible. Global standards for reporting are the only way to ensure a coordinated global response to social and environmental concerns. The Global Reporting Initiative (GRI) provides the basis for such standardization through its 2002 Sustainability Reporting Guidelines ('GRI Guidelines'). The GRI Guidelines are the best known and most widely used example of 'triple bottom line reporting' – reporting that encompasses financial, social and environmental performance.[43] They consist of a general reporting framework applicable to all corporations,[44] as well as a series of sector-specific supplements.[45] As more and more countries begin to strengthen and expand their corporate reporting requirements, the GRI is increasingly being used as a reference point. For example, all companies listed on the Johannesburg Stock Exchange have been required to report on social performance in accordance with the GRI Guidelines since September 2003.[46] Use of the GRI Guidelines is also promoted through cooperative engagement with other government-approved initiatives addressed to TNCs, such as the OECD's Guidelines for Multinational Enterprises and the Global Compact.[47] For most companies, however, subscribing to the GRI remains entirely voluntary. Moreover, while the GRI Guidelines provide guidance, there is no accreditation or external evaluation, so that compliance with its standards remains patchy.[48]

2.   United Nations Draft Code for Transnational Corporations

By the 1960s, UN agencies were making clear their determination to become concerned with the question of how global business enterprises should behave. The UN General Assembly made clear this concern in its Declaration on Social Progress and Development.[49] An early effort by the United Nations to adopt a voluntary code on policies of transnational enterprises was aborted in the 1960s,[50] but not abandoned. In 1974, during the era when the debate surrounding the 'new international economic order' dominated discourse in the United Nations,[51] the UN Economic and Social Council (ECOSOC) established the Commission on Transnational Corporations, charged with developing a multinational code of conduct for transnational corporations.[52] A series of draft codes were produced over the next 16 years,[53] the last draft being produced in 1990. While recognizing some rights for investors, the 1983 and 1990 draft codes emphasized the need for foreign investors to obey host country law, follow host country economic policies and avoid interference in the host country's domestic political affairs.[54]

By 1990, polarization had developed between developing countries which were pushing for mandatory rules for TNCs and an emphasis on the municipal law of the host state, on the one hand, and developed nations seeking a voluntary set of broader guidelines inspired by international law, on the other. The 1990 Draft UN Code of Conduct for TNCs, which was broad-ranging and ambitious, was never adopted, and the drafting process was abandoned by 1994.[55]

Although never finalized as a legal instrument, the Draft UN TNC Code of Conduct still has normative value. In particular, the drafting process and the debates surrounding the Code provide valuable evidence of state practice in relation to such things as the need for corporations to adhere to human rights standards. The drafting experience also contributed to later efforts to express standards of conduct for TNCs, including the Global Compact and the UN Draft Norms discussed below.

3. ILO Tripartite Declaration

By the 1970s, when the Draft UN TNC Code was being developed and debated, another UN agency, the International Labour Organization (ILO), was also concerning itself with the behaviour of big business. By 1977, the ILO had secured the Tripartite Declaration of Principles concerning Multinational Enterprises and Social Policy ('ILO Tripartite Declaration').[56] The ILO Tripartite Declaration begins by making clear its voluntary status, stating that 'its provisions shall not limit or otherwise affect obligations arising out of ratification of any ILO Convention'.[57]

The ILO Tripartite Declaration also has lesser legal status than ILO Conventions. This is because it was adopted by the ILO Governing Body, which has a limited membership of governments and workers' and employers' organizations at any one time. Its adoption as a Declaration by the Governing Body gives it a lesser legal status than if it were a Convention adopted by the ILO Annual Conference composed of all ILO member states. Its lesser legal status is also emphasized by the many words throughout the Declaration which emphasize its non-binding and unenforceable nature – terms such as 'encourage', 'commended' and 'recommended'. For example, the dispute resolution mechanism in the ILO Tripartite Declaration, to the extent that there is one, involves 'requests for interpretation' of its terms, and does not result in a legally binding outcome for any of the parties involved.[58]

The ILO Tripartite Declaration is directed to member governments of the ILO, in their capacities as both home and host countries of TNCs, and employers and trade unions within those countries, reflecting the tripartite structure of the organization. In line with the role and purpose of the ILO, the Declaration is confined to the area of labour standards, and focusses particularly upon promotion and security of employment, equality of opportunity and treatment, training, wages and conditions, child labour, freedom of association and collective bargaining. The principles are drawn from ILO Conventions which are binding on states that ratify them under international law. However, the ILO Declaration expresses these principles in terms of their application to corporate entities rather than to governments.

The adoption of the ILO Tripartite Declaration as a non-binding instrument emphasizes the politically charged nature of any attempt to regulate company employment practices at the international level. Not surprisingly therefore, the ILO Tripartite Declaration has so far revealed itself as, at best, a weak and ineffective instrument for achieving change.[59]

The ILO Declaration creates a procedure that asks governments, workers' and employers' organizations to respond at regular intervals to questions relating to its implementation. It also provides for publication of a summary of the replies by the ILO. In November 2005, the Sub-Committee on Multinational Enterprises of the ILO published a summary of results from its *Eighth Survey on the Effect Given to the Tripartite Declaration of Principles concerning Multinational Enterprises and Social Policy.*[60] The questions contained in the Eighth Survey related specifically to the years 2000–2003, a period during which foreign direct investment (FDI) inflows reached a historical record of US$1.4 trillion in 2000, before declining three years in a row from 2001 to 2003.[61] By 2003, global FDI inflows had declined to US$632 billion[62] while at the same time countries continued to liberalize their FDI regimes. In the single year 2003, it was reported that there had been 244 changes in laws and regulations affecting FDI, of which 220 were deemed to be measures favouring FDI. In comparison, there were 150 changes in laws and regulations affecting FDI in 2000, of which 147 were more favourable towards FDI.[63]

In keeping with past practice, the Eighth Survey questionnaire was sent both to governments and to the most representative national employers' and workers' organizations in all member states. Unfortunately, neither France, which became the largest recipient of FDI among industrialized countries in 2003, nor Australia, another large recipient of FDI, nor the United States, whose cumulative inflows and outflows during 2000–2003 were larger than those of any other country, replied.[64] In fact, only 62 countries replied by the survey response deadline, as compared to 52 countries for the First Survey (1980); 62 for the Second (1983); 68 for the Third (1986); 70 for the Fourth (1989); 73 for the Fifth (1992); 74 for the Sixth (1996); and 100 for the Seventh (2001).[65] This reveals one of the major defects of the ILO Declaration as an instrument purporting to establish global standards: not even half of the membership of the United Nations (currently 192 members) is represented as willing to subject itself to ILO scrutiny via the mechanism of the survey.

4.   United Nations Global Compact

The Global Compact initiative was announced by the then UN Secretary-General Kofi Annan at the World Economic Forum in Davos, Switzerland, in January 1999, and formally launched at the United Nations Headquarters in July 2000. The Global Compact allows not just TNCs and business organizations, but also public sector bodies, cities, academic institutions, NGOs and labour organizations, to sign up to a set of ten universally accepted principles in the areas of human rights, labour standards, the environment and, since early 2005, anti-corruption.[66] The Ten Principles are that businesses should:

1. support and respect the protection of internationally proclaimed human rights within their sphere of influence;
2. make sure that they are not complicit in human rights abuses;
3. uphold the freedom of association and the effective recognition of the right to collective bargaining;
4. uphold the elimination of all forms of forced and compulsory labour;
5. uphold the effective elimination of child labour;
6. eliminate discrimination in respect of employment and occupation;
7. support a precautionary approach to environmental challenges;
8. undertake initiatives to promote greater environmental responsibility;
9. encourage the development and diffusion of environmentally friendly technologies; and
10. work against all forms of corruption, including extortion and bribery.

The ten principles are drawn from four of the most important (because universally accepted) international legal instruments:

*   the Universal Declaration of Human Rights;[67]
*   the International Labour Organization's Declaration on Fundamental Principles and Rights at Work;[68]
*   the Rio Declaration on Environment and Development;[69]
*   the United Nations Convention Against Corruption.[70]

By June 2010, the Global Compact had grown to include more than 7,700 participants, including over 5,300 business participants from 130 countries.[71] Business participants include both corporations (250 or more full time employees) and small-and-medium-sized enterprises (SMEs, defined as those employing between 10 and 250 full-time employees). The initiative followed the failure of earlier draft codes of conduct to obtain treaty status,[72] and complements efforts by individual UN organizations such as ECOSOC, the ILO and the Human Rights Commission to formulate standards of behaviour for TNCs.

By participating in the Global Compact, TNCs agree to incorporate its ten principles into their day-to-day operations and to report publicly on their implementation, for instance in annual reports. The original requirement to report directly to the Global Compact Secretariat annually was replaced in 2005 with a public reporting requirement. One of the explicit commitments that a company makes when joining the Global Compact is to submit annual Communications on Progress (COP) using reporting indicators such as the Global Reporting Initiative (GRI) Guidelines. The COP must be placed on the UN Global Compact website and shared widely with the company's stake-holders.[73] A violation of the Global Compact Policy on COP will result in a change in a participant's status from 'active' to 'non-communicating' to 'inactive', and eventually results in the delisting of the participant. As of October 2009, over 1,000 companies had been delisted from the Global Compact website,[74] and a significant proportion of those remaining are labelled as having 'Non-communicating COP Status'. For example, of the 605 businesses (all sectors) from France listed as participants in the Global Compact on 1 June 2010, there were 154 with a non-communicating COP status.[75] Of the 260 American business participants listed on that date, only 182 were listed as active.[76]

The COP public reporting requirement was introduced as one of a number of 'integrity measures' in 2005. The Global Compact Integrity Measures were largely a response to criticisms of the Compact as ineffective, toothless or a 'blue-wash'. It was said that the United Nations was simply allowing companies to benefit from their association with a UN programme, without imposing on them any legal obligation to make any meaningful changes to their operations.[77] In addition to introducing the public reporting requirement, the Global Compact Integrity Measures extended the strict rules on the use of UN logos to the Global Compact logo,[78] and also introduced for the first time a complaints mechanism. Section 4 of the Integrity Measures creates a complaints process for 'credible complaints of egregious abuse of the Global Compact's overall aims and principles'.[79] The focus of the complaints system is on engagement with the company and working with it to achieve change or, in the words of the Integrity Measures, to 'align the actions of the company with its commitments to the Global Compact principles'. The strongest remedy under the complaints process is designation as an 'inactive' partici-pant'[80] – the same sanction applied to companies that fail to comply with the public reporting COP policy requirements.

Despite its lack of teeth, the Global Compact does perform a valuable facil-itative role. It takes fundamental principles from broadly accepted UN instru-ments and distils them into an easily digested form. This facilitative role is enhanced by the development of practical guides for corporate managers, such as the *Guide for Integrating Human Rights into Business Management*.[81] Developed by the Business Leaders Initiative on Human Rights, the UN Global Compact and the Office of the High Commission on Human Rights, this Guide presents the process of implementing human rights protection in business processes in management-friendly language, rather than the language of international law. Other guidance material includes training notes and manuals on business and human rights, guidelines on the establishment of grievance mechanisms and reporting and risk-assessment guidelines.[82] The Global Compact Human Rights Working Group has also developed and endorsed a series of notes on good business practices on human rights.[83] These Good Practice Notes, as they are known, seek to identify general approaches recognized by companies and stakeholders as being good for both business and human rights. Examples include the Good Practice Note on *Setting up a Multi-Stakeholder Panel as a Tool for Effective Stakeholder Dialogue*[84] and the Good Practice Note on *How Business Can Encourage Governments to Fulfil their Human Rights Obligations*.[85]

One interesting question which remains to be explored is whether corpora-tions from nations with a 'stakeholder-focussed' model of corporate gover-nance are more willing or more able to participate in the Global Compact than those from states where a shareholder-focussed, Anglo-US system of corpo-rate regulation prevails. By 1 June 2010, 168 business organizations from the United Kingdom, 45 enterprises from Australia and 268 from the United States were represented in the Global Compact business participant list. France, in contrast, was represented by 605 business participants, but Germany by only 142 businesses; 105 business participants in the Global Compact on 1 June 2010 came from Japan, 162 from mainland China, and 153 from India. There were also 104 Swedish and 115 Italian enterprises on the Global Compact business participants list.[86]

The proportion of all TNCs that have signed up as Global Compact partic-ipants remains extremely low. The media appears at least partly to blame for this. While mainstream media are all too quick to expose problems in the UN hierarchy, such as corrupt involvement in the Iran oil-for-food programme and other problems at the top,[87] positive UN initiatives such as the Global Compact are more often ignored.[88]

5.   United Nations Human Rights Norms for TNCs

In 1998, the UN Sub-Commission on the Promotion and Protection of Human Rights[89] began work on an instrument to identify and draw together from the various sources of international law the existing human rights obligations which could be said to apply to TNCs.[90] In August 2003, the Sub-Commission formally approved the instrument known as the Norms on the Responsibilities of Transnational Corporations and Other Business Enterprises with regard to Human Rights[91] ('Draft Norms'). When the Draft Norms came before the UN Commission on Human Rights at its 60th Session in 2004, however, they were met with a frosty reception and a great deal of controversy. The business world was particularly offended by the suggestion that the negative impacts of corporate activity required regulation at the international level. Particularly objectionable was the idea that TNCs might be held legally accountable for the actions of others, including suppliers, users of their products and even governments. The corporate lobby therefore rose to action and primed their governments in preparation for the April 2004 session of the Human Rights Commission.[92]

When the Commission considered the Draft Norms for the first time on 20 April 2004, they were surrounded by so much controversy that they were effectively put on hold by the Commission, and a decision made to engage in further consultation.[93] At its 61st Session in 2005, the Commission recommended a two-year mandate for a Special Representative of the Secretary-General (SRSG) 'on the issue of human rights and transnational corporations and other business enterprises', to report back to the Commission on some of the issues raised by the Draft Norms. That recommendation was duly acted upon, and an appointment was made in July 2005.[94]

(a)   Basic provisions

The Draft Norms and their accompanying Commentary were compiled and drafted by the Sub-Commission as a statement of the human rights obligations of transnational corporations. The Norms begin by making clear that:

> States have the primary responsibility to promote, secure the fulfilment of, respect, ensure respect of, and protect human rights recognised in international as well as national law, including ensuring that transnational corporations and other business enterprises respect human rights.[95]

Recognizing that relying on state responsibility alone is inadequate to protect human rights, particularly in the context of TNC activities transcending the control of any one state, the Draft Norms then go on to provide that:

> Within their respective spheres of activity and influence, transnational corporations and other business enterprises have the obligation to promote, secure the fulfilment

of, respect, ensure respect of, and protect human rights recognised in international as well as national law.[96]

The Norms then list 36 specific international human rights instruments, taking up the human rights obligations considered most relevant to companies, and applying them directly to TNCs and other business enterprises, 'within their respective spheres of activity and influence'.[97] The human rights obligations applicable to TNCs and other business enterprises are identified in articles 2–14 of the Draft Norms (the 'content' provisions), and include equality of opportunity and non-discriminatory treatment; the right to security of person and recognized labour rights such as the provision of a safe and healthy workplace and adequate wages, and freedom of association and collective bargaining. The content provisions also prohibit corporations from participating in or benefiting from international crimes against the person, including war crimes, torture and forced labour.[98] There is also a prohibition on receiving bribes,[99] a requirement to observe fair business practices and product safety,[100] and requirements relating to environmental protection[101] and the realization of economic, social and cultural rights.[102]

The Draft Norms were innovative in at least three respects, and it is these particular features which have made them so highly controversial. First, the Draft Norms go well beyond existing human rights law, both in the content of the rights they enumerate, and in the scope of their purported application. Second, the Norms seek to extend implementation and enforcement obligations to non-state entities, and provide novel mechanisms for ensuring that these obligations are met. Third, the concept of a TNC's 'sphere of influence', used to delineate the boundaries of a TNC's obligations, is a relatively novel and potentially slippery concept which has generated much dispute.

(b) Moving outside the boundaries of traditional human rights law
The first way in which the Draft Norms go outside the currently accepted boundaries of human rights law is in the content of the rights it enumerates. In particular, rights associated with consumer protection, the environment and corruption are usually accepted as being already covered by different areas of law, and questions have been raised as to the value or appropriateness of including these rights in a human rights instrument. As David Kinley and Rachel Chambers have noted, the answer may be that given the inadequacy of national protection in these areas in many states, and the interrelation between the enjoyment of these rights and 'mainstream' human rights, TNCs should be held to clear international standards with respect to these rights.[103]

In relation to economic, social and cultural rights, these have always been limited by the concepts of 'available resources', 'progressive realization' and 'appropriate means' when applied to states.[104] That is, the state duty to ensure the realization of economic, social and cultural rights is subject to the right of each state to decide how best to make use of available resources, to determine what means are most appropriate to bring about such realization, and to determine the rate at which particular measures are to be introduced. There is no such limitation in the Draft Norms on the obligation of TNCs to contribute to the realization of social, economic and cultural rights.[105]

But the real departure of the Draft Norms from traditional international law lies in its application to non-state parties. As further noted below, international law traditionally only applies to states. The Draft Norms not only apply to non-state transnational corporations, they also extend to 'business enterprises' having any relation with a transnational corporation or carrying out activities with impacts that are 'not entirely local'.[106] The term 'other business enterprise' is defined to include any contractor, sub-contractor, supplier, licensee or distributor of a TNC, regardless of the legal form of the enterprise or the relationship involved.[107] The enforcement provisions provide that TNCs should include the Draft Norms in all contracts with suppliers and other business partners, thus establishing contractual liability within a company's supply chain. But no detail is provided as to the length or depth of the TNC's own liability for abuses occurring up or down the supply chain, although such liability clearly exists. For example, the Draft Norms provide that a TNC shall not 'benefit from' certain serious human rights abuses,[108] but do not define the boundaries of this duty. This raises the question of whether and to what extent a TNC should be held liable for serious abuses committed by a sub-contractor or supplier?

The Draft Norms also provide that 'Security arrangements for transnational corporations and other business enterprises shall observe international human rights norms as well as the laws and professional standards of the country or countries in which they operate'.[109] There is, however, no means provided for determining the extent to which a TNC should be held liable for the failure of security arrangements from which it benefits to meet such standards.

Paragraph 11 of the Draft Norms provides that 'Transnational corporations and other business enterprises shall refrain from any activity which supports, solicits, or encourages States or any other entities to abuse human rights. They shall further seek to ensure that the goods and services they provide will not be used to abuse human rights'. However, no indication is provided of exactly what is required of a TNC to ensure, for example, that its mere presence does not encourage an abusive government to continue its reign of terror, or to ensure that the products it produces are not misused or used illegally by the perpetrators of human rights abuses. Nor does the concept of 'sphere of influence' provide a solution to this uncertainty, for reasons further explored below.

(c) Implementation and enforcement mechanisms for non-state entities
The ambitious scope of the Draft Norms would not be so objectionable to business if they were intended simply as statements of principle. But the Norms are framed in mandatory terms, backed by mechanisms for implementation and enforcement. Such terms are commonplace in relation to state obligations found in human rights treaties, such as the International Covenant on Civil and Political Rights.[110] But the Norms seek to extend implementation and enforcement obligations to non-state entities and provide novel mechanisms for ensuring these obligations are met. The general provisions of implementation require TNCs and other business enterprises to adopt, disseminate and implement internal operational rules in compliance with the Norms and also to incorporate the Norms in contracts with other parties.[111] There are provisions for the internal and external monitoring and verification of companies' application of the Norms, including the use of either a new or an existing UN monitoring mechanism.[112] In addition, states are called on to establish and reinforce a legal framework for ensuring that the Norms are implemented, although the wording of paragraph 17 ('should' rather than 'shall') suggests that this is not an obligatory or normative provision. Monitoring and verification is backed up by a reparation provision, which obliges companies to provide prompt, effective and adequate reparations to those affected by a TNC's failure to comply with the Norms. The reparation provision reflects a similar provision in the ILC's Draft Articles on State Responsibility,[113] and is also in line with principles of compensation recognized in legal systems throughout the world. As further argued below, the concept of reparation is thus one which could usefully and legitimately be retained in relation to TNC human rights responsibilities.[114]

(d) The 'sphere of influence' concept
All previous instruments aimed at delineating the responsibilities of TNCs in a global context have grappled with the need to define the boundaries of such responsibilities. The United Nations Global Compact achieves this through use of the concept of 'sphere of influence'. The concept was, in fact, first introduced by the Global Compact, and has since entered the lexicon of corporate social responsibility (CSR) discourse. The 'sphere of influence' concept was then taken up in the Draft Norms. The use of this concept to demarcate respective spheres of responsibility is not found in other international law instruments, and is not one familiar to international lawyers outside of the CSR context. Its definition and application, especially its legal connotations, have been the subject of heated debate and some confusion.[115]

The concept of sphere of influence seeks to establish the scope of corporate responsibility for human rights issues based on the extent of a particular business's influence.[116] As originally conceived, the concept was intended to help companies 'support and respect the protection of internationally proclaimed human rights' within and beyond their workplaces. To promote this aim, the Global Compact developed a model to visualize the sphere of influence, which a number of companies then adopted. The model consists of a set of concentric circles, mapping stakeholders in a company's value chain: with employees in the innermost circle, then moving outward to suppliers, the marketplace, the community and governments. The model made the implicit assumption that the 'influence', and thus presumably the responsibility, of a company declines as one moves outward from the centre. The Draft UN Human Rights Norms later used the phrase 'within their respective spheres of activity and influence' in defining the limits of TNC obligations to 'promote, secure the fulfilment of, respect, ensure respect of and protect human rights recognized in international as well as national law'.[117]

The sphere of influence model has helped companies to consider their roles in society beyond the workplace, and what actions to take in order to respect and support human rights. For example, a survey of the Fortune Global 500 firms conducted by the SRSG showed that respondents appeared to prioritize their obligations to stakeholders in approximately the order envisaged by the model – one significant variation being that firms in the extractive sector placed communities ahead of supply chains.[118] Sphere of influence remains a useful metaphor for companies in thinking about their human rights impacts beyond the workplace and in identifying opportunities to support human rights, which is what the Global Compact seeks to achieve.[119] But there are major problems with the sphere of influence concept as a tool for defining the parameters of TNC responsibilities.

The main problem is that the sphere of influence model of concentric circles is imprecise in a number of different ways. First, there is the problem that:

> If the only difference is that governments have a comprehensive set of obligations, while those of corporations are limited to their 'spheres of influence' ... how are the latter [obligations] to be delineated? Does Shell's sphere of influence in the Niger Delta not cover everything ranging from the right to health, through the right to free speech, to the rights to physical integrity and due process.[120]

Philip Alston asks 'what are the consequences of saddling [corporations] with all of the constraints, restrictions, and even positive obligations which apply to governments?'[121] His answer raises concerns that the 'sphere of influence' formula, as expressed in the Draft Norms, could undermine corporate autonomy, risk-taking and entrepreneurship. Ruggie agrees, and further argues that the formula's possible impact on the roles and responsibilities of governments is 'equally troubling'.[122] Ruggie argues that imposing the full range of duties on TNCs directly under international law 'by definition reduces the discretionary space of individual governments' within the scope of their duties to secure the fulfilment of human rights.[123] But governments have, according to Ruggie, a legitimate need to exercise discretion, make trade-offs and balance decisions in determining best how to secure human rights. This is especially the case when it comes to those economic, social and cultural rights over which TNCs may have a great deal of influence. Ruggie is particularly concerned that imposing overlapping human rights duties on both states and TNCs could 'generate endless strategic gaming and legal wrangling on the part of governments and companies alike'.[124] Furthermore, 'where governance is weak to begin with, shifting obligations onto corporations to protect and even fulfil the broad spectrum of human rights may further undermine domestic political incentives to make governments more responsive and responsible to their own citizenry, which surely is the most effective way to realize rights'.[125]

The concept of influence is also imprecise because it does not differentiate stakeholders whose rights could be affected negatively by a company's practices, such as communities, from actors over whose actions a TNC might have some degree of influence, whether suppliers, communities or governments. This ambiguity conflates two very different meanings of influence: one is impact, where the TNC's activities or relationships are causing human rights harm; the other is whatever leverage a company may have over actors that are causing harm. The first falls within accepted parameters of a TNC's responsibilities to be aware of the impact of its actions (due diligence).[126] The exercise of leverage, however, does not usually fall within the scope of a TNC's obligations.

The Global Compact sphere of influence concept 'implies that the more control, authority or influence a business has over a situation giving rise to human rights abuses (or the means to improve respect for human rights) the greater the business responsibility to act'.[127] Anchoring TNC responsibility in influence defined as leverage like this is problematic, because it requires assuming, in moral philosophy terms, that 'can implies ought'. However, TNCs cannot be held responsible for the human rights impacts of every entity over which they may have some leverage. TNCs have potential leverage in many cases where they are neither contributing to nor a causal agent of the harm in question. Nor is it even desirable to require TNCs to act wherever they have influence, particularly over governments. Asking companies to support human rights voluntarily where they have influence is one thing; but attributing responsibility to them on that basis alone is another.[128] The concept of sphere of influence thus becomes particularly problematic when used in the context of norms framed in mandatory terms, such as in the case of the Draft Norms.

The SRSG has also argued in relation to the Draft Norms, that influence as a basis for assigning responsibility invites manipulation. This is so because influence can only be defined in relation to someone or something. Thus, it is itself subject to influence. A government can deliberately fail to perform its duties in the hope or expectation that a company will yield to social pressures to promote or fulfil certain rights, demonstrating why state duties and corporate responsibilities must be defined independently of each other.[129]

When operationalization of the sphere of influence concept has been discussed further, it has been through the concept of 'proximity': 'The "sphere of influence" of a business entity tends to include the individuals to whom it has a certain political, contractual, economic or geographic proximity. Every business entity, whatever its size, will have a sphere of influence; the larger it is, the larger the sphere of influence is likely to be.'[130] But the precise meaning of proximity remains unclear. What constitutes 'political proximity', for example? The most intuitive meaning of proximity – geographic – can be misleading. Clearly, companies need to be concerned with their impact on workers and surrounding communities, but their activities can equally affect the rights of people far away from the source, as, for example, violations of privacy rights by Internet service providers can endanger dispersed end-users. The example of Google's dilemma in deciding to withdraw from China also provides an example of how a government in pursuit of its own agenda can hijack the rational pursuit of profits by a TNC, to the detriment of human rights. It is not proximity that determines whether or not human rights impacts fall within a TNC's sphere of responsibility, but rather the TNC's web of activities and relationships.[131]

In attempting to 'clarify' the concept of sphere of influence and its implications, the SRSG explored the possibility of redefining corporate 'influence' in terms of 'control' or 'causation'. However, he concluded that those concepts, in turn, may be too restrictive for companies that seek to not only respect rights but also to voluntarily 'support' them, as, for example, in the context of the Global Compact.[132]

Furthermore, the concepts of control or causation could wrongly limit the baseline responsibility of companies to respect rights. As further explored in Chapter 6, the responsibility to respect requires that TNCs exercise due diligence to identify, prevent and address adverse human rights impacts related to their activities. If the scope of due diligence were defined by control and causation this could imply, for example, that companies were not required to consider the human rights impacts of suppliers they do not legally control, or situations where their own actions might not directly cause harm but indirectly contribute to abuse.

These considerations led the SRSG to conclude that, while sphere of influence remains a useful metaphor for TNCs to think more broadly about their human rights responsibilities and opportunities, it is of limited utility in clarifying the specific parameters of their responsibility to respect human rights.[133]

(e) Status of the Draft Norms

The SRSG found in his 2006 Interim Report that despite the claim by some that the Draft Norms were no more than 'a restatement of international legal principles applicable to companies', there was in fact no basis in existing law to support the obligations for private actors set out in the Norms. He concluded that:

> What the Norms have done, ..., is to take existing State-based human rights instruments and simply assert that many of their provisions are now binding on corporations as well. But that assertion itself has little authoritative basis in international law – hard, soft or otherwise.[134]

Nor do the Draft Norms have any formally binding status in their own right. And given the effective criticism of the Draft Norms by the SRSG, they probably never will. But they have now become part of a larger corpus of normative statements contributing to the emergence of customary law in this area. Given the significant amount of opposition to the Draft Norms, their value as evidence of customary law (state practice and *opinio juris*)[135] remains weak at the moment; but custom evolves, and so may the status of the Norms.

6. OECD Guidelines for Multinational Enterprises

Partly in response to developments in other multinational organizations at the time, the Organisation for Economic Co-operation and Development (OECD) drafted its own set of Guidelines for Multinational Enterprises in 1976.[136] The current version of the OECD Guidelines dates from 2000. The Guidelines describe themselves as 'recommendations addressed by governments to multinational enterprises'.[137] As an instrument emanating from a group of industrialized countries[138] where most TNCs are based, the Guidelines serve as a statement of the standards expected by home governments of their corporations operating abroad. Enterprises[139] are invited to adopt the guidelines in their management systems and incorporate the principles into their corporate operations. Chapter I of the Guidelines is careful to stress, however, that 'Observance of the Guidelines by enterprises is voluntary and not legally enforceable'. Other chapters of the Guidelines cover a wide range of issues, including labour and environmental standards, corruption, consumer protection, technology transfer, competition and taxation.

The revised 2000 version of the OECD Guidelines established a system for lodging complaints and settling disputes. Anyone can lodge a complaint about a TNC's activities to the National Contact Point (NCP) of the country where the relevant conduct occurred, or the country where the TNC is based, if either of those countries have adopted the Guidelines. If the NCP considers that a complaint warrants investigation, it will investigate the matter and attempt to facilitate resolution between the relevant parties in accordance with the Guidelines. If the parties involved do not reach agreement on the issues raised by the complaint, the NCP will issue a statement and make recommendations on the implementation of the Guidelines. While NCPs can recommend that some measure of restitution or remedial action be taken, recommendations in general are non-binding and cannot be enforced.[140]

NCPs can also request assistance from the OECD Investment Committee, which can issue a clarification of the application of the Guidelines in particular circumstances.[141] Clarifications are made publicly available but do not generally name the enterprise involved. This is in line with the OECD's desire to avoid taking on a quasi-judicial or punitive role. The OECD views the Guidelines as a 'problem solving' mechanism rather than a means of holding TNCs to account.[142]

The Investment Committee oversees the NCP dispute resolution process. It considers annual reports submitted by NCPs, deals with requests from NCPs for clarifications and other forms of assistance, considers submissions by adhering countries or advisory bodies on whether an NCP has correctly interpreted the Guidelines in specific instances, and issues clarifications in response to such submissions where necessary.[143]

Following the adoption of the current version of the Guidelines in 2000, 207 requests to consider specific instances had been filed with NCPs by the time of the June 2009 Annual Meeting of the NCPs.[144] Of these, 146 specific instances had been taken up for consideration by NCPs, mostly involving issues of labour rights under Chapter IV of the Guidelines. 114 of the 146 specific instances taken up for consideration since 2000 had been concluded or closed by June 2009.[145]

One example of a complaint under the OECD Guidelines is the complaint that was lodged with the Australian NCP by a coalition of NGOs[146] in June 2005 against Global Solutions Limited (Australia) (GSL). GSL was the Australian subsidiary of a UK-based enterprise which operated immigration detention centres for the Australian government. The complaint explicitly invoked the human rights provision in the Guidelines and alleged that GSL had violated that provision by detaining children indefinitely, acquiescing in mandatory detention of asylum seekers and treating detainees inhumanely.[147] The complaint was largely framed in terms of GSL's complicity in Australia's violations of international human rights law in relation to the implementation of its policy of mandatory detention for asylum seekers. The Australian NCP issued its 'final statement' in April 2006.[148] The NCP began by ruling out of consideration significant issues concerning the human rights complicity of Australia's immigration detention regime.[149] In addressing the complaint through mediation between the parties, however, the NCP was still able to address a number of practical issues relating to the treatment of detainees.[150]

The mediation process allowed the complainants to secure GSL's agreement to incorporate human rights standards into future contracts and to use those standards as 'the appropriate framework for a service delivery model in all areas of detention and deportation'.[151]

7.   ISO Standards and Guidelines

The International Organization for Standardization (ISO) is a network of the national standards bodies of 157 countries.[152] It is well recognized as the world's leading developer of International Standards of all types, based on consensus among relevant categories of stakeholder and among countries. ISO standards include standards relating to occupational health and safety,[153] food safety,[154] sustainability[155] and environmental management systems.[156] There are also standards governing managerial and organizational practice generally. The most well known of the ISO standards setting out requirements for good management practices is ISO 9001:2000. This general guideline has, since 2000, been supplemented by new standards based on the same generic model but developed to meet the needs of specific sectors or addressing specific challenges.[157]

In 1997, the multi-stakeholder NGO Social Accountability International (SAI) was founded to develop the first globally recognized accreditation standard relating to social responsibility.[158] The most recent version of SAI's SA8000 Standard for socially responsible employment practices dates from 2008.[159] The SA8000 Standard prescribes specific performance standards which are audited and certified in line with other recognized systems for certifying compliance to international standards such as ISO 9000, ISO 14000 and the Forest Stewardship Council.[160] SA8000 Standards cover nine key areas of workplace norms, and are based on various ILO Conventions, the Universal Declaration of Human Rights and the UN Convention on the Rights of the Child.[161] A facility wishing to seek certification to SA8000 must apply to one of the 19 auditing firms and certification bodies accredited by Social Accountability Accreditation Services (SAAS).[162] Accredited facilities are required to produce an annual report detailing compliance with the SA8000 code of practice. As of 31 December 2009, there were 2,103 SA8000-accredited facilities from 63 different countries and employing 1,213,796 employees.[163]

ISO 26000 Guidance on Social Responsibility, Draft International Standard

At its General Assembly in Stockholm, Sweden, in September 2002, the ISO decided that the time had come to consider the value of developing management standards relating to corporate social responsibility (CSR).[164] This resolution recognized the value of the ISO 14001 environmental management system standard in improving the efficiency of corporate environmental management, and built on a 2001 report prepared by the ISO Consumer Policy Committee on the value of CSR standards.[165] In 2003, the multi-stakeholder ISO Ad Hoc Group on Social Responsibility (SR) which had been set up by ISO's Technical Management Board (TMB) completed an extensive overview of SR initiatives and issues worldwide.[166] In 2004, ISO held an international multi-stakeholder conference on whether it should launch SR work. The positive recommendation of this conference led to the establishment in late 2004 of the ISO Working Group on Social Responsibility (ISO WG SR) to develop a new ISO Standard, to be designated ISO 26000.[167]

By the time the ISO 26000 Guidance on Social Responsibility was published as a Draft International Standard in September 2009, 91 countries and 42 organizations with liaison status were participating in the ISO WG SR under the joint leadership of the ISO members for Brazil (ABNT) and Sweden (SIS).[168] Six main stakeholder groups were thus involved throughout the drafting process: industry, government, labour, consumers, non-governmental organizations, and service support research. The ISO WG SR also aimed throughout for a geographical and gender balance of participants.[169] At its Eighth Plenary Meeting on 17–21 May 2010, the ISO WG SR approved the Draft ISO 26000 for processing as a Final Draft International Standard (FDIS), and reaffirmed its desire for publication of the fully fledged ISO Standard to occur in November 2010, following a two-month FDIS vote by ISO member countries in August/September 2010.[170]

The two most notable features of Draft ISO 26000 are, first, that, like the Global Compact initiative, it is not limited to corporations, but is intended for use by organizations of all types, in both public and private sectors. Second, ISO 26000 is a guidance document, not a formal management system Standard. It does not contain requirements, and cannot be used as a certification standard like ISO 9001:2000 and ISO 14001:2004. The guidance itself is careful to note that 'It is not intended or appropriate for certification purposes or regulatory or contractual use. Any offer to certify, or claims to be certified, to ISO 26000 would be a misrepresentation of the intent and purpose of the International Standard'.[171]

The guidance in ISO 26000 draws on best practice from existing public and private sector SR initiatives. It was designed to be consistent with and complement relevant declarations and conventions of the United Nations and its constituents, including the ILO, with whom the ISO established a Memorandum of Understanding (MoU) to ensure consistency with ILO labour standards. ISO also signed MoUs with the UN Global Compact Office and with the OECD to enhance their cooperation in the development of ISO 26000.[172] The Draft ISO 26000 contains sections covering:

1. scope;
2. terms, definitions and abbreviated terms;
3. understanding social responsibility;
4. principles of social responsibility;
5. recognizing social responsibility and engaging stakeholders;
6. guidance on social responsibility core subjects;
7. guidance on integrating social responsibility throughout an organization.[173]

The Draft ISO 26000 also includes an 'informative' Annex (Annex A) which comprises a detailed table setting out examples of SR initiatives and tools under four different categories: inter-governmental, multi-stakeholder, single stakeholder and sectoral initiatives. A summary of each initiative and a website address (URL) is provided. The Draft Standard is also accompanied by a diagram to provide a 'Schematic overview of ISO 26000'.[174]

In a *Note on ISO 26000 Guidance Draft Document*, issued shortly after the first Draft ISO was published in 2009, the SRSG welcomed the development of the new ISO guidance, which he described as both important and complex. But he was critical of the fact that the concept of 'sphere of influence' was used in different parts of the Draft ISO in different and inconsistent ways.[175] In the section on human rights in ISO 26000 (clause 6.3), noted the SRSG, the reference to 'sphere of influence' is used in a way which indicates that while the concept 'can be a useful metaphor for companies to employ in identifying opportunities to support human rights, influence by itself is not an appropriate basis on which to attribute specific social responsibilities'.[176] However, this same message was not repeated in other parts of the 2009 Draft ISO 26000. For example, clause 5 entitled 'Recognising social responsibility and engaging stakeholders' contained a sub-clause (5.2.3) titled 'Social responsibility and the organization's sphere of influence' which, in the 2009 Draft, states that 'Generally, the responsibility for exercising influence increases with the ability to influence'.[177] This sentiment is repeated later in clause 7, entitled 'Guidance on integrating social responsibility throughout an organization'. In sub-clause 7.3.2.1, on 'Assessing an organization's sphere of influence', the 2009 text states that 'there will be situations where an organization's ability to influence others will be accompanied by a responsibility to exercise that influence'.[178]

Noting that this internal inconsistency in the 2009 Draft ISO 26000 could 'send mixed and confusing messages to companies seeking to understand their social responsibilities, and to stakeholders seeking to hold them to account', the SRSG urged the ISO WG SR to review all references to sphere of influence in the Draft ISO 26000 to ensure internal consistency and also to ensure consistency with the SRSG's own 'Protect, Respect and Remedy' Framework for business and human rights.[179]

This advice appears to have been taken on board. The May 2010 Final Draft of the ISO 26000 guidance has been significantly changed in those places where reference to the sphere of influence concept is made. Sub-clause 5.2.3 on 'Social responsibility and an organization's sphere of influence' no longer implies that an ability to exercise influence indicates a responsibility to do so. Instead, the new sub-clause 5.2.3 now provides that:

> An organization does not always have a responsibility to exercise influence purely because it has the ability to do so. For instance, it cannot be held responsible for the impacts of other organizations over which it may have some influence if the impact is not a result of its decisions and activities. However, there will be situations where an organization will have a responsibility to exercise influence. These situations will be determined by the extent to which an organization's relationship is contributing to negative impacts.[180]

In addition, sub-clause 5.2.3 now expressly recognizes the importance of 'due diligence' – a concept which forms an important part of the SRSG's 'Protect, Respect and Remedy' Framework. The May 2010 ISO 26000 guidance document now provides that:

> When assessing its sphere of influence and determining its responsibilities, an organization should exercise due diligence in order to avoid contributing to negative impacts through its relationships.[181]

There is also, in the 2010 Final Draft, a whole new sub-clause 7.3.1 titled 'Due diligence' – a concept which was not even mentioned in the counterpart clause 7 of the 2009 Draft ISO 26000.[182]

8. Protect, Respect and Remedy: Framework of the Secretary-General's Special Representative on Business and Human Rights

In the aftermath of debate and controversy generated by the Draft Norms, the UN Commission on Human Rights created a two-year mandate for a Special Representative of the Secretary General on the Issue of Human Rights and Transnational Corporations and Other Business Enterprises (SRSG) in 2005.[183] The mandate of the SRSG, Professor John Ruggie, was extended for the first time in 2007. At its June 2008 session, the UN Human Rights Council was unanimous in welcoming the 'Protect, Respect and Remedy' Framework for managing business and human rights as developed by the SRSG, and his mandate was extended for a second time in 2008, to run until 2011.[184] The work of the SRSG, and in particular his 'Protect, Respect, and Remedy' Framework, has thus become the primary focus of the debate on the international responsibilities of TNCs. The SRSG's 'Protect, Respect and Remedy'

Framework emphasizes three main elements: the state duty to protect against human rights abuses by third parties, including business; the corporate responsibility to respect human rights; and the need for more effective access to remedies.[185]

The duty of states to protect human rights is well accepted, and the SRSG is on uncontroversial ground when he argues that states should retain the primary responsibility for the realization of human rights.[186] In his role as SRSG, Ruggie advocates greater cooperation between states in discharging the duty to protect in this context. State approaches to the protection of human rights should be harmonized as much as possible, in order to deal with the particular problems caused by the globalized nature of TNCs.[187] This suggestion becomes particularly important in light of the evolving area of international law governing state responsibility for extra-territorial violations by TNCs of international human rights law.

(a)   State responsibility for extra-territorial violations by corporations of international human rights law

States routinely provide support and assistance to their corporate nationals in their global trade and investment ventures. While states may not intend to allow corporate nationals to violate human rights in their extra-territorial operations, by their actions or omissions, states may facilitate or otherwise contribute to a situation in which such violations by a corporation occur. As McCorquodale and Simons demonstrate, the extra-territorial activities of TNCs that violate international human rights law can give rise to significant home state responsibility in international law.[188] Under customary international law, if an act or omission can be attributed to a state and there has been a breach of an international legal obligation, by that act or omission, then the state is responsible for that breach. This has been codified in the International Law Commission's Articles on the Responsibility of States for International Wrongful Acts.[189]

Under these rules, a state is responsible for the actions and omissions of its executive, legislative, judicial and other state organs and officials, including police, military, immigration and similar officials. In addition, the general law of state responsibility provides for the possibility of attribution to a state of the acts committed by its corporate nationals in violation of international law giving rise to international responsibility in two situations: first, where a state empowers a corporation to exercise elements of public authority;[190] second, where a corporation acts on the 'instructions of, or under the direction or control of' a state.[191] In addition, where the state, through aiding or assisting corporate activity, is complicit in the commission of an internationally wrongful act committed by another state or by the corporation itself, then the state will be internationally responsible.[192]

In all of these cases, such acts will be attributable to the state even where they are committed outside the territory of that state. This is because state obligations, including those arising under international human rights law, are not territorially confined. The major international human rights treaties expressly extend state obligations both to individuals within a state's territory and to those individuals who are subject to a state's jurisdiction.[193] This means that a state may be held responsible under certain circumstances for the acts and omissions of its agents which produce effects or are undertaken outside that state's territory. In the case of a corporate 'agent', this will be the case to the extent that the exercise of governmental authority is involved, and regardless of the extent of any ownership of the corporation by the state.[194]

The extra-territorial activities of AWB Ltd, an Australian corporation, provide an example of this type of situation. AWB Ltd began as a governmental agency (the Australian Wheat Board) with, *inter alia*, the sole responsibility for the marketing and export of Australian wheat around the world; and it retained this power upon being privatized in 1998.[195] AWB Ltd was active in the Iraqi Oil for Food programme managed by the United Nations, being the largest supplier of food to that programme. A 2005 investigation into that programme led to, *inter alia*, allegations that AWB Ltd was involved in the bribery of Iraqi officials in order to sell Australian wheat, contrary to UN resolutions and with clear impacts on the human rights of Iraqis, including the right to food.[196] These allegations were found to be substantiated both by a Royal Commission[197] and by an Australian court,[198] but without expressly deciding whether some of the actions of AWB Ltd were attributable to the Australian government.[199] However, the circumstances of the case clearly gave rise to the possibility of attribution, and illustrate the way in which actions of privatized government entities generally might be attributable to a state.[200]

(b)   The corporate responsibility to respect human rights
So far as the TNC responsibility to respect human rights is concerned, Ruggie explains that '[t]o respect rights essentially means not to infringe on the rights of others, put simply, to do no harm'.[201] The SRSG then explains that in order to discharge their duty to respect human rights, TNCs must engage in due diligence.

The scope of this duty of due diligence includes an assessment of the harm that the operations of TNCs might cause 'in their capacity as producers, service providers, employers, and neighbours'.[202] It further requires that TNCs assess 'whether they might contribute to abuse through the relationships connected to their activities, such as with business partners, suppliers, State agencies and other non-State actors'.[203]

(i) Due diligence and the responsibility to respect   In May 2008, the SRSG presented a *Report Clarifying the Concepts of 'Sphere of Influence' and 'Complicity'* to the Human Rights Council. That Report concluded that the sphere of influence concept is of 'limited utility in clarifying the specific parameters' of TNCs' responsibility to respect human rights.[204] In particular, the sphere of influence concept was 'considered too broad and ambiguous a concept to define the scope of due diligence required to fulfil the responsibility to protect'.[205] In contrast, avoiding complicity was viewed by the SRSG as 'an essential ingredient in the due diligence carried out to respect human rights'.[206]

In defining the scope of human rights due diligence, the SRSG's May 2008 Report went on to outline an alternative process that is inevitably 'inductive and fact-based', but guided by three basic principles.[207] The first principle is that TNCs should consider the country contexts in which their business activities take place, and should identify any specific human rights challenges that they may pose. Relevant information is usually available from reports by workers, NGOs, governments and international agencies.[208] The analysis should include relevant national laws and international obligations as they relate to human rights, and potential gaps between international standards and national law and practice.[209]

Second, TNCs should consider what human rights impacts their own activities may have within the relevant country contexts in which they occur. A company should analyse the actual and potential impacts arising from its activities on employees, consumers, local communities and other affected groups. The production process itself, the products or services the company provides, its labour and employment practices, the provision of security for personnel and assets, and the company's lobbying or other political activities, all need to be scrutinized in light of their human rights impacts. The company should determine which of its policies and practices may harm human rights, and adjust them accordingly to prevent harm from occurring.[210]

The third principle is that TNCs should consider whether they might contribute to human rights abuses through the relationships connected to their activities, such as with business partners, suppliers, state agencies and other non-state actors. How far or how deep this process must go will depend on the circumstances.[211] The aim is to ensure that the company is not implicated in third party harm to rights through its relationships with such parties. According to the SRSG, the possibility of complicity:

> can arise from a company's business activities, including the provision or contracting of goods, services and even non-business activities, such as lending equipment or vehicles. Therefore, a company needs to understand the track records of those entities with which it deals in order to assess whether it might contribute to or be associated with harm caused by entities with which it conducts, or is considering

conducting business or other activities. This analysis of relationships will include looking at instances where the company might be seen as complicit in abuse caused by others.[212]

Risk impact assessment is thus a fundamental element of business human rights due diligence under the SRSG Framework. The OECD has established a Risk Awareness Tool for Multinational Enterprises in Weak Governance Zones ('RA Tool').[213] The RA Tool includes questions that TNCs should ask 'when considering actual or prospective investments in weak governance zones'.[214] The questions cover 'obeying the law and observing international relations; heightened managerial care; political activities; knowing clients and business partners; speaking out about wrongdoing; and business roles in weak governance societies – a broadened view of self interest'.[215]

Recognizing that risk impact assessment is not limited to weak governance zones, the SRSG has recommended that the RA Tool should be made more use of and incorporated into the OECD Guidelines for more general use. In his speech to the June 2008 OECD NCP Convention, the SRSG also recommended that the home countries of TNCs should play a more active role in providing information and oversight of their TNCs' activities in weak governance zones, making use of the RA Tool:

> [E]ven though the OECD's work on weak governance zones is not part of the Guidelines, it has much to offer. The human rights regime cannot be expected to function as intended when a country is engulfed in civil war, for instance. In such situations, the home countries of multinationals should play a more active role in providing information about human rights risks and, especially where the investment involves home country support, in providing greater oversight.[216]

One way of enhancing the interaction between the OECD Guidelines and the RA Tool, even in the absence of formal integration, is for NCPs to make use of the RA Tool throughout the process of handling specific instance complaints.[217] In this way, the RA Tool would be integrated into TNC due diligence practices through the activities of the NCPs. In the *Afrimex* case, for example, the UK NCP expressly recommended that Afrimex should integrate the RA Tool into its corporate policies and management practices.[218] In finding that Afrimex had failed to apply adequate due diligence to its supply chain, the NCP also expressly referred to the SRSG's 'Protect, Respect and Remedy' Framework.[219]

Afrimex involved importation of minerals by the UK company from the Democratic Republic of the Congo (DRC), a weak governance zone. The case illustrates the importance of due diligence in the assessment of cases involving alleged TNC complicity in 'supply chain' human rights abuses. A complaint lodged by NGO Global Witness in February 2007 claimed that Afrimex's trade in minerals had contributed to human rights abuses in war-torn eastern DRC. It alleged that Afrimex had made payments to the rebel group Rassemblement congolais pour la démocratie-Goma (RDC-Goma), who controlled the area and committed grave human rights abuses. Global Witness also alleged that the company had bought minerals produced in very harsh conditions, including forced and child labour.[220] The UK NCP found that Afrimex had failed to apply sufficient due diligence to its supply chain. Afrimex's suppliers included SOCOMI, a company with close business and family ties with Afrimex, and two other suppliers who had paid taxes and licence fees to RCD-Goma. The NCP stated that these payments contributed to the ongoing conflict. It found that, as the only significant customer of SOCOMI in 2000–2001, 'Afrimex was the reason that SOCOMI traded in minerals and therefore Afrimex is responsible for SOCOMI paying the licence fees and taxation to RCD-Goma'.[221] The NCP found that Afrimex's reliance on oral assurances from suppliers and one written statement amounted to insufficient due diligence, that these assurances lacked substance and were not underpinned by any checks. It held that Afrimex 'did not apply sufficient due diligence to the supply chain and failed to take adequate steps to contribute to the abolition of child and forced labour in the mines or to take steps to influence the conditions of the mines'.[222] Afrimex's failure to apply any conditions on its suppliers during the war was, according to the NCP, 'unacceptable considering the context of the conflict and human rights abuses taking place'.[223] Similarly, in 2009, the UK NCP noted that Vedanta Resources had failed to exercise adequate human rights due diligence in its operations in India.[224]

The SSRG makes a lot of sense when he rejects the 'sphere of influence' concept and prefers an alternative concept of 'due diligence' when outlining the corporate responsibility to respect human rights.[225] Due diligence requires reasonable steps by TNCs to identify, prevent and address the actual or potential adverse impacts of their activities and relationships.[226] The concept of due diligence is already well entrenched and understood in company law and practice.[227] It is not a fixed sphere, nor is it based on influence.[228] Its relevance in the context of human rights, as in other contexts, is now broadly recognized, and is defined by what is reasonable in that context. Thus, as already noted above, the Draft ISO 26000 guidance on social responsibility now contains an entire section outlining the meaning of due diligence in line with the SRSG's Framework.[229] The OECD's 2009–2010 periodic review of its Guidelines for Multinational Enterprises is also being influenced by the SRSG's Protect, Respect and Remedy Framework.

9.   2010 Update of the OECD Guidelines for Multinational Enterprises

Periodic review of the OECD Guidelines is provided for in the OECD Declaration on International Investment and Multinational Enterprises[230] and the June 2000 Decision of the OECD Council on the Implementation Procedures of the OECD Guidelines for Multinational Enterprises.[231] At their Annual Meeting in June 2009, NCPs recommended that adhering states should review their experience with the Guidelines since 2000 with a view to defining terms of reference for updating the Guidelines.[232] At the June 2009 OECD Council Meeting at Ministerial level, ministers welcomed 'further consultation on the updating of the OECD Guidelines to increase their relevance and clarify private sector responsibilities'.[233] It was recognized that the landscape for international investment and TNCs has changed significantly since 2000. In particular, non-OECD countries are attracting a larger share of world investment and TNCs from non-adhering states have grown in importance.[234] In addition, the financial crisis and the loss of confidence in open markets, the need to address climate change, and the need to pay renewed attention to failing development goals all indicated a need for a new look at the Guidelines.

A broad-based process of consultation was initiated by the OECD Investment Committee on 8 December 2009 as part of the revision process.[235] Consultation partners included non-government stakeholders, including the Business and Industry Advisory Committee (BIAC), the Trade Union Advisory Committee (TUAC) and OECD Watch, recognized experts and specialized business and civil society groups; interested non-adhering countries (notably China, India, Indonesia, South Africa and Southeast Asia); internal OECD bodies and international organizations responsible for key instruments referred to in the Guidelines, including the ILO, the UN Global Compact, the GRI and the ISO.[236]

One of the consultation partners involved in the early part of the consultation process was the International Bar Association's Working Group on the OECD Guidelines for Multinational Enterprises (IBA WG).[237] In response to an invitation to prepare and directly submit a response to the OECD, the IBA WG submitted a detailed response, in line with the OECD consultation terms of reference, on 29 January 2010.[238] I was a member of the IBA WG and found the whole process of reviewing the Guidelines in light of their history since 2000 fascinating. One of the most notable features of the Working Group process was the degree of consensus that was reached on the need for reform to the Guidelines, and in particular the amount of agreement that reforms should be designed to bring the OECD Guidelines in line with the SRSG's 'Protect Respect and Remedy' Framework. This was particularly the case in the two areas of supply chains and human rights.

(a) Supply chains

The 2000 review of the Guidelines significantly expanded their applicability to supply chains in both Guideline-adhering and non-adhering countries. In 2003, however, the OECD Investment Committee issued a statement providing that the Guidelines are part of the OECD Declaration on International Investment and Multinational Enterprises, and by so doing limited the applicability of the Guidelines to supply chains cases involving an actual investment, or where an investment nexus exists.[239] In the absence of clarification on what constitutes an investment nexus, NCPs have rejected complaints because of the lack of an investment nexus.[240] The IBA WG therefore recommended the introduction of a new Chapter in the Guidelines dealing specifically with TNCs'[241] relationships with their supply chains. The new chapter should make clear that the proper extent of a TNC's obligations with respect to its supply chain should be defined by the TNC's due diligence, in line with the SRSG Framework. As the SRSG has noted: 'The challenge for buyers is to ensure they are not complicit in violations by their suppliers. How far down the supply chain a buyer's responsibility extends depends on what a proper due diligence process reveals about prevailing country and sector conditions, and about potential business partners and their sourcing practices'.[242]

The IBA WG also recommended that the proposed new Supply Chain Chapter of the Guidelines should incorporate paragraph 10 of existing Chapter II of the Guidelines, which states that enterprises should:

> Encourage, where practicable, business partners, including suppliers and sub-contractors, to apply principles of corporate conduct compatible with the Guidelines.[243]

The IBA WG also recommended, however, that a significant change be made to the existing Commentary which guides the interpretation of paragraph 10. The Commentary on General Principles in paragraph 10 uses the word 'influence' in the following context:

> The *influence* enterprises may have on their suppliers or other business partners is normally restricted to the category of products or services they are sourcing, rather than to the full range of activities of suppliers or business partners. Thus, the scope of *influencing* business partners and the supply chain is greater in some instances than in others. In cases where direct *influence* of business partners is not possible, the objective could be met by means of dissemination of general policy statements. (emphasis added).[244]

The term 'influence', however, is inconsistent with the SRSG Framework. As noted above, the SRSG has explicitly declined to use the term 'influence', or 'sphere of influence', to define the scope of a company's responsibility to respect human rights. Consequently, the IBA WG recommended that the Commentary to the Guidelines be revised in a manner consistent with the SRSG Framework.[245]

(b) Human rights

The OECD Guidelines currently contain only one brief reference to human rights, in paragraph 2 of Chapter II, the General Policies chapter of the Guidelines. Paragraph 2 provides that enterprises should 'Respect the human rights of those affected by their activities consistent with the host government's international obligations and commitments'. The IBA WG felt that this was grossly inadequate and recommended in its report that a new and detailed chapter dealing with human rights is required.[246] It was recommended that the new Human Rights chapter should encourage TNCs to conduct human rights due diligence in accord with the SRSG Framework, should identify the sources of international human rights standards to be followed, and should set out guidelines to help enterprises identify, prevent and address the human rights impacts of their operations.[247] The Guidelines should specify that a proper due diligence process would involve, *inter alia*, undertaking human rights risk impact assessments and monitoring, and regular reporting by TNCs on their human rights performance.[248] It was also recommended that the Human Rights chapter should, like the current Environment chapter of the Guidelines, encourage TNCs to engage with members of communities before and throughout the lifecycle of an investment/project.[249] The IBA WG was not able to reach consensus on the nature of the engagement which should be required of TNCs. Some members were happy to recommend that TNCs should 'consult' with local host communities, while others felt that TNCs should be required to obtain the 'free, prior and informed consent' of any local community affected by a large footprint project.[250] The IBA WG was united, however, in recommending that TNCs be encouraged to establish company-level grievance mechanisms, in line with the third pillar of the SRSG Framework – the need for access to remedies.[251]

Other parts of the IBA WG response to the OECD consultation process deal with issues of disclosure,[252] anti-corruption,[253] environment,[254] consumer interests,[255] risk awareness[256] and, importantly, aspects of the complaints handling and dispute resolution process that require improvement.[257]

E. ROLE OF INVESTORS, CREDITORS AND CONSUMERS

Currently for most TNCs that adopt company, industry or international codes of conduct, compliance remains essentially voluntary. A failure to report violations of code standards, or even an open statement that such violations have occurred, is unlikely to carry any serious sanction. Being rendered inactive on the Global Compact list, having the company's SR8000 certification removed, or otherwise receiving bad publicity can certainly impact negatively on a

TNC's bottom line, but companies have long become adroit at containing such costs. What is needed to give global standards genuine force and meaning are standardized, independent, *monitoring* and *verification* mechanisms.

Local NGOs, industry watchdog groups and independent trade unions are examples of groups that have become instrumental in carrying out monitoring and verification activities, but they are often poorly funded and lack formal investigatory powers. NCPs established under the OECD Guidelines have also become useful monitors, but can only operate in the context of specific complaints. As a result, the monitoring and verification activities of investors, creditors and consumers who can affect the TNC's bottom line are often much more effective than other similar mechanisms in influencing TNC behaviour. The example of the Equator Principles, which facilitate independent monitoring by creditors of projects being implemented by borrowers, has already been discussed. Yet the Equator Principles remain confined in their application to large project finance contracts. More influential in terms of the number of TNCs involved are investor-initiated ethical investment guidelines.

Socially responsible investment

Investment organizations and other share-market participants have responded to investor concerns about corporate behaviour by developing a number of selective indexes that require companies to demonstrate compliance with prescribed standards. The FTSE4Good Index Series, for example, requires that companies provide evidence showing compliance with 'Inclusion Criteria' in five areas: environmental sustainability, stakeholder relationships, human rights, supply-chain labour standards and countering bribery.[258] The global investment group Dow Jones has developed a number of 'Sustainability Indexes', including the Dow Jones Sustainability World Index,[259] a number of regional sustainability indexes and the Dow Jones Islamic Market Sustainability Index.[260] The DJSI World Index is derived from the Dow Jones World Index and represents approximately the top 10 per cent of companies from individual sectors based on a 'corporate sustainability score'.[261] Companies are assessed against sustainability best practice guidelines using information obtained from four key sources: SAM Questionnaires distributed to CEOs and heads of investor relations; company documentation; media and stakeholder reports; and personal contact with companies.[262] The DJSI fact-sheet emphasizes that 'transparency is a key principle for the Dow Jones Sustainability Indexes'. At the same time, however, companies are encouraged to participate in the sustainability assessment process on the basis that 'confidentiality' of information is assured,[263] and on the basis of a principle of 'trust' that means 'no "naming and shaming" of laggards'.[264]

The growth in ethical investment funds and indexes since the late 1990s is all part of a growing recognition throughout the financial community of its non-financial roles and responsibilities. The UN's 2006 Principles for Responsible Investment (PRI),[265] aimed at all types of financial institutions, exhort signatories to be more aware of environmental, social and governance issues in financial management. According to Donald MacDonald, the Chair of the PRI Initiative, in his 2007 Progress Report:

> The most important contribution the PRI has made is to reinforce and promote the paradigm that environmental, social and corporate governance issues matter to the financial performance of companies, and that mainstream investors have a responsibility to take these issues seriously and, where appropriate, act to address them.[266]

The desire to be included in an approved list of investment targets provides an incentive for companies to bring their activities, policies and practices (including reporting practices) into line with guidelines established by sustainability and social responsibility indexes. These ethically targeted investment funds then play a monitoring and verification role to the extent that they are able to scrutinize continuing corporate compliance with their guidelines. In addition, these investment funds also play an 'enforcement' role when they demonstrate a willingness to suspend, cease or reconsider their associations with companies that are involved even indirectly in harmful activities. Along with their published investment policies, such funds also publish their divestment and delisting decisions, with direct implications for investor decisions in the broader market.[267]

The Norwegian Government Pension Fund Global (NGPF) provides one example of an ethical investment fund with significant status in the investment world.[268] The Council on Ethics for the NGPF issues recommendations on request by the Ministry of Finance as to whether an investment may be at odds with a set of specially tailored ethical guidelines, as well as whether it might constitute a violation of Norway's obligations under international law.[269] The NGPF ethical guidelines are promoted through the use of three mechanisms: first, through the exercise of ownership rights – the overall objective of Norges Bank's exercise of ownership rights for the NGPF is to safeguard the Fund's long-term financial interests; at the same time, however, '[t]he exercise of ownership rights shall mainly be based on the UN's Global Compact and the OECD Guidelines for Corporate Governance and for Multinational Enterprises';[270] second, through observation of companies which are placed on the Ministry's observation list; and third, through the exclusion of companies on the advice of the Council on Ethics. Expressly excluded from the NGPF 'investment universe' are companies that 'either themselves, or through entities they control, produce weapons that through normal use may violate fundamental humanitarian principles' and, since early 2010, companies that produce tobacco. In addition, the Ministry of Finance may, on the advice of the

Council on Ethics, exclude companies from the investment universe of the NGPF 'if there is an unacceptable risk that the company contributes to or is responsible for, serious or systematic human rights violations;[271] serious violations of individuals' rights in situations of war or conflict; severe environmental damages; gross corruption; other particularly serious violations of fundamental ethical norms'.[272]

In 2006, following consideration of allegations that Wal-Mart was 'implicit in violations of human rights and labour rights in its business operations', the Norwegian Ministry of Finance announced the NGPF's divestment of the company based on recommendations from the Council of Ethics. The Ministry said that the Fund would 'incur an unacceptable risk of contributing to serious or systemic violations of human rights by maintaining its investments in the company'.[273] Thus, the Norwegian governments' concern is not only about investing in companies which may be complicit in abuses, but also that the Fund itself may be considered to have contributed to abuse through its association with such companies.[274]

More recently, in January 2010, the Norwegian Ministry of Finance announced the decision to exclude 17 companies that produce tobacco from the NGPF, based again on a recommendation from the Fund's Council on Ethics.[275] When the Graver Committee proposed the original ethical guidelines in 2004, there was debate on whether or not to exclude tobacco producers from the Fund. It was eventually decided that tobacco should not be excluded. Since that time, the WHO Framework Convention on Tobacco Control has entered into force, and the Norwegian Tobacco Act has been tightened. It was in light of these and other international and national developments that the Council of Ethics recommended the exclusion of tobacco. When the Minister took this recommendation to the *Storting* (Norwegian Parliament), the move was supported. The new rule for negative screening of tobacco producers excludes all production of tobacco, regardless of the percentage of business represented by tobacco production. This means it will be possible to exclude more companies than just those listed under the industrial classification 'tobacco' by the index providers.[276]

Other governments which have established ethical guidelines for their pension funds include Sweden and Holland. In other jurisdictions, governments have regulated the criteria that may be applied and the information that must be reported by those claiming to abide by responsible investment criteria.[277] The broad and growing range of ethical investment schemes means that there is significant variation in the criteria applied. While such schemes clearly have the potential to influence and even improve corporate behaviour, they remain much more of a complementary approach to improving selected human rights, environmental and other outcomes, than an enforcement mechanism as such. Even assuming greater alignment between the various ethical investment schemes and international legal norms, the absence of recourse and remedies for victims of corporate abuses of human rights means that ethical investment remains, at best, a complementary oversight mechanism.[278]

NOTES

1. Peter Henley, 'Were corporate tsunami donations made legally?' (2005) 30:4 *Alternative Law Journal* 154.
2. Bhopal Medical Appeal and Sambhavna Trust, 'What happened in Bhopal', available at www.bhopal.org/whathappened.html. See also www.bhopal.com/.
3. CFMEU Construction and General, *James Hardie Scandal* (2nd edn), available at www.cfmeu-construction-nsw.com.au/pdf/JamesHardieScandal2ndEdition150804.pdf.
4. 'Corporate social responsibility, companies in the news, BP', available at www.mallenbaker.net/csr/CSRfiles/bp.html. See also Dennis M. Patten, 'Intra-industry environmental disclosures in response to the Alaskan oil spill: a note on legitimacy theory' (1992) 17:5 *Accounting, Organizations and Society* 471.
5. See e.g. www.mallenbaker.net/csr/CSRfiles/; Australian Centre for Corporate Social Responsibility, www.accsr.com.au; CSR International, www.csrinternational.org; Business for Social Responsibility, www.bsr.org; CSR360 Global Partner Network, www.csr360gpn.org; AccountAbility: Institute of Social and Ethical Accountability, www.accountability.org; Ethical Performance, www.ethicalperformance.com; Business Ethics: The Magazine of Corporate Responsibility, www.business-ethics.com; Corporate Social Responsibility in Asia (CSR Asia), www.csr-asia.com and Corporate Social Responsibility in China (China CSR), www.ChinaCSR.com.
6. See e.g. FTSE4Good Indices, available at Corporate Responsibility Index, www.corporate-responsibility.com.au; AA1000 Assurance Standard 2008, www.accountability.org; Jantzi Social Index, www.jantziresearch.com; Calvert Social Index, www.calvert.com/sri.html; E Capital Partners Ethical Index, available at www.ecpindices.com and the Ethibel Sustainability Index, available at www.ethibel.org/subs_e/4_index/main.html. For discussion see Bertelsmann Foundation, *Who is Who in Corporate Social Responsibility Rating? A Survey of Internationally Established Rating Systems that Measure Corporate Responsibility* (July 2006), available at www.bertelsmann-stiftung.de/bst/de/media/Transparenzstudie2006.pdf.
7. Henley, above n. 1 and Therese Wilson, 'The pursuit of profit at all costs: corporate law as a barrier to corporate social responsibility' (2005) 30:6 *Alternative Law Journal* 278, 279–80. Wilson notes that Australian companies making donations to the tsunami relief effort included National Australia Bank, the Commonwealth Bank, Foster's Group, Visy Industries, Westfield Group, Travelex and News Corporation.
8. For example, following the bombing incident on 1 October 2005, both Qantas and Telstra immediately announced they would provide special concessions to help those affected by the bombings return home from Bali, delay or alter flights booked to travel to Bali and communicate with relatives at no cost.
9. CNNMoney.com, 'Corporate Katrina gifts could top $1B: Report: Donations from companies, customers exceed $500M; likely to top record $750 in 9/11 gift giving' (13 September 2005), available at http://money.cnn.com/2005/09/13/news/fortune500/katrina_donations/.
10. Parija Bhatnagar, 'Wal-Mart redeems itself, but what's next: Experts say quick response to Katrina has softened its image some but deeper problems remain' (9 September 2005), available on 28 May 2010 at http://money.cnn.com/2005/09/09/news/fortune500/walmart_image/index.htm.
11. E.P. Mendes and J.A. Clark, 'The five generations of corporate codes of conduct and their impact on corporate social responsibility' (18 September 1996), available at www.cdp-

hrc.uottawa.ca/eng/publication/centre/five.php. See also Gerald Acquaah-Gaisie, 'Enhancing corporate accountability in Australia' (2000) 11 *Australian Journal of Corporate Law* 139.

12. All of the Company Codes of Conduct cited here are available at 'Self-Imposed Company Codes' published on University of Minnesota Human Rights Library webpage accessed on 28 May 2010 at http://www1.umn.edu/humanrts/business/sicc.html. See also discussion at Global Business Responsibility Resource Centre, 'Human Rights', available at www1.umn.edu/humanrts/links/gbrhumanrts.html.

13. *Ibid.*

14. *Ibid.*

15. Steven R. Ratner, 'Corporations and human rights: a theory of legal responsibility' (2001) 111 *Yale Law Journal* 443, 463, citing 'Human rights and Unocal: our position', available at www.unocal.com/responsibility/humanrights/hrl.htm. See now Chevron, 'About our human rights policy' (April 2010), available at 28 May 2010 at www.chevron.com/documents/pdf/AboutOurHumanRightsPolicy.pdf. See also Prince of Wales Business Leaders Forum and Amnesty International, *Human Rights: Is It Any of Your Business?* (2000), reviewed by Delwin Roy for *Alliance Magazine* at www.alliancemagazine.org/en/content/human-rights-%E2%80%93-it-any-your-business-amnesty-internationalprince-wales-business-leaders-forum.

16. Ann Florini, 'Business and global governance: the growing role of corporate codes of conduct' (2003) 21:2 *Brookings Review* 4. See also actrav Bureau for Workers' Activities, International Labour Organization, 'Corporate Codes of Conduct', available at http://actrav.itcilo.org/actrav-english/telearn/global/ilo/code/main.htm.

17. The Australian Minerals Industry Code for Environmental Management was originally launched in December 1996. The Code was substantially revised in 1999 and replaced by an updated Code, the Australian Minerals Industry Code for Environmental Management 2000. The 2000 Code was formally retired on 1 January 2005 and replaced by *Enduring Value*, the Australian Minerals Industry Framework for Sustainable Development: see the Minerals Council of Australia, www.minerals.org.au/environment/code.

18. For example, when the Australian-controlled Esmeralda Corporation's mining operations affected millions of people after a cyanide spill in Romania in the late 1990s, the Australian mining industry 'was at pains to point out that Esmeralda was not signatory to the Code, nor a member of the Minerals Council of Australia': Ingrid Macdonald, 'The limits of corporate codes of conduct' (2002) 7:3 *Mining Monitor* (September) 9, citing Minerals Policy Institute, *Corporate Code of Conduct Bill Mineral Policy Submission to Senate Inquiry* (2000).

19. Details including history and discussion available at www.voluntaryprinciples.org/.

20. The seven states are Canada, Netherlands, Norway, Republic of Colombia, Switzerland, United Kingdom and United States. NGO participants include Amnesty International, Oxfam and Human Rights Watch, while corporate participants include BP, BHP Billiton, Chevron, ExxonMobil, Rio Tinto and Shell: see www.voluntaryprinciples.org/participants/.

21. Voluntary Principles on Security and Human Rights, available at www.voluntary principles.org/.

22. *Ibid.* For discussion, see Judith Richter, *Holding Corporations Accountable: Corporate Conduct, International Codes and Citizen Action* (2001) (a UNICEF commissioned study). See also S. Prakash Sethi, 'Standards for corporate conduct in the international arena: challenges and opportunities for multinational corporations' (2002) 107:1 *Business and Society Review* 20.

23. Kimberley Process Certification Scheme, details and discussion available at www.kimberleyprocess.com/.

24. Extractive Industries Transparency Initiative, available at www.eitransparency.org.

25. Text of the Equator Principles (July 2006) available at www.equator-principles.com/documents/Equator_Principles.pdf.

26. See www.equator-principles.com/. There were 67 institutions listed as EPFIs on 29 May 2010.

27. Equator Principles, above n. 25, Principle 4. This is now a stricter requirement than

contained in the original 2003 version of the Equator Principles, which simply required 'Management Plans' for Category B projects 'whenever appropriate'.

28. 'Leading banks announce adoption of Equator Principles', Media Release, 4 June 2003, available at http://equator-principles.com/pr030604.shtml.
29. Equator Principles, above n. 25, 'Scope'.
30. *NGO Collective Analysis of the Equator Principles* (April 2003), Pt 3(a), available at www.globalpolicy.org/socecon/ffd/2003/06ngos.htm.
31. Equator Principles, above n. 25, Principle 3.
32. *Ibid.*
33. *Ibid.* Principle 8 'Covenants', notes that 'An important strength of the Principles is the incorporation of covenants linked to compliance'.
34. *Ibid.* Principle 8(d).
35. IFC's Policy and Performance Standards Review and Update Process, outlined at www.ifc.org/policyreview.
36. *NGO Collective Analysis of the Equator Principles*, above n. 30.
37. Michael Posner and Justine Nolan, 'Can codes of conduct play a role in promoting workers' rights' in Robert J. Flanagan and William B. Gould IV, *International Labor Standards: Globalization, Trade, and Public Policy* (Stanford University Press, 2003) 207–26.
38. *Ibid.* See also Judith Richter, *Holding Corporations Accountable: Corporate Conduct, International Codes and Citizen Action* (2001) (a UNICEF commissioned study).
39. Examples include MediaGlobal, www.mediaglobal.org/, GlobalAware Independent Media, http://orgs.tigweb.org/globalaware-independent-media/, reclaimthemedia, www.reclaim themedia.org/ and *Mining Monitor* (published by the Mineral Policy Institute). For discussion see David Vogel, *The Market for Virtue: The Potential and Limits of Corporate Social Responsibility* (2005) and Judith Richter, *Holding Corporations Accountable: Corporate Conduct, International Codes and Citizen Action* (2001).
40. *Ibid.*
41. Raj Patel, *The Value of Nothing: How to Reshape Market Society and Redefine Democracy* (Black Inc., 2009) 48, citing Juan Martinez-Alier, *The Environmentalism of the Poor: A Study of Ecological Conflicts and Valuation* (Edward Elgar, 2002).
42. For discussion, see Owen E. Herrnstadt, 'What's missing from voluntary codes of conduct?' (2000–2001) 16 *The Labor Lawyer* 349.
43. For discussion and analysis see Proving and Improving, 'Global Reporting Initiative (GRI) Guidelines' information page, available at www.proveandimprove.org/new/tools/griguidelines.php.
44. In the general guidelines of the GRI, social performance is broken up into sections on labour practices and decent work, human rights, society and product responsibility. The performance indicators (supported by Indicator Protocols) within these sections are comprehensive and drawn from UN human rights instruments, ILO Conventions and the ILO Tripartite Declaration concerning Multinational Enterprises and Social Policy, and the OECD Guidelines for Multinational Corporations. See also www.globalreporting.org/.
45. Sector specific supplements exist for the following sectors: Financial Services, Electric Utilities, Mining and Metals, Food Processing and the NGO sector: www.globalreporting.org/ReportingFramework/ReportingFrameworkDownloads/.
46. Justine Nolan, 'Corporate accountability and triple bottom line reporting: determining the material issues for disclosure' in Gerald Acqaah-Gaisie and Val Clulow (eds), *Enhancing Corporate Accountability: Prospects and Challenges* (2006) 196.
47. Global Reporting Initiative, *Synergies between the OECD Guidelines for Multinational Enterprises (MNEs) and the GRI 2002 Sustainability Reporting Guidelines* (June 2004), available at www.oecd.org/dataoecd/25/26/35150230.pdf; *The 9 UN Global Compact Principles and Selected 2002 GRI Sustainability Reporting Guidelines Core Performance Indicators* (19 January 2004), available at http://commdev.org/content/document/detail/ 768/.
48. Nolan, above n. 46; Proving and Improving website, above n. 43.
49. Declaration on Social Progress and Development, GA Res 2542 (XXIV), UNGAOR, 24th Sess., UN Doc. A/Res/24/2542 (11 December 1969), available at www.un-documents.net/a24r2542.htm.

50. Virginia A. Leary, '"Form follows function": formulations of international labor standards – treaties, codes, soft law, trade agreements' in Robert J. Flanagan aand William B. Gould IV (eds), *International Labor Standards: Globalization, Trade, and Public Policy* (Stanford University Press, 2003) 179–206, 194.

51. Among the principal instruments to come out of this era were: the Declaration on the Establishment of a New International Economic Order, GA Res. 3201 (S-VI), UN Doc. A/RES/3201(S-VI) (1 May 1974); the Programme of Action on the Establishment of a New International Economic Order, GA Res. 3202 (S-VI), UN Doc. A/RES/3202(S-VI) (1 May 1974) and the Charter of Economic Rights and Duties of States, GA Res. 3281 (XXIX), UN Doc. A/RES/3281(XXIX) (12 December 1974).

52. Discussed in Sean Murphy, 'Taking multinational corporate codes of conduct to the next level' (2005) 43 *Columbia Journal of Transnational Law* 389. The United Nations Centre on Transnational Corporations was terminated in 1994, and the Intergovernmental Commission on Transnational Corporations absorbed into the United Nations Conference on Trade and Development in the same year: Murphy at 405.

53. See e.g. 1983 Draft Code, UN Doc. E/1983/17/Rev.1, Annex II (1983 draft), reproduced at (1984) 23 ILM 626.

54. *Ibid*; Draft United Nations Code of Conduct for Transnational Corporations, UN Doc. E/1990/94 (1990) ('Draft UN TNC Code'). For discussion see Steven R. Ratner, 'Corporations and human rrights: a theory of legal responsibility' (2001) 111 *Yale Law Journal* 443 and Larry Catá Backer, 'Multinational corporations, transnational law: The United Nation's Norms on the Responsibilities of Transnational Corporations as harbinger of corporate responsibility in international law' (2005) 37 *Columbia Human Rights Law Review* 287.

55. Adam McBeth, *International Economic Actors and Human Rights* (Routledge, 2010) 264–5, citing Draft UN TNC Code. See also UN Doc. E/1983/17/Rev.1, Annex II (1983 draft), reproduced at (1984) 23 ILM 626. Ratner, *ibid.*, 458–60, argues that the drafting process for the Draft Code was abandoned in the 1990s due to a shift in the economic strategy of many developing countries, from an assertive attitude towards TNCs, to a desire to attract foreign direct investment: 'The Draft UN Code of Conduct, which, its advocates hoped, would become a treaty, was effectively discarded in the early 1990s as the South retreated from assertive policies regarding economic development'.

56. The Tripartite Declaration of Principles concerning Multinational Enterprises and Social Policy is claimed by the ILO to be 'the first successfully elaborated and universally applicable instrument on the subject of Multinational Enterprises'. It was adopted by the Governing Body of the ILO in November 1977. See further www.ilo.org/public/english/employment/multi/promact/tridecla.htm.

57. ILO, Tripartite Declaration of Principles concerning Multinational Enterprises and Social Policy (Geneva, 2006), available at www.ilo.org/wcmsp5/groups/public/—ed_emp/—emp_ent/documents/publication/wcms_094386.pdf.

58. Procedure for the Examination of Disputes concerning the Application of the Tripartite Declaration of Principles concerning Multinational Enterprises and Social Policy by Means of Interpretation of its Provisions, adopted by the Governing Body of the ILO at its 232nd Session (Geneva 1986), (1986) LXIX *ILO Official Bulletin* (Series A, No. 3), 196–7 (replacing Part IV of the Procedures adopted by the Governing Body at its 214th Session (November 1980), (1981) LXIV *ILO Official Bulletin* (Series A, No. 1) 86–90).

59. Bob A. Hepple QC, *Labour Laws and Global Trade* (Hart Publishing, 2005) 83.

60. *Eighth Survey on the Effect Given to the Tripartite Declaration of Principles concerning Multinational Enterprises and Social Policy*, '(a) Introduction' and '(b) Summary of reports submitted by governments and by employers' and workers' organizations (Part II)', ILO Governing Body Subcommittee on Multinational Enterprises, 294th Sess., GB.294/MNE/1/1 (November 2005) and GB.294/MNE/1/2 (November 2005).

61. *Follow-up to and Promotion of the Tripartite Declaration of Principles concerning Multinational Enterprises and Social Policy*, '(a) Eighth Survey on the effect given to the Tripartite Declaration of Principles concerning Multinational Enterprises and Social Policy: analytical reports of the Working Group on the reports submitted by governments and by

employers' and workers' organizations (Part I)', ILO Governing Body Subcommittee on Multinational Enterprises, 295th Sess., GB.295/MNE/1/1 (March 2006), para. 8; also noting that by the end of 2003 there were approximately 61,000 parent companies of multi-national enterprises (MNEs) with 900,000 foreign affiliates globally. These foreign affili-ates were in turn estimated to employ around 54 million people worldwide. MNEs were estimated to directly employ 105 million people worldwide.

62. *Ibid.* Table 2.
63. ILO Governing Body, Subcommittee on Multinational Enterprises, 295th Sess., GB.295/MNE/1/1 (March 2006) para. 13.
64. *Eighth Survey on the Effect Given to the Tripartite Declaration of Principles concerning Multinational Enterprises and Social Policy*, '(a) Introduction', above n. 60, paras 1–8.
65. *Ibid.* paras 3–4.
66. Global Compact, www.unglobalcompact.org/ (2000, amended June 2004).
67. Adopted by the UN General Assembly on 10 December 1948, UN. Doc A/811. The vote was 48 for and none against, with eight states abstaining. As Brownlie notes, 'The Declaration is not a legally binding instrument *as such*, ... [but has] status as an authorita-tive guide, produced by the General Assembly, to the interpretation of the Charter. In this capacity the Declaration has considerable indirect legal effect': Ian Brownlie (ed.) *Basic Documents in International Law* (4th edn, 1995) 255.
68. Adopted at the end of the ILO's International Labour Conference held in Geneva in June 1998. Participants at the conference comprised not only member countries, but also trade unions and employer organizations. The vote was 273 in favour with 43 abstentions. See ILO Provisional Record 20A, 86th Session (Geneva 1998). Also adopted was a follow-up mechanism to promote adherence to the declaration by ILO members.
69. (1992) 31 ILM 874. The Rio Declaration is a non-binding statement of principles emerging from the United Nations Conference on Environment and Development, Rio de Janeiro, Brazil, 3–14 June 1992.
70. UN Doc. A/58/422. The Convention was adopted by the General Assembly on 31 October 2003. Regional economic integration organizations can also become signatories to the Convention in accordance with art. 67(2), and the European Community became such a signatory on 15 September 2005. The Convention entered into force on 14 December 2005, in accordance with art. 68(1), 'on the ninetieth day after the date of deposit of the thirtieth instrument of ratification, acceptance, approval or accession'. As at 20 February 2006, there were 140 signatories to the Convention, and 47 states had become full parties to the Convention.
71. Global Compact.
72. Peter T. Muchlinski, 'Attempts to extend the accountability of transnational coporations: the Role of UNCTAD' in Menno T. Kamminga and Saman Zia-Zarifi (eds), *Liability of Multinational Corporations under International Law* (Kluwer Law International, 2000) 102–5. See also Steven R. Ratner, 'Corporations and human rights: a theory of legal respon-sibility' (2001) 111 *Yale Law Journal* 443, 458–60.
73. United Nations Global Compact, *Policy for the 'Communication on Progress' (COP)* (updated 2009), available at www.unglobalcompact.org/docs/communication_on_progress/COP_Policy.pdf.
74. '1,000 companies delisted by UN Global Compact since 2008'; *Global Compact News and Events*, New York, 7 October 2009, available at www.unglobalcompact.org/NewsAndEvents/news_archives/2009_10_07.html.
75. Participant Search, www.unglobalcompact.org/ParticipantsAndStakeholders/.
76. Participant Search, www.unglobalcompact.org/ParticipantsAndStakeholders/.
77. See e.g. Mahmoud Monshipouri, Claude Welch and Evan Kennedy, 'Multinational corpo-rations and the ethics of global responsibility: problems and possibilities' (2003) 25 *Human Rights Quarterly* 965, 981.
78. Use of the United Nations name and logo was already governed by GA Res. 92(1), UN Doc. A/RES/92(1) (7 December 1946). However, the policy for the use of the specific Global Compact name and logo only became prominent with the introduction of the Integrity Measures.

79. United Nations Global Compact, *Global Compact Integrity Measures*, available at www.globalcompact.org/AboutTheGC/gc_integrity_measures.pdf.

80. *Ibid.* section 4(c) and section 4.

81. 2nd edn, UNGC/BLIHR/OHCHR (2009), www.integrating-humanrights.org/.

82. See 'Some key business and human rights guidance materials and how to use them' (March 2010), available at www.unglobalcompact.org/docs/issues_doc/human_rights/Resources/ Some_key_business_and_human_rights_guidance_materials_and_how_to_use_them.pdf. See also Business an Human Rights Resource Centre, www.business-humanrights.org/.

83. UN Global Compact Releases Good Practice Notes on Human Rights (New York, 30 March 2010), available at www.unglobalcompact.org/news/18-03-30-2010.

84. Endorsed by the United Nations Global Compact Human Rights Working Group on 29 March 2010, available at www.unglobalcompact.org/docs/issues_doc/human_rights/ Resources/Stakeholder_Panels_Good_Practice_Note.pdf.

85. Endorsed by the United Nations Global Compact Human Rights Working Group on 29 March 2010, available at www.unglobalcompact.org/docs/issues_doc/human_rights/ Resources/Governments&HumanRights_Good_Practice_Note.pdf.

86. See Participant Search, www.unglobalcompact.org/participants/search. Norway had 42 participants and Israel had 15.

87. See e.g. Caroline Overington, 'Europe and US divided over support', *Sydney Morning Herald*, 4 December 2004; Sean Aylmer, 'US antagonism subverts Annan agenda', *Financial Review*, 31 March 2005; Mark Coultan, 'Annan's reform agenda shaky after son's scandal', *The Age*, 2 April 2005; Mark Coultan, 'War of the world', *Sydney Morning Herald*, 2 April 2005; Tony Walker, 'Company email names Annan', *Financial Review*, 16 June 2005; Mark Coultan, 'Annan's conflict over son's scandal', *The Age*, 31 March 2005; Mark Coultan, 'Rueful Annan cleared of role in son's sins', *Sydney Morning Herald*, 31 March 2005. In the United States, see the substantial Fox News coverage of the probes carried out by Paul Volker (on behalf of the United Nations) and the US Justice Department into the involvement of various individuals (including Koji Annan, son of the UN Secretary-General) in the UN Oil-for-Food programme: available at www.foxnews.com.

88. In stark contrast to the many articles discussing scandals at the United Nations, a search conducted on 1 June 2010 on the *New York Times* website using the search term 'UN Global Compact' since 1981 found only 24 hits. A search using 'UN Global Compact' found only 12 hits for all articles since 1851: http://query.nytimes.com/search/sitesearch?query= %22UN+Global+Compact%22&more=date_all.

89. The Sub-Commission on the Promotion and Protection of Human Rights was created by the UN Economic and Social Council (UNESCO) in 1947 as a think-tank for the UN Human Rights Commission. The Sub-Commission's membership comprises 26 independent experts who are nominated by their countries, with the remit to study cases of human rights violations, examine obstacles to human rights protection and develop new standards: UNCHR Res. E/1371, *The Prevention of Discrimination and the Protection of Minorities, Report of the Fifth Session of the Commission on Human Rights*, E/CN.4/350 at para 13(A) (1949).

90. For a description by one of the principal drafters of the Norms, which includes a detailed history of the process that led to their adoption, see David Weisbrodt and Maria Kruger, 'Norms on the Responsibilities of Transnational Corporations and Other Business Enterprises with regard to Human Rights' (2003) 97 *American Journal of International Law* 901.

91. UN Doc. E/CN.4/Sub.2/2003/12/Rev.2 (2003), approved on 13 August 2003 by UN Sub-Commission on the Promotion and Protection of Human Rights Res. 2003/16, UN Doc. E/CN.4/Sub.2/2003/L.11 at 52; copy available at www.umn.edu/humanrts/links/norms-Aug2003.html.

92. For discussion of this history see David Kinley, Justine Nolan and Natalie Zerial, 'The politics of corporate social responsibility: reflections on the United Nations Human Rights Norms for Corporations' (2007) 25 *Company and Securities Law Journal* 30.

93. For discussion of the polarized debate between business alliances (such as the International Chamber of Commerce and the International Organisation of Employers (IOE)) on the one

hand, and human rights advocates and NGOs on the other, see David Kinley and Rachel Chambers, 'The UN Human Rights Norms for Corporations: the private implications of public international law' (2006) 6:3 *Human Rights Law Review* 447 (especially Part D 'Origins, compilation and drafting of the Norms').

94. Office of the High Commissioner for Human Rights, 'Human rights and transnational corporations and other business enterprises', Human Rights Res. 2005/69 (20 April 2005). Adopted by a recorded vote of 49 votes to 3 with 1 abstention. See ch. XVII, E/CN.4/2005/L.10/Add17. On 25 July 2005, the Economic and Social Council adopted Decision 2006/273 approving the Commission's request. On 28 July 2005, the Secretary-General appointed Professor John Ruggie as his Special Representative. See also 'Mandate of the Special Representative of the Secretary-General on the issue of human rights and transnational corporations and other business enterprises', Human Rights Council, Resolution 8/7, 28th Meeting (18 June 2008), adopted without a vote.

95. Draft Norms on the Responsibilities of Transnational Corporations and Other Business Enterprises with regard to Human Rights, E/CN.4/Sub.2/2003/12 (2003). See Part A 'General obligations', art. 1. See also Preamble, para. 3.

96. *Ibid.*

97. *Ibid.* Preamble, para. 4.

98. *Ibid.* Part C 'Right to security of persons', art. 3.

99. *Ibid.* Part E 'Respect for national sovereignty and human rights', art. 11.

100. *Ibid.* Part F 'Obligation with regard to consumer protection', art. 13.

101. *Ibid.* Part G 'Obligation with regard to environmental protection', art. 14.

102. *Ibid.* arts 12 and 14.

103. David Kinley and Rachel Chambers, *The UN Human Rights Norms for Corporations: The Private Implications of Public International Law*, University of Sydney, Sydney Law School Legal Studies Research Paper No. 07/06 (February 2007) 7–8, n. 20 (available at http://ssrn.com/abstract=944153)

104. For example, art. 2 of the International Covenant on Economic, Social, and Cultural Rights, opened for signature 16 December 1966, 993 UNTS 3 (entered into force 3 January 1976), provides that 'Each State Party to the Present Covenant undertakes to take steps, individually and through international assistance and co-operation, ... to the maximum of its available resources, with a view to achieving progressively the full realization of the rights recognized in the present Covenant by all appropriate means'.

105. Article 12 of the Draft Norms provides that 'Transnational corporations and other business enterprises shall respect economic, social and cultural rights as well as civil and political rights and contribute to their realization, in particular the rights to development, adequate food and drinking water, the highest attainable standard of physical and mental health, adequate housing, privacy, education, freedom of thought, conscience, and religion and freedom of opinion and expression, and shall refrain from actions which obstruct or impede the realization of those rights'.

106. Article 21 of the Draft Norms provides that 'These Norms shall be presumed to apply, as a matter of practice, if the business enterprise has any relation with a transnational corporation, the impact of its activities is not entirely local, or the activities involve violations of the right to security as indicated in paragraphs 3 and 4'.

107. Article 21 also provides that 'The phrase "other business enterprise" includes any business entity, regardless of the international or domestic nature of its activities, including a transnational corporation, contractor, subcontractor, supplier, licensee or distributor; the corporate, partnership, or other legal form used to establish the business entity; and the nature of the ownership of the entity'.

108. Article 3 of the Draft Norms provides that 'Transnational corporations and other business enterprises shall not engage in nor benefit from war crimes, crimes against humanity, genocide, torture, forced disappearance, forced or compulsory labour, hostage-taking, extrajudicial, summary or arbitrary executions, other violations of humanitarian law and other international crimes against the human person as defined by international law, in particular human rights and humanitarian law'.

109. Article 4 of the Draft Norms.

110. Opened for signature 16 December 1966, 999 UNTS 171 (entered into force 23 March 1976) (ICCPR). See in particular art. 2 of the ICCPR which provides that each state party to the ICCPR undertakes to ensure to all individuals within its territory and subject to its jurisdiction the rights recognized in the ICCPR. In addition, state parties undertake to take necessary steps to adopt legislative or other measures necessary to give effect to those rights, to ensure that persons whose rights are violated have an effective remedy, and to ensure that such remedies are enforced when granted. See also the reporting obligations imposed upon the states parties by art. 40 of the ICCPR.
111. Article 15 of the Draft Norms provides that 'As an initial step towards implementing these Norms, each transnational corporation or other business enterprise shall adopt, disseminate and implement internal rules of operation in compliance with the Norms. Further, they shall periodically report on and take other measures fully to implement the Norms and to provide at least for the prompt implementation of the protections set forth in the Norms. Each transnational corporation or other business enterprise shall apply and incorporate these Norms in their contracts or other arrangements and dealings with contractors, subcontractors, suppliers, licensees, distributors, or natural or other legal persons that enter into any agreement with the transnational corporation or business enterprise in order to ensure respect for an implementation of the Norms'.
112. Article 16 of the Draft Norms provides that 'Transnational corporations and other business enterprises shall be subject to periodic monitoring and verification by United Nations, other international and national mechanisms already in existence or yet to be created, regarding application of the Norms. This monitoring shall be transparent and independent and take into account input from stakeholders (including non-governmental organizations) and as a result of complaints of violations of these Norms. Further, transnational corporations and other business enterprises shall conduct periodic evaluations concerning the impact of their own activities on human rights under these Norms'.
113. *Draft Articles on Responsibility of States for Internationally Wrongful Acts*, adopted by the International Law Commission at its 53rd Session (2001), Official Records of the General Assembly, 56th Session, Supplement No. 10 (A/56/10), chp.IV.E.1) ch. II, arts 34–9.
114. See Chapter 6, nn. 49, 50 and accompanying text.
115. See e.g., John Ruggie, *Report of the United Nations High Commissioner on Human Rights on the Responsibilities of Transnational Corporations and Related Business Enterprises with regard to Human Rights*, E/CN.4/2005/91 (15 February 2005) para. 52(e). See also John Ruggie, 'Business and human rights: the evolving international agenda' (2007) 101:4 *American Journal of International Law* 819; John Ruggie, *Clarifying the Concepts of 'Sphere of Influence' and 'Complicity*, report to Human Rights Council, UN Doc. A/HRC/8/16 (15 May 2008) and Surya Deva, 'UN's Human Rights Norms for Transnational Corporations and Other Business Enterprises: an imperfect step in the right direction?' (2004) 10 *ILSA Journal of International an Comparative Law* 493.
116. Office of the High Commissioner for Human Rights, United Nations Global Compact, E-Learning, Module 2, www.unssc.org/web/hrb/details.asp?mod=2&sec=2&cur=1.
117. Draft Norms, Part A 'General obligations', art. 1.
118. John Ruggie, *Business and Human Rights: Mapping International Standards of Responsibility and Accountability for Corporate Acts, Report of the Special Representative of the Secretary-General on the Issue of Human Rights and Transnational Corporations and Other Business Enterprises*, UN Doc. A/HRC/4/035/Add.3 (9 February 2007).
119. See www.global.compact.org/AboutTheGC/TheTenPrinciples/index.html.
120. Philip Alston, 'The "not a Cat" syndrome: can the international human rights regime accommodate non-state actors?' in Philip Alston (ed.), *Non-State Actors and Human Rights* (OUP, 2005) 3, 13–14.
121. *Ibid.* 14.
122. John Ruggie, 'Business and human rights: the evolving international agenda' (2007) 101:4 *American Journal of International Law* 819, 826.
123. *Ibid.*
124. *Ibid.*
125. *Ibid.*

126.   John Ruggie, *Protect Respect and Remedy: A Framework for Business and Human Rights, Main Report of the Special Representative of the Secretary-General on the Issue of Human Rights and Transnational Corporations and Other Business Enterprises*, UN Doc. A/HRC/8/5 (7 April 2008) available at www.reports-and-materials.org/Ruggie-report-7-Apr-2008.pdf, 19, para. 68. See also *Clarifying the Concepts of 'Sphere of influence' and 'Complicity'*, report to the Human Rights Council, A/HRC/8/16 (15 May 2008).
127.   OHCHR, UN Global Compact, E-Learning, Module 2, www.unssc.org/web/hrb/details.asp?mod=2&sec=1&cur=1.
128.   Ruggie, A/HRC/8/5 (7 April 2008), above n. 126, para. 69 and John Ruggie, *Clarifying the Concepts of 'Sphere of Influence' and 'Complicity'*, report to the Human Rights Council, UN Doc. A/HRC/8/16 (15 May 2008) para. 13.
129.   Ruggie, A/HRC/8/5 (7 April 2008) para. 70 and A/HRC/8/16 (15 May 2008) para. 14.
130.   *Report of the United Nations High Commissioner for Human Rights on the Responsibilities of Transnational Corporations and Related Business Enterprises*, UN Doc. E/CN.4/2005/91.
131.   Ruggie, A/HRC/8/16 (15 May 2008), above n. 126, para. 15.
132.   *Ibid.* para. 16.
133.   *Ibid.* para. 18.
134.   John Ruggie, *Interim Report of the Special Representative of the Secretary-General on Business and Human Rights*, UN Doc. E/CN.4/2006/97 (22 February 2006) para. 60.
135.   Statute of the International Court of Justice, art. 38(b).
136.   Steven R. Ratner, 'Corporations and human rights: a theory of legal responsibility' (2001) 111 *Yale Law Journal* 443, 457, citing *Development and International Economic Co-operation: Transnational Corporations*, UN ESCOR, 2nd Sess., UN Doc. E/1990/1994 (1990); Draft United Nations Code of Conduct on Transnational Corporations, UN ESCOR, Spec. Sess., Supp. No. 7, Annex II, UN Doc. E/1983/17/Rev. 1 (1983). See also Peter T. Muchlinski, 'Attempts to extend the accountability of transnational corporations: the role of UNCTAD' in Menno T. Kamminga and Saman Zia-Zarifi (eds), *Liability of Multinational Corporations under International Law* (2000) 97; and Leary, above n. 50, 194.
137.   OECD Guidelines for Multinational Enterprises, DAFFE/IME/WPG(2000)15/FINAL (31 October 2001), Preamble. Text, commentary and clarifications available at www.olis.oecd.org/2000doc.nsf/LinkTo/NT00002F06/$FILE/JT00115758.PDF.
138.   When the revised version of the Guidelines were released in June 2000, adhering governments included those of all OECD members, as well as Argentina, Brazil, Chile and the Slovak Republic: Note 1, Declaration on International Investment and Multinational Enterprises, 27 June 2000. By January 2010, there were 42 adhering governments from both OECD and non-OECD states.
139.   For the sake of consistency with the rest of this book, TNC is used here instead of the term multinational enterprise as used in the OECD Guidelines. There is no essential difference between the term multinational enterprise as used in the Guidelines and the term TNC as used here. According to para. 3 of the 'Concepts and Principles' section of the Guidelines: 'A precise definition of multinational enterprise is not required for the purposes of the Guidelines. These usually comprise companies or other entities established in more than one country and so linked that they may co-ordinate their operations in various ways. While one or more of these entities may be able to exercise a significant influence over the activities of others, their degree of autonomy within the enterprise may vary widely from one multinational enterprise to another. Ownership may be private, state or mixed. The Guidelines are addressed to all the entities within the multinational enterprise (parent companies and/or local entities). According to the actual distribution of responsibilities among them, the different entities are expected to co-operate and to assist one another to facilitate observance of the Guidelines.'
140.   *Implementation Procedures of the OECD Guidelines for Multinational Enterprises* (June 2000), Part C, 'Implementation in specific instances'. See also *Commentary on the Implementation Procedures of the OECD Guidelines for Multinational Enterprises* paras 13–20. Full text of both available at www.olis.oecd.org/olis/2000doc.nsf/LinkTo/NT00002F06/$FILE/JT00115758.PDF.

141. *Implementation Procedures of the OECD Guidelines for Multinational Enterprises* (June 2000), Part II 'The Committee on International Investment and Multinational Enterprises', para. 4.
142. *Human Rights, Alternative Dispute Resolution and the OECD Guidelines for Multinational Enterprises*, Briefing note for the participants at the Workshop on Accountability and Dispute Resolution, Kennedy School of Government, Harvard University 11–12 April 2007, available at www.oecd.org/dataoecd/42/11/38297552.pdf.
143. OECD, *2009 Annual Meeting of the National Contact Points, Report by the Chair* (16–17 June 2009), Part I 'Overview', available at www.oecd.org/dataoecd/41/25/43753441.pdf.
144. *Ibid.* Part IV 'Active use of the "specific instance" facility', IV.a 'Number of specific instances'.
145. *Ibid.*
146. The NGOs involved were Rights and Accountability in Development (RAID), the Human Rights Council of Australia, Children Out of Detention (ChildOut), the Brotherhood of St Laurence and the International Commission of Jurists.
147. RAID *et al.*, *Submission to the Australian National Contact Point for the OECD Guidelines for Multinational Enterprises Concerning Global Solutions (Australia) Pty Ltd* (June 2005) ('GSL complaint') 2–3, available at www.hrca.org.au/OECD.pdf.
148. Australian National Contact Point for the OECD Guidelines for Multinational Enterprises, *Statement by the Australian National Contact Point 'GSL Specific Instance'* (6 April 2006), contained in OECD, *2006 Annual Meeting of the National Contact Points, Report by the Chair* (20–21 June 2006) 59–65.
149. *Ibid.* para. 5.
150. *Ibid.* attachment B, *Agreed Outcomes of Mediation Meeting.*
151. *Ibid.* attachment B, para. 3.
152. At 1 July 2008.
153. See e.g. *Guide for addressing environmental issues in product standards* (2nd edn) ISO 15743:2006; *Safety of machinery: Lubricants with incidental product contact, hygiene requirements* ISO 21469:2006 and *Welding and allied processes: health and safety*, wordless precautionary labels for equipment and consumables used in arc welding and cutting ISO 17846:2004.
154. See e.g., *Food safety management systems: requirements for any organization in the food chain* ISO 22000:2005 and *Food safety management systems: guidance on the application of ISO 22000* ISO/TS 2204:2005.
155. See e.g., *Sustainability in building construction: general principles* ISO 15392:2008.
156. The most well-known of the ISO's standards setting out requirements for quality environmental management systems is ISO 14001:2004 *Environmental management systems: requirements with guidance for use* (2nd edn). ISO 14001:2004 is supported by a number of guidelines standards including ISO 14004:2004 *Environmental management systems: general guidelines on principles, systems and support techniques* (2nd edn).
157. See e.g., ISO/TS 16949:2002 (for the automotive sector); ISO/TS 29001:2007 (petroleum and gas sector) and ISO 31000 (risk awareness and evaluation).
158. SAI, www.sa-intl.org. SAI was founded by the corporate social responsibility research organization Council on Economic Priorities (CEP).
159. SA8000:2008, available at www.sa-intl.org/_data/n_0001/resources/live/2008Std EnglishFinal.pdf.
160. 'Envisioning change: how we got started', SAI, above n. 158.
161. See www.sa-intl.org and see also www.bdsglobal.com/tools/system_sa.asp.
162. SAAS began work as a department within SAI in 1997 and was formally established as its own not-for-profit organization in 2007: see www.saasaccreditation.org/.
163. See www.saasaccreditation.org/certfacilitieslist.htm.
164. IISD 2010 20th, ISO 26000 (CSR Guidance), available at www.iisd.org/standards/csr.asp.
165. *Ibid.*
166. ISO, *ISO and Social Responsibility* (2008), available at www.iso.org/iso/social responsibility.pdf.
167. *Ibid.*

168. ISO, 'Future ISO 26000 standard on social responsibility published as Draft International Standard' (14 September 2009), available at www.iso.org/iso/pressrelease.htm?refid= Ref1245.
169. *Ibid.*
170. ISO, 'ISO 26000 on social responsibility approved for release as Final Draft International Standard' (26 May 2010), available at www.iso.org/iso/pressrelease.htm?refid=Ref1321.
171. Draft ISO 26000 Guidance on Social Responsibility, ISO/TMB SR N 191 (21 May 2010) ISO/DIS 26000 (Unedited Draft) IDTF_N115, clause 1 'Scope', at lines 233–5.
172. ISO, 'Future ISO 26000 standard on social responsibility published as Draft International Standard', above n. 168.
173. Draft ISO 26000 Guidance on social responsibility, above n. 171.
174. *Ibid.* ix, lines 175–7.
175. John Ruggie, *Note on ISO 26,000 Guidance Draft Document* (November 2009), available at www.business-humanrights.org/Links/Repository/641199.
176. *Ibid.*
177. Draft International Standard ISO/DIS 26000, ISO/TMB/WG SR 172 (September 2009). Voting on the 2009 draft began on 14 September 2009 and ended on 14 February 2010.
178. *Ibid.*
179. John Ruggie, *Note on ISO 26,000 Guidance Draft Document* (November 2009).
180. Draft ISO 26000 Guidance on social responsibility, above n. 171.
181. *Ibid.*
182. Draft International Standard ISO/DIS 26000, ISO/TMB/WG SR 172 (September 2009). Note, however, that clause 6 of the 2009 Draft does refer to due diligence as an important concept in the context of its 'Human rights' clause, clause 6.3. Due diligence is expressly dealt with in sub-clause 6.3.3. Sub-clause 6.3.3.1 describes what is involved in a proper due diligence process, while sub-clause 6.3.3.2 of the 2009 Draft outlines expectations placed on organizations in relation to due diligence. These sub-clauses have been edited as part of creating the new sub-clause 7.4.3, but their content remains essentially unchanged in the 2010 Draft ISO/DIS 26000 Guidance.
183. Office of the High Commissioner for Human Rights, 'Human rights and transnational corporations and other business enterprises', Res. 2005/69 (20 April 2005), above n. 94.
184. Human Rights Council, *Mandate of the Special Representative of the Secretary-General on the Issue of Human Rights and Transnational Corporations and Other Business Enterprises*, UN Doc. A/HRC/RES/8/7 (18 June 2008).
185. John Ruggie, *Protect, Respect and Remedy: A Framework for Business and Human Rights, Report of the Special Representative of the Secretary-General on the Issue of Human Rights and Transnational Corporations and Other Business Enterprises*, UN Doc. A/HRC/8/5/ (7 April 2008) Summary.
186. *Ibid.* para. 27. See also Adam McBeth, *International Economic Actors and Human Rights* (Routledge 2010) chs 2 and 3; Gillian Triggs, *International Law: Contemporary Principles and Practice* (LexisNexis Butterworths, 2006) ch. 14.
187. Ruggie, above n. 185, paras 33–46; John Ruggie, *Business and Human Rights: Towards Operationalizing the "Protect, Respect and Remedy" Framework, Report of the Special Representative of the Secretary-General on the Issue of Human Rights and Transnational Corporations and Other Business Enterprises*, UN Doc. A/HRC/11/13 (22 April 2009) paras 38–43.
188. Robert McCorquodale and P. Simons, 'Responsibility Beyond Borders: State Responsibility for Extraterritorial Violations by Corporations of International Human Rights Law' (2007) 70:4 *Modern Law Review* 598.
189. International Law Commission, *Draft Articles on the Responsibility of States for Internationally Wrongful Acts, Report of the International Law Commission on the Work of its 53rd Session*, UN GAOR. 56th Sess. Supp. No. 10, UN Doc. A/56/10 (SUPP) (August 2001). Not all of the ILC Articles can be considered to be customary international law, though most of them, including those relevant to a state's responsibility for the extra-territorial acts of TNCs under its jurisdiction, have been adopted by international tribunals as reflective of customary international law: see H. Duffy, 'Towards global responsibility

for human rights protection: a sketch of international developments' (2006) 15 *Interights Bulletin* 104. See also J. Crawford, *The International Law Commission's Articles on State Responsibility: Introduction, Text and Commentaries* (CUP, 2002).

190. ILC, Draft Articles on the Responsibility of States for Internationally Wrongful Acts (2001) art. 5 'Conduct of persons or entities exercising elements of governmental authority'.

191. *Ibid.* art. 8 'Conduct directed or controlled by a state'.

192. *Ibid.* art. 6 'Conduct of organs placed at the disposal of a state by another state' and art. 16 'Aid or assistance in the commission of an internationally wrongful act'. For discussion see J. Quigley, 'Complicity in international law: a new direction in the law of state responsibility' (1986) 57 *British Yearbook of International Law* 77; E. Noyes and B.D. Smith, 'State responsibility and the principle of joint and several liability' (1988) 13 *Yale Journal of International Law* 225.

193. See e.g., American Convention on Human Rights 1969, art. 1(1) and European Convention on Human Rights 1950, art. 1. The UN Convention on Economic, Social and Cultural Rights and the African Charter of Human and Peoples' Rights have no similar express jurisdictional clause, though it is assumed they would also apply to a state's jurisdiction: see the Committee on Economic and Social and Cultural Rights General Comment No. 8, *The Relationship between Economic Sanctions and Respect for Economic, Social and Cultural Rights*, UN Doc. E/C.12/1997/8 (12 December 1997) para. 7. Article 2(1) of the UN Convention on Civil and Political Rights refers to both territory and jurisdiction. The Human Rights Commission (as it then was) has clarified that the state's obligations extend to both individuals within a state's territory as well as to those who are not within the state's territory but who are subject to its jurisdiction: HRC General Comment No. 31(80), *Nature of the General Legal Obligation Imposed on States Parties to the Covenant*, UN Doc. CCPR/C/21/Rev.1/Add.13 (26 May 2004) para. 3.

194. ILC Draft Articles on Responsibility of States for Internationally Wrongful Acts, with commentaries (2001), text adopted by the International Law Commission at its 53rd Session, and submitted to the General Assembly as a part of the Commission's report covering the work of that session (A/56/10). The report, which also contains commentaries on the Draft Articles, appears in (2001) II *Yearbook of the International Law Commission* Part 2, as corrected. See art. 5 and accompanying commentary.

195. See Wheat Marketing Act 1989 (Cth) and for discussion of the privatization process and its implications see Geoff Cockfield and Linda Botterill, 'From the Australian Wheat Board to AWB Ltd: collective marketing and privatisation in Australia's export wheat trade', paper delivered at the Public Policy Network Summer Conference, 1–2 February 2007, Flinders Institute of Public Policy and Management, Adelaide, South Australia; available at www.socsci.flinders.edu.au/fippm/ppnsummerconference2007/papers/CockfieldAnd Botterill.pdf.

196. *Final Report of the Independent Inquiry Committee into the United Nations Oil-for-Food Programme (Report on the Manipulation of the Oil-for-Food Programme)* (27 October 2005) 269; available at www.iic-offp.org/story27oct05.htm.

197. The Royal Commission chaired by Terence Cole reported on 24 November 2006: see *Inquiry into Certain Australian Companies in relation to the UN Oil-for-Food Program*, available atwww.ag.gov.au/agd/www/UNoilforfoodinquiry.nsf.

198. *AWB Ltd v Cole (No. 5)* [2006] FCA 1234.

199. The narrow terms of reference of the Cole inquiry prevented it from considering closely any attribution to the Australian government: *Inquiry into Certain Australian Companies in relation to the UN Oil-for-Food Program*, 'Terms of Reference', available at www.ag.gov.au/agd/WWW/unoilforfoodinquiry.nsf/Page/Terms_of_Reference.

200. McCorquodale and Simons, above n. 188, 607.

201. John Ruggie, *Clarifying the Concepts of 'Sphere of Influence' and 'Complicity'*, report to Human Rights Council, UN Doc. A/HRC/8/16 (15 May 2008) para. 3.

202. *Ibid.* para. 19.

203. *Ibid.*

204. *Ibid.* para. 18.

205. *Ibid.* Summary.

206. *Ibid.*
207. *Ibid.* para. 19.
208. *Ibid.* para. 20, citing *Guide to Human Rights Impact Assessment and Management*, Road-testing Draft, a joint publication of the International Financial Corporation, the Global Compact, and the International Business Leaders Forum (June 2007) 31, available at www.unglobalcompact.org/docs/news_events/8.1/HRIA_final.pdf.
209. Ruggie, above n. 201.
210. *Ibid.* para. 21.
211. *Ibid.* para. 19.
212. *Ibid.* para. 22.
213. *OECD Risk Awareness Tool for Multinational Enterprises in Weak Governance Zones* (2006),available at www.oecd.org/dataoecd/26/21/36885821.pdf.
214. *Ibid.* Introduction at 13.
215. *Ibid.* 13.
216. Quoted in IBA Working Group on the OECD Guidelines for Multinational Enterprises, *Response to the OECD Consultation on an Update of the OECD Guidelines for Multinational Enterprises* (31 January 2010) para. 54.
217. *Ibid.*
218. *Final Statement by the UK National Contact Point for the OECD Guidelines for Multinational Enterprises: Afrimex (UK) Ltd* (28 August 2008) available at www.oecd.org/dataoecd/40/29/43750590.pdf, Summary of NCP Decision, 1.
219. *Ibid.* NCP Recommendations, para. 64.
220. *Ibid.* Summary of NCP Decision.
221. *Ibid.* para. 38.
222. *Ibid.*
223. *Ibid.* para. 47.
224. *Final Statement by the UK National Contact Point for the OECD Guidelines for Multinational Enterprises: Vedanta Resources plc* (25 September 2009), available at www.berr.gov.uk/files/file53117.doc.
225. Ruggie, A/HRC/8/16 (15 May 2008), above n. 201, para. 25.
226. *Ibid.* para. 23.
227. For discussion, see Jonathan Clough and Carmel Mulhern, *The Prosecution of Corporations* (2002) ch. 5. As Clough and Mulhern note, corporate responsibility for a failure to act is a well-established basis of liability, particularly in the area of workplace safety. The authors' description of the 'corporate duty to take reasonable steps' is also akin to and overlaps with the SRSG's description of the corporate duty of 'due diligence': Ruggie, A/HRC/8/16 (15 May 2008), above n. 201, para. 23.
228. Ruggie, A/HRC/8/16 (15 May 2008), above n. 201, para. 25.
229. Draft ISO 26000 Guidance on Social Responsibility (May 2010), above n. 171, clause 7.3.1.
230. OECD, *Declaration on International Investment and Multinational Enterprises* (27 June 2000) para. VI. A booklet (2008) containing the text of all four parts of the Declaration, titled *OECD Guidelines for Multinational Enterprises*, is available at www.oecd.org/dataoecd/56/36/1922428.pdf.
231. *Ibid.* Part II, section III (at 311 of 2008 booklet)..
232. OECD, '2010 update of the OECD Guidelines for Multinational Enterprises' (as updated 31 May 2010), available at www.oecd.org/document/33/0,3343,en_2649_34893_44086753_1_1_1_1,00.html.
233. *Ibid.*
234. *Ibid.* The term 'non-adhering states' refers to states that have not signed up to the OECD Declaration on International Investment and Multinational Enterprises and so have not established a National Contact Point or declared their agreement with the principles set out in the Guidelines.
235. *Ibid.* See also OECD, *Consultation on an Update of the OECD Guidelines for Multinational Enterprises*, 'Agenda and Consultation Note', OECD Conference Centre, Paris France, 8 December 2009.

236. *Ibid.* para. 27.
237. The IBA WG was created in November 2009 in response to a call for consultation by the UK Department of Business Innovation and Skills (BIS) (which acts as the British NCP for the Guidelines), issued in October 2009. The WG submitted its report to the BIS on 30 November 2009, and that report was read by many at the 9 December 2009 OECD Meeting. As a result, the OECD invited IBA WG to submit a report directly to it, by the end of January 2010, under its own public consultation terms of reference.
238. IBA Working Group on the OECD Guidelines for Multinational Enterprises, *Response to the OECD Consultation on an Update of the OECD Guidelines for Multinational Enterprises* (31 January 2010), available at www.**iba**net.org/Document/Default.aspx? DocumentUid=33298df5-4c58 ('IBA WG Report').
239. *Ibid.* para. 10.
240. *Ibid.*
241. Called MNEs in the IBA WG Report but referred to as TNCs here for the sake of consistency.
242. John Ruggie, *Business and Human Rights: Towards Operationalizing the 'Protect, Respect and Remedy' Framework*, UN Doc. A/HRC/11/13 (22 April 2009) para. 75, cited in IBA WG Report, para. 11.
243. OECD Guidelines, above n. 230, Part I, ch. II 'General policies', para. 10.
244. *Ibid.* Part III 'Commentaries', para. 10.
245. IBA WG Report, above n. 238, para. 13.
246. *Ibid.* para. 14.
247. *Ibid.* paras 15–17.
248. *Ibid.* para. 20.
249. *Ibid.* para. 21.
250. *Ibid.*
251. *Ibid.* para. 22.
252. *Ibid.* paras. 24–31.
253. *Ibid.* paras. 32–41.
254. *Ibid.* paras 42–46.
255. *Ibid.* paras 47–51.
256. *Ibid.* paras 54–58.
257. *Ibid.* paras 59–90.
258. *FTSE4Good Index Series Inclusion Criteria*, available at www.ftse.com/Indices/FTSE4Good_Index_Series/Downloads/FTSE4Good_Inclusion_Criteria.pdf.
259. *Dow Jones Sustainability Indexes*, 'DJSI World Key Facts', available at www.sustainability-index.com/07_htmle/indexes/djsiworld_keyfacts.html.
260. For information, see 'sustainability investing', available at www.sam-group.com/htmle/djsi/islamic.cfm.
261. *Dow Jones Sustainability Indexes*, 'DJSI World Key Facts', above n. 259.
262. *Dow Jones Sustainability Indexes*, 'Information Sources', available at www.sustainability-index.com/07_htmle/assessment/infosources.html.
263. SAM Research AG, *Dow Jones Sustainability Indexes Key Facts* (April 2010), available at https://secure2.sam-group.com/online/documents/DJSI_KeyFacts_2006_final.pdf; jsessionid=1EF90CAE562753C4FAF9596BB64C6F67.
264. *Ibid.* See also *Dow Jones Sustainability World Index*, 'Factsheet, April 2010', available at www.sustainability-index.com/djsi_pdf/publications/Factsheets/SAM_IndexesMonthly_DJSIWorld.pdf.
265. Principles available at www.unpri.org/principles/.
266. David Kinley, *Civilising Globalisation: Human Rights and the Global Economy* (CUP, 2009) 172, citing PRI Initiative, *PRI Report on Progress 2007: Implementation, Assessment and Guidance* (July 2007) 5; available at www.upri.org/report07/PRIReportOnProgress 2007.pdf.
267. See e.g., 'BP removed from the Dow Jones Sustainability Indexes' (Zurich, 1 June 2010) available at www.sustainability-index.com/djsi_pdf/news/PressReleases/20100531_Statement%20BP%20Exclusion_Final.pdf.

268. For information see Government Pension Fund Global, www.nbim.no/en/About-us/ Government-Pension-Fund-Global/.
269. See s. 4(3) of the *Guidelines for Observation and Exclusion from the Government Pension Fund Global's Investment Universe*, adopted by the Ministry of Finance on 1 March 2010 pursuant to Act No. 123 of 21 December 2005 relating to the Government Pension Fund, s. 7.
270. Ministry of Finance, 'Ethical Guidelines for the Government Pension Fund – Global', information available at www.regjeringen.no/en/dep/fin/Selected-topics/the-government-pension-fund/responsible-investments/the-ethical-guidelines.html?id=434894.
271. Such as murder, torture, deprivation of liberty, forced labour, the worst forms of child labour and other child exploitation: s. 2(3) of the Guidelines for Observation and Exclusion from the Government Pension Fund Global's Investment Universe, above n. 269, section 7, available at www.regjeringen.no/en/sub/styrer-rad-utvalg/ethics_council/ethical-guidelines.html?id=425277.
272. *Ibid.* See also John Ruggie, *Clarifying the Concepts of 'Sphere of Influence' and 'Complicity'*, UN Doc. A/HRC/8/16 (15 May 2008) para. 65, citing Ministry information on the Ethical Guidelines available at www.regjeringen.no/en/dep/fin/Selected-topics/andre/Ethical-Guidelines-for-the-Government-Pension-Fund-Global-/The-Ethical-Guidelines.html?id=434894.
273. Ministry of Finance Press Release, 'Two Companies – Walmart and Freeport – are being excluded from the Norwegian Government Pension Fund – Global's investment universe', 6 June 2006, available at www.regjeringen.no/en/dep/fin/Press-Center/Press-releases/2006/Two-companies-Wal-Mart-and-Freeport-.html?id=104396.
274. Ruggie, A/HRC/8/16 (15 May 2008), above n. 272, para. 66.
275. Ministry of Finance Press Release 1/2010, 'Tobacco producers excluded from Government Pension Fund Global', 19 January 2010, available at www.regjeringen.no/en/dep/fin/press-center/Press-releases/2010/Tobacco-producers-excluded-from-Government-Pension-Fund-Global.html?id=591449. See now s. 2(1)(b) of the Guidelines, above n. 270.
276. *Ibid.*
277. Justine Nolan, 'Corporate accountability and triple bottom line reporting: determining the material issues for disclosure' in Gerald Acquaah-Gaisie and Val Clulow (eds), *Enhancing Corporate Accountability: Prospects and Challenges* (2006) 183–205. See also Adam McBeth, *International Economic Actors and Human Rights* (Routledge, 2010) 292–3.
278. *Ibid.*

3. The state and the multinational corporation: the investment relationship

A. THE GLOBAL NATURE OF THE MODERN CORPORATION

There is no doubt that TNCs can and do act like participants in an international community. They exert increasing global influence and power, and can and do influence the outcomes of global inter-governmental meetings and the drafting of global agreements.[1] Moreover, it stands to reason that the larger the global corporation, the more influence it can bring to bear on national governments and on the outcomes of international negotiations:

> the largest 500 corporations in the world control 25% of the global economic output. The powers of company management can and do affect others significantly: 'Managers now have more power than most sovereign governments to determine where people will live; what they will do, if any [sic]; what they will eat, drink, and wear; what sorts of knowledge they will encourage; and what kinds of society their children will inherit.'[2]

As former Australian Prime Minister Malcolm Fraser noted during his 2001 Deakin Lecture, governments are being downsized while global corporations are growing ever larger and more powerful.[3] Governments are losing, if they have not already lost, the ability to regulate or constrain the behaviour of corporations. This process is being propelled by the increasing consolidation of corporate power through global mergers and acquisitions. The decade since 2000 has seen an unprecedented number of cross-border mergers and acquisitions around the world,[4] resulting in an expanding network of relations between TNCs and host governments.

The relationship between any TNC and the foreign host state where its investments are located inevitably involves a tension between:

(i) on the one hand, the right, indeed the duty of corporate directors to protect and maximize the legitimate property rights and expectations of the corporation. This tension comes into sharpest focus in the context of foreign investment law, as both host governments and home states attempt to regulate the behaviour of multinational corporations; and

(ii) on the other hand, the right, indeed the duty of the state to regulate for the wellbeing of its citizenry and the orderly exploitation of environmental resources.

B.   PROTECTING THE RIGHTS OF FOREIGN INVESTORS

In any relationship between a foreign investor TNC and a host state there is a need to protect the foreign TNC from unfair regulatory actions by the host government. In this respect, the priorities of international law have evolved considerably in the post-Second World War era. The emphasis since the 1950s upon a state-driven model for economic development has given way to the power of TNCs and the movement across national boundaries of capital, labour and knowledge.[5] The 1990s saw a number of developments which effectively shifted the balance in favour of the investor by restricting host countries' ability to control and regulate foreign investment. Within the WTO, the Agreement on Trade-Related Investment Measures (TRIMs) establishes a number of restrictions on the ability of host governments to maximize the benefits of foreign investment for the local economy.[6] The OECD tried in the late 1990s to conclude a Multilateral Agreement on Investment (MAI)[7] and when that failed moves were made to include foreign investment on the agenda for the Development Round of trade negotiations through the Doha Declaration of November 2001.[8] The topic was abandoned in July 1994, reflecting yet again the all-too-familiar traditional clash of interests between developing and developed nations – with developed, capital-exporting countries championing the interests of foreign investors, and desiring the maximum mobility of capital, while developing, capital-importing countries wished to protect the sovereign autonomy of host governments, and their ability to maximize areas of legitimate comparative advantage.[9]

Despite the absence of a WTO agreement on investment, the interests of foreign investors remain well protected. Under the Convention Establishing the Multilateral Investment Guarantee Agency (MIGA) (an arm of the World Bank Group), guarantees may be issued to investors against non-commercial risk.[10] In addition, TNCs are able to bring claims against foreign host states where their foreign investment interests are located under a number of specific bilateral and multilateral trade and investment treaties. The most important of these treaties is the 1965 Convention on the Settlement of Investment Disputes between States and Nationals of Other States,[11] under which the International Centre for the Settlement of Investment Disputes (ICSID) has jurisdiction over legal disputes arising directly out of an investment between a contracting state and a national from another contracting state.

International law focuses primarily on the sovereign nation-state when it imposes duties and responsibilities. Thus, multilateral investment treaties (MITs) and bilateral investment treaties (BITs) do not directly impose legal requirements on TNCs in the conduct of their foreign investment activities. Instead, such treaties operate by regulating the ability of host government signatories to exercise the full range of their sovereign powers. In particular, they limit the ability of host governments to take action, including through direct expropriation, affecting the property rights of foreign investors. Thus, the law of foreign investor protection has often been preoccupied with the task of distinguishing between compensable expropriation of foreign investment property, on the one hand, and non-compensable regulatory action by a host government, on the other.[12]

There is no doubt today that under customary international law states have the right to expropriate the property of foreign investors. That right is, however, subject to four conditions:[14]

1. The expropriation must be undertaken for a public purpose;[14]
2. The expropriation must be non-discriminatory;[15]
3. The expropriation must comply with principles of due process of law (also known as 'natural justice');[16] and
4. Compensation for the expropriation must be paid to the foreign investor.[17]

One important and influential example of a MIT which incorporates these principles is the North American Free Trade Agreement (NAFTA). Chapter 11 of the NAFTA seeks to ensure for investors of one state party the right to claim certain minimum standards of treatment 'in accordance with international law, including fair and equitable treatment and full protection and security': article 1105.[18] Examples of BITs serving to protect the interests of foreign investors include the 1,400 page long Free Trade Agreement concluded between the United States and Singapore[19] and the Australia–United States Free Trade Agreement[20] which followed shortly thereafter. What is interesting is that in spite of the lengthy attention to detail in both of these BITs, many matters of foreign investment law have not been defined or clarified, and are left, instead, to customary international law to decide.

A dispute that went to arbitration under the terms of the NAFTA Agreement in 1997 demonstrates the clash between the interests of foreign investors, on the one hand, and local measures for environmental protection, on the other. In *Metalclad Corporation v United Mexican States*,[21] the claimant, Metalclad Corporation, a US company, had invested in Mexico through a Mexican subsidiary in the development and operation of a hazardous waste landfill site.

Prior to Metalclad's investment in the Mexican subsidiary, the company had obtained what appeared to be all of the required permits from the relevant Mexican authorities. Metalclad began construction of the landfill in 1994, largely on the strength of representations made by the Mexican federal government, which was involved throughout the project, that all relevant regulatory conditions had been fulfilled, and construction of the site was completed in 1995. The federal government made clear that it 'was satisfied that this project was consistent with, and sensitive to, its environmental concerns'.[22] Despite this, however, local citizens held demonstrations near the landfill site as construction neared completion, and the local municipality refused to issue a municipal permit, on the ground, *inter alia*, that the landfill would cause adverse environmental effects. The ICSID tribunal established in accordance with Chapter 11 of the NAFTA found that the refusal by the municipality to grant Metalclad a permit constituted a measure equivalent to expropriation. The level of interference with the company's operations was found to be complete since the measure 'involve[d] the complete frustration of the operation of the landfill and negate[d] the possibility of any meaningful return on Metalclad's investment'.[23] In ordering that Mexico pay approximately US$17 million in damages to Metalclad, the tribunal appears to have adopted a somewhat broader definition of expropriation than is found in other foreign investment decisions, even those concerning the same provisions of NAFTA. The tribunal held that expropriation under article 1110 of NAFTA:

> includes not only open, deliberate and acknowledged takings of property, such as outright seizure or formal or obligatory transfer of title in favour of the host State, but also *covert and incidental interference with the use of property which has the effect of depriving the owner, in whole or in significant part, of the use or reasonably-to-be-expected economic benefit of the property* even if not necessarily to the obvious benefit of the host state.[24]

The decision in *Metalclad* clearly has implications not only for future disputes arising under the NAFTA, but also for foreign investor claims arising under other MITs and BITs, such as the Australia–United States Free Trade Agreement, article 11.7 of which deals with issues of 'Expropriation and Compensation' in virtually identical terms to the NAFTA.[25]

C.   SHIELDING LOCAL COMMUNITIES FROM THE CONSEQUENCES OF TNC ACTIVITIES

The *Metalclad* case also demonstrates the way in which protection of foreign investor interests overlaps with a second aspect of the relationship between TNCs and host states: the relationship which arises when host governments seek to protect local communities from the potentially detrimental impacts of foreign investor activities. All too often, when communities in developing countries are detrimentally affected by the activities of foreign TNCs their chances of obtaining effective legal redress in their own jurisdiction is hamstrung by poor environmental and labour regulations, often combined with an ineffective or even corrupt legal system. The Special Representative of the Secretary-General (SRSG) has described the 'far-reaching effects' of BITs and host government agreements (the contracts between governments and foreign investors for specific projects), which may constrain the ability of states to adopt legitimate policy reforms, including for human rights.[26]

An example of the impact that foreign investment can have on local legal systems can be found in the relationship between Australian TNC Broken Hill Proprietary (since 2001 known as BHP Billiton, hereafter BHP) and the government of Papua New Guinea (PNG). The PNG government has yet to put in place effective environmental regulations controlling the disposal of mine waste into local rivers. This lack is further compounded by laws specifically designed to prevent local landowners and residents taking action against foreign mine operators. The Ok Tedi Mine Continuation (Ninth Supplementary) Act of 2001 ('Ninth Ok Tedi Act')[27] is one such law.

The Ninth Ok Tedi Act allowed BHP to offload its 52 per cent share of the Ok Tedi Mine (which was scheduled to close in 2010) into a development trust, in return for being insulated from future liabilities for environmental damage. The Act also gave effect to community mine continuation agreements (CMCAs) which were designed to negate any claims by landowners against BHP, including the claim for damages by 34,000 landowners against BHP which had been instituted before the Supreme Court of Victoria, Australia, in 1994.[28]

In 1996, BHP had made an out-of-court settlement that included payment of approximately AUS$40 million in compensation as well as the dredging of tailings from the river in an attempt to limit further damage. The legal action was reinstated in April 2000 when two landowner leaders claimed that BHP had breached the terms of the settlement. In particular, they claimed that the provision requiring investigation of the need for a tailings dam to prevent further tailings entering the river system had not been complied with.[29]

By passing the Ninth Ok Tedi Act, the PNG government effectively deprived both itself and PNG landowners of any right to take any action against BHP Billiton or Ok Tedi Mine Ltd (OTML) over the effects of the company's mining activities. So far as the state itself was concerned, the Act provides that 'neither the State nor any Government Agency may take, pursue, or in any way support Proceedings against a BHP Billiton Party in respect of an Environmental Claim'.[30] The PNG government thus willingly limited the state sovereignty of PNG in favour of a global corporation with an annual income larger than the Papua New Guinea GDP of 2001, the year the legislation was passed. Nor in the absence of government support were local landowners able to take action against BHP on their own behalf. With the passing of the new legislation, the CMCAs were able to bypass any class action by expressly exempting BHP 'from all and any demands and claims arising directly or indirectly from the operation of the mine'.[31] Another provision ensures that 'the signature ... by a person representing or purporting to represent a community or clan or that person's delegate, binds all of the members of that community or clan'.[32]

Within days after the Ninth OK Tedi Act was passed, the then former Prime Minister of PNG, Sir Michael Somare, challenged the constitutional validity of the legislation before the PNG Supreme Court, on the basis that the legislation was unreasonable and breached the constitutional provision guaranteeing equality for all PNG citizens.[33] Legal actions in both Victoria and PNG then stalled, however, as lawyers in both countries became drawn into CMCA negotiations in circumstances where the original 1996 settlement had already bound the most capable public interest lawyers in PNG from becoming involved in any further legal actions against the company.[34]

Sir Michael Somare was elected Prime Minister of PNG again in 2002. This meant that, as the government is a major shareholder in Ok Tedi Mining Ltd, he found himself with a significant conflict of interest in bringing OTML before the courts. The constitutional case was consequently withdrawn. A simultaneous court action by landowners led by Gabia Gagarimabu, an MP from the Western Province of PNG, was settled out of court in 2004 on the advice of law firm Slater and Gordon as part of the settlement of the action which had previously been instituted in the Victorian Supreme Court.[35]

More recently, the PNG government has passed amendments to the Forestry Act 1991 and, on 28 May 2010, to the Environment and Conservation Act 2000, to effectively rule out future legal action by land owners against major resource projects.[36] Amendments to the Environment and Conservation Act now give the director of the Office of Environment and Conservation wide-ranging powers to grant various certificates relating to environmental plans submitted by investors. These powers are then supplemented by provisions ensuring that complying certificates issued by the director will be final and 'may not be challenged or reviewed in any court or tribunal, except at the instigation of an Authorization Instrument'.[37] The changes to the legislation follow complaints from the mining industry after landowners won a temporary injunction preventing the Chinese-owned Ramu nickel mine from dumping waste into the sea off Madang.[38] A Madang landowners group lodged a legal challenge against the controversial environmental law changes in the PNG Supreme Court on 6 June 2010.[39] The claim is that the amendments breach various human rights guaranteed under PNG's 1975 Constitution, and also breach the ILO's Indigenous and Tribal Peoples Convention 1989,[40] which was ratified by the PNG parliament in 2000.[41]

Papua New Guinea is far from being the only developing nation where global corporations have effectively evaded legal liability for the harmful consequences of their business operations. An even more striking example is the negotiations (or lack of them) between Union Carbide and Indian workers in Bhopal, India, who were injured, or whose relatives had been killed, following a 2–3 December 1984 gas leak. The leak from a Union Carbide plant exposed half a million people to 27 tons of the deadly gas methyl isocyanate. Thousands of people were killed as a result of their exposure to the gas; estimates of how many range from 3,800 according to Union Carbide, to 15,000 according to municipal workers who picked up bodies in the days following the disaster. More than 120,000 people still suffer from ailments, including blindness and breathing difficulties, caused by the accident and subsequent pollution at the plant site.[42]

At the time of the accident, the Bhopal plant was owned and operated by Union Carbide India, Ltd (UCIL), an Indian company in which Union Carbide Corporation held a controlling interest of just over half the stock.[43] Despite investigations into the cause of the accident, conflicting claims about responsibility are still being made over 20 years later. According to the Union Carbide website:

> Shortly after the gas release, Union Carbide launched an aggressive effort to identify the cause. A thorough investigation was conducted by the engineering consulting firm Arthur D. Little. Its conclusion: the gas leak could only have been caused by deliberate sabotage. Someone purposely put water in the gas storage tank, causing a massive chemical reaction. Process safety systems had been put in place that would have kept the water from entering the tank by accident.[44]

The Bhopal Medical Appeal website has quite a different story to tell:

> The plant, which never reached its full capacity, proved to be a losing venture and ceased active production in the early 1980s. However, vast quantities of dangerous chemical remained: three tanks continued to hold over 60 tons of methyl isocyanate, or MIC for short. Although MIC is a particularly reactive and deadly gas, the Union Carbide plant's elaborate safety system was allowed to fall into disrepair. The management's reasoning seemed to be that since the plant had ceased all production, no threat remained. Every safety system that had been installed to prevent a leak of MIC – at least six in all – ultimately proved inoperative.
>
> Regular maintenance had fallen into such disrepair that on the night of December 2nd, when an employee was flushing a corroded pipe, multiple stopcocks failed and allowed water to flow freely into the largest tank of MIC. Exposure to this water soon led to an uncontrolled reaction; the tank was blown out of the concrete sarcophagus and spewed a deadly cloud of MIC, hydrogen cyanide, mono methyl amine and other chemicals that hugged the ground. Blown by the prevailing winds, this cloud settled over much of Bhopal.[45]

It wasn't until 1989 that Union Carbide, in a partial settlement with the Indian government, agreed to pay out some US$470 million. The victims of the disaster weren't consulted in the settlement discussion, and those who did receive compensation were paid around US$300–500 each. This equals about five years' worth of medical expenses, or to view it from another direction, about 3 cents for each Union Carbide shareholder.[46]

In 1991, the local government in Bhopal charged Warren Anderson, Union Carbide's CEO at the time of the disaster, with manslaughter. However, Mr Anderson has never stood trial before an Indian court. He has, instead, evaded an international arrest warrant and a summons to appear before a US court. For years, Mr Anderson's whereabouts were unknown, and it wasn't until August 2002 that Greenpeace found him in the Hamptons.[47] In 2010, when his fellow directors were sentenced by a local court in Bhopal to two years' imprisonment, Warren Anderson was living in the United States.[48] The Union Carbide Corporation was itself charged with culpable homicide, but the US parent firm has consistently refused to appear before an Indian court.

In 1994, Union Carbide sold its majority interest in UCIL to MacLeod Russell (India) Ltd of Calcutta, and UCIL was renamed Eveready Industries India, Ltd. According to Union Carbide, '[a]s a result of the sale of its shares in UCIL, Union Carbide retained no interest in – or liability for – the Bhopal site, and … the state government of Madhya Pradesh assumed control of the site and its remediation' in 1998.[49] The opposite view is put forward by the Bhopal Medical Appeal and Sambhavna Trust and other supporters of Bhopal victims. They argue that Union Carbide remains liable for environmental damages, which were never addressed in the 1989 settlement, and that these liabilities became the property of the Dow Corporation, following its 2001 purchase of Union Carbide.[50] Dow Corporation, however, has consistently maintained that it is not liable for any aspect of the Bhopal accident.[51]

On 7 June 2010, over 25 years after the Bhopal gas leak occurred, former Chairman of Union Carbide of India Keshub Mahindra plus seven others were convicted for the tragedy and sentenced to two years' prison each. The accused were held guilty under sections of the Indian Penal Code relating to causing death by negligence, culpable homicide not amounting to murder, and gross negligence.[52] The Indian unit of Union Carbide was fine Rs 500,000. Meanwhile, the site has not been properly cleared up, local people continue to suffer from health problems without adequate medical care, survivors of the gas leak are still awaiting more adequate compensation and both Dow Chemical and its US subsidiary Union Carbide continue to deny the jurisdiction of the Indian courts.[53]

TNCs not only have greater resources than local communities, they also have greater mobility. One TNC which has used its legal mobility to evade liabilities is the asbestos manufacturer, James Hardie. From the 1920s until

1987, companies in the James Hardie Group were involved in the manufacture, distribution and mining of asbestos and asbestos products throughout Australia. Asbestos was widely used in building products, insulation, pipes and brake linings. By 1938, the health effects of inhaling asbestos dust were known by the company. If there was any doubt at that stage, the effects were evaluated and publicized almost 20 years later in a 1957 medical journal article. From then on it was clear that asbestos caused lung cancer, asbestosis, mesothelioma and pleural diseases following either occupational or environmental exposure to the fibres. It was not until another 20 years later, in 1977, that labels were put on Hardie's asbestos products warning that 'breathing asbestos dust may cause serious damage to health including cancer'.[54]

Two subsidiaries of the parent company James Hardie Industries Ltd (JHIL), Amaca and Amaba, had previously manufactured products made from asbestos. On 15 February 2001, these two subsidiaries were separated from JHIL and transferred to a newly established Medical Research and Compensation Foundation (MRCF) for no monetary value. The establishment of the fund was announced by JHIL on 16 February 2001 in a statement which informed readers that the purposes of the new fund were 'to compensate sufferers of asbestos-related diseases with claims against two former James Hardie subsidiaries and fund medical research aimed at finding cures for these diseases'.[55] The statement also reassured readers that:

> The Foundation has sufficient funds to meet all legitimate compensation claims anticipated from people injured by asbestos products that were manufactured in the past by two former subsidiaries of JHIL ... The ... Foundation ... will be completely independent of JHIL and will commence operation with assets of $293 million.[56]

This latter reassurance was particularly important for JHIL shareholders who were becoming anxious about the introduction of a proposed new Australian Accounting Standard likely to come into force at the end of October 2001 and which would require that the total of the Group's estimated asbestos liabilities (discounted to present value) be disclosed in JHIL's accounts. This gave a degree of urgency to the need to separate out the asbestos liabilities from the Group. The second factor was a public relations aspect: if the separation could be effected at the same time as the announcement of the Group's Third Quarter results, the inclusion of information about the Group's cutting loose its asbestos liabilities – a matter which might otherwise attract undesirable publicity – would be muted by its mingling with 'business news'.

The separation meant that JHIL would be able to continue business supposedly free from the stigma of asbestos liabilities. Shortly afterwards, JHIL also took measures to move its operations offshore, enabling it to focus upon its largest growth markets which were by then outside of Australia, while also allowing it to leave any asbestos compensation liabilities behind it in

Australia. In October 2001, a scheme of arrangement was approved by the Australian courts whereby the holding company of JHIL became James Hardie Industries NV (JHI NV), a Dutch company.[57]

In order for James Hardie to be allowed to relocate to the Netherlands, it had to provide assurances to the Australian courts that there would be enough assets left in the MRCF to meet all future asbestos-related liability claims. The net assets of the two subsidiary groups that had been transferred to the MRCF in fact amounted to approximately AUS$293 million, most of which lay in real estate and loans. This amount exceeded the 'best estimate' of AUS$286 million in asbestos liabilities contained in an actuarial report commissioned by James Hardie as part of the establishment of the MRCF. By the end of October 2001, however, and despite assurances to the contrary given by both James Hardie CEO Peter McDonald and by the firm's lawyers, a revised actuarial report showed that liabilities for asbestos-related disease would actually reach $574.3 million. The fund sought extra funding from JHI NV and was offered AUS$18 million if the MRCF acquired JHIL, which by this time was a shell company with no operations and AUS$18 million in assets. The MRCF rejected this offer. Asbestos liabilities were subsequently again revised upwards to AUS$751.8 million in 2002 and then AUS$1.573 billion in 2003. As the cost of liabilities continued to rise, it became increasingly clear that the MRCF was inadequately funded and that many eligible victims would miss out on receiving compensation.[58]

On 12 February 2004, the NSW Cabinet Office commissioned a special committee to investigate the formation of the MRCF. The terms of reference for the inquiry, headed by David Jackson QC, included an examination of the separation of the MRCF from James Hardie, along with an examination of the corporate restructuring of James Hardie following this separation, to determine whether these movements affected the ability of the MRCF to meet expected asbestos liabilities. The report, which was finally released in September 2004, found that JHI NV was under no legal obligation to provide for the compensation shortfall of its former subsidiaries despite its direct involvement in jeopardizing the health of workers, their families and the community. The only obligation James Hardie had to the victims of its products was an ethical one.[59]

It took months of social pressure from unions, political parties, victims and victims' support groups, along with prominent media exposure, before James Hardie, after initially refusing to accept any extra-legal liability, finally agreed to participate in a statutory scheme to cover compensation claims. The Jackson Inquiry supported such a scheme which would see JHI NV contribute to a government-run compensation system. Unions, the NSW government and victims' support groups initially all opposed the scheme, fearing that claims would be capped, and called for full, unconditional compensation.[60] In the result, a series of non-binding and binding agreements were reached between James Hardie, victims' groups, unions and the government to facilitate funding for victim compensation. The Australian Securities and Investments Commission (ASIC) also pursued the directors of James Hardie in the NSW Supreme Court for breaches of the Corporations Act. Although the ASIC initially sought a fine of between AUS$1.47 million and AUS$1.81 million for James Hardie CEO Peter MacDonald, he was eventually fined just AUS$350,000 for deceptive conduct over asbestos compensation. Non-executive board members were fined as little as AUS$30,000. Mr MacDonald was also disqualified from managing a company for 15 years and the others for between five and seven years.[61]

The *James Hardie* case provides a good example of how most TNCs now conduct their operations through often complex structures of holding and subsidiary firms. Other well-known examples include Unocal, which conducted its operations in Burma through wholly-owned subsidiaries, and Talisman, which conducted its operations in the Sudan through a consortium of oil companies called the Greater Nile Petroleum Operating Company Ltd (GNPOC). The rationale for interposing subsidiaries is easily understood – it minimizes risk and insulates the parent. The principle of separate corporate identity ensures that the parent will generally not be liable for the conduct of a subsidiary, despite the 'commercial reality that every holding company has the potential and, more often than not, in fact does, exercise complete control over a subsidiary'.[62] In addition, the principle of limited liability further insulates the parent by ensuring that its liability as a shareholder is limited to the unpaid amount of its investment in the subsidiary. As Jonathan Clough has noted, 'the extension of this principle, designed to protect investors in the enterprise, to the enterprise itself is one of the most significant factors in the success of [TNCs] because it allows risks to be transferred to the (often under-capitalized) subsidiary'.[63]

Along with many other examples, the *James Hardie* case also illustrates the mobility of the corporate form: the ability of firms to threaten relocation of their businesses and jobs to alternative jurisdictions if local regulatory constraints on corporate behaviour become too restrictive or detrimentally affect the corporate quest for profits. It is this mobility which is often put forward as an argument against the introduction of national reforms aimed at imposing standards of behaviour on foreign corporations in the local jurisdiction. Host states are often keen to encourage the entry of large direct investment proposals of the kind that TNCs are in a position to put forward, and conversely are often reluctant to impose obligations or standards of behaviour on foreign investors that might drive them away. As a result, victims of harmful TNC activities seeking redress typically find themselves in a legal jurisdiction where standards for TNC behaviour are set dismayingly low. When added to the further advantages bestowed on TNCs by their ability to pay for seemingly endless litigation, it is not surprising that litigation against TNCs is rare, and successful litigation even rarer.

Nevertheless, civil litigation under the local laws of a host state does take place, and remains the simplest way for victims to seek redress for harms inflicted by a TNC. Most often, such litigation once initiated is quickly settled out of court, especially where the TNC concerned has a reputation worth preserving. Settlement out of court is a risk minimization strategy for the TNC, and typically leaves victim plaintiffs with less than adequate compensation. The *Bhopal* and *James Hardie* cases both provide examples of this.

Civil actions against TNCs in respect of rights violations also face a number of significant procedural and legal obstacles to success. These obstacles mostly stem from the principle of separate legal personality which views the corporation as a separate and independent legal actor from its directors, managers and owners. The attribution of personhood to the corporate form in effect creates a fictitious wall behind which the law will generally not look to assign responsibility to individuals for the actions of the corporation. Only in very limited circumstances, such as where a corporate structure has been established solely or primarily to avoid existing contractual duties, have courts been prepared to treat the person in control of a company as if he or she were the company itself.[64] In the absence of such special circumstances, directors, officers or employees acting in 'the best interests of the corporation' are not held responsible for corporate activities having negative social and/or environmental consequences.[65] Likewise, the concept of limited liability limits the liability of shareholders to the extent of their investment: the putative 'owners' of the corporation thus become divorced from the consequences of the activities of the firm, just as the shareholders of Union Carbide remained unaffected by events occurring in Bhopal, India.

The notion of corporate separate personhood also allows parent companies to shield themselves from liability for the activities of subsidiary corporations. As a separate legal person, the subsidiary corporation alone is held separately liable for the results of its actions. Courts will not generally look behind the subsidiary firm to assign liability to the parent corporation, even in cases where the parent corporation was involved in decisions leading to the subsidiary's actions.[66] The parent corporation is a 'shareholder' and, like any other shareholder, benefits from the protection of limited liability. This helps to explain the common practice of creating a 'shell' corporation to protect directors, officers, shareholders and corporate assets from liabilities accrued by other parts of the corporate group.

The *Bhopal* and *James Hardie* cases are just two examples of how, even in states which are politically stable and have a well-developed legal system, local remedies for harms caused by the operations of foreign TNCs are either unavailable or ineffective. The ability of TNCs to incorporate in one country while seeking out opportunities in one or more other countries is crucial to their success. Moreover, the opportunities sought by TNCs are increasingly to be found in the developing world where resources are plentiful, labour is cheap, and regulation weak or non-existent. As will be further discussed in Chapters 4, 5 and 6, however, some developing countries are beginning to realize that the costs of allowing TNCs to operate unregulated can outweigh the benefits provided by their presence. Some states are beginning to regulate at least the worst aspects of TNC behaviour, beginning with behaviour that is so bad it can be categorized as criminal. In Indonesia, for example, a country which has not historically prosecuted corporations for criminal behaviour, the Law Concerning Environmental Management passed in 1997 made it possible to sue TNCs for 'environmental crimes'.[67] The 1997 law was replaced by improved mechanisms for protecting the environment and harsher penalties for polluters and violators under Law No. 32 of 2009 on Environmental Protection and Management.[68] In other countries also, both civil and legal scrutiny of TNC activity, particularly the environmental effects of such activities, is increasing.[69]

In sharp contrast to the improved standards of scrutiny in some developing nations are those countries euphemistically labelled by the OECD as 'weak governance zones' where the most egregious abuses of human rights occur. A weak governance zone is defined by the OECD as 'an investment environment in which governments are unable or unwilling to assume their responsibilities'.[70] By definition, the legal system in such environments is virtually absent or at best inefficient and corrupt. Local litigation against harmful TNC behaviour is therefore either not possible at all or unrealistic at best. Not surprisingly, therefore, a growing number of developing country victims and victims' support groups have pursued the alternative and more controversial approach of suing in the home state of the TNC. These cases, and the legislation which makes such actions possible, are the focus of Chapter 4.

NOTES

1. It has even been claimed that the WTO's Agreement on Trade Related Intellectual Property Rights (TRIPS) 'was the brainchild of senior executives at 12 US corporations including, in particular, the pharmaceutical giant Pfizer': Dr Thomas Faunce (Senior Lecturer ANU Medical School, Lecturer ANU Faculty of Law), 'FTA bushwack threatens fifty years of equality in Australian health', *Canberra Times*, 4 December 2003. See also David Kinley and Justine Nolan, 'Trading and Aiding Human Rights: Corporations in the Global Economy' (2008) 25:4 *Nordic Journal of Human Rights Law* 353,
2. Michael Spisto, 'Stakeholder interests in corporate governance: is a new model of governance a change for the better for South Africa, Part 1' (2005) 18 *Australian Journal of Corporate Law* 129, 131, citing P. Goldenberg, 'IALS company law lecture – shareholders v stakeholders: the bogus argument' (1998) 19:2 *The Company Lawyer* 34.

3. Malcolm Fraser, Melbourne Festival Deakin Lecture address, 'My Country 2050', delivered at the Capitol Theatre on 20 May 2001, broadcast on ABC Radio National 21 May 2001, at 14, available at www.abc.net.au/rn/deakin/docs/fraser.doc.

4. Steven Brakman, Harry Garretsen and Charles Van Marrewijk, *Cross-Border Mergers and Acquisitions: The Facts as a Guide for International Economics*, CESifo Working Paper Series No. 1823 (October 2006), available at SSRN, http://ssrn.com/abstract=940348.

5. Gillian Triggs, *International Law: Contemporary Principles and Practices* (2006) para. 8.107, citing T. Walde, 'A requiem for the "New International Economic Order": the rise and fall of paradigms in international economic law' in N. Al-Nauimi and R. Meese (eds), *International Legal Issues Arising under the United Nations Decade of International Law* (1995) 1301, 1335.

6. Specifically, art. 2.1 of the TRIMs Agreement prohibits trade-related investment measures that are inconsistent with the national treatment or quantitative restriction principles embodied in arts III and XI of the GATT, respectively. This means that host states cannot, for example, make it a condition for foreign investment approval that the investor should buy domestic products for its operations, or that the investor should agree to export a minimum percentage of goods produced by the investment project: see Agreement on Trade Related Investment Measures, Annex, 'Illustrative list', available at www.wto.org/english/docs_e/legal_e/18-trims.pdf. See also *Indonesia – Autos*, Panel Report, WTO Doc. WT/DS54/R, WT/DS59/R and WT/DS64/R, adopted 23 July 1998.

7. For discussion see David Kinley, *Civilizing Globalization: Human Rights and the Global Economy* (2009) 55–7.

8. Jurgen Kurtz, 'The Doha Declaration and prospects for investment negotiations in the WTO' (2004) 1:2 *Transnational Dispute Management*.

9. *Ibid*.

10. Convention Establishing the Multilateral Investment Guarantee Agency, opened for signature 11 October 1985, 1508 UNTS 99 (entered into force 12 April 1988). See also Kinley, above n. 7, 100, noting the enormous growth in size of the MIGA since the late 1990s.

11. Opened for signature 18 March 1965, 575 UNTS 159 (entered into force 14 October 1966), with over 130 contracting states.

12. Gillian Triggs, *International Law: Contemporary Principles and Practices* (2006) paras 8.108, 8.112–8.115.

13. L. Yves Fortier, CC, QC and Stephen L. Drymer, 'Indirect expropriation in the law of international investment: I know it when I see it, or caveat investor' (2005) 13:1 *Asia Pacific Law Review* 79, 81.

14. Triggs, above n. 12, para. 8.114. See also art. 4 of the UN General Assembly Declaration on Permanent Sovereignty over Natural Resources, GA Res. 1803 (XVII) GAOR 17th Sess., Supp. 17, 15, which provides that 'Nationalisation, expropriation or requisitioning shall be based on grounds or reasons of public utility, security or the national interest which are recognised as overriding purely individual or private interests, both domestic and foreign'.

15. *Ibid*. paras 8.114–8.115.

16. *Ibid*. paras 8.110–8.111.

17. *Ibid*. paras 8.116–8.117. The main controversy here concerns the standard of compensation to be paid. Developed states have long maintained the position that an expropriation is not legal unless it complies with the so-called Hull formula (after US Secretary of State Cordell Hull) which provides that '[T]he right to expropriate property is coupled with and conditioned on the obligation to make adequate, effective and prompt compensation'. Developing states, on the other hand, have consistently rejected the Hull formulation in favour of the view that questions of compensation for expropriation are for domestic laws and tribunals. The Calvo Doctrine as this theory was known (after the Argentine jurist Carlos Calvo) is enshrined in art. 2(2)(c) of the 1974 UN General Assembly Charter of the Economic Rights and Duties of States, GA Res. 3281, 29 UN GAOR Supp. No. 31), which provides that '[i]n any case where the question of compensation gives rise to controversy, it shall be settled under the domestic law of the nationalizing State and by its tribunals'.

18. Canada–Mexico–United States Free Trade Agreement (NAFTA), opened for signature 17 December 1992 (entered into force 1 January 1994). The minimum standards of treatment

provided for in Chapter 11 require, *inter alia*, that 'Each party shall accord to investors of another Party treatment no less favourable, than that it accords, in all like circumstances, to investors of any other Party or of a non-Party with respect to the establishment, acquisition, expansion, management, conduct, operation, and sale or other disposition of investments': (art. 1103, 'Most favoured nation treatment'). National treatment of foreign investors, that is, treatment 'no less favourable' than that accorded to local investors in the host state, is required by art. 1102.

19. United States – Singapore Free Trade Agreement, opened for signature 6 May 2003 (entered into force 1 January 2004).
20. Australia–United States Free Trade Agreement, opened for signature 18 May 2004 (entered into force 1 January 2005). For discussion see Andrew Clarke and Xiang Gao, 'Bilateral free trade agreements: a comparative analysis of the Australia-United States FTA and the forthcoming Australia-China FTA' (2007) 30:3 *UNSW Law Journal* 842; Susan Hawthorne, 'The Australia-United States Free Trade Agreement (AUSTA): free trade and war in the creation of the New American Empire', *Global Research*, 1 August 2003, available at www.globalresearch.ca/index.php?context=va&aid=765; and Centre for International Economics, *Economic Impacts of an Australia-United States Free Trade Area* (prepared for the Australian Department of Foreign Affairs and Trade, June 2001), available at www.dfat.gov.au/publications/aus_us_fta/aus_us_fta.pdf.
21. *Metalclad Corp. v United Mexican States*, ICSID Case No. ARB (AF)/97/1, Award, 30 August 2000, reprinted in (2001) 16 *ICSID Rev.* 1 (Arbitrators: Sir Elihu Lauterpacht, Benjamen R Civilette, Jose Luis Siqueiros). Reasons for judgment of 2 May 2001 (2001) BCSC 1529; (2004) 6 ICSID Rep. 53; available at www.worldbank.org/icsid/cases/mm-award-e.pdf. For commentary see Todd Weiler, '*Metalclad v Mexico*: a play in three parts' (2001) 2 *Journal of World Investment* 685. See also Fortier and Drymer, above n. 13, 89.
22. ICSID Case No. ARB(AF)/97/1, Award, 30 August 2000, 27, para. 98.
23. *Ibid*. para. 30, 13.
24. *Ibid*. para. 28, 103 (emphasis added).
25. For examples of similar toxic waste dump project proposals giving rise to tensions and conflicts of interests in the Australian context see: 'Toxic waste creates political hazards', *The Age*, 22 May 2004; 'Communities to continue fight against toxic waste dump', ABC Rural Radio, 7 October 2005; Catherine Munro, 'We were conned, say toxic waste dump opponents', *The Age*, 23 August 2004; Irene Scott, 'Toxic waste dump rally photographs', ABC Mildura, 16 September 2005.
26. John Ruggie, *Business and Human Rights: Further Steps Towards the Operationalization of the 'Protect, Respect and Remedy' Framework*, UN Doc. A/HRC/14/27 (9 April 2010) para. 20.
27. Text of the Ninth OK Tedi Act, available atwww.paclii.org/legis/consol_act/mtmcsaa 2001589/.
28. For discussion see 'BHP deal faces Supreme Court today in Australia and PNG', *MAC: Mining and Communities*, 18 December 2001; 'The front: the Big Ugly at Ok Tedi' (2002) 23:1 *Multinational Monitor*; Stuart Kirsch, 'Litigating Ok Tedi (again)' (2002) 26:3 *Cultural Survival Quarterly*, Special Issue: *Melanesia: The Future of Tradition*, and Bob Burton, 'PNG law shields BHP from Ok Tedi liabilities' (2002) 6:4 *Mining Monitor* 1. For the company view, see BHP Billiton corporate website, bhpbilliton.com, 'BHP Billiton withdraws from Ok Tedi Copper Mine and establishes Development Fund for benefit of Papua New Guinea people'. Release No. 06/02, 8 February 2002, available at www.bhpbilliton.com/bb/investorsMedia/news/2002/bhpBillitonWithdrawsFromOkTediCo pperMineAndEstablishesDevelopmentFundForBenefitOfPapuaNewGuineaPeople.jsp.
29. *Gargarimabu v BHP OK Tedi* [2001] VSC 304, 27 August 2001 and *Gagarimabu v Broken Hill Proprietary Co. Ltd and Another* [2001] VSC 517, 21 December 2001. Both decisions available at www.austlii.edu.au/au/cases/vic/VSCA.
30. Mining (Ok Tedi Mine Continuation (Ninth Supplement)) Agreement Act (2001), s. 5(1).
31. Bob Burton, 'PNG law shields BHP from Ok Tedi liabilities' (2002) 6:4 *Mining Monitor* 1. See also s. 8 of the Act which governs the execution of community mine continuation agreements.

32. Burton, above n. 31.
33. *Ibid.*
34. *Ibid.*
35. See *Gargarimabu v BHP OK Tedi* [2001] VSC 304, 27 August 2001 and *Gagarimabu v Broken Hill Proprietary Co. Ltd and another* [2001] VSC 517, 21 December 2001. Both decisions available at www.austlii.edu.au/au/cases/vic/VSCA.
36. 'Greenpeace accuses PNG govt over new environment laws', ABC Radio Australia, Pacific Beat, 7 June 2010, available at www.radioaustralia.net.au/pacbeat/stories/201006/s2920632. htm.
37. 'Papua New Guinea: indigenous people lose out on land rights', *IRIN News* (a project of the UN Office for the Coordination of Humanitarian Affairs), 1 June 2010, available at www.irinnews.org/.
38. 'PNG landowners sue over environment law: Miners, bas companies immune from prosecution', *Pacific Islands Report*, 7 June 2010, available at http://pidp.eastwestcenter.org/pireport/2010/June/06-08-04.htm.
39. *Ibid.*
40. Convention concerning Indigenous and Tribal Peoples in Independent Countries, General Conference of the ILO 76th Session, adopted on 27 June 1989 (entered into force 5 September 1991).
41. *IRIN News*, above n. 37.
42. Bhopal Medical Appeal and Sambhavna Trust, 'What happened in Bhopal', available at www.bhopal.org/whathappened.html. See also www.bhopal.com/.
43. The other stockholders included Indian financial institutions and thousands of private investors in India: www.unioncarbide.com/bhopal.
44. See www.unioncarbide.com/bhopal.
45. See www.bhopal.org/whathappened.html.
46. 'Union Carbide's Bhopal fallout' in Dorothy Wentworth-Walsh, *A Room in Bombay and Other Stories* (Pluto Press Australia, 2005) ch. 2, 167, 174.
47. See www.bhopal.org/whathappened.html.
48. 'India jails seven over Bhopal', *Bangkok Post*, 7 June 2010, available at www.bangkokpost.com/breakingnews/180476/india-jails-seven-over-bhopal.
49. Seee www.unioncarbide.com/bhopal.
50. See www.bhopal.org/whathappened.html.
51. Amnesty International, 'India: first convictions for 1984 Union Carbide disaster too little, too late' (7 June 2010), aailale at www.amnesty.org/en/for-media/press-releases/india-first-convictions-1984-union-carbide-disaster-too-little-too-late-20-1; story available at www.amnesty.org/en/news-and-updates/first-convictions-1984-union-carbide-disaster-bhopal-too-little-too-late-2010-06-07.
52. 'Two years in prison for eight convicted in Bhopal gas tragedy', NDTV, Press Trust of India, 7 June 2010, available at www.ndtv.com/news/india/bhopal-gas-tragedy-all-eight-accused-convicted-30253.php.
53. *Ibid.* See also BBC News, 'Bhopal gas leaks not enough, say campaigners', BBC News, 7 June 2010, available at http://news.bbc.co.uk/2/hi/south_asia/10260109.stm and Iftikhar Gilani, 'Bhopal tragedy accused sentenced to 2 years in prison: former chairman of Union Carbide USA goes scot free', *Daily Times*, 8 June 2010, available at www.dailytimes.com.pk/default.asp?page=2010\06\08\story_8-6-2010_pg7_35.
54. This account of the James Hardie asbestos liabilities and related corporate restructurings substantially derived from Christina Jarron, 'The social control of business', paper presented at the Enhancing Corporate Accountability Prospects and Challenges Conference, Melbourne, 8–9 February 2006, published in Gerald Acquaah-Gaisie and Val Clulow (eds), *Conference Proceedings* (Monash University School of Business and Economics and Department of Business Law and Taxation, 2000) 155, 167–8.
55. ASX–James Hardie Industries Ltd Media Release, 'James Hardie resolves its asbestos liability favourably for claimants and shareholders', 16 February 2001, available at www.asx.com.au/asx/statistics/displayAnnouncement.do?display=text&issuerId=602&announcementId=645410.

56. *Ibid.*
57. Jarron, above n. 54. See also David Jackson, *Report of the Special Commission of Inquiry into the Medical Research Fund and Compensation Foundation* (Cabinet Office, Sydney, 2004), available at www.dpc.nsw.gov.au/__data/assets/pdf_file/0020/11387/PartA.pdf (hereafter the Jackson Inquiry Report).
58. Jarron, above n. 54, 168–9. See also Jackson Inquiry Report, 9, 30–1.
59. Jackson Inquiry Report, paras 1.8, 1.21 and 1.23, available at www.dpc.nsw.gov.au/__data/assets/pdf_file/0020/11387/PartA.pdf.
60. On 21 December 2004, a voluntary Heads of Agreement was reached between the ACTU, Unions NSW, and the NSW government which would see James Hardie pay compensation to asbestos disease sufferers over a period of 40 years. The non-binding agreement placed an annual limit on payments by James Hardie, set at 35 per cent of the company's free cash flow. When compensation payments exceed this limit, funds would be accessed from a 'buffer' account worth approximately AUS$250 million. More negotiations concluded with the signing of a final binding Principal Agreement on 1 December 2005, effectively securing an open-ended funding commitment from James Hardie and providing AUS$4.5 billion dollars for asbestos compensation as well as funding for asbestos education and medical research: George Wright, 'Unions welcome signing of James Hardie asbestos compensation deal' (1 December 2005), available at ACTU campaigns website accessed at www.actu.asn.au/public/campaigns/ jameshardie/ jh_1dec05.html. See also Susannah Greenleaf, 'Campaign for James Hardie asbestos victims much harder nnder new IR laws' (1 December 2005), available at ACTU campaign website accessed, www.actu.asn.au/ public/campaigns/jameshardie/1dec05_jh_2ndrelease. html.
61. Lisa Martin, 'Court rulings "vindicate" Bernie Banton', *Sydney Morning Herald*, 20 August 2009. See also 'Bernie Banton dead', *Sydney Morning Herald*, 27 November 2007.
62. *Briggs v James Hardie & Co.* (1989) 16 NSWLR 549, 577. The situation is otherwise where the relevant conduct is carried out by an unincorporated division of an incorporated entity. *Poller v Columbia Broad Sys Inc.*, 284 F.2d 599 (DC Cir. 1960).
63. Jonathan Clough, 'Punishing the parent: corporate criminal complicity in human rights abuses' (2008) 33:3 *Brooklyn Journal of International Law* 899, 916; citing Phillip E. Blumberg, *The Multinational Challenge to Corporation Law* (OUP, 1993) 58–60.
64. In *Salomon v A. Salomon and Co. Ltd* [1897] AC 22, the House of Lords for the first time recognized the company as an entity separate from those that own and manage it. The decision was affirmed by the Australian High Court in *Industrial Equity Ltd v Blackman* (1977) CLR 567. See also *Jones v Lipman* [1962] 1 All ER 442 and Brendan Sweeny and Jennifer O'Reilly, *Law in Commerce* (2nd edn, 2004) ch. 12.
65. The business judgement rule essentially operates to protect directors from possible liability for bad decisions. The rule provides that directors are presumed to have taken decisions in good faith and in the best interest of the company unless there is compelling evidence proving otherwise: *Aronsen v Lewis*, 473 A2d 805, 812 (1984). In Australia, the business judgement rule has been codified in s. 180(2) of the Corporations Act 2001 (Cth) which provides that a director or other officer of a corporation who makes a business judgement is assumed to have exercised the legally required degree of care and diligence if they make that decision in good faith and for a proper purpose. See also Chapter 1, n. 25.
66. See e.g., *Industrial Pioneer Concrete Services Ltd v Yelnah Pty Ltd* (1987) 5 ACLC 467, where the NSW Supreme Court refused the invitation to treat the holding company and the subsidiary company as one and the same. The holding company and its subsidiary were separate legal entities and must be treated as such. There were good commercial reasons to have separate companies and, therefore, it could not be said that a separate corporation had been established for the sole or dominant purpose of evading a contractual or fiduciary obligation: Sweeny and O'Reilly, above n. 64, 353–4.
67. Law concerning Environmental Management (Law No. 23 of 1997), available at http://sunsite.nus.edu.sg/apcel/dbase/indonesia/primary/inaem.html.
68. Fadjar Kandar and Deny Sidharta, 'New environmental law: better protection or more legal hurdles for industry', *ALB Legal News*, 31 May 2010, available at http://asia.legalbusinessonline.com/industry-updates/indonesia-soemadipradja-taher/new-environmental-law-better-protection-or-more-legal-hurdles-for-industry/46199.

69. For discussion see Neil Hawke, 'Corporate environmental crime: why shouldn't directors be liable?' (1997) 13 *London Journal of Canadian Studies* 12.
70. OECD, *OECD Risk Awareness Tool for Multinational Enterprises in Weak Governance Zones* (adopted by the OECD Council on 8 June 2006), Preface. Appendix I, Glossary of Terms, elaborates on this summarized definition: 'Weak governance zones are defined as investment environments in which public sector actors are unable or unwilling to assume their roles and responsibilities in protecting rights (including property rights), providing basic public services (e.g. social programmes, infrastructure development, law enforcement and prudential surveillance) and ensuring that public sector management is efficient and effective. These "government failures" lead to broader failures in political, economic and civic institutions that are referred to as weak governance'. Identifying characteristics of weak governance zones are also outlined.

4. Extra-territorial legislation and corporate liability

Transnational cases based on harm caused to communities in developing countries by TNCs have recently been litigated in several home states. This chapter examines these cases, and explores how governments and courts in home states have sought to render locally incorporated TNCs legally liable for the effects of their business activities overseas.

Many capital exporting nations have attempted to overcome the legal obstacles discussed in Chapter 3, so that parent companies can no longer escape from liability for the actions of their overseas subsidiaries. In particular, legislators have passed, or tried to pass, extra-territorial legislation aimed at regulating the activities of local corporations abroad. Such legislation has included regulatory 'codes of conduct' for local corporations drafted to have extra-territorial effect, and statutes aimed at extending the local law of torts to facilitate prosecution of local parent companies for wrongs occurring overseas. Most states also have laws imposing criminal liability on corporations for offences such as money laundering and corruption (especially bribery). The whole question of the extent to which corporations, as legal persons, can be held criminally liable is dealt with in Chapter 5. This chapter explores civil law avenues for rendering TNCs liable for harms caused by their activities outside the home state.

A. THE LEGALITY OF EXTRA-TERRITORIAL LEGISLATION AND THE EXERCISE OF STATE JURISDICTION UNDER INTERNATIONAL LAW

The main obstacles to the enactment of extra-territorial legislation making parent companies liable for the harmful effects of their activities overseas have been political, not legal. The enactment of extra-territorial legislation in such a context can be justified on a number of bases founded in international law principles.[1]

1. The Territorial Principle

There is a general presumption that criminal laws can be applied throughout the territory of the state that enacted the law. This territorial principle is almost universally recognized and is the most common basis for the exercise of criminal jurisdiction. The territorial principle has been interpreted broadly to allow state A to exercise criminal jurisdiction in respect of an offence when only part of the offence was committed in state A, even if the offence originated in, or its effects were felt within, a different state or states.[2] It also allows the exercise of criminal jurisdiction in respect of complicity,[3] where the act of complicity occurs in state A, even though the principal offence takes place elsewhere.

2. The Nationality Principle

Second, there is the ability of any state to exercise jurisdiction in respect of its own nationals for acts committed anywhere in the world. For the purposes of this principle, international law recognizes a 'firm distinction between the separate entity of the company and that of the shareholder'. International law also recognizes that the nationality of a company is the state in which the company is incorporated, regardless of the nationality of the company's owners (shareholders).[4] States are therefore free to legislate in respect of the activities of any entity incorporated within the territory of that state, wherever those activities take place.

3. The Universal Principle

The principle of universal jurisdiction recognizes the right of any country to exercise jurisdiction over a defendant with respect to 'universal crimes' such as piracy, genocide and war crimes. Jurisdiction may be exercised irrespective of the nationality of the defendant or the locus of the offence. The sweeping nature of this jurisdiction is justified by reference to the egregious nature of the offending conduct and the need to limit the availability of safe havens for those accused of such crimes. A growing number of countries have provided for their courts to exercise universal jurisdiction with respect to crimes under the Rome Statute of the ICC (the Rome Statute).[5] However, given the need for the defendant to have some presence in the jurisdiction in order to be prosecuted, it is argued that the territorial or nationality bases of jurisdiction provide sounder rationales for extra-territoriality in the context of corporate defendants.

4. The SRSG's 'Extraterritoriality Matrix'

In August 2010, the Special Representative of the Secretary General (SRSG) presented his third report on the implementation of his mandate to operationalize the 'protect, respect and remedy' framework.[6] Part III of this report discusses the issue of extraterritoriality in the business and human rights context. The discussion begins by noting the often highly controversial nature of extraterritorial legislation, and describes an increasing recognition of the need to 'unpack' the concept of extraterritoriality in the business and human rights context.[7] The importance of the SRSG's discussion in this report lies in its presentation of an heuristic 'extraterritoriality matrix' with two rows and three columns. Its two rows represent: (a) domestic measures with extraterritorial implications; and (b) direct extraterritorial jurisdiction over actors or activities abroad. The three columns represent: (c) public policies relating to companies (such as corporate social responsibility and public procurement policies, export credit rating criteria or consular support); (d) regulation (through corporate law, for instance); and (e) enforcement actions (adjudicating alleged breaches and enforcing judicial and executive decisions). The combination of these rows and columns yields six types of 'extraterritorial' forms, each in turn offering a range of options, not all of which are equally likely to trigger objections from other states, particularly when driven by international consensus.

B. NON-CRIMINAL LITIGATION AGAINST TNCs FOR TRANSNATIONAL HARMS

1. Role of NGOs, Civil Society Groups, Public Interest Lawyers and the Media

A preliminary and very important point to make about home country civil law suits against TNCs for the harmful effects of their overseas operations is the vital role played by civil society groups and the media. Without support and assistance from NGOs, many plaintiffs would have neither the information nor financial wherewithal to take their claim to court. Likewise, without the willingness and expertise of public-interest lawyers, litigation against TNCs would be unlikely to proceed, and far less likely to result in a payout for affected victims. In addition, without the risk of media exposure (a form of naming and shaming) many TNCs would have no incentive to either settle such claims or alter their behaviour. Groups such as the New York-based Centre for Constitutional Rights,[8] OECD Watch,[9] Amnesty International,[10] Jubilee 2000 SA,[11] the Spain-based Asociación Pro Derechos Humanos de España,[12] the Mineral Policy Institute[13] and the Nigerian Movement for the Survival of the Ogoni People[14] have been instrumental in initiating, funding and supporting litigation on behalf of the victims of corporate harms. For example, in 2004, Earth Rights International, the Center for Constitutional Rights and the International Human Rights Law Clinic at the University of Virginia School of Law filed an amicus brief on behalf of Vietnamese villagers allegedly harmed by Agent Orange, a herbicide used by the US government during the Vietnam War. The action was brought against a number of US companies that manufactured the herbicide.[15]

Jedrzej Frynas has examined the dramatic increase in social and environmental litigation against African-based TNCs in the two decades since 1990. He finds that one important factor in this increase has been a crucial combination of public-interest pressure groups and the media publicity which is a 'key weapon in [their] armoury'.[16] Frynas also highlights the increased professional ability of legal counsel in both Western and non-Western litigation against TNCs, and the impact of changing social attitudes on judges.[17] He finally demonstrates, however, that the support of global NGOs for such litigation has been, at best, uneven, focussing on those cases which can be litigated in either the Western home state of a TNC and/or in a non-Western legal system inherited from a common law colonial past. Thus, litigation in Africa has so far focussed on a few countries – South Africa, Nigeria, Namibia – rather than the continent's poorest states.[18] The presence of greater financial and legal support, combined with the generally higher figure of compensation payments (settled and court-awarded), serve to make the United States the most attractive venue for litigation in many cases, followed by the United Kingdom and/or Australia where the parent TNC lacks a US presence.[19] Thus, many of the cases examined below help to illustrate both the advantages and shortcomings of the US legal system as it relates to TNC liability for extra-territorial harms.

2.   Common Law and Other Non-statutory Actions against TNCs for Transnational Harms

Ever since limited liability was extended to corporate groups, courts have struggled to articulate a principled basis on which to mitigate its more extreme consequences by rendering the parent liable for the conduct of the subsidiary.[20] Principles of common law negligence have been applied in cases where decisions taken in the home state allegedly caused tortious harms occurring overseas. Principles of agency liability have also been used in such cases, as well as so-called (international) enterprise liability.

(a)   Tort and negligence claims
Human rights abuses and other harms caused by TNC activities can often be classified as ordinary torts. For example, loss of life can give rise to wrongful death suits, while torture or cruel and inhuman treatment may give rise to assault and battery claims. The tort of negligence may also be relevant, for

example where a TNC fails to take due care to ensure adequate safety standards in its factories or mines, or when a TNC engages military personnel to defend its installations when it should be aware that such an engagement is likely to result in injuries to others.[21]

In the United States, initiating proceedings under ordinary tort jurisdiction in cases involving overseas harms caused by TNC activity may have several advantages over other avenues for such litigation. For example, US courts can hear claims brought by US victims of transnational torts, while jurisdiction over claims brought under the Alien Tort Claims Act (ATCA) only exists where the claimant is a foreign national. There is also no need in tort cases to establish that the alleged wrong qualifies as a breach of the law of nations, as is also required in ATCA claims. Transnational tort litigation has, however, all too often been dismissed by the court. As further discussed below, one of the most common grounds for dismissal has been *forum non conveniens*, a principle which allows courts to stay or dismiss proceedings more appropriately heard in a foreign jurisdiction.[22]

In the United States and other common law jurisdictions, plaintiffs claiming compensation for the tort of negligence must establish the existence of a duty of care owed to the plaintiff, and a breach of that duty. In the case of TNC defendants, the duty of care can be owed by the subsidiary company in the country where the tort occurred, and/or by the parent company. For example, both Exxon Mobil and its Indonesian subsidiary were sued in relation to acts of killing and torture committed by Indonesian public security forces hired by the company to protect its facilities. The court found sufficient evidence to entitle plaintiffs to a jury trial on whether either or both of the defendants was directly liable for negligently hiring, retaining and supervising the security forces.[23] Similarly, in *Bowoto v Chevron Texaco*, both Chevron Texaco and its Nigerian subsidiary were sued for negligence under California law, on the basis of an alleged failure to train and supervise the Nigerian security forces and police called in to suppress protests against Chevron's Nigerian operations, resulting in injury to the plaintiffs.[24]

In England, plaintiffs have sought to make parent companies directly liable in negligence for harms caused by their foreign subsidiary operations. Such claims have alleged that business policies pursued in the head offices of British corporations caused serious human rights abuses in the developing countries where their subsidiaries operated. In *Connelly v RTZ*, for example, an English parent company was sued in relation to injuries in a uranium mine operated by its Namibian subsidiary.[25] In *Lubbe v Cape plc*, a number of South African nationals sued the English parent of a mining company for asbestos-related injuries.[26] In both cases, the plaintiff was required to establish that the TNC parent had failed to use reasonable care to protect person(s) from foreseeable harm, resulting in injury.

With regard to the meaning of reasonable care, a number of cases have confirmed that commonly accepted social and industry standards drawn from industry custom, administrative regulations, statutes or internationally accepted guidelines can help to define what is reasonable.[27] There is thus a significant overlap between the common law negligence concept of a duty to exercise reasonable care, and the duty to exercise human rights due diligence forming part of the SRSG's 'Protect, Respect and Remedy' Framework. As the SRSG's Framework gains broader acceptance, it is certainly possible that the Framework's notion of a duty to exercise due diligence will be cited by courts as an appropriate standard of care in negligence cases involving TNCs.[28]

In his 2009 Report, the SRSG identified the concern raised by some corporate counsel that rather than reduce risks for companies, exercising human rights due diligence could actually increase a TNC's risk of liability. In particular, the process of due diligence, it was feared, could lead to the discovery of facts that might increase the TNC's exposure to tort liability claims by victims of human rights abuses.

The short answer to such fears, however, is that human rights due diligence enables a TNC to identify potential human rights risks and address them before they occur. As the SRSG suggests, only through a process of due diligence which integrates the common features of legal and societal benchmarks can TNCs become aware of, prevent and address risks of complicity.[29] While there are no guarantees that acting with due diligence will protect a company from legal liability or public allegations, it should go a long way toward improving the company's ability to recognize and act on risks of complicity, and to highlight to stakeholders that it is serious about not contributing to the abuses of others.[30] So far as negligence claims are concerned, the fulfilment of a company's due diligence obligations can also be put forward as evidence that the company's duty of care has been satisfied. The exercise of due diligence thus reduces the company's exposure to litigation risk, and provides the basis for a defence against any claims that might be filed.

In the context of supply chain liability, there may currently be an important difference between the concept of duty of care in common law negligence claims, and the duty of due diligence forming part of the SRSG's Framework. The duty of TNCs to respect human rights under the SRSG's Framework clearly encompasses a duty to assess its supply chain relationships for the possibility of complicity in human rights abuses, and to manage any such possibility.[31] So far, however, municipal courts applying negligence principles have refused to go beyond the idea that contract partners are separate entities, and that TNCs cannot be held liable for the abusive behaviour of those entities with which they have even strong contractual links. In *Sinaltrainal v Coca Cola*,[32] for example, the plaintiffs alleged that the two corporate defendants,

Coca Cola US and its subsidiary Coca Cola Columbia, were responsible for the actions of their contractual partner, Bebidas, a small bottling company. The court ultimately dismissed the case against the two Coca Cola companies after examining the Bottler's Agreement between those two companies and Bebidas. The contract was a typical franchise agreement, which gave Coca Cola rights regarding the protection of its product in the marketplace (e.g. quality control, use of trademark, etc.). The Agreement did not impose upon Coca Cola 'a duty to monitor, enforce or control labour policies at' Bebidas.[33] Thus, the *Sinaltrainal* District Court was unwilling to look behind the contract to examine whether Coca Cola's control over Bebidas' operations was more than formally recorded in the contract. It remains to be seen whether increasing acceptance of the SRSG's Framework will have an influence on the 'duty of care' concept as applied in such cases at the municipal level.[34]

(b) Agency cases

Many plaintiffs, including victims of negligence and other torts, have relied on agency principles in seeking to render a parent company not directly liable, but liable as principal for the actions (or omissions) of its overseas agent(s) – typically its overseas subsidiaries. In tort claims based on agency principles there must be proof that the principal asked the agent to act on the principal's behalf, that the agent agreed to so act, and that the principal retained the right to control relevant activities of the agent.[35]

An example of a case where an agency-principal relationship was held *not* to have been sufficiently established is *In Re South African Apartheid Litigation* where the case against Fujitsu for aiding and abetting arbitrary denationalization was dismissed for insufficient allegations of an agency relationship between Fujitsu and its subsidiary.[36] In contrast is the 2004 case of *Bowoto v Chevron Texaco*, where the plaintiffs alleged that Nigerian government security forces, which committed various international crimes in responding to a protest on one of Chevron's Nigerian offshore oil platforms, were acting as agents of Chevron's Nigerian subsidiary, which in turn was acting as agent of two of Chevron's US companies.[37] Illston J held that there was sufficient evidence to conclude that Chevron Nigeria Ltd (CNL) was the agent of Chevron Texaco (Chevron). In particular, Illston J was influenced by the volume, timing and content of certain communications between Chevron and CNL; the degree to which Chevron actively participated in the security policy of CNL; the large number of common officers between the companies; the importance of CNL for the overall success of Chevron's operations; and evidence that CNL was acting within the scope of its purported agency.

Conduct is within an agent's scope of authority if it is reasonably related to the tasks that the agent was required to perform, or reasonably foreseeable in the light of the principal's business or the agent's job responsibilities. Even misconduct that violates a company policy, or doesn't benefit the company, may still be within the agent's scope of authority if the action was committed in the course of a series of acts authorized by the principal or the conduct arose from an inherent risk created by the work. Furthermore, even if the misconduct was outside the scope of the agent's authority, the principal can ratify it afterwards if it knows, or should have known, of material facts relating to the conduct and then adopts or approves it. For example, Illston J in *Bowoto v Chevron Texaco* found that Texaco could be liable under a theory of ratification, holding that a company can ratify, and become liable for, even the actions of an entity that was not its agent at the time that the event took place. Illston J also indicated that a failure to take adequate steps to investigate or remedy the misconduct can constitute ratification in some circumstances.[38]

(c)   International enterprise liability (multinational group liability)

Multinational group liability views related corporations as one single juridical unit or enterprise, and ascribes responsibility for the actions of one corporation to all corporations in that legal unit. It recognizes that when a parent and its subsidiary are part of an economically integrated enterprise, there is, in effect, one corporate actor. In so doing it allows a court to pierce the corporate veil and impose liability on the parent for the conduct of the group. The concept of international enterprise liability has been adopted, albeit with limited success, in several areas of both the US and Canadian legal systems.[39] In Canada the international enterprise liability approach has been adopted in contaminated sites legislation and related case law, but the common law has expressly rejected the principle.[40] In the US also, judicial support for the concept of integrated group liability is rare.

3.   Extra-Territorial Legislation Facilitating Civil Prosecution of TNCs

(a)   Introduction

In nearly all jurisdictions legislation exists aimed at facilitating the prosecution of corporations and/or their officers for particular offences. Under the US Age Discrimination in Employment Act of 1967, for example, when an employer controls a corporation incorporated in a foreign country, any prohibited practice by that corporation is presumed to be the conduct of the employer. The determination of whether an employer controls a corporation is based upon four factors: 'the interrelation of operations, common management, centralized control of labour relations, and common ownership or financial control of the employer and the corporation'.[41]

While most legislative efforts to deal with issues of transnational corruption in business have been based on criminal law approaches, non-criminal approaches to the problem of corruption also exist. For example, a Civil Law

Convention on Corruption (CLCC) was approved by the Council of Europe in 1999.[42] The CLCC entered into force on 1 November 2003, and represents the world's first attempt to define common international rules in the field of civil law and corruption. In particular, it requires contracting parties to provide in their domestic law 'for effective remedies for persons who have suffered damage as a result of acts of corruption, to enable them to defend their rights and interests, including the possibility of obtaining compensation for damage'.[43] As at March 2010, 34 states have ratified the CLCC, while an additional eight States have signed without ratification.[44]

(b)   US Alien Tort Claims Act

Also called the Alien Tort Statute, the US Alien Tort Claims Act (1789)[45] (ATCA) is a US federal law which provides that: 'The district courts shall have original jurisdiction of any civil action by an alien for a tort only, committed in violation of the law of nations or a treaty of the United States'. The ATCA thus gives US federal courts jurisdiction over claims by aliens for torts in violation of the law of nations.

The ATCA is unique to the United States and has gained notoriety as perhaps the most ambitiously drafted piece of extra-territorial legislation in the world. Yet for a number of reasons, the ATCA has proved surprisingly ineffective in actually bringing TNCs to account for human rights abuses occurring abroad. This is despite the fact that since the path-breaking *Doe v Unocal* litigation in 1997, more than 50 cases have been brought against companies under the ATCA alleging corporate involvement in human rights abuses. Most cases lodged against TNCs under the ATCA, however, have been dismissed outright or settled prior to trial. Corporations such as Texaco,[46] Monsanto and Union Carbide[47] have all too often been able to employ a strategy of 'wearing down' the opposition by dragging cases out before finally settling for sums much less than originally claimed.

By 2010, the ATCA had resulted in only three jury trials in cases involving TNCs, resulting in two verdicts in favour of the defendants, and one for the plaintiffs. These jury trials included the case against Chevron arising from its use of security forces to protect its oil platforms in Nigeria.[48] The other case resolved in favour of the defendant involved a claim against Drummond Coal Company arising from killings at its mines in Columbia,[49] while the case resolved in favour of the plaintiffs was against a Bangladeshi company for its role in the arrest and torture of a business rival by a paramilitary.[50] The case against Unocal settled in 2005 essentially in favour of the plaintiffs, but on confidential terms.[51]

Another more recent example of a prominent settlement outcome from ATCA litigation is the June 2009 US$15.5 million settlement paid by Royal Dutch Petroleum Company (RDP) and Shell Transport and Trading (Shell) to family members of Ken Saro-Wiwa and other residents of the Ogoni region of the Niger delta. Ken Saro-Wiwa had been arrested and hanged, and others had also been killed and injured, in the early 1990s when the government of Nigeria used violent means to quell protests against the environmental effects associated with Shell's oil-mining operations. Family members, along with other residents of the Ogoni region involved in the protests, sued RDP, Shell, a company official and a Nigerian affiliate, alleging that they acted in concert with the Nigerian government's conduct, including torture, cruel inhuman and degrading treatment, summary execution, arbitrary arrest and detention, and crimes against humanity.[52]

Enacted in 1789, the ATCA was largely ignored until the 1980s, when human rights lawyers began to use it as the basis for civil claims against perpetrators of torture, genocide, war crimes and other crimes under international law. It was in 1980 that the landmark decision in *Filartiga v Peña-Irala*[53] held that the ATCA does provide a cause of action for non-US victims of corporate human rights abuses amounting to a violation of international law. In *Filartiga*, Judge Irving R. Kaufman of the Court of Appeals for the Second Circuit held that the ATCA afforded subject matter jurisdiction over the claim by two citizens of Paraguay that a former Paraguayan police inspector-general tortured and killed a member of their family in Paraguay, in violation of the customary international law prohibition against official torture.[54]

Since *Filartiga*, the scope of the ATCA has been expanded by a number of district and circuit decisions.[55] For example, accountability was extended beyond actual perpetrators to those in a position of command responsibility in *Xuncax v Gramajo*.[56] In *Kadic v Karadzic*, ATCA liability was extended to officials of de facto, yet unrecognized governments.[57] The Second Circuit in *Kadic* also confirmed that the ATCA could ground certain actions against individuals acting in a private rather than official capacity. More importantly for the purposes of this book, in the 1997 case of *Doe v Unocal* (1997),[58] it was held for the first time that ATCA actions could lie against private corporations.

In *Unocal* (1997), Paez J of the Central California District Court permitted the plaintiffs, a group of Burmese farmers, to proceed with an ATCA suit against Unocal, a Californian energy corporation, alleging that Unocal, acting through its partners in the Burmese military and police forces, had committed a range of egregious human rights abuses, including forced labour, forced relocations, torture, rape and murder in conducting its Yandana gas pipelines project in southern Burma.[59] Since the *Unocal* (1997) decision, there have been many more ATCA cases brought against multinational corporations, most alleging that the defendants worked with or supported governments that engaged in human rights violations. Defendants in this second wave of ATCA litigation have included Chevron (for conduct related to protests in the Niger delta),[60] Rio Tinto (for slave labour and other claims related to copper mines in Papua New Guinea),[61] a Boeing subsidiary (for claims related to extraordinary rendition),[62] Pfizer (for non-consensual medical experimental in Nigeria),[63] a variety of companies for crimes committed in the Second World War,[64] and others.

Class actions have also been brought under the ATCA. One recent example is *Khulumani et al. v Barclay National Bank et al.* The case began in 2002 when 87 victims of apartheid in South Africa attempted to bring 23 TNCs, including major bank, automobile and computer companies, to account in a US federal court for 'aiding and abetting' the apartheid regime.[65] The case was dismissed in 2004, but re-emerged in the New York Second Circuit Court of Appeals on 24 January 2006.[66] In 2007, the US Court of Appeals for the Second Circuit, in a two to one decision, permitted class actions under the ATCA by the South Africans against 50 corporations, including Citigroup, General Electric, EI DuPont de Nemours and IBM, for allegedly aiding and abetting apartheid discrimination.[67] This decision, largely in favour of the plaintiffs, was handed down despite the fact that both the US and South African governments sided with the defendant companies in opposing the appeal, and calling for the dismissal of the case.[68] Further legal actions by the defendants to dismiss the proceedings failed at the Supreme Court level in May 2008,[69] after which the cases were remanded to the US District Court in New York City for further proceedings.

(i)   Violation of the law of nations   In the absence of a treaty ratified by the United States, a successful plaintiff under the ATCA must establish that an accepted norm of customary international law has been violated. In the 2004 case of *Sosa v Alvarez-Machain*,[70] the court affirmed the decision in *Filartiga*[71] which had been under attack from opponents of ATCA claims, and so the decision in many ways represented a victory for foreign victims of corporate abuses. The court also held, however, that the ATCA was confined to cases where the alleged offence was one widely accepted as constituting a violation of customary international law. In the words of the court, the ATCA only allows US courts to recognize private claims for violations of those international law norms that have a 'definite content and acceptance amongst civilized nations'.[72] The court then went on to hold that arbitrary detention by an agent of the Drug Enforcement Administration (DEA), as alleged by the Mexican plaintiff, was not actionable under the ATCA because it was not a violation of a universally recognized norm of customary international law.[73] Yet there remains disagreement as to what constitutes an international norm having a 'definite content and acceptance amongst civilized nations'.

In *Rodolfo Ullonoa Flores and others v Southern Peru Copper Corp.*,[74] the court held that the plaintiffs had failed to establish the existence of any customary law 'right to life' or 'right to health'. Nor was there any basis for a claim relying on a customary international law rule against *intra*national pollution.[75] In *Wiwa v Shell*, the district court held that claims based on the right of peaceful assembly did not meet the *Sosa* standard (a conclusion shared by the district court in the *Bowoto* litigation). However, the *Wiwa* court did allow the other claims to go forward under the ATCA, including claims alleging crimes against humanity, extra-judicial killing, cruel, inhuman and degrading treatment and arbitrary arrest and detention. The Eleventh Circuit, on the other hand, in *Aldana v Del Monte Fresh Produce* (2005), even while purportedly applying *Sosa*, saw 'no basis in law to recognize Plaintiff's claim for cruel, inhuman, degrading treatment or punishment'.[76] District courts in other circuits have rejected such a narrow application of the ATCA.[77]

In 2004, a number of individuals brought a class action against Titan Corporation and other Department of Defense contractors working at Abu Ghraib prison in Iraq.[78] The claim brought under the ATCA alleged violations of customary international law including torture, cruel, inhuman and degrading treatment, enforced disappearance, arbitrary detention, crimes against humanity and war crimes. After two court transfers and a number of appeals, the Court of Appeals for the District of Columbia, in a judgment issued on 11 September 2009, found that the plaintiffs' ATCA claims could not be brought against contractors because they are not 'state actors', and were in any event pre-empted under 'battlefield pre-emption'.[79] The plaintiffs did not want to argue that the corporate defendants were 'state actors' because of the sovereign immunity defence implications that such an argument would raise. Garland J, however, issued a strong and closely argued dissent in *Saleh v Titan Corporation*, and the plaintiffs filed a petition for a writ of certiorari in the US Supreme Court on 26 April 2010.[80]

In *Khulumani*, the plaintiffs had to argue that establishing a system of apartheid was a violation of customary international law. Apartheid is expressly defined as a crime against humanity by article 7(1)(j) of the Rome Statute. Because the United States has not ratified that treaty, it was argued that article 7(1)(j) represented a codification of customary international law.[81] The argument relating to apartheid was not dealt with by the Second Circuit Court of Appeal in *Khulumani*, but a majority of judges did turn to the Rome Statute[82] for guidance on the standard for aiding and abetting liability in international law.[83] Most, but not all, of the plaintiffs' claims in relation to aiding and abetting apartheid were dismissed by Southern District of New York Judge Shira Scheindlin in April 2009, while other claims were allowed to proceed.[84]

(ii)   Violation of a treaty of the United States   ATCA claims have hardly ever been based on an alleged violation of a 'treaty of the United States'. The problem for plaintiffs arises from the peculiarly American distinction between

'self-executing' and 'non self-executing' treaties. Norms included in self-executing treaties, and drafted in self-executing form, become part of US law. Norms contained in non-self-executing treaties, however, do not. The US executive has therefore developed a practice of issuing a declaration upon ratification that treaties, including human rights treaties, are not self-executing.

The question therefore arises whether or not norms found in such treaties are actionable under the ATCA on the basis that they form part of customary international law, as was argued in the *Khulumani* South African apartheid litigation. This was also the approach adopted in *Saro-Wiwa v Royal Dutch Shell* where (following a 2009 Second Circuit precedent from *Abdullahi v Pfizer*),[85] the court accepted that non-self-executing (and non-binding) treaties can serve as evidence of customary international law. This is consistent with *Sosa*, which reasoned that non-self-executing treaties cannot *themselves* establish the relevant rule of international law, but did not deny they could form part of the evidence demonstrating the existence of a customary norm.[86]

(iii) Requirement of state action Most international law human rights norms only apply in the context of governmental action. Only a small number of human rights norms apply in the absence of state action. These include genocide, certain war crimes, piracy, slavery, forced labour and aircraft hijacking – all of which can give rise to direct individual liability under international law. Article 25 of the Rome Statute also serves to render directly liable any individual who 'aids, abets, or otherwise assists' in the commission of a war crime or crime against humanity.[87]

Outside of such special cases, however, private actors can only be held liable under the ATCA if a sufficient connection exists between the private actor and abuses committed by a government or, alternatively, between the private actor's abusive acts and a government. Most of the ATCA cases brought against companies in the United States to date have thus been based on allegations of complicity, where the actual perpetrators were public or private security forces, other government agents, armed factions in civil conflicts, or other such actors. A 2008 survey conducted by the Office of the High Commissioner for Human Rights (OHCHR) for the SRSG mapped allegations made against companies, and found that 41 per cent of the 320 cases (from all regions and sectors) in the sample alleged *indirect* forms of company involvement in various human rights abuses.[88] Less frequently, plaintiffs have alleged that corporations themselves have engaged in human rights abuses, with the approval or assistance of the government.[89]

Although the case law so far is limited, for aiding and abetting claims under the ATCA courts have required: (1) assistance by an act or omission with a substantial effect on the commission of an international crime by a third party (*actus reus*); and (2) depending on the legal standard applied, knowledge or intent (*mens rea*). As to the *actus reus* requirement of assistance, in *Re South African Apartheid Litigation*, the district court required a close causal link between the assistance and the commission of the international crime, distinguishing between products that were specifically tailored to help support various aspects of apartheid, and others that were merely fungible commodities.[90] Thus, aiding and abetting claims against three multinational banks were dismissed altogether. The court held that making loans to the South African government and buying its defence forces bonds were not sufficient to make the banks complicit in the South African government's crimes against the law of nations.[91] Similarly, the automotive defendants' sale of general purpose vehicles to the South African government and its agencies could not form the basis for a claim of aiding and abetting any violation of the law of nations.[92]

In contrast, those claims which the district court held *were* sufficient to proceed to litigation on the merits included:

- alleged aiding and abetting torture and cruel, inhuman or degrading treatment and apartheid by Daimler AG, General Motors Corporation and Ford Motor Company's providing information about anti-apartheid activists to the South African Security Forces, facilitating their arrests, providing information for use by interrogators and participating in interrogations;[93]
- alleged aiding and abetting extra-judicial killing and apartheid by Rhienmetall Group AG's selling armaments and related equipment and expertise to the South African government with knowledge that they would be used for extra-judicial killings to sustain apartheid;[94]
- alleged aiding and abetting arbitrary denationalization and apartheid by IBM and Fujitsu Ltd's sale of computer hardware and support to the South African government with knowledge of the latter's use of same to register individuals, strip them of their citizenship, segregate them within South Africa, produce identity documents and effect denationalization.[95]

(iv)   Knowledge or intent   The major uncertainty remaining in ATCA litigation concerns the requirement for plaintiffs to establish that the defendant either knew or intended that its actions would make it complicit in the commission of a violation of the law of nations. The courts have consistently required evidence of the state of mind, or the *mens rea* of the defendant, but the question remains whether the test for ATCA liability is knowledge or intent. The Supreme Court has not ruled on this point (as at June 2010) and the lower court decisions are in disagreement.[96] The district court in the *South African Apartheid Litigation* appeared to favour a knowledge test. It held that

the *mens rea* requirement meant that the defendant has to 'know that its actions will substantially assist the perpetrator in the commission of a crime or tort in violation of the law of nations'.[97] The court further concluded that knowledgeable employees for the purpose of attribution to a corporate defendant need not be managers or more senior executives in the defendant corporation.[98] In contrast is the case of *Presbyterian Church v Talisman*,[99] where the district court followed an intent-based standard in an ATCA claim against an oil and gas company arising out of human rights crimes committed by the Sudanese government.[100]

Evidence that human rights due diligence has been exercised will be relevant in all aiding and abetting cases, regardless of whether the correct test for ATCA liability is knowledge or intent.[101] If the intent standard is applied when establishing corporate complicity, *Talisman* shows that proof that a company exercised due diligence to prevent human rights crimes can potentially be used to counter an allegation of wrongful intent. In *Talisman*, the court granted summary judgment to the defendants expressly noting that the company had advocated unsuccessfully several times for the government to adopt better human rights practices and to stop using the company's air strips.[102] In other words, evidence that the company had exercised human rights due diligence was instrumental in enabling that company to avoid liability for complicity in Sudanese government human rights abuses.

If the correct standard for ATCA liability is based on knowledge alone, then plaintiffs have an easier task than if required to prove intent. Especially given that ATCA cases typically involve crimes affecting large numbers of people and information in the public arena, knowledge should be relatively easy to establish. Senior managers thus have every incentive to put into place due diligence procedures rigorous enough to identify anything untoward going on at lower levels of the company. Any such due diligence process also needs to take into account the fact that knowledge need not be actual, it can be constructive. Thus, the company need only know sufficient facts to make a reasonable person conclude that a crime of the type which occurred is likely. For example, in the *Unocal* case, which involved allegations of corporate complicity in international crimes against Burmese villagers by the Burmese military, the record showed that Unocal could be charged with knowledge of such crimes from numerous sources.[103]

(v) Kiobel v Royal Dutch Petroleum: another round in the fight over corporate liability under the ATCA   On 17 September 2010, the Second Circuit dismissed a putative class action brought by Esther Kiobel, the wife of a member of the 'Ogoni Nine' who was executed in 1995 along with Nigerian author and environmentalist Ken Saro-Wiwa.[104] The plaintiffs alleged that Royal Dutch Petroleum Company and Shell Transport and Trading Company, acting through

a Nigerian subsidiary, aided and abetted the Nigerian dictatorship's violent suppression of protests against oil exploration and development activities in the Ogoni region of the Niger Delta.

In the *Kiobel* majority opinion, Judge Cabranes, joined by Chief Judge Jacobs, essentially held that corporations are not subject to suit under the ATCA. They reasoned that 'the fact that corporations are liable as juridical persons under domestic law does not mean they are liable under international law [and, therefore, under the ATCA]'.[105] Because no international tribunal has ever held a corporation either actually or potentially liable for violating customary international law, they concluded that international law violations by corporations (as opposed to individuals) do not give rise to subject matter jurisdiction under the ATCA.[106] The majority discovered support for this finding in the words of the Nuremburg judgment reasoning that '[c]rimes against international law are committed by men, not by abstract entities'.[107]

The point being made by the Nuremburg Tribunal, however, was not that abstract entities (states) could not be held liable for breaches of international law, but that individuals could *also* be held liable for such breaches. Moreover, as Judge Leval (who concurred in the result in *Kiobel*) pointed out, other ATCA cases have involved legal consequences for juridical (non-natural) entities. For example, the early ATCA case of *Hilao v Estate of Marcos* involved the actions of an individual, but the legal consequences were borne by his estate, a juridical entity.[108] For Judge Leval, this was an entirely appropriate application of domestic law: international law governed the substance of the violation, and domestic law governed the attribution of liability.[109] Judge Leval preferred to hold in favour of the defendant by relying on the finding in *Presbyterian Church of Sudan v Talisman Energy* that international law requires purposefully – not just knowingly – aiding and abetting a violation. He found that the complaint before the court did 'not contain allegations supporting a reasonable inference that [Royal Dutch and Shell] acted with a purpose of bringing about the alleged abuses'.[110]

It is probably only a matter of time before the Supreme Court weighs in on legal questions arising from cases brought against corporations under the ATCA. Until it does, however, or until either the Second Circuit takes action *en banc* or Congress acts to clarify the liability of corporations, corporations cannot be subject to suit under the ATCA in the Second Circuit or in other circuits that adopt its reasoning.[111] Yet as Chimène Keitner points out, this may in fact give a boost to cases under the ATCA against individuals who become involved in international law crimes when acting on behalf of a TNC or on behalf of a foreign State. And this, in turn, should give both foreign officials and corporate executives reason for pause.[112]

(c) Jurisdiction under 28 USC s. 1331 and the Torture Victim Protection Act

Even in the absence of the ATCA, transnational human rights cases may also come before US federal courts under the courts' 'federal question' jurisdiction and/or under the Torture Victim Protection Act (TVPA). US federal district courts are given jurisdiction over matters arising under the Constitution and/or federal laws by USC Title 28 s. 1331.[113] 'Federal laws' include self-executing treaties ratified by the United States. The relevance of this federal 'treaty' jurisdiction has been significantly curtailed, however, by the US executive practice noted above of issuing a declaration upon ratification that treaties, including human rights treaties, are not self-executing.

So far as the status of customary international law is concerned, the orthodox view is that customary international law constitutes enforceable federal common law, so long as there is no relevant statutory law in the area. Federal statutes prevail over inconsistent custom. As federal statute law is quite comprehensive, there is little scope for the application of customary international law. Nevertheless, custom provided a basis for federal jurisdiction in *Bodner v Banque Paribas*, where the complaints of the US plaintiffs against a French bank for looting of their possessions during the Second World War (a war crime) were accepted under s. 1331.[114] Claims under s. 1331 typically have a substantial overlap with ATCA claims. Its main importance thus lies in providing a cause of action for victims of TNC activity who are US nationals and thus lack standing under ATCA.

Also having a significant overlap with ATCA claims are claims arising under the Torture Victim Protection Act of 1991.[115] The TVPA provides for a civil cause of action for acts of torture and extra-judicial killings, when committed by individuals 'under actual or apparent authority, or color of law, of any foreign nation' against aliens or US citizens. Again, like 28 USC s. 1331, the TVPA provides a cause of action to US nationals who lack standing under the ATCA. Otherwise, however, the TVPA is much more limited than the ATCA. Not only does it apply to only a portion of the international law violations covered by the ATCA, it cannot apply to any private acts of torture or extra-judicial killings due to its explicit state action requirement. The TVPA also explicitly requires plaintiffs to 'exhaust adequate and available remedies in the place in which the conduct giving rise to the claim occurred' prior to bringing a TVPA claim in a US court.[116] Finally, it also contains an explicit statute of limitations clause excluding all actions not commenced within ten years of the cause of action arising.[117]

A further limitation of the TVPA which has only recently become evident is that it may not be applicable to corporations at all, but only to natural persons. In a September 2010 development closely related to the finding in *Kiobel v Royal Dutch Petroleum* (discussed above) that corporations are not

subject to suit under the ATCA, the Ninth Circuit in *Bowoto v Chevron* held
that the use of the term 'individual' in the TVPA precluded the application of
that statute to corporations.[118] Whether and when this decision will be overturned by a superior circuit or the Supreme Court (or by Congress) remains to
be seen.

4.   Procedural Obstacles to TNC Liability for Transnational Harms

In nearly all transnational human rights litigation against TNCs the nationality
of the defendant TNC has provided a basis for courts in the home state to exercise jurisdiction. What has been a challenge for plaintiffs, however, is overcoming a number of private international law concepts which can be used by
defendants to prevent the case proceeding. These concepts include the doctrine
of *forum non-conveniens*, the doctrine of state action, the political question
doctrine and the discretionary ability of courts to dismiss a claim with transnational implications on the basis of comity.

(a)   *Forum non conveniens*

(i)   Introduction   The question of *forum non conveniens* arises whenever
litigation concerning the same bundle of rights has been, or could be, initiated
in more than one legal system. In the context of TNC liability, litigation may
have been initiated in both the host state and the home state. An application for
a stay of proceedings in the home state on the ground of *forum non conveniens*
is typically made by a corporate defendant, with a view to requiring that the
claim made by the plaintiff in the proceedings be litigated in some other jurisdiction. For example, in *Abad v Bayer Corp*,[119] Argentinian plaintiffs filed
products liability actions against US manufacturers for injuries sustained in
Argentina. The plaintiffs alleged that they (a group of haemophiliacs or their
descendants) were infected with the AIDS virus because the defendant manufacturers of the clotting factor taken as treatment by the plaintiffs had failed to
eliminate the virus from the donors' blood used to make the clotting factor.
The defendant corporation successfully requested that the US district court
dismiss the case on the basis of *forum non conveniens*, thus obliging the plaintiffs to pursue their claim in the Argentinian courts.

In the majority of common law states, including the United Kingdom and
those jurisdictions which inherited their common law system from the United
Kingdom,[120] the doctrine of *forum non conveniens* is interpreted to focus on
the search for a clearly more appropriate forum. In considering whether to or
not to decline jurisdiction, courts following the UK version of the *forum non
conveniens* doctrine will usually apply a version of the two-stage test developed in *Spiliada Maritime Corp. v Cansulex Ltd*.[121]

The first stage of the *Spiliada* test requires the court to determine whether (in the words of Lord Goff) there is:

> some other available forum, having jurisdiction, which is the appropriate forum for the trial of the action, i.e. in which the case may be tried more suitably for the interests of all the parties and the ends of justice.[122]

Lord Goff went on to define a 'more appropriate forum' as being one 'with which the action (has) the most real and substantial connection'. Factors making a forum more appropriate in this sense include the law governing the relevant transaction, the places where the parties respectively reside or carry on business[123] and/or the place where a particular harm the subject of litigation was suffered. Other considerations relevant when determining whether or not a case is more appropriately tried in an alternative forum, include:

- whether or not justice can be done in the other forum at 'substantially less inconvenience or expense' (such as the availability of witnesses) than in the local forum;[124]
- whether or not the plaintiff has a 'legitimate personal or juridical advantage' in having the proceedings heard in the domestic forum.[125] Such advantages may include an earlier trial, a more complete procedure of discovery, better recovery of damages, a power to award interest, or a more generous limitation period. But the mere fact that the plaintiff has such an advantage is not decisive.

Where the defendant has been served in the local jurisdiction, the burden of establishing the existence of a more suitable alternative forum rests on the defendant. In the case of a plaintiff seeking to invoke the statutory jurisdiction of the local court based upon service outside the jurisdiction, the onus is reversed. Leave to proceed with the action will not be granted unless the plaintiff shows that the local court is clearly the more appropriate forum.[126]

If the first stage of the *Spiliada* inquiry leads the court to conclude that there is some other available forum which prima facie is more appropriate for the trial of the action, a court applying the *Spiliada* test will ordinarily grant a stay unless the plaintiff can show that justice requires that a stay should nevertheless not be granted.[127] In this second stage, the court will concentrate its attention not only on factors connecting the proceedings with the foreign or local forum, but also on whether the plaintiff will obtain justice in the foreign jurisdiction.[128] It is only if the plaintiff can establish that substantial justice will not be done in the appropriate forum that a stay will be refused.[129] A stay order might be made notwithstanding that the plaintiff would be defeated by a time bar in the other jurisdiction; but where a plaintiff has acted reasonably in commencing the proceedings in the local court, and has not acted unreasonably in failing to commence proceedings within time in the other jurisdiction, the plaintiff should not be deprived of the advantage of having the proceedings heard in the domestic court. Where a stay would otherwise be appropriate and the time limitation in the foreign jurisdiction is dependent on the defendant invoking the limitation, it can be made a condition of the stay that the defendant must waive the time bar in the foreign jurisdiction.[130]

(ii)   Australia and the 'clearly inappropriate forum' test   Not all common law jurisdictions have followed the English courts' approach. In Australia, for example, the law makes it harder for a defendant to obtain a stay of proceedings on the ground of *forum non conveniens*. Under the test laid down in the 1990 majority High Court decision of *Voth v Manildra Flour Mills Pty Ltd*,[131] the defendant seeking a stay order must prove that the local court is a *clearly inappropriate forum* for hearing the case before it. This will only be the case if continuation of the proceedings in that court would be oppressive, in the sense of 'seriously and unfairly burdensome, prejudicial or damaging', or vexatious, in the sense of 'productive of serious and unjustified trouble and harassment'.[132]

The 'clearly inappropriate' version of *forum non conveniens* has been controversial ever since it was adopted by the High Court in 1990. However, the courts so far appear to have had little inclination for abandoning the 'clearly inappropriate' test,[133] and the legislature, with one exception for cases involving New Zealand,[134] has not seen fit to override it.[135]

(iii)   United States and forum non conveniens   Courts in the United States apply yet another version of the doctrine. It was in 1947 that the US Supreme Court adopted a general doctrine of *forum non conveniens* to be applied in all courts exercising federal jurisdiction.[136] Thirty states, the District of Columbia and all US territories engage in an analysis effectively identical to that undertaken in federal courts, and 13 others employ a factor-based analysis very similar to the federal one. Significantly, if a US court decides that it is *forum non conveniens*, it dismisses the case rather than merely staying it, although it may, in some cases, make the dismissal a conditional one.[137]

In the American context, the doctrine of *forum non conveniens* may be invoked by either the court or on a party's motion. It permits a court to decline to exercise its jurisdiction if the court finds that it is a 'seriously inconvenient' forum and the interests of the parties and the public will be best served by remitting the plaintiff to another, more convenient forum, that is available.

Just as in other common law states, a US court will not lightly disturb a plaintiff's choice of forum. However, this plaintiff-friendly approach is reserved for US plaintiffs only, and it has been held that foreign plaintiffs deserve less deference in their choice of forum.[138] This makes ATCA plaintiffs particularly vulnerable to *forum non conveniens* defences.

If the court determines that an adequate alternative forum does exist, then a number of public and private elements are then considered in deciding whether to dismiss the proceedings on the basis of *forum non conveniens*. These factors were identified by the US Supreme Court in *Gulf Oil Corp. v Gilbert*,[139] and have been summarized by Del Duca and Zaphiriou as follows:

> The private factors included: relative ease of access to sources of proof, availability and cost of obtaining witnesses, possibility of view of the premises, and all other practical problems that make a trial easy, expeditious, and inexpensive. The public factors included: administrative difficulties from court congestion, local interest in having localised controversies decided at home; interest in applying familiar law, avoidance of unnecessary problems in conflicts of laws or in the application of foreign law; and the unfairness of burdening citizens in an unrelated forum with jury duty.[140]

For example, claims against Southern Peru Copper with regard to alleged environmental damage in Peru were dismissed on *forum non conveniens* grounds when the court found that Peru was the more appropriate forum for the plaintiff's litigation.[141]

Dismissal on *forum non conveniens* grounds is more likely where the applicable law governing the plaintiff's claim is held to be the law of the overseas jurisdiction where the tort occurred. Here we find that US courts have not gone as far as Australian courts in their refusal to apply local law in proceedings involving foreign torts. In the Australian case of *Regie Nationale des Usines Renault SA v Zhang*,[142] the High Court confirmed that the governing law in cases involving foreign torts is the law of the *lex loci delicti* – the place where the harm was inflicted. Such a finding makes it more likely that a case involving a foreign tort will be dismissed on *forum non conveniens* grounds. Of course, as discussed above, this is counter-balanced in the Australian context by the fact that *forum non conveniens* is less easily argued by defendants than in the United States, England and other similar jurisdictions.

(b) Sovereign immunity

Sovereign immunity bars most ATCA claims brought directly against governments, against current or former heads of state, or against state agencies or instrumentalities acting in pursuance of state policy. The doctrine of foreign sovereign immunity arises from the sovereign equality of all states under international law. It provides that a state and its instrumentalities (including its incorporated instrumentalities) are generally immune from the jurisdiction of the courts of another state. Until the mid-twentieth century, sovereign immunity from the jurisdiction of foreign courts was almost absolute. However, as governments and state enterprises became more and more active in commercial activities in the modern era, private entities interacting with foreign states attacked complete sovereign immunity as fundamentally unfair in eliminating judicial recourse and favouring state companies.[143]

The United States and some Western European nations reacted by adopting a 'restrictive' approach to foreign sovereign immunity. The restrictive theory of state immunity provides that foreign states are immune from jurisdiction for their 'public acts' (*acta jure imperii*) but are not immune from jurisdiction for their 'private acts' (*acta jure gestionis*), including commercial activities. The United States codified the restrictive approach to state immunity through the Foreign Sovereign Immunities Act of 1976 (FSIA).[144] Two years later, the United Kingdom passed similar legislation: the State Immunity Act 1978. Similar legislation also exists in Australia,[145] Canada[146] and elsewhere, but many countries, including, for example, Sweden and Germany, do not have such legislation, although both their courts and their administrative authorities have expressly accepted the restrictive ('relative')[147] theory of sovereign immunity.[148]

In addition to domestic laws, attempts have been made to develop multilateral treaties governing foreign sovereign immunity issues. The Council of Europe adopted a European Convention on State Immunity and an Additional Protocol that became effective in June 1976. At the time of writing in April 2010, there are eight ratifications/accessions to the European Convention, while Portugal has signed without yet ratifying. More recently, the United Nations General Assembly approved the UN Convention on Jurisdictional Immunities of States and Their Property ('State Immunity Convention') on 2 December 2004. The Convention essentially codifies the customary international law of state immunity, and thus provides for exceptions to state immunity in similar terms to the FSIA. Unlike the FSIA, however, there is no exception to immunity for proceedings relating to state expropriation of foreign property, nor is there an exception for acts of state-sponsored terrorism, as was inserted into the FSIA in 2008.[149]

The State Immunity Convention is drafted to enter into force on the 30th day following deposit of the 30th instrument of ratification, approval or accession. As at 15 June 2009, however, there were only 28 signatories and six instruments of ratification. It seems unlikely, therefore, that the State Immunity Convention will become the basis for development of new international norms in the field of state immunity any time soon.

So far as TNCs are concerned, state-owned companies are just as likely as their privately owned counterparts to be organized in complex legal structures with holding companies and numerous tiers of subsidiaries partly or fully owned by the parent. Article 10 of the State Immunity Convention recognizes that states are separate from the independent commercial entities, such as state enterprises, that they might establish for commercial purposes. A state enterprise that has an independent legal personality and is capable of suing or being sued, and of acquiring, owning or possessing and disposing of property (including property which that state has authorized it to operate or manage), cannot generally claim state immunity, but this does not affect the immunity from jurisdiction enjoyed by the state which established it.

Until 2003, the position of many US courts was that corporations indirectly owned by a foreign state through intermediary parent corporations could claim immunity under the FSIA if they could demonstrate that they were an instrumentality of the state. In 2003, however, the Supreme Court reversed this presumption, and held that indirect ownership is not sufficient to justify a claim of immunity under the FSIA. In *Dole Food Co. v Patrickson* the Supreme Court concluded that 'the State must itself own a majority of the shares of a corporation if the corporation is to be deemed an instrumentality of the state under the provisions of the FSIA'.[150]

Dole Food was followed by the District Court of New York in the 2005 decision of *Burnett v Al Baraka Inv. and Dev. Corp.*[151] That case involved a number of individuals and entities alleged to have provided support for the operations of al Qaeda, Osama bin Laden and international terrorism. One of the defendants was the National Commercial Bank (NCB), established in 1950 as the first commercial bank of Saudi Arabia. Since 1999, the NCB had been majority owned by the Public Investment Fund (PIF), an administrative unit of the Saudi Ministry of Finance. The court confirmed that:

> the Kingdom of Saudi Arabia's ownership of the NCB must be direct for NCB to enjoy immunity under the FSIA. That is, NCB will not be deemed an instrumentality of the Kingdom if the PIF ..., its majority owner, is determined to be an agency, instrumentality or organ of the Kingdom.[152]

The court went on to find that only if PIF was found to be a political subdivision of the Saudi government could it be said that NCB was directly owned by the Kingdom of Saudi Arabia. The evidence showed that PIF could sue and be sued as, and generally held property on behalf of, the Saudi Ministry of Finance, a political sub-division of the Saudi government. On the other hand, the PIF's emphasis on commercial projects, the fact that it was created by royal decree, the fact that it was supervised by the Kingdom's Council of Ministers and staffed with government employees all pointed to a finding that the PIF was an organ of the Saudi government, rather than a political sub-division. Since the court was unable to determine whether the PIF qualified as an organ or political sub-division of the Kingdom of Saudi Arabia, it felt bound to grant additional limited jurisdictional discovery to explore PIF's function, organizational structure and place within the Kingdom of Saudi Arabia.[153]

(c)   Act of state doctrine

In *Banco Nacional de Cuba v Sabbatino*,[154] the US Supreme Court stated that the act of state doctrine prevents US courts from inquiring into the legitimacy of public acts committed by a recognized foreign sovereign power within its own territory.[155] The constitutional underpinnings of this doctrine reflect the judiciary's concerns regarding separation of powers, particularly that US courts sitting in judgment on a foreign state may be interfering with the conduct of foreign policy by the President and Congress.[156]

In other cases, the act of state doctrine has been held to preclude the US court from adjudicating a claim on the basis that to do so would require the court to invalidate a foreign sovereign's official acts within its own territory. There must be (1) an official act of a foreign sovereign, (2) performed within its own territory and (3) a claim before the court seeking relief that would require the court to declare the foreign sovereign's act invalid.[157] The court must also consider a number of other factors, including whether or not the government which perpetrated the challenged act of state is still in existence, the degree of codification or consensus concerning the relevant area of international law and the implications of the case and issues it raises for US foreign relations. For example, in *Sarei and others v Rio Tinto*, the court concluded that:

> Rio Tinto's liability is premised on its alleged joint venture with the PNG government, as codified in the Copper Act, and on the purported actions the two took jointly to construct, operate, and reopen the mine on Bougainville. Certain of those alleged activities clearly involved official acts of the PNG government – e.g. conferring a mining concession on Rio Tinto and allowing Rio Tinto to exercise eminent domain powers to dispossess the native people of Bougainville. Were the court to conclude that Rio Tinto was a state actor, and that its conduct violated the law of nations, it would, *a fortiori*, have to conclude that PNG's official acts were invalid as well.[158]

The court therefore held that the plaintiffs' claims based on racial discrimination and alleged environmental torts were precluded by the act of state doctrine.

As the key question for US courts appears to be whether a court decision might impede US foreign relations policy, the act of state doctrine is less likely to be applied in a human rights context if the foreign state's human rights record has already been publicly denounced by the US government. It is also less likely to apply where the impugned foreign act is that of a former government, especially if the conduct of that former government has been repudiated by the contemporary government.[159]

In a number of cases where 'act of state' has arisen, the views of the US State Department have been sought to provide evidence of the executive government's own view of whether the litigation at hand would unduly interfere in its conduct of foreign affairs. Such submissions can be crucial to the court's decision to accept or dismiss the case. In *Rio Tinto*, for example, the court in dismissing allegations of racial discrimination and breaches of UNCLOS[160] due to act of state, said:

> [P]laintiffs have not cited and the court has not found, a single case in which a court permitted a lawsuit to proceed in the face of an expression of concern such as that communicated by the State Department here. The is probably because to do so would have the potential to embarrass the executive branch in the conduct of its foreign relations and 'the major underpinning of the act of state doctrine is ... [to] foreclose' such a possibility.[161]

In contrast is the case of *Presbyterian Church v Talisman Energy*,[162] where the court did not request a US State Department brief. This left the court free to decide that the alleged acts of genocide, war crimes, torture and enslavement were so universally condemned that they could not be properly classified as acts of state. In rejecting the defendant's argument that the case should be dismissed for act of state, the court also took a sceptical view of the supposedly detrimental impact that the litigation would have on US foreign policy in Sudan.[163]

The 'act of state' doctrine appears to have significantly smaller scope in England than in the United States. While the paramount issue regarding 'act of state' under US law is the need to prevent litigation that would interfere with the executive's conduct of foreign affairs, in England there is less of a desire to avoid clashes with the foreign policy of the British government. Rather, the *raison d'etre* behind the doctrine as applied by English courts is a desire to respect the legitimate acts of foreign nations. This focus on legitimacy means that English courts are less likely to characterize breaches of international human rights law as 'acts of state'.[164]

In *Banco Nacional de Cuba v Sabbatino*, the district court held that the act of state doctrine is inapplicable when the questioned act violated international law.[165] The trial court in *Sarei v Rio Tinto* agreed, holding that while orders given by military commanders during wartime are commonly viewed as official sovereign acts, where those commands do not involve acts of legitimate warfare, the act of state doctrine no longer bars adjudication of the matter.[166] Thus, the act of state doctrine could not preclude the court considering the claim based on the allegation that Bougainville islanders, 'died by the thousands because a blockade deprived them of access to needed medical supplies, PNG soldiers tortured, raped and pillaged, and other human rights violations and atrocities occurred'.[167] The court did hold, however, that another principle, the political question doctrine, did preclude the consideration of the plaintiffs' claim in this regard.

(d)   Political question

The political question doctrine restricts the justiciability of questions which are essentially political in nature, and therefore deemed more properly dealt with by the executive and legislative branches of government. The criteria for applying the doctrine remain vague, and it appears to arise whenever a case raises matters that are simply 'too political ... to handle'.[168] It is very similar to the 'act of state' doctrine in its preoccupation with the notion of the separation of powers. That is, the political question doctrine is used to prevent the court intruding too much into the political realm more properly occupied by the legislature and the executive. Also like the act of state doctrine, the political question doctrine inevitably arises when a case impinges on governmental foreign policy.[169]

In *Iwanowa v Ford Motor Co*,[170] a complaint against a US company concerning use of slave and forced labour in Nazi Germany in the Second World War, the court dismissed the case, *inter alia*, on political question grounds because the issue of compensation for grievances arising out of the war had been dealt with by the political branches of government in concluding post-war reparation treaties. Claims against Japanese companies for alleged forced labour in the Far East during the Second World War were similarly dismissed.

In *Sarei v Rio Tinto*, the State Department's brief, arguing that continued litigation against Rio Tinto would imperil an important foreign policy objective of the United States, was crucial to the trial court's decision to dismiss the entire case on 'political question' grounds, including the claim based on allegations of war crimes and crimes against humanity.[171] Following the 2002 trial court ruling in *Rio Tinto*, however, the Supreme Court published its decision in *Sosa v Alvarez-Machain*,[172] and that decision affected the Ninth Circuit Court of Appeals 2007 decision in *Rio Tinto*. By a two to one majority, the Ninth Circuit disagreed with the district court's political question analysis, and remanded for the district court to further consider the plaintiffs' claims for racial discrimination and environmental damage under the UNCLOS.[173]

(e)   Comity

Comity is a further obstacle that a plaintiff is likely to face. International comity has been defined as 'the recognition which one nation allows within its territory to the legislative, executive or judicial acts of another nation'.[174] Under the doctrine of international comity, courts may exercise a discretion to defer to the laws or interests of a foreign country and decline to exercise the jurisdiction they otherwise have. Whether or not the discretion should be exercised is a matter of what is reasonable, convenient and expedient in the circumstances.[175] In August 2005 the district court in *Presbyterian Church of Sudan v Talisman Energy Inc.* refused to dismiss the suit against Talisman on comity grounds, as urged by the US and Canadian executive government authorities.[176] The court found an insufficient nexus between Canada's foreign policy and the specific allegations in the complaint because the litigation did not require judging Canada's policy of constructive engagement with the Sudan, but 'merely' judging 'whether Talisman acted outside the bounds of customary international law while doing business in Sudan'.[177] The court also observed that Canadian courts are unable to consider civil suits for violations of the law of nations.[178]

Yet there is little evidence that ATCA and other human rights claims against TNCs do in fact harm the United States' foreign relations. For example, the *Wiwa* case does not appear to have created any friction between the United States and the government of Nigeria. Indeed, a key plaintiff in Wiwa, Ken Saro-Wiwa's son, worked as a special adviser to the Nigerian government on international affairs during and after the campaign to sue Shell for complicity in his father's death.[179]

C.   CONCLUSION

Not surprisingly given the significant procedural obstacles faced by civil litigants in claims against TNCs for transnational wrongs, most such claims have so far been unsuccessful. The exact number of civil proceedings initiated against TNCs, and the ratio of successful and unsuccessful outcomes in different countries, is a subject which deserves further research. A comparative study into the different rates of success in civil versus criminal proceedings against TNCs is also needed. A cursory overview of recorded cases appears to indicate, however, that criminal prosecutions against TNCs for wrongful acts outside the home state have generally been more successful than civil proceedings. There appear to be a number of reasons for this. First, the state which is typically responsible for initiating criminal prosecutions has more resources to devote to pursuing such actions than do victims of TNC harms seeking civil compensation. Prosecution authorities also tend to take a conservative approach in selecting cases for prosecution, so that only those cases most likely to result in a conviction are pursued. One result is that the determining feature of a decision to prosecute is more likely to be the presence of evidence likely to satisfy a criminal standard of proof, than the nature of the crime or the amount of damage wrought. Finally, most countries tend to have more and stronger legislation for dealing with corporate crimes, particularly those relating to money laundering and corruption, than for facilitating civil claims by victims of corporate wrongs. The next chapter therefore examines this important aspect of criminal law in light of its obvious relevance to the question of TNC accountability for transnational wrongs.

NOTES

1. For a general overview, see Gillian Triggs, *International Law: Contemporary Principles and Practices* (2006) ch. 7, 342–80.
2. *Lotus (France v Turkey)* (1927) PCIJ Rep., Ser. A, No. 10.
3. John Ruggie, *Clarifying the Concepts of 'Sphere of Influence' and 'Complicity'*, UN Doc. A/HRC/8/16 (15 May 2008) para. 26 *et seq.*
4. *Barcelona Traction, Light and Power Co. (Belgium v Spain)* [1970] ICJ Rep., available at www.icj-cij.org.
5. Rome Statute of the International Criminal Court, opened for signature 17 July 1998, 2187 UNTS 3 (entered into force 1 July 2002). See further Leila Nadya Sadat, 'The International Criminal Court Treaty enters into force' (2002) *ASIL Insights* (April) available at www.asil.org/insights/insigh86.htm.
6. John Ruggie, Report of the Special Representative of the Secretary-General on the issue of human rights and transnational corporations and other business enterprises UN Doc A/65/310 (19 August 2010).
7. *Ibid.*, paras. 22–23.
8. See http://ccrjustice.org/.
9. See http://oecdwatch.org/.
10. See http://www.amnesty.org/.
11. Jubilee 2000 SA is the South African-based affiliate of a global pressure group campaigning for cancellation of Third World debt. See further Cyrus Rustomjee, *Jubilee South Africa: A Case Study for the UKZN Project Entitled Globalisation, Marginalisation and New Social Movements in post-Apartheid South Africa* (2004) and Richard Walker and Nicoli Nattrass, '"Don't owe, won't pay!": a critical analysis of the Jubilee SA position on South African government debt' (2002) 19:4 *Development Southern Africa* 467.
12. Seee www.apdhe.org/.
13. See www.mpi.org.au. See also http://eyeonmining.wordpress.com/.
14. See www.mosop.org/.
15. Earth Rights International, 'Federal Court: ATCA can be used against corps. Complicit in abuse' (16 March 2005), available at www.earthrights.org/amicus/federal-court-atca-can-be-used-against-corps-complicit-abuse. In a March 2005 decision, however, the court dismissed the case on the basis that the use of Agent Orange during the Vietnamese war was not a violation of a universally recognized (customary) international law, as required under the Alien Tort Claims Act.
16. Jedrzej George Frynas, 'Social and environmental litigation against transnational firms in Africa' (2004) 42:3 *Journal of Modern African Studies* 363, 378.
17. *Ibid.*, 373–5.
18. *Ibid.*, 372.
19. *Ibid.*, 372–3.
20. Jonathan Clough, 'Punishing the parent: corporate criminal complicity in human rights abuses' (2008) 33:3 *Brooklyn Journal of International Law* 899, 916, citing Phillip I. Blumberg, *The Law of Corporate Groups: Substantive Law* (1987) 3–39, 55–62 (providing a history of the evolution of the corporate form, and in particular of corporate groups).
21. *John Doe et al. v Exxon Mobil Corp. et al.*, 573 Supp. 2d 16 (DDC 2008).
22. See e.g. *Flores v Southern Peru Copper*, 253 F. Supp. 2d 510, 544 (FDNY 2002), where the court held the case should be dismissed because 'Peru provides an adequate alternative forum for plaintiffs' claims' and because public and private interest factors weighed heavily in favour of the Peruvian forum.
23. *John Doe et al. v Exxon Mobil Corp. et al.*, 573 Supp. 2d 16 (DDC 2008) (federal statutory claims against Exxon, including under the Alien Tort Claims Act, were earlier dismissed), dismissed under a seldom-used doctrine denying standing for non-citizens in common law claims, 2009 US Dist LEXIS 90237 (DDC 2009). Plaintiffs have appealed the case.
24. *Bowoto v Chevron Texaco*, 2007 WL 2349536 (ND Cal. 2007) 23–4. For further discussion of tort jurisdiction in the context of human rights actions against US TNCs, see Sarah

Joseph, *Corporations and Transnational Human Rights Litigation* (Hart Publishing, 2004) ch. 3.

25. [1998] AC 854 (HL). The case was ultimately dismissed for being filed outside the applicable statute of limitations in *Connelly v RTZ*, QBD (Judge Wright), 4 December 1998. See also Greg Dropkin, 'Door slams shut on former Rössing worker', *The Namibian*, 7 December 1998.

26. *Lubbe v Cape Plc* [2000] 4 All ER 268 (HL). The case was eventually settled in early 2002, with payment completed in 2003: see P. Muchlinski, 'Holding multinationals to account: recent developments in English litigation and the Company Law Review' (2002) 23:6 *Company Lawyer* 168, 169 and Sarah Joseph, *Corporations and Transnational Human Rights Litigation* (Hart Publishing, 2004) 120, n. 54.

27. Jennifer A. Zerk, *Multinationals and Corporate Social Responsibility* (CUP, 2006) ch. 5, noting that 'in identifying the substantive obligations of the parent company, the courts will take account of the general state of knowledge about the risks posed by the particular industry, process or technology and how to minimize them. To this end, home state regulatory requirements, codes of conduct, industry "best practice", safety cases and risk control manuals are likely to be important sources of evidence': 220–1.

28. Ruggie, above n. 3, paras. 52–3, 71–2.

29. *Ibid.*, para. 32.

30. *Ibid.*

31. *Ibid.*, para. 22.

32. 256 F. Supp. 2d 1345 (SD Fla. 2003).

33. *Ibid.*

34. For discussion see Joseph, above n. 24, 142–3, citing M. Davies, 'Just (don't) do it: ethics and international trade' (1997) 21 *Melbourne University Law Review* 601, 614–20.

35. John F. Sherman III and Amy K. Lehr, 'Human rights due diligence: is it too risky?' (2010) *CSR Journal* (January) 6, 8, noting further that such a relationship can be inferred by the parties' conduct, and its existence is highly fact-specific; citing *Bowoto v Chevron Texaco*, 312 F. Supp. 2d 1229 (ND Cal., 23 March 2004).

36. *In re South African Apartheid Litigation*, 633 F. Supp. 2d 117 (SD NY 2009).

37. *Bowoto v Chevron Texaco*, 2007 WL 2349536 (ND Cal. 2007) 15–16. Although the plaintiffs in this case ultimately lost the jury trial (*Bowoto v Chevron Corp.*, 1 December 2008), their claims survived motions to dismiss and for summary judgment: *Bowoto v Chevron Corp.*, No. C99-02506SI, 2006 WL 2455752 (ND Cal., 22 August 2006); *Bowoto v Chevron Corp.*, No. C99-02506SI, 2007 WL 800940 (ND Cal., 14 March 2007).

38. Sherman III and Lehr, above n. 35, 8, citing *Bowoto v Chevron Texaco*, 'Instructions to Jury', Case 3:99-civ-0506-SI, Doc. 2252, 28 November 2005, 29–33, 37–9. See also (US) *Restatement (Third) of the Law of Agency*, s. 4.06 (Ratification), comment d.

39. Aurora Institute, *Submission to the Canadian Democracy and Corporate Accountability Commission* (17 June 2001), available at www.aurora.ca/docs/Accountability CommSubmisssion.pdf.

40. For further discussion, see Joseph, above n. 24, 138–42. Joseph notes that the concept of multinational group liability is also found in the Argentinian Draft Code of Private International Law, which in art. 10 provides that TNCs will be regulated 'on the basis of their economic unity and regardless of the legal separation between the various companies within the group': at 140, n. 72, citing Peter Muchlinski, *Multinational Enterprises and the Law* (2nd edn, Blackwell, 1999) 138-9. The text of the whole Draft Code is available at (1985) 24 ILM 269.

41. Age Discrimination in Employment Act, 29 USC s. 623(h)(3).

42. See Civil Law Convention on Corruption, CETS No. 174, opened for signature Strasbourg, 4 November 1999 (entered into force 1 November 2003).

43. *Ibid.*, art. 1.

44. *Ibid.* Table showing status of ratifications and signatures as at 21 March 2010, available at http://conventions.coe.int/Treaty/Commun/ChercheSig.asp.

45. 28 USC 1350.

46. In the case of Texaco, for example, the company offered US $176 million to settle,

representing the largest cash settlement ever to resolve a discrimination case, but 'it's not a princely sum to dole out over five years for a corporation with revenue of more than $30 billion': Aurora Institute, above n. 39, 9, citing Robert Sherrill, 'The year ('97) in corporate crime', *The Nation*, 7 April 1997, available at www.thenation.com/article/year-97-corporate-crime.

47. In the case of the 1984 Union Carbide gas leak in Bhopal, India, it took until 1989 for Union Carbide to move from its original offer of US$7 million compensation to victims in 1985, to final payment of US$470 million to the Indian government, in accordance with an order handed down by the Supreme Court of India in February 1989. (US$420 million was paid by Union Carbide Corporation, and the Indian rupee equivalent of US$50 million was paid by Union Carbide India Ltd): Lauren Farrow, 'A soft verdict for corporate polluters', *New Matilda*, 15 June 2010, available at http://newmatilda.com/print/8690.

48. *Bowoto v Chevron* No. 3:99-cv-02506 (ND Cal) (jury verdict reached on 1 December 2008). See also 'Case profile: Chevron lawsuit (re Nigeria)', Business and Human Rights Resource Centre, available at www.business-humanrights.org/Categories/Lawlawsuits/Lawsuitsregulatoryaction/ LawsuitsSelectedcases/ChevronlawsuitreNigeria?batch.

49. *Estate of Rodriguez v Drummond* No. CV-03-BE-0575 (ND Ala) (jury verdict reached on 26 July 2007). See also 'Case profile: Drummond lawsuit', Business and Human Rights Resource Centre, available at www.business-humanrights.org/Categories/Lawlawsuits/Lawsuitsregulatoryaction/LawsuitsSelectedcases/DrummondlawsuitreColombia. See also 'Ga. court upholds verdict in Columbian killings' (29 December 2008), available at www.wtvy.com/georgianews/headlines/36865629.html. Also available at http://bit.ly/ i77K8.

50. Ross Todd, 'Fulbright wins Alien Tort case for Bangladeshi businessman', *American Lawyer*, 10 August 2009, first appeared on *American Lawyer Litigation Daily Blog*, available at http://tiny.cc/DGpbu. See also summary of verdict in *Nayeem Mehtab Chowdhury Chowdhury et al. v WorldTel Bangladesh Holding Ltd and Amjad Hossain Khan* (defendants), Duke Copeland Court Reporters, noting plaintiff's verdict for US$1.5 million compensatory damages and US$250,000 in punitive damages, and citing Case No. 1:08-cv-01659-BMC, US District Court for the Eastern District of New York, King County, available at More Law Lexapedia, www.morelaw.com/verdicts/case.asp?n=1:08-cv-01659-BMC&s=NY&d=40919.

51. Marc Lifsher, 'Unocal settles human rights lawsuit over alleged abuses at Myanmar pipeline', *Los Angeles Times*, 22 March 2005.

52. Ingrid Wuerth, 'Wiwa v Shell: the $15.5 million settlement' (2009) 13:14 *ASIL Insight* (9 September), noting that Ken Saro-Wiwa was hanged in 1995 and the case was brought in a US federal court in 1996.

53. 630 F. 2d 876 (2d Cir. 1980).

54. *Rodolfo Flores et al. v Southern Peru Copper Corp.*, F. 2d 13, n. 17 (2d Cir. 2003, 29 August 2003), citing 630 F.2d at 887.

55. For discussion, see Joseph, above n. 24, 55–60.

56. 886 F. Supp. 162 (D. Mass 1995), especially at para. 171, relying in part on *Forti v Suarez-Mason*, 672 F. Supp. 1531 (ND Cal. 1987) where the court held an Argentinian general responsible for acts of brutality committed by military personnel under his command, available at www.uniset.ca/other/cs5/886FSupp162.html.

57. *Kadic v Karadzic*, 70 F. 3d 232 (2d Cir. 1995). The case involved a claim against de facto Bosnian Serb government officials for atrocities during the Yugoslavian conflict.

58. 963 F. Supp. 880 (CD Cal. 1997).

59. See description of facts in *John Doe 1 v Unocal Corp.*, 2002 US App. LEXIS 19263 (9th Cir. 2002) 14193–5.

60. *Bowoto v Chevron Corp.*, 557 F. Supp. 2d 1080 (ND Cal. 2008).

61. *Sarei v Rio Tinto*, 550 F. 3d 822 (9th Cir. 2008).

62. *Mohammed et al. v Jeppesen* (ND Cal., No. 5:07-cv-02798), Complaint, available at www.aclu.org/pdfs/safefree/mohamed v jeppesen 1stamendedcomplaint.pdf.

63. *Abdullahi v Pfizer*, 562 F. 3d 163 (2d Cir. 2009) (holding that case against Pfizer alleging non-consensual medical experimentation on children in Nigeria could go forward under the ATCA).

64. *In re Holocaust Victim Assets Litigation* 105 F. Supp. 2d 139 (EDNY 2000) (application for settlement approved).
65. *Khulumani et al. v Barclays National Bank et al.*, Case CV 25952 (EDNY 2002). See also 'Apartheid lawsuits 'too broad'', 7 November 2003, available at www.news24.com/.
66. Lloyd Coutts, 'Apartheid business verdict goes to US appeal court on Tuesday', *Business Report*, 22 January 2006, aavailable at www.busrep.co.za/. See also Wendell Roelf, 'Khulumani: SA govt "putting profits before people"', *Mail and Guardian online*, 24 January 2006, available at www.mg.co.za/; 'Apartheid reparations appeal under way', 165 *Legalbrief Africa*, 30 January 2006, available at www.legalbrief.co.za/; 'Apartheid lawsuit back in court', 24 January 2006,available at www.news24.com/.
67. *Khulumani v Barclay National Bank*, 504 F. 3d 254 (2d Cir. 2007).
68. 'Setback for apartheid-era reparations suits', 158 *Legalbrief Africa*, 26 January 2006, aavailable at www.legalbrief.co.za/. See also 'Late bid to get government to pull out of apartheid reparations case', *Legalbrief Today*, 23 January 2006, available at www.legalbrief.co.za/; Ray Faure, 'Activists to protest apartheid-reparations affidavit', *Mail and Guardian online*, available at www.mg.co.za/; and Ernest Mabuza, 'US judge deals blow to apartheid claims cases', *Business Day online*, 26 January 2006, available at www.businessday.co.za/.
69. On 12 May 2008, the Supreme Court affirmed the Second Circuit's decision of 27 November 2007 denying the defendants' motion. The Second Circuit's decision had to be affirmed because four justices had recused themselves (probably due to their ownership of stock in some of the corporate defendants) so that the Court no longer had the quorum of six Justices required by 28 USC s. 2109 and Supreme Court Rules, rule 4(2).
70. *Sosa v Alvarez-Machain*, 542 US 692 (2004).
71. *Filartiga v Peña-Irala*, 630 F. 2d 876 (2d Cir. 1980).
72. *Sosa v Alvarez-Machain*, 542 US 692 (2004). For commentary, see Ingrid Wuerth, 'Wiwa v Shell: the $15.5 million settlement' (2009) 13:14 *ASIL Insight* (September).
73. *Sosa v Alvarez-Machain*, 542 US 692 (2004). See also 'ACTA lives!' (29 June 2004), EarthRights International, available at www.earthrights.org/.
74. 414 F. 3d 233 (US Ct App. 2d Cir., decided 29 August 2003) paras 74, 84 and 86.
75. Noting that because the plaintiffs had not alleged the defendants' conduct had an effect outside the borders of Peru, the court did not need to consider the customary international law status of transnational pollution: at 31, n. 29.
76. *Aldana et al. v Del Monte Fresh Produce Na Inc. et al.*, 416 F. 3d 1242; 2005 US App. LEXIS 13504, 3. An application for rehearing *en banc* was rejected in *Aldana v Del Monte Fresh Produce NA Inc.*, 452 F. 3d 1284 (11th Cir. 2006) (with a strong dissent from Barkett J).
77. *Bowoto v Chevron Corp.*, 557 F. Supp. 2d 1080 (ND Cal. 2008). But contra *In re South African Apartheid Litigation*, 346 F. Supp. 2d 538 (SD NY 2004), where the District Court for the Southern District of New York rejected the argument that defendants could be held liable under the ATCA for aiding and abetting. This decision was overturned, however, by the Second Circuit Court of Appeal in *Khulumani*, 504 F. 3d 254 (2d Cir. 2007) and found little support amongst other district courts. See also *Khulumani*, 2009 WL 960078, 9–10.
78. *Saleh v Titan Corp.*, 361 F. Supp. 2d 1152 (SD Cal. 2005). Discussed in Juli Schwartz, '*Saleh v Titan Corporation*: the Alien Tort Claims Act: more bark than bite? Procedural limitations and the future of ATCA litigation against corporate contractors' (2006) 37 *Rutgers Law Journal* 867.
79. *Saleh v Titan Corp.*, Case 08-7008, Doc. 1205678, 11 September 2009, 29–30, available at http://ccrjustice.org/files/Titan_Decision%209%2011%2009.pdf. See also 'Saleh *et al.* v Titan *et al.*', Center for Constitutional Rights, available at http://ccrjustice.org/ourcases/current-cases/saleh-v.-titan. Plaintiffs' petition for rehearing *en banc* was denied on 25 January 2010.
80. *Saleh v Titan Corp.*, dissenting judgment at 32–69. See also 'Saleh *et al.* v Titan *et al.*', Center for Constitutional Rightsaccessed available at http://ccrjustice.org/ourcases/current-cases/saleh-v.-titan. Prior to the filing of the petition for certiorari, the US DC Circuit denied the plaintiffs' petition for rehearing *en banc* on 25 January 2010.
81. *In Re South African Apartheid Litigation*, 346 F. Supp. 2d 538 (SD NY 2004).

82. Rome Statute of the International Criminal Court, opened for signature 17 July 1998, 2187 UNTS 3 (entered into force 1 July 2002), art. 25(3)(c).

83. *Kulumani*, 504 F. 3d 254, 277 (Judge Katzmann); 504 F. 3d 254, 333 (Judge Korman). Judge Korman was the dissenting judge who was loath to accept corporate responsibility under international law at all, but he did accept that the international law standard for aiding and abetting liability would be the standard set out in the Rome Statute, as Judge Katmann identified. By contrast, Judge Hall, finding that both customary international law and federal common law included standards of accessorial liability, preferred to use federal common law standards: *ibid.* 287–8, reasoning that 'when international law and domestic law speak on the same doctrine, domestic courts should choose the latter'.

84. Mark Hamblett, 'Judge narrows claims in apartheid torts case against multinational corporations' (11 April 2009) Axis of Logic World News Law.com, available at www.axisoflogic.com/artman/publish/printer_55422.shtml.

85. *Abdullahi v Pfizer*, 562 F. 3d 163 (2d Cir. 2009).

86. Ingrid Wuerth, 'Wiwa v Shell: the $15.5 million settlement' (2009) 13:14 *ASIL Insight* (September).

87. For example, art. 25(3)(c) of the Rome Statute provides that a person can be held criminally responsible for a crime against humanity under art. 7 of the Statute if that person 'For the purpose of facilitating the commission of such a crime, aids, abets, or otherwise assists in its commission or its attempted commission, including providing the means for its commission'.

88. John Ruggie, *Report of the SRSG on the Issue of Human Rights and Transnational Corporations and Other Business Enterprises, Addendum: Corporations and Human Rights: A Survey of the Scope and Patterns of Alleged Corporate-related Human Rights abuse*, UN Doc A/HRC/8/5/Add.2 (23 May 2008).

89. *Doe I v Unocal*, 395 F. 3d 932 (9th Cir. 2002), vacated *en banc*, 395 F. 3d 978 (9th Cir. 2003); *Khulumani*, 504 F. 3d 254 (2d Cir. 2007); *American Isuzu Motors Inc. v Ntsebeza* (No. 07-919, affirmed 2008 WL 117862), 76 USLW 3405 (12 May 2008) (in which the Supreme Court affirmed the Second Circuit's judgment on the basis of 28 USC s.1, lack of quorum).

90. Sherman and Lehr, above n. 35, 7, citing *In Re South African Apartheid Litigation*, 617 F. Supp. 2d 228, 262 (SD NY 2009).

91. *In Re South African Apartheid Litigation*, 633 F. Supp. 2d 117, 269 (SD NY 2009).

92. *Ibid.*, 267.

93. *Ibid.*, 264, 296.

94. *Ibid.*, 269–70, 296.

95. *Ibid.*, 265, 268, 296. Although the sale of computer hardware, software and support for the government's use in the individual registration system was *not* sufficient to form the basis of a claim against IBM and Fujitsu for alleged aiding and abetting of cruel, inhuman and degrading treatment: at *ibid.* 265.

96. Compare *Presbyterian Church of Sudan v Talisman*, 582 F. 3d 244 (2d Cir. 2009) (intent standard) with *Doe I v Unocal*, 395 F. 3d 932, 947 (9th Cir. 2002) (knowing assistance standard). The *Unocal* opinion was withdrawn following the grant of an *en banc* petition for review and settlement by the parties: John R. Crook (ed.), 'Contemporary practice of the United States relating to international law, Notes: tentative settlement of ATCA human rights suits against Unocal' (2005) 99 *American Journal of International Law* 497.

97. *In Re South African Apartheid*, 617 F. Supp. 2d 228, 259–62. Quoted in Mark Hamblett, 'Judge narrows claims in apartheid torts case against multinational corporations' (11 April 2009), Axis of Logic, World News, available at www.axisofligic.com/artman/publish/printer_55422.shtml. For analysis of the lower court's reasoning in *Khulumani* on the issue of *mens rea* in aiding and abetting liability, see Hugh King, 'Corporate accountability under the Alien Tort Claims Act' (2008) 9:2 *Melbourne Journal of International Law* 472. See also *Khulumani v Barclays Bank*, 504 F. 3d 254 (2d Cir. 2007).

98. *In Re South African Apartheid Litigation*, 617 F. Supp. 2d 228, 262, n. 184 (SD NY 2009).

99. *Presbyterian Church of Sudan v Talisman Energy, Inc.*, 453 F. Supp. 2d 633, 657 (SD NY 2006), affirmed 582 F. 3d 244 (2d Cir. 2009).

100. Sherman and Lehr, above n. 35, 8, citing *Presbyterian Church of Sudan v Talisman Energy, Inc.*, 453 F. Supp. 2d 633, 657 (SD NY 2006), affirmed 582 F. 3d 244 (2d Cir. 2009).
101. Lucien J. Dhooge, 'Due diligence as a defense to corporate liability pursuant to the Alien Tort Statute' (2008) 22:2 *Emory International Law Review* 455.
102. *Presbyterian Church of Sudan v Talisman Energy, Inc.*, 453 F. Supp. 2d 633, 657 (SD NY 2006), affirmed 582 F. 3d 244 (2d Cir. 2009) (see 14-15 of the 2 October 2009 judgment).
103. *Doe I v Unocal*, 110 F. Supp. 2d 1294 (CD Cal. 2000), reversed in part, affirmed in part, and remanded, 395 F. 3d 932 (9th Cir. 2002) (opinion withdrawn following settlement and prior to *en banc* ruling). This withdrawn opinion is not precedential, but nevertheless provides guidance regarding how courts will approach aiding and abetting liability: Sherman and Lehr, above n. 35, 8, n. xv. See further Crook , above n. 96, 497–8.
104. *Kiobel v Royal Dutch Petroleum*, No. 06-4876-cv, 2010 WL 3611392 (2d Cir., 17 September 2010).
105. *Ibid.* 6 (majority opinion).
106. *Ibid.* 9. On 4 December 2009, a three-judge panel consisting of Judges Cabranes, Hall and Livingston spontaneously requested supplemental briefing on this issue in the pending appeal in *Balintulo v Daimler AG*, No. 09-2778 (2d Cir.) framing the question as 'whether customary international law recognizes corporate criminal liability': Chimene I. Keitner, '*Kiobel v Royal Dutch Petroleum*: another round in the fight over corporate liability under the Alien Tort Statute' (2010) 14:30 *ASIL Insight* (30 September).
107. *Kiobel v Royal Dutch Petroleum*, above n. 102, 7, quoting *United States v Goering*, International Military Tribunal, Nuremburg, Judgment of 30 September 1946, reprinted in (1946–1947) 6 FRD 69, 110, available at www.uniset.ca/other/cs4/6FRD69.html.
108. *Kiobel v Royal Dutch Petroleum*, above n. 104, 23, n. 12 (Leval J, concurring), citing *Hilao v Estate of Marcos*, 103 F. 3d 767, 776–7 (9th Cir. 1996).
109. *Kiobel v Royal Dutch Petroleum*, above n. 104, 44 (Level J, concurring).
110. *Ibid.* 74 (Level J, concurring). See *Presbyterian Church of Sudan v Talisman Energy Inc.*, 582 F. 3d 244 (2d Cir. 2009).
111. For example, less than ten days before the Second Circuit issued its opinion in *Kiobel*, a California district court reached the same conclusion: see *Doe I v Nestle No. 2*, 05-cv-05133, 121–60 (DC Cal., 8 September 2010). The question of corporate liability was discussed briefly during oral argument before the Ninth Circuit *en banc* in *Sarei v Rio Tinto*, No. 02-56256 (argued 21 September 2010), but other issues have so far predominated in that case; audio recording available at www.ca9.uscourts.gov/media/view_subpage.php?pk_id=0000006103.
112. Keitner, above n. 106, n. 30.
113. US Code Title 28, Part IV, ch. 85, s. 1331 'Federal question' provides 'The district courts shall have original jurisdiction of all civil actions arising under the Constitution, laws, or treaties of the United States'.
114. *Bodner v Banque Paribas*, 114 F. Supp. 2d 117, 127 (FDNY 2000) 127. But *contra Xuncax v Gramajo*, 886 F. Supp. 162, 193–4 (D Mass. 1995). See also Joseph, above n. 24, 77–8.
115. Torture Victim Protection Act of 1991, Pub. L 102-256, 12 March 1992, 106 Stat. 73. USC Title 28, Part IV, ch. 85, s. 1350.
116. *Ibid.*, s. 2(b). In relation to exhaustion under the ATCA, see *Sarei v Rio Tinto*, 550 F. 3d 822 (9th Cir. 2008) where the US Court of Appeals for the 9th Circuit, sitting *en banc* with 11 judges, addressed just one issue: whether a plaintiff seeking ATCA relief must show that he or she exhausted all local remedies or that seeking such local relief would be infeasible or futile. For discussion see 'Jonathan Drimmer on *Sarei v Rio Tinto* 550 F.3d 822 (9th Cir. 2008), *LexisNexis Emerging Issues Analysis*, 4 June 2009.
117. *Ibid.*, s. 2(c).
118. *Bowoto v Chevron*, No. 09-15641, 13–17 (9th Cir., 10 September 2010).
119. *Carlos Abad et al. v Bayer Corp. et al.*, No. 08-1504, 08-2146 (appeal from US DC for the Southern District of Indiana, No. 04 C 5812, Sarah Evans Barker, Judge), 1 May 2009, available at www.intheiropinion.com/uploads/file/abad.pdf (district court judgment affirmed by Posner, Evans and Tinder, Circuit Judges).
120. These jurisdictions include Hong Kong, Malaysia, New Zealand and Singapore.

121. [1987] AC 460.
122. *Ibid.* 476.
123. *Ibid.* 477–8.
124. Per Lord Goff (dissenting) [1987] 477–8; approved in *Voth v Manildra Flour Mills Pty Ltd* (1990) 171 CLR 538, 564–5.
125. *Spiliada*, above n. 121 ([1987] AC 460), per Lord Goff, 482–4; another passage approved in *Voth v Manildra Flour Mills Pty Ltd* (1990) 171 CLR 538, at 564–5.
126. *Spiliada*, above n. 121, 481.
127. *Lubbe v Cape Plc (No. 2)* [2000] 4 All ER 268, 275, per Lord Billingham.
128. *Ibid.* 275. See also *Bayer Polymers Co. Ltd v Industrial and Commercial Bank of China, Hong Kong Branch* [2000] 1 HKC 805.
129. *Spiliada*, above n. 111, per Lord Goff, 482; *Connelly v RTZ Corp Plc* [1998] AC 854, 873, per Lord Goff; *Lubbe v Cape Plc (No. 2)* [2000] 4 All ER 268, 275, per Lord Bingham.
130. See cases listed above n. 129. For discussion see Binda Sahni, 'Limitations of access at the national level: *forum non conveniens*' (2006) 9 *Gonzaga Journal of International Law* 119.
131. (1990) 171 CLR 538.
132. *Oceanic Sun Line Special Shipping Co. v Fay* (1988) 165 CLR 197, 247, per Deane J.
133. *Henry v Henry* (1996) 185 CLR 571; 135 ALR 564; *Regie Nationale de Usines Renault SA v Zhang* (2002) 210 CLR 491, 187 ALR 1; *Dow Jones & Company Inc. v Gutnick* [2002] HCA 56; *Puttick v Tenon Ltd* (2008) 250 ALR 482.
134. See Trans-Tasman Proceedings Act 2010. The Act gives effect to Australia's obligations under the Agreement on Trans-Tasman Court Proceedings and Regulatory Enforcement signed with New Zealand on 24 July 2008. Article 8.1 of the Agreement creates a 'more appropriate forum' test which must be applied whenever a stay is being sought and the other forum in question is in New Zealand. When determining which court is more appropriate, the court must have regard to the following factors: (a) where the parties and the witnesses live; (b) which jurisdiction's law is to be applied; and (c) whether there is an agreement between the parties to the proceeding about the court or place where proceedings should be heard. See also Civil Law (Wrongs) Act 2002 (ACT), s. 220; and Jurisdiction of Courts (Foreign Land) Act 1989 (NSW), ss. 3–4.
135. For discussion, see M. Davies, A.S. Bell and P.L.G. Brereton (eds), *Nygh's Conflict of Laws in Australia* (8th edn, LexisNexis Butterworths,2010) ch. 8. See also Dan Jerker B. Svantesson, 'In defence of the doctrine of *forum non conveniens*' (2005) 35:2 *Hong Kong Law Journal* 395.
136. *Gulf Oil Corp. v Gilbert*, 330 US 501, 67 S Ct 839 (1947); *Koster v American Lumbermens Mutual Casualty Co.,* 330 US 518, 67 S Ct 828 (1947).
137. *Carlos Abad et al. v Bayer Corp. et al.*, No. 08-1504, 08-2146, above n. 109. For discussion, see Martin Davies, 'Time to change the federal *forum non conveniens* analysis' (2002) 77 *Tulsa Law Review* 309.
138. *Piper Aircraft Co. v Reyno*, 454 US 235 (1981); *King v Cessna Aircraft* (CA 11th Cir., 27 March 2009)), Appeal from the US District Court for the Southern District of Florida, available at www.ca11.uscourts.gov/opinions/ops/200811033.pdf.
139. 330 US 501 (1947).
140. James Fawcett (ed..), *Declining Jurisdiction in Private International Law* (Clarendon Press, 1995) 403.
141. *Flores v Southern Peru Copper*, 253 F. Supp. 2d 510, S44 (FD NY 2002). The Circuit Court did not review the *forum non conveniens* decision in *Flores v Southern Peru Copper*, 343 F. 3d 140 (2d Cir. 2003).
142. (2002) 210 CLR 491.
143. For discussion see Gillian Triggs, *International Law: Contemporary Principles and Practices* (2006) ch. 7, 380–92.
144. Passed in 1976 and codified at USC Title 28, ss. 1330, 1332, 1391(f), 1441(d), and 1602–11.
145. Foreign States Immunities Act 1985 (Cth).
146. State Immunity Act RSC 1985, c. S-18.
147. The German submission to the Council of Europe's Database on State Practice regarding

State Immunities uses the term 'relative immunity' rather than restrictive immunity. It is clear, however, that the German courts accept what I have called a restrictive doctrine of sovereign immunity as accepted in international customary law and codified in the European Convention on State Immunity.

148. See the Swedish and German submissions (2005) to the Database on State Practice regarding State Immunities, maintained by the Council of Europe, Human Rights and Legal Affairs section, available at www.coe.int/t/e/legal_affairs/legal_co-operation/public_international_law/state_immunities.

149. USC Title 28 s. 1605A 'Terrorism exception to the jurisdictional immunity of a foreign state'. For discussion see Daniel Bryer, 'Liability under the anti-terrorism exception to the Foreign Sovereign Immunity Act: an expanding definition of "material support or resources"' (2007–2008) 11:2 *Gonzaga Journal of International Law* 1.

150. *Dole Food Co. v Patrickson*, (01-593) 538 US 468 (2003), certiorari dismissed, affirmed No 01-594, reported 251 F. 3d 795.

151. 349 F. Supp. 2d 765, US District Court SD New York, 18 January 2005, *RICO Business Disputes Guide* (CCH) para. 10,804. See also *Filler v Hanvit Bank* where the defendants were commercial banks majority-owned by the Korean Deposit Insurance Corporation (KDIC), a 'government institution' run by the Korean Ministry of Finance and the Economy of the Republic of Korea. The court held that as KDIC was itself an organ of the Korean government, the two defendant banks could not themselves claim that status: *Gary B. Filler and Lawrence Perlman v Hanvit Bank, Chohung Bank and Sinhan Bank*, US Ct. App. 2d Cir., 6 August 2004, available at http://caselaw.lp.findlaw.com/data2/circs/2nd/037861p.pdf.

152. 349 F. Supp. 2d 765, 790. US District Court SD New York, 18 January 2005.

153. *Ibid.*

154. 376 US 398 (1964).

155. *Ibid.* 423–7.

156. Brad J. Kieserman, 'Profits and principles: promoting multinational corporate responsibility by amending the Alien Tort Claims Act' (1998–1999) 48 *Catholic University Law Review* 881, 908.

157. *Sarei et al. v Rio Tinto plc and Rio Tinto Ltd*, 221 F. Supp. 2d 1116 (CD Cal. 9 July 2002), citing *Credit Suisse v United States Dist. Court for the Central Dist. of Cal*, 130 F. 3d 1342, 1346 (9th Cir. 1997); *Banco Nacional de Cuba v Sabbatino*, 376 US 398 (1964); *WS Kirkpatrick & Co. v Environmental Tectonics Corp. International*, 493 US 400 (1990), and *Doe III v Unocal Corp.*, 70 F. Supp. 2d 1073, 1076 (CD Cal. 1999).

158. On appeal by the plaintiffs, a three-judge panel of the Ninth Circuit held, by majority, that most of the plaintiffs' claims could be tried in the United States, and that a corporation can be vicariously liable for the acts of government actors: *Sarei v Rio Tinto*, 487 F. 3d 1193 (9th Cir. 2007). See further above n. 116.

159. For example, the act of state doctrine did not apply in *Bigio v Coca Cola*, 239 F. 3d 440, 451 (2d Cir. 2000); *Wiwa*, 2002 No. 96 Civ. 8386, 2002 US Dist. LEXIS 3293 (SD NY 22 February 2002) 93–4; or *Bodner v Banque Paribas*, 114 F. Supp. 2d 117 (ED NY 2000). In each case, the acts of the former governments of Egypt, Nigeria and France, respectively, had been expressly repudiated by the contemporary governments of those states.

160. United Nations Convention on the Law of the Sea, UN Doc. A/Conf 62/122; (1982) 21 ILM 1261 (entered into force 16 November 1994).

161. *Sarei v Rio Tinto*, 221 F. Supp. 2d 1116, 1192 (CD Cal. 2002), citing *Alfred Dunhill of London Inc. v Republic of Cuba*, 425 US 682, 697 (Sup. Ct 1976), cited in Joseph, above n. 24, 41–2.

162. 244 F. Supp. 2d 289 (SD NY 2003) and see also *Presbyterian Church of Sudan v Talisman Energy, Inc.*, 374 F. Supp. 2d 331 (SD NY 2005) where the district court also denied Talisman's motion to dismiss. Talisman's next attempt to move for judgment on the pleadings was, however, based on a letter from the US Attorney with attachments from the Department of State and Embassy of Canada expressing concern with the litigation: *Presbyterian Church of Sudan v Talisman Energy, Inc.*, No. 1 Civ. 9882(DLC), 2005 WL 2082846, 1 (SD NY 30 August 2005). Despite this letter, the district court again denied Talisman's motion.

163. But note that on 12 September 2006 the district court did grant Talisman's motion for summary judgment as to all claims: *Presbyterian Church of Sudan v Talisman Energy, Inc.*, 453 F. Supp. 2d 633 (SD NY 2006), holding that the plaintiffs had failed to establish Talisman's purposeful complicity in human rights abuses. This decision was affirmed by the US Court of Appeals for the 2nd Circuit on 2 October 2009: *Presbyterian Church of Sudan v Talisman Energy, Inc.* (Docket No. 07-0016-cv).

164. Joseph, above n. 24, 121, citing M. Byers, 'English courts and serious human rights violations abroad: a preliminary assessment' in M. Kamminga and S. Zia-Zarifi (eds), *Liability of Multinational Corporations under International Law* (Kluwer Law International, 2000) 241, 247. See also *Oppenheimer v Cattermole* [1976] AC 249, 278 (HL). In *Oppenheimer*, the House of Lords refused to give effect to a Nazi nationality law that deprived Jews outside Germany of their nationality.

165. 193 F. Supp. 375; affirmed by the Court of Appeals, 307 F. 2d 845. The Court of Appeal decision was, however, reversed by the US Supreme Court on the ground that the act of state doctrine applies and is desirable with regard to a foreign expropriation, even though the expropriation allegedly violates customary international law: *Banco Nacional de Cuba v Sabbatino*, 376 US 398 (1964).

166. 487 F. 3d 1193 (9th Cir. 2007).

167. *Sarei v Rio Tinto*, 221 F. Supp. 2d 1116; 2002 US Dist LEXIS 16235 (at 66 of the judgment). The claims based on discrimination and the UNCLOS were, however, dismissed under the act of state doctrine, as well as under the political question doctrine.

168. Joseph, above n. 24, 44–5, citing L. Brilmayer, 'International law in American courts: a modest proposal' (1991) 100 *Yale Law Journal* 2277, 2305.

169. *Ibid.*

170. F. Supp. 2d 424 (DNJ 1999). Also dismissed due to expiry of the ten-year statute of limitations period.

171. For discussion, see Joseph, above n. 24, 45–6.

172. *Sosa v Alvarez Machain*, 542 US 692 (2004).

173. *Sarei v Rio Tinto*, 487 F. 3d 1193 (9th Cir. 2007). See also *Presbyterian Church v Talisman Energy*, 244 F. Supp. 2d 289, 348 (SD NY 2003). But note *Sarei v Rio Tinto*, 550 F. 3d 822 (9th Cir. 2008) and *Presbyterian Church of Sudan v Talisman* (US Ct App. 2d Cir., 2 October 2009), Docket No. 07-0016-cv.

174. *Hilton v Guyot*, 159 US 113, 164 (1895).

175. See *Restatement (Third) of the Foreign Relations Law of the United States* (2005) s. 403(1).

176. *Presbyterian Church of Sudan v Talisman Energy Inc.*, No. 01 Civ 9882 (DLC), 2005 WL 2082846, 1 (SD NY 30 August 2005).

177. *Ibid.* 5–8. See also *Bigio v Coca Cola Co.* (2d Cir. 2006) Docket No. 05-2426, where the US Court of Appeals reversed and remanded the judgment of the US District Court for the Southern District of New York which had dismissed the complaint on grounds of international comity and *forum non conveniens*: *Bigio v Coca-Cola Co.*, No. 97 Civ. 2858, 2005 US Dist LEXIS 1587 (SD NY 3 February 2005).

178. *Ibid.* 7. See also *Presbyterian Church of Sudan v Talisman* (US Ct App. 2d Cir., 2 October 2009)), Docket No. 07-0016-cv, 19–20.

179. Catherine Boyle, 'Portrait: Ken Saro-Wiwa', *Sunday Times*, 26 May 2009, available at http://business.timesonline.co.uk/tol/business/industry_sectors/natural_resources/article6364435.ece.

5. Corporate criminal liability for extra-territorial harms

A. INTRODUCTION: THE EXERCISE OF CRIMINAL JURISDICTION

As long ago as 1927, the Permanent Court of International Justice (PCIJ)[1] considered the question of whether the exercise of criminal jurisdiction by a state should be governed by different principles to those governing the exercise of civil jurisdiction. The court began by noting that the application of different rules to the exercise of criminal jurisdiction 'might be the outcome of the close connection which for a long time existed between the conception of supreme criminal jurisdictions and that of a State and also by the especial importance of criminal jurisdiction from the point of view of the individual'. The court concluded that:

> Though it is true that in all systems of law the principle of the territorial character of criminal law is fundamental, it is equally true that all or nearly all of these systems of law extend their action to offences committed outside the territory of the State which adopts them, and they do so in ways which vary from State to State.[2]

Since the Second World War, globalization has seen an expansion of the willingness of states to enact and implement extra-territorial criminal legislation with extra-territorial effect, and to make such legislation applicable to legal persons as well as natural persons. Thus, in 2006 a comprehensive survey of national legislation in 16 countries from a variety of legal traditions (the Fafo Institute Survey) found not only that most countries permit legal persons to be prosecuted for criminal offences, but also that there has been widespread adoption of international criminal law at the national (domestic) level.[3] Since the coming into effect of the Rome Statute establishing the International Criminal Court, a significant number of states have also passed legislation to provide for the investigation and prosecution of the serious crimes falling under the jurisdiction of the ICC, and many have ensured that such legislation extends to legal persons.

B. EXTRA-TERRITORIAL CRIMINAL LEGISLATION APPLICABLE TO TNCs

1. Overview

The 2006 Fafo Institute Survey collected information from 16 countries as to their domestic laws relating to the accountability of TNCs.[4] The results of the survey revealed that the surveyed countries had all enacted, to differing degrees, some form of extra-territorial legislation aimed at regulating the activities of TNCs. The results of the survey also indicated that most countries permit legal persons to be prosecuted for criminal offences. The significance of such a finding is that state practice within the domestic laws of many countries, across a variety of legal systems and traditions, has expanded criminal laws to include corporate entities. It is not inconceivable that the generation of such state practice will become an important underpinning of the emerging international customary law of TNC responsibility.

The Fafo Institute Survey found that it is prevailing practice to apply criminal liability to (corporate) legal persons in 11 of the countries surveyed: Australia, Belgium, Canada,[5] France, India, Japan, the Netherlands, Norway, South Africa, the United Kingdom and the United States. In five countries (Argentina, Germany, Indonesia, Spain and the Ukraine) current jurisprudence does not recognize corporate criminal liability. In two of those countries (Argentina and Indonesia), the national legislature has ignored conceptual issues and has adopted specific statutes making legal persons liable for important crimes (e.g., environmental crimes, commercial crimes, corruption and terrorism). Germany has an interesting statute (Gesetz über Ordnungswidrigkeiten, Administrative Offences Act, s. 30) under which a legal person whose representative has committed a crime or an administrative offence may be held liable for payment of the monetary penalty imposed upon such representative.[6]

While the manner in which a business entity or legal person may be found liable for a crime varies from jurisdiction to jurisdiction, one of the key features found in most domestic legislation is a requirement that an employee have a certain status within a company and be acting within the scope of her employment when committing the alleged illegal act. Furthermore, many statutes specify how and when the necessary criminal 'intent' (*mens rea*) can be attributed to the business entity.

Various countries have developed different methods for attributing the actions of a responsible employee or board member to a company for purposes of finding intent and imposing criminal liability. Australia's Criminal Code is perhaps the most extensive, and provides that fault may be attributed to a body corporate that 'expressly, tacitly, or impliedly authorised or permitted' the commission of a criminal offence.[7] There are four ways of establishing that such authorization took place:

(a)   proving that the body corporate's board of directors intentionally, knowingly or recklessly carried out the relevant conduct, or expressly, tacitly or impliedly authorized or permitted the commission of the offence; or

(b)   proving that a high managerial agent of the body corporate intentionally, knowingly or recklessly engaged in the relevant conduct, or expressly, tacitly or impliedly authorized or permitted the commission of the offence; this basis of liability is subject to a defence of due diligence under s. 12.3(3);

(c)   proving that a 'corporate culture'[8] existed within a body corporate that directed, encouraged or tolerated or led to non-compliance with a relevant provision of the Criminal Code;

(d)   proving that the body corporate failed to create and maintain a 'corporate culture' that required compliance with a relevant provision of the Criminal Code; if this is proven, the corporation can be held to have authorized a breach of that provision.[9]

The Fafo Institute Survey also found that all of the 16 countries surveyed have statutes in place that address corporate complicity. Although the wording of the relevant statutory language varies from country to country, complicity – or aiding and abetting another in the commission of a crime – was found to be a crime in itself in the domestic law of every one of the countries surveyed, and the survey authors concluded that it was likely that complicity (i.e. aiding and abetting the criminal acts of another) is a crime in the laws of most countries throughout the world.

Most statutes define criminal complicity using concepts such as 'aiding', 'abetting', 'accessory' (e.g. Japan, Germany), 'solicitation', 'facilitation', etc. Those which define 'aiding' do so in such terminology as 'aid and abet by providing the opportunity, the means or information to commit a crime' (the Netherlands, Indonesia), or 'aids, abets, counsels, commands, induces or procures' (United States). Differences exist in the rules governing the *actus reus* and *mens rea* requirements for criminal complicity. With regards to the *mens rea* requirement in domestic criminal laws, many countries, including the Netherlands and Germany for example, have accepted the international criminal law standard of 'knowledge' for establishing the criminal guilt of a defendant (including corporate defendants) charged with complicity.[10]

2.   US RICO Statute

In the United States, the Racketeer Influenced and Corrupt Organizations Act

(RICO),[11] provides not only for extended criminal penalties, but also establishes a civil cause of action for acts performed as part of an ongoing criminal organization. Under RICO, a person associated with an enterprise guilty of a pattern of racketeering can be charged with racketeering. A pattern of racketeering is established if the enterprise has committed any two of 35 crimes within a ten-year period. A defendant found liable under RICO is susceptible to triple damages and the plaintiff's legal costs, as well as to criminal penalties. While RICO defendants are usually individuals associated with a criminal enterprise (which may be a corporation), an action under RICO also lies against a corporate defendant that has acted in concert with one or more partners in the commission of alleged crimes.

Like a number of other federal criminal statutes, the RICO is silent as to whether it applies extra-territorially. RICO's reach to extra-territorial conduct has been a source of disagreement among the federal circuit courts. There is a presumption that Congressional legislation 'unless a contrary intent appears, is meant to apply *only* within the territorial jurisdiction of the United States'.[12] However, some courts have avoided the impact of this presumption by finding that where extra-territorial acts have substantial effects inside the United States, the court may exercise jurisdiction. In *United States v Philip Morris* (2009), the DC Circuit Court reasoned that:

> [b]ecause conduct with substantial domestic effects implicates a state's legitimate interest in protecting its citizens within its borders, Congress's regulation of foreign conduct meeting this 'effects' test is '*not* an *extraterritorial* assertion of jurisdiction'.[13]

In *Wiwa v Royal Dutch Petroleum Co* (2002),[14] the plaintiffs claimed that the defendants violated RICO in that they engaged in an enterprise in the Ogoni oilfields with the Nigerian military and an unaffiliated company, Willbros West Africa, to perform acts such as murder (of environmental protestors), arson, extortion and bribery. As the defendants' racketeering activities allegedly forced the plaintiffs to sell and therefore abandon their property and businesses, the plaintiffs had suffered relevant damage for the purposes of RICO. The relevant effects inside the United States were that (i) 40 per cent of the oil extracted from the relevant operations was exported to the United States, and (ii) the defendants hoped to gain a significant competitive advantage from the lower production costs entailed in their 'unlawful exploitation of the Ogoni oil fields'. The court accepted that these economic effects inside the United States could give rise to RICO jurisdiction.[15]

3. Indonesia and Criminal Liability for Environmental Damage

In Indonesia, the Penal Code, which was inherited from the Dutch colonial period and dates from early 1900, does not recognize the legal entity as a subject of criminal law. It was not until 1955 that Indonesia enacted a Law on Economic Crimes[16] which does allow a legal entity to be subject to criminal liability. Other legislation recognizing legal entities as subject of criminal law has also been enacted.[17] However, the relevant provisions have rarely been invoked, as traditionally when a legal entity has been involved in a crime, the responsible director(s) or other person in charge has been brought to court on the basis of personal responsibility. This is similar to the practice in countries where legal persons cannot be prosecuted, where it is still possible to pursue management and directors of companies that are complicit in internationally-recognized crimes.

In Indonesia, the traditional reluctance of the authorities to prosecute corporations under criminal laws was recently overcome when TNC Newmont Mining was criminally prosecuted for violations of Indonesian Law No. 23 (1997) on the environment. Article 41 of that law makes it a criminal offence for any natural or legal person to intentionally or negligently pollute the environment. The first trial for alleged breach of article 41 involved the Indonesian mining joint venture of Newmont Mining, located in Buyat Bay, North Suluwesi.[18] It was alleged that certain gold mine wastes pumped offshore by PT Newmont Minahasa Raya (PTNMR) contained toxic levels of a variety of poisons, which caused illness in a local fishing village. Prior to the criminal case under Law No. 23 of 1997, a civil lawsuit was submitted by the Indonesian Environment Ministry in March 2005 demanding that PTNMR and its president director, Richard Ness, pay compensation of US$117.68 million for lost income and environmental damage and US$16.3 million for damaging Indonesia's reputation.[19] The South Jakarta District Court threw out the lawsuit in November 2005, ruling that under the terms of the government's contract with PTNMR, any dispute must be settled through international arbitration or conciliation. The matter was eventually settled for US$30 million.[20] An independent scientific panel was also established under a 'Goodwill Agreement' entered into by the Indonesian government and PTNMR to monitor the seawater quality and environmental health of Buyat Bay.[21]

The criminal lawsuit was brought in August 2005 alleging that PTNMR and Richard Ness were guilty of intentionally or negligently polluting Buyat Bay with toxic tailings waste from the now exhausted gold mine. The charges stemmed from police and environmental group accusations that the company pumped potentially lethal amounts of mercury and arsenic into Buyat Bay, near its mining site in Minahasa regency, causing local villagers to suffer skin diseases, neurological disorders and other health problems. After one of the longest criminal proceedings in Indonesian history lasting 21 months, the Manado District Court, in a decision handed down by a panel of five judges on 24 April 2007, ruled that PTNMR and its president Richard Ness had not polluted Buyat Bay, and both the company and Ness were cleared of all charges.[22] The Public Prosecutor then appealed to the Supreme Court in May 2007, in response to which PTNMR filed a counter-memorandum objecting to the appeal.[23] In October 2008, a panel of Supreme Court judges was assigned to consider the appeal.[24]

In addition, on 22 March 2007, an NGO Wahana Lingkungan Hidup Indonesia (WALHI) filed a civil lawsuit against PTNMR and Indonesia's Ministry of Energy and Mineral Resources and Ministry for the Environment, alleging pollution from the disposal of mine tailings into Buyat Bay, and seeking a court order requiring PTNMR to fund a 25-year monitoring programme in relation to Buyat Bay. In December 2007, the court ruled in PTNMR's favour and found that WALHI's allegations of pollution in Buyat Bay were without merit. WALHI appealed this decision to the Indonesian Supreme Court in October 2008.[25]

Indonesian Law No. 23 of 1997 was replaced in 2009 by Law No. 32 on Environmental Protection and Management.[26] Although the new Environmental Law includes many of the provisions and practices of the 1997 Environmental Law and its implementing regulations, it also contains certain key changes. As with many other new laws issued in Indonesia, the implementation of the new Environmental Law is largely dependent on the issuance of implementing regulations to be issued by 3 October 2010, within a year of the new Law's entry into effect.[27] Key improvements under the 2009 Environmental Law include the addition of a new requirement for entities to obtain an environmental permit, which is a prerequisite to obtaining other relevant business permits. An environmental permit may be revoked by the issuing authority or the State Administrative Court in certain circumstances, including where the permit holder fails to meet requirements specified in a relevant environmental impact assessment statement or recommended environmental management and monitoring effort.[28] Holders of environmental permits must set aside funds to be used as a type of environmental bond for the purpose of environmental rehabilitation and recovery. Entities whose activities are likely to have a significant impact on the environment or entities that are suspected of non-compliance with environmental regulations must also carry out periodic environmental audits.[29]

Indonesia's new Environmental Law also gives more rights to community and environmental NGOs to file legal claims concerning environmental pollution or damage, as well as providing for immunity from prosecution or civil claims for any person who fights for a sustainable and healthy environment.[30] In addition to increased administrative and criminal penalties for violations of its provisions, the 2009 Environmental Law also imposes penalties on government officials who grant environmental permits without following proper procedures.[31]

4. International Treaties and Corporate Criminal Liability

A great deal of extra-territorial criminal legislation is based upon international treaties. One of the most important of these treaties is the United Nations Convention against Transnational Organized Crime (CATOC), adopted by General Assembly Resolution 55/25 of 15 November 2000. The CATOC is now the main international instrument in the fight against transnational organized crime.[32] It entered into force on 29 September 2003, and is supplemented by three Protocols targeting specific areas and manifestations of organized crime: the Protocol to Prevent, Suppress and Punish Trafficking in Persons, Especially Women and Children; the Protocol Against the Smuggling of Migrants by Land, Sea and Air; and the Protocol Against the Illicit Manufacturing of and Trafficking in Firearms, their Parts and Components and Ammunition.[33]

Other treaties forming the basis of extra-territorial legislation have focussed upon combating transnational corruption and money laundering activities. The Rome Statute of the International Criminal Court has also provoked new national legislation providing for the exercise of local jurisdiction in respect of the serious crimes listed in the Statute.[34] When criminal legislation is based upon the terms of an international treaty there is a greater degree of uniformity in different jurisdictions around the world, and the implementation of such legislation is more likely to receive international acceptance and assistance. Anti-money laundering and anti-corruption legislation provide good examples of such legislation.

(a) Anti-money laundering legislation

Following Senate-level investigations carried out in 1999–2001, US anti-money laundering legislation was significantly strengthened with the passing of Title III of the USA Patriot Act in 2001,[35] also known as the International Money Laundering Abatement and Financial Anti-Terrorism Act of 2001. It stands on its own as a separate Act of Congress as well as being part of the USA Patriot Act, and is an amended version of the 1986 Money Laundering Control Act and the 1970 Bank Secrecy Act. The earlier Acts tended to focus on preventing money laundering and international cash flow as it related to the drug trade, to gambling, smuggling, or other types of criminal activity. In the 2001 version, the focus has shifted towards money laundering as a means of financing international terrorism. Among other key provisions, Title III obligates US financial institutions to exercise due diligence when opening and administering accounts for foreign political figures, and deems corrupt acts by foreign officials as an allowable basis for US money laundering prosecutions. It is also a federal crime to 'knowingly provid[e] material support or resources to a foreign terrorist organization'.[36]

In Europe, as elsewhere, early money laundering legislation was primarily directed towards drug-related crimes. More recently, in October 2005 the European Parliament and Council approved the Third EU Money Laundering Directive to expand and modernize the coverage of earlier Directives providing for a coordinated approach to combating money laundering.[37] The terms of the Third Directive, which have now been implemented throughout the EU,[38] expressly recognize the need for significant penalties, including criminal penalties, to combat the laundering of money from all types of crimes, and by all types of financial institutions. Article 41 also recognizes that such penalties must be adapted and extended to legal persons which 'are often involved in complex money laundering or terrorist financing operations'.[39]

It was in a case involving Riggs Bank[40] that US and EU anti-money laundering provisions came into play simultaneously. On 15 July 2004, the US Senate published a Report on its investigations into the *Enforcement and Effectiveness of the PATRIOT Act*.[41] The Report included a detailed case study of money laundering and corruption offences committed by and within Riggs Bank. These offences included using shell companies and hiding accounts from federal regulators so as to allow the former Chilean dictator Augusto Pinochet to retain access to much of his fortune during the period 1994–2004, including periods during which Pinochet was in prison and on trial for crimes against humanity. Riggs Bank was also the bank into which much of the oil revenues from Equatorial Guinea were paid until the Bank was investigated by the US Senate. The investigation revealed that Riggs Bank accounts based at the embassy to the United States of Equatorial Guinea were allowed to make large withdrawals without properly notifying federal authorities. At least US$35 million was siphoned off by long-time dictator of Equatorial Guinea, Teodoro Obiang Nguema Mbasogo, his family and senior officials of his regime.[42]

In the United States, Riggs Bank was fined US$25 million in May 2004 for violations of money-laundering laws.[43] In February 2005, the bank and the Allbritton family also agreed to pay US$9 million to Pinochet victims for concealing and illegally moving Pinochet money out of Britain.[44] No similar payment was ever made with regard to Equatorial Guinea.

Meanwhile, in Spain, a Spanish magistrate indicted certain principal officers of Riggs Bank for violating Spanish court orders to freeze assets of General Augusto Pinochet. Spanish lawyers representing victims of Pinochet initiated the Riggs Bank indictment as Spanish law, unusually, makes it possible for citizens to initiate a criminal complaint. This law also enabled the NGO Asociación Pro Derechos Humanos de España (APDHE) to submit a formal complaint (Querella) to Instructing Judge Baltasar Garzon against the Obiang family for embezzlement of the Equatorial Guinea funds.[45] The following day, on 23 October 2008, the case was referred to the office of the National

Criminal Court Prosecutor (Fiscal de la Audiencia Nacional), which found there was a case to answer and transferred the case, in turn, to the Pre-Trial Investigative Court in Las Palmas, Gran Canaria, the location of the Banco Santander account where the money was received.[46]

The Spanish Penal Code makes it a crime for anyone to acquire, convert or transfer property knowing such property was purchased using proceeds from a serious crime, or for anyone to perform any other act to conceal or disguise the unlawful origin of funds or to aid another person who has participated in a crime in evading the legal consequences of the crime. The fact that the crime (e.g., the embezzlement that occurred in the Riggs Bank cases) has been committed abroad is irrelevant because the Spanish Penal Code grants jurisdiction to the Spanish courts over money laundering cases occurring in Spain, regardless of where the underlying crime occurred.[47]

Despite the terms of article 41 of the Third EU Directive on Money Laundering, there remains a vigorous debate in Spain over whether it is appropriate to impose criminal liability on corporations.[48] Spanish criminal law still does not allow for the imposition of corporate criminal liability per se, and those against altering this situation argue that corporate entities are incapable of engaging in conduct, of possessing a criminal mental state, or of suffering the physical pain associated with punishment. On the other hand, modern advocates of corporate criminal responsibility contend that corporations are indeed capable of organizing themselves in a way that is relevant to the criminal law, that they do possess certain organizational awareness that meets the *mens rea* standard of knowledge/criminal intent, and that corporations may suffer the pain associated with social stigma.[49] This debate possibly helps to explain Spain's failure to implement the terms of the Third Directive by 2009, although a draft implementation Act was released on 3 April 2009 for consultation prior to presentation to Parliament.[50]

Corporations are, however, subject to various types of non-criminal sanctions and civil liability under the Spanish Criminal Code.[51] In addition, as a means of combating national and international organized criminal activity, article 129 of the Spanish Criminal Code provides for five derivative (or ancillary) consequences that may be imposed upon legal persons for certain types of offences. The sanctions that may be imposed pursuant to this provision include the temporary or permanent closure of business premises; suspension of business activities for up to five years;[52] winding up of the legal person; prohibition on the conduct of certain types of business, and/or placing the legal person under temporary judicial administration.[53] These measures are similar to penalties for corporate persons proposed by the European Union in several Council Framework Decisions adopted since 2000.[54] In addition, article 31.2 of the Spanish Criminal Code was amended in 2004 to establish joint and several liability of corporations for payment of criminal fines imposed on their managers.[55] The sanctions provided for in articles 129 and 31 of the Criminal Code are, however, seldom imposed by Spanish courts, and when they are it is usually for conduct related to environmental crimes. Many commentators tend to view such sanctions as administrative-style penalties that can be imposed on dangerous corporations.[56]

(b)   Anti-bribery and anti-corruption laws

International conventions also play a key role in addressing the worldwide and cross-border nature of corruption. It is precisely because transnational corruption thrives on differences in regulations among countries that harmonization of national legislation is of the utmost importance. International anti-corruption conventions are thus more essential than ever in an increasingly interconnected world. The range of anti-corruption conventions and instruments that exist today are the result of an international consensus that emerged in the 1990s. Since then, the international legal framework prohibiting bribery and other forms of corruption has expanded dramatically.

At the UN level, it was on the 16 December 1996 that the United Nations adopted a Declaration Against Corruption and Bribery in International Commercial Transactions.[57] The Declaration, which is non-binding, nonetheless purports to commit UN members to criminalize bribery in an effective and coordinated manner, and to deny tax deductibility for bribes. Approximately a year later, the 1996 UN Declaration was endorsed by the (then) 29 member states of the Organisation for Economic Co-operation and Development (OECD) adopting the Convention on Combating Bribery of Foreign Public Officials in International Business Transactions ('OECD Anti-Bribery Convention').[58] In adopting this convention, OECD members agreed to establish legislation criminalizing the bribing of foreign public officials by the end of 1998.[59] By 2010, all of the 31 members of the OECD, plus seven non-member countries (Argentina, Brazil, Bulgaria, Estonia, Israel, Slovenia and South Africa) had adopted the OECD Anti-Bribery Convention.[60] However, enforcement of its provisions remains uneven. For example, in October 2008, an OECD working group strongly criticized the United Kingdom for failing to bring its anti-bribery laws in line with the OECD Anti-Bribery Convention and other international standards. The UK government responded with a new draft Bribery Bill[61] which was introduced into the House of Lords on 19 November 2009. The UK Bribery Act 2010 received Royal Assent on 8 April 2010. In addition to codifying and clarifying existing law, the Act also introduces several new offences including, for the first time, the specific offence of bribing a foreign official, and provisions to enhance corporate liability.[62]

The OECD Anti-Bribery Convention was supplemented in 1997 by the OECD Council's Revised Recommendation of the Council on Bribery in International Business Transactions.[63] This Recommendation was succeeded in 2009 by the Recommendation of the Council for Further Combating Bribery of Foreign Public Officials in International Business Transactions,[64] which in turn was amended by the Council in 2010 to reflect the inclusion of Annex II, *Good Practice Guidance on Internal Controls, Ethics and Compliance*.[65] Sections IV–VII of the 2009 Recommendation deal with 'Criminalisation of Bribery of Foreign Public Officials'. Annex I of the 2009 Recommendation, *Good Practice Guidance on Implementing Specific Articles* of the OECD Anti-Bribery Convention, contains specific recommendations on implementing art. 2 of the Convention concerning responsibility of legal persons. This is further supplemented by Part A 'Good Practice Guidance for Companies' in Annex II of the Recommendation.[66] The 2009 Recommendation falls short, however, of recommending the imposition of criminal penalties on corporate entities found guilty of corruption offences.

Within the European context, and also in 1997, the Ministers of Justice of the Council of Europe recommended that efforts be intensified to ensure the adoption of a Criminal Law Convention on Corruption[67] to provide for a coordinated criminalization of corruption offences and for enhanced cooperation in the prosecution of offences. The Convention opened for signature in 1999, and entered into force on 1 July 2002. By June 2010, there were 43 parties to the Criminal Law Convention on Corruption, while seven states (including the United States and Mexico as non-EU members) had signed without ratification.[68]

Meanwhile, the UN General Assembly recognized that a formally binding and therefore more effective version of the Declaration Against Bribery and Corruption was desirable, and so in 2000 established an ad hoc committee for the negotiation of such an instrument.[69] The UN Convention Against Corruption was adopted by the General Assembly in October 2003,[70] and entered into force on 14 December 2005 with 140 signatories.[71] By June 2010, the Convention Against Corruption had 145 parties, including both states and regional organizations such as the European Union.[72] Article 26 of the Convention obliges states parties to 'adopt such measures as may be necessary ... to establish the liability of legal persons for participation in the offences established' in accordance with the Convention. In recognition of the difficulty some legal systems have with recognizing the criminal liability of corporations, however, article 26 further provides that the liability of legal persons for offences described in the Convention 'may be criminal, civil or administrative'.[73]

In the United States it is noticeable that the Foreign Corrupt Practices Act 1977[74] (FCPA) has been more successful than the Alien Tort Claims Act (ATCA) in terms of the number of successful prosecutions brought under it. Jonathan Clough suggests that the FCPA provides a model for legislative reform aimed at enabling the successful prosecution of parent companies for human rights abuses committed by their overseas operations.[75] In particular, the two major attributes of the FCPA which make it a good model for reforming legislation elsewhere are first, the way it has been specifically designed to apply to corporate legal persons, and second, the way it makes use of a variety of bases of jurisdiction to extend its coverage as broadly as possible.

The FCPA imposes criminal liability on corporations with respect to certain practices involving the bribery of foreign officials. Under section 78dd-3a(a) of the FCPA, it is an offence for any person, 'while in the territory of the United States, corruptly to make use of the mails or any means or instrumentality of interstate commerce or do any other act in furtherance of [a prohibited transaction]'. 'Person' for these purposes is defined to include both individuals and companies, including companies incorporated outside the United States that have a principal place of business within the United States. Under section 78dd-2(a) of the FCPA it is an offence for any domestic US concern, 'or for any officer, director, employee, or agent of such domestic concern, to make use of the mails or any means or instrumentality of interstate commerce corruptly in furtherance of [certain prohibited transactions relating to foreign officials]'. The FCPA also applies to conduct of a 'United States person' acting outside the United States, whether or not the person 'makes use of the mails or any means or instrumentality of interstate commerce'.[76]

C.   ROME STATUTE OF THE INTERNATIONAL CRIMINAL COURT AND DOMESTIC LEGAL SYSTEMS

As of June 2010, 111 states had ratified or acceded[77] to the Rome Statute, while a further 38 states had signed but not ratified the treaty.[78] The Rome Statute obliges states parties to pass procedural legislation to facilitate cooperation with the ICC in the investigation and prosecution of crimes, including the arrest and surrender of suspects. Part 9 of the Statute requires all states parties to 'ensure that there are procedures available under their national law for all of the forms of cooperation which are specified under this Part'. By April 2006, 39 states parties had legislation in place implementing Rome Statute cooperation obligations, while a further 27 state parties had draft legislation aimed at implementing cooperation obligations.[79]

Under the Rome Statute's complementarity principle, the International Criminal Court only has jurisdiction over cases where the relevant state is unwilling or unable to investigate and, if appropriate, prosecute the case itself.[90] Therefore, many states have passed national legislation to provide for the investigation and prosecution of crimes that fall under the jurisdiction of the ICC. By April 2006, over 33 countries had passed complementarity legislation, while draft legislation implementing complementarity obligations existed in another 37 states.[81]

Even in those countries which are not party to the Rome Statute (including Japan, India, Indonesia, Ukraine and the United States), there is legislation incorporating one or more of the three Rome Convention crimes into its domestic legislation. This wide-spread pattern of incorporation is significant in that it makes clear that some of the important limitations on the jurisdiction of the ICC under the Rome Convention have been eliminated by domestic legislation. In particular, article 25 of the Rome Statute limits the ICC's jurisdiction to crimes by individuals (natural persons). In contrast, many countries which have incorporated international criminal law into their domestic statutes include legal persons within the coverage of their international criminal law legislation.[82]

In addition, the domestic criminal statutes of many countries apply extra-territorially to cover grave breaches of international criminal law (ICL) either committed by or causing injury to their own nationals. This is the case in 11 of the 16 countries surveyed by the Fafo Institute: Argentina, Australia, Belgium, Canada, Germany Japan, Norway, South Africa, Ukraine, United Kingdom and United States.[83] In a few cases, such as India, the international criminal law statutes of the home country apply only to their own nationals' acts abroad.[84]

The domestic ICL statutes of some countries extend to grave breaches of ICL throughout the world through application of the concept of universal jurisdiction. Whereas article 12(2) of the Rome Statute limits the ICC's own jurisdiction to crimes committed by nationals of states parties and crimes committed on the territory of state parties, domestic ICL legislation in several countries is applicable universally. Australia, Canada,[85] South Africa,[86] New Zealand,[87] the Netherlands,[88] Spain[89] and United Kingdom[90] are examples of countries where crimes legislation applies to persons who commit grave breaches of ICL anywhere in the world, irrespective of the nationality of the perpetrators or the victims.

D. CONCLUSION

Significant differences exist between jurisdictions in national approaches to corporate liability. Some countries recognize that principles of criminal liability can be applied to legal persons, while other legal systems have difficulty in accepting such an approach. Some legislatures have been concerned with facilitating compensation for victims of wrongful acts, while other governments have been more concerned with ensuring the perpetrators of such acts are punished. Such differences send conflicting signals to TNCs as to the standards of behaviour expected of them and the principles of liability that they can expect will be applied to their actions. Jurisdictional differences also encourage forum shopping by both plaintiffs and corporate defendants. What therefore needs to be explored is the possibility of internationally agreed standards for TNC responsibility, akin to the rules for state responsibility that already exist in international law. In Chapters 6 and 7, I explore this possibility.

NOTES

1. The predecessor of the International Court of Justice (ICJ) established under the League of Nations Charter. The Statute of the PCIJ later became the basis for the Statute of the ICJ, which is an integral part of the United Nations Charter.
2. *SS Lotus*, PCIJ Ser. A No. 10 (1927) 17.
3. Anita Ramasastry and Robert C. Thompson, *Commerce, Crime and Conflict: Legal Remedies for Private Sector Liability for Grave Breaches of International Law: A Survey of Sixteen Countries*, Fafo Report 536 (Norway, September), Norway; available at www.fafo.no/pub/rapp/536/536.pdf ('Fafo Institute Survey'). This survey followed an earlier pilot study of five countries, Fafo and International Peace Academy, *Business and International Crimes: Assessing the Liability of Business Entities for Grave Violations of International Law* (Fafo, 2003), available at www.fafo.no/liabilities/467.pdf.
4. Fafo Institute Survey, above n. 3.
5. Canadian Criminal Code (RS 1985, c-46), s. 1 and Interpretation Act, RS 1985, c. 1-21, s. 35. For a discussion of the Canadian approach to criminal corporate liability, particularly how *mens rea* is determined, see *Canadian Dredge & Dock Co. v The Queen* [1985] 1 SCR 662 (SCC).
6. Fafo Institute Survey, above n. 3, 15.
7. Commonwealth Criminal Code Act 1995 (Cth), s. 12.3.
8. The term corporate culture means an attitude, policy, rule, course of conduct or practice existing within the body corporate generally or in the part of the body corporate in which the relevant activities take place.
9. Commonwealth Criminal Code Act 1995 (Cth), s. 12.3.
10. Fafo Institute Survey, above n. 3, ' Summary of findings', 17–22, noting that under international criminal law, as set forth by the International Criminal Tribunals for Rwanda and the former Yugoslavia, the appropriate *mens rea* for determining the guilt of an accomplice is 'knowledge'; citing *Prosecutor v Jean-Paul Akayesu*, Case No. ICTR-96-4-T, 2 September 1998, para. 90, report available at www.fafo.no/liabilities. Compare art. 25 of the Rome Statute of the International Criminal Court, opened for signature 17 July 1998, 2187 UNTS 3 (entered into force 1 July 2002), which provides, *inter alia*, for individual liability in respect of international law crimes whenever a person 'contributes to the commission or attempted commission of such a crime by a group of persons acting with a common purpose ... [where] the contribution is intentional and ... [is] made in the knowledge of the intention of the group to commit the crime'. Article 25(2)(c) also expressly provides for aiding and abetting liability where the act of aiding or assisting is 'For the purpose of facilitating the commission of ... a crime [within the jurisdiction of the Court]'.
11. RICO was enacted by s. 901(a) of the Organized Crime Control Act of 1970 (Pub L 91-452, 84 Stat 922, enacted 15 October 1970). RICO is codified as Title 18 Chapter 96 of the United States Code, 18 USC ss. 1961–1968.
12. *British American Tobacco (Investments) Ltd v United States*, Petition for a Writ of Certiorari, 08-980 (February 2010) at i, citing *EEOC v Arabian Am Oil Co.*, 499 US 244, 248 (1991). Discussed in Robert G. Morvillo and Robert J. Anello, 'Federal RICO Statute: extraterritorial reach and other recent issues', 243:64 *New York Law Journal*, 6 April 2010.

13. 566 F. 3d 1095, 1130 (DC Cir. 2009), citing *Laker Airways v Sabena, Belgian World Airlines*, 731 F. 2d 909 (DC Cir. 1984) (emphasis in original).
14. *Wiwa v Royal Dutch Petroleum Co.*, No. 96 Civ. 8386, 2002 US; Dist LEXIS 3293 (SD NY 2002, unreported).
15. *Ibid.*
16. Law No. 7/ Drt/1955.
17. Indonesian legislation recognizing legal entities as subjects of criminal law include: Law No. 4 of 1982 on Environment (amended by Law No. 23 of 1997 and by Law No. 32 of 2010 on Environmental Protection and Management); Law No. 5 of 1997 on Psychotropic Drugs; Law No. 22 of 1997 on Narcotics; Law No. 10 of 1998 on Banking; Law No. 31 of 1999 on Corruption as amended by Law No. 20 of 2001;Law No. 15 of 2002 on Terrorism; Law No. 23 of 2004 on Child Protection; and Law No. 15 of 2003 on Money Laundering.
18. Fafo Institute Survey, above n. 3, 'Indonesia: Survey Questions and Responses', 4; available at www.fafo.no/liabilities/CCCSurveyIndonesia06Sep2006.pdf.
19. 'Newmont to pay $30 million to end civil law suit' (16 February 2006), MAC: Mines and Communities website, available at www.minesandcommunities.org/article.php?a=1380.
20. *Ibid.*
21. Fidelis E. Satriastanti, 'Newmont didn't pollute Buyat, new study finds', *Jakarta Globe*, 24 May 2010, available at www.thejakartaglobe.com/home/newmont-mining-didnt-pollute-buyat-new-study-finds/376713.
22. Dorothy Kosich, 'Newmont Minahasa Raya's Richard Ness cleared by Indonesian court over gold mine' (24 April 2007), Mineweb, available at www.mineweb.net/mineweb/view/mineweb/en/page68?oid=19984&sn=Detail.
23. Fact Sheet, *No. Grounds for Appeal in the Buyat Bay Case*, available at www.buyatbayfacts.com/pdfs_docs/TrialFactSheet91907.pdf. 'Indonesia prosecutors challenge Newmont verdict' (8 May 2007), *Terra Daily*, available at www.terradaily.com/reports/Indonesia_Prosecutors_Challenge_Newmont_Verdict_999.html.
24. Newmont Mining Corporation, *Annual Report 2008*, 'Notes to the Financial Statements', Note 33 'Commitments and contingencies (PT Newmont Minahasa Raya (PTNMR) – 80% Newmont owned', available at http://investor.shareholder.com/newmont/AR2008/note33.cfm.
25. *Ibid.*
26. Fadjar Kandar and Deny Sidharta, 'New environmental law: better protection or more legal hurdles for industry', *ALB Legal News*, 31 May 2010, available at http://asia.legalbusinessonline.com/site-search/new-environmental-law-better-protection-or-more-legal-hurdles-for-industry/46199. See also 'Pertamina not ready to follow the Law No. 32/2009' (5 April 2010), available at http://www.tenderoffer.biz/news/281-headline/3064-pertamina-not-ready-to-follow-the-law-no-322009.html.
27. Kandar and Sidharta, above n. 26.
28. *Ibid.*, noting also that the 2009 Environmental Law retains the requirement that any entity whose activities are likely to have a significant impact on the environment must submit either an environmental impact assessment statement (AMDAL) or an environmental management effort (UKL) and an environmental monitoring effort (UPL), as applicable, to the relevant authority for approval or recommendation.
29. *Ibid.*
30. *Ibid.*
31. *Ibid.*, also noting that environmental permits (*Izin Lingkungan*) may be granted by the Minister for the Environment, governor or regent/mayor, as applicable.
32. UN Doc. A/Res/55/25 (8 January 2001), opened for signature 15 December 2000. Copy of the Convention available at United Nations Convention Against Transnational Organized Crime and its Protocols, available at http://www.unodc.org/unodc/en/treaties/CTOC/index.html?ref=menuside.
33. *Ibid.* art. 37(2) providing that states must become parties to the Convention itself before they can become parties to any of the Protocols.
34. Joanna Kyriakakis, 'Corporate criminal liability and the ICC Statute: the comparative law challenge' (2009) 56 *Netherlands International Law Review* 333.

35. International Money Laundering Abatement and Financial Anti-Terrorism Act, Title III of the US Patriot Act of 2001, Public Law 107-56 (26 October 2001) is intended to facilitate the prevention, detection and prosecution of international money laundering and the financing of terrorism. It primarily amends portions of the Money Laundering Control Act of 1986 and the Bank Secrecy Act of 1970. It is divided into three subtitles. The first deals primarily with strengthening banking rules against money laundering, especially on the international stage. The second concerns communication between law enforcement agencies and financial institutions, as well as expanding record keeping and reporting requirements. The third subtitle deals with currency smuggling and counterfeiting, including quadrupling the maximum penalty for counterfeiting foreign currency. USA Patriot Act is an acronym for the Uniting and Strengthening America by Providing Appropriate Tools Required to Intercept and Obstruct Terrorism Act of 2001.

36. 18 USC s. 2339B(a)(1). See also *Holder v Humanitarian Law Project*, No. 08-1498, US Supreme Court, 21 June 2010.

37. Directive 2005/60/EC of the European Parliament and of the Council of 26 October 2005 on the prevention of the use of the financial system for the purpose of money laundering and terrorist financing, as amended by Directive 2008/20/EC of the European Parliament and of the Council of 11 March 2008.

38. National provisions communicated by Member States concerning Directive 2005/60/EC: 'National execution measures', available at http://eur-lex.europa.eu/LexUriServ/ LexUriServ.do?uri=CELEX:72005L0060:EN:NOT.

39. Article 41 provides '41. The importance of combating money laundering and terrorist financing should lead Member States to lay down effective, proportionate and dissuasive penalties in national law for failure to respect the national provisions adopted pursuant to this Directive. Provision should be made for penalties in respect of natural and legal persons. Since legal persons are often involved in complex money laundering or terrorist financing operations, sanctions should also be adjusted in line with the activity carried on by legal persons'.

40. A US bank later taken over and renamed as PNC Bank.

41. US Senate Permanent Subcommittee on Investigations, Committee on Governmental Affairs, *Money Laundering and Foreign Corruption: Enforcement and Effectiveness of the PATRIOT Act: Case Study Involving Riggs Bank* (released in conjuction with the Permanent Subcommittee on Investigations hearing on 15 July 2004), available at http://hsgac. senate.gov/public/_files/ACF5F8.pdf.

42. *Ibid.* 7–8, 98–105.

43. PRMIA, *Riggs Bank*, available at http://prmia.org/pdf/Case_Studies/Riggs_Bank_Short_ version_April_2009.pdf.

44. Terence O'Hara, 'Allbrittons, Riggs to pay victims of Pinochet', *Washington Post*, 26 February 2005; see also *Fair Finance Watch/Inner City Press*, available at www.innercity press.org/finwatch.html. See also Global Witness, *Undue Diligence: How Banks Do Business with Corrupt Regimes* (March 2009): Riggs Bank's involvement in Equatorial Guinea is discussed in ch. 3 of this extensive and well-researched report.

45. Open Society Institute and Soros Foundations Network, 'APDHE v Obiang Family', available at www.soros.org/initiatives/justice/litigation/obiangfamily.

46. *Ibid.*, noting further that on 6 February 2009, Judge Garzón issued an order ratifying the determination of the Prosecutor requiring transfer of the case to the Pre-Trial Investigative Court (*Juzgado de Instrucción*) in Las Palmas. See also Global Witness, *Undue Diligence: How Banks Do Business with Corrupt Regimes* (March 2009).

47. Money laundering is criminalized pursuant to art. 301 of the Spanish Penal Code on the basis of the Vienna and Palermo Conventions. Terrorist financing is criminalized pursuant to art. 571 of the Spanish Penal Code, and this criminalization is largely in line with international standards: eStandardsForum, *Anti-Money Laundering/ Combating Terrorist Financing Standard: Spain*, Report of the Financial Action Task Force (last updated September 2008), available at www.estandardsforum.org/spain/standards/anti-money-laundering-combating-terrorist-financing-standard.

48. Carlos Gómez-Jara Díez and Luis E. Chiesa, 'Spanish criminal law' in Kevin Jon Heller and

Markus Dirk Dubber (eds), *The Handbook of Comparative Criminal Law* (Stanford University Press, 2009) 26. Electronic copy available at http://ssrn.com/abstract=1317689.

49. Michael G. Faure aand Günter Heine, *Criminal Enforcement of Environmental Law in the European Union* (Kluwer Law International, 2005) 1–5; Carlos Gómez-Jara Díez, 'Corporate criminal liability in the 21st century: are all corporations equally capable of wrongdoing?' (5 January 2010), available at SSRN, http://ssrn.com/abstract=1531468.

50. See IBA, 'Overview of the implementation of the Third Money Laundering Directive', available at www.anti-moneylaundering.org/EuropeanChart.aspx, noting further that in a press release of 16 October 2008 (Ref. IP/08/1522), the European Union advised that the European Commission had decided to refer Spain (along with Belgium, Ireland and Sweden) to the European Court of Justice over non-implementation of the Third Money Laundering Directive. This referral officially opened the litigation procedure in relation to the matter. Then, in a press release of 29 December 2009 (Ref. IP/09/159) the European Union advised that reasoned opinions would be sent to Spain (and Poland) for not laying down effective, proportionate and dissuasive penalties in national law as required by the Directive.

51. For example, art. 120.3 of the Spanish Criminal Code renders corporations civilly liable for harm resulting from the commission of an offence within their commercial establishment, if at the time of the offence the corporation was not abiding by applicable regulations. Furthermore, art. 120.4 of the Code holds corporations responsible in tort for the actions of their employees within the scope of their employment. In such cases, the corporate entity is held strictly liable and there is no need to show that the harm took place as a result of negligence.

52. Gómez-Jara Díez and Chiesa, above n. 47, 26–7; noting also that these first two sanctions may be imposed as pre-emptive measures.

53. Uria Menéndez, *Criminal Liability of Companies Survey: Spain* (Lex Mundi, 2008), available at www.lexmundi.com/images/lexmundi/PDF/Business_Crimes/Crim_Liability_Spain.pdf.

54. For example, Council Framework Decision 2003/568/JHA of 22 July 2003 on combating corruption in the private sector; Council Framework Decision 2004/68/JHA of 22 December 2003 on combating the sexual exploitation of children and child pornography; and Council Framework Decision 2005/222/JHA of 24 February 2005 on attacks against information systems.

55. Gomez-Jara Diez and Chiesa, above n. 47, 26–7. See also Menendez, above n. 52, 9.

56. Gomez-Jara, Diez and Chiesa, above n. 47, 27.

57. GA Res. 51/191, UN GAOR, 86th Plen Mtg, UN Doc. A/RES/51/191 (16 December 1996).

58. Adopted by the Negotiating Conference on 21 November 1997, opened for signature 17 December 1997 (entered into force 15 February 1999), text available at www.oecd.org/dataoecd/4/18/38028044.pdf. Discussed in Martijn Wilder and Michael Ahrens, 'Australia's implementation of the OECD Convention on Combating Bribery of Foreign Public Officials in International Business Transactions' (2001) *Melbourne Journal of International Law* 22.

59. Twelve of the 16 countries included in the 2006 Fafo Institute Survey were signatories to the OECD Anti-Bribery Convention. The exceptions were India, Indonesia, South Africa and the Ukraine. South Africa acceded to the Convention by instrument of accession dated 19 June 2007: OECD Anti-Bribery Convention, 'Ratification status as of March 2009', available at www.oecd.org/dataoecd/59/13/40272933.pdf. The Fafo Institute Survey found that at least six of the countries surveyed had anti-bribery statutes in place implementing the terms of the OECD Convention: Argentina, Australia, Japan, the Netherlands, South Africa and United States. With the exception of Argentina, the statutes of all these countries apply to legal persons: Fafo Institute Survey, above n. 3, 26–7.

60. OECD Anti-Bribery Convention, 'Ratification status as of March 2009', available at www.oecd.org/dataoecd/59/13/40272933.pdf.

61. The Bill was published in draft form on 25 March 2009 for pre-legislative scrutiny by a Joint Committee of both Houses of Parliament and received Royal Assent, as the Bribery Act 2010, on 8 April 2010. Copy of both the Bill and the Act plus related documentation available at the UK Ministry of Justice, www.justice.gov.uk/publications/bribery-bill.htm.

62. Phil Taylor, 'UK Bribery Bill: the long arm of the Crown' (February 2010), China Law and Practice, available at www.chinalawandpractice.com/Article/2384642/UK-Bribery-Bill-The-long-arm.

63. Adopted on 23 May 1997 as[C(97)123/FINAL.

64. Adopted by the Council on 26 November 2009; text available at www.oecd.org/dataoecd/11/40/44176910.pdf.

65. Full text of the 2009 Recommendation of the Council for Further Combating Bribery of Foreign Public Officials in International Business Transactions, including both Annexes, available at www.oecd.org/dataoecd/11/40/44176910.pdf.

66. *Ibid.*

67. CETS No. 173, opened for signature in Strasbourg on 27 January 1999 (entered into force 1 July 2002).

68. Criminal Law Convention on Corruption CETS No. 173, 'Chart of signatures and ratifications', available at http://conventions.coe.int/Treaty/Commun/ChercheSig.asp?NT=173&CM=1&DF=23/06/2010&CL=ENG.

69. UN Doc. GA Res. 55/61 (4 December 2000).

70. UN Doc. A/58/422, GA Res. 58/4 (31 October 2003).

71. In accordance with art. 68(1), the Convention Against Corruption entered into force following the deposit of the 30th instrument of ratification: 'Background of the United Nations Convention Against Corruption', available at http://www.unodc.org/unodc/en/treaties/CAC/index.html.

72. United Nations Convention against Corruption, 'Table of signature, ratification, Acceptance, approval, accession, succession', available atwww.unodc.org/unodc/en/treaties/CAC/signatories.html.

73. UN Doc. A/58/422, GA Res. 58/4 (31 October 2003); full text available at www.unodc.org/documents/treaties/UNCAC/Publications/Convention/08-50026_E.pdf.

74. The US Foreign Corrupt Practices Act, 15 USC ss. 78dd-1 *et seq.* (1977) as amended by the International Anti-Bribery and Fair Competition Act of 1998, Public Law No. 105-366, 112 Stat. 3302. The Act imposes extra-territorial criminal liability with respect to certain practices involving the bribery of foreign officials.

75. Jonathan Clough, 'Not-so innocents abroad: corporate criminal liability for human rights abuses' (2005) 11:1 *Australian Journal of Human Rights* 1.

76. 15 USC s. 78dd-1(g).

77. ICC, 'The states parties to the Rome Statute', available at ICC, www.icc-cpi.int/Menus/ASP/states+parties/, further noting that of the 111 states parties, 30 come from Africa, 15 from Asia, 24 from Latin America and the Caribbean, 17 from Eastern Europe and 25 from Western Europe and other areas. See also United Nations Treaty Collection, Rome Statute of the International Criminal Court, 'Status as at 23 June 2010', available at treaties.un.org/Pages/ViewDetails.aspx?src=TREATY&mtdsg_no=XVIII-10&chapter=18&lang=en

78. UN Status of Treaties, available at *ibid.* Note, however, that three of these 38 signatory states, the United States, Israel and Sudan, have 'unsigned' the Rome Statute, indicating that they no longer intend to become states parties and, as such, they have no legal obligations arising from their signature of the Statute. Indonesia, Nepal and Guatemala have indicated an intention to accede to the Rome Convention.

79. Amnesty International, *The International Criminal Court: Summary of Draft and Enacted Implementing Legislation* (April 2006), available at http://www.amnestyusa.org/document.php?lang=e&id=ENGIOR400412006.

80. Rome Statute, art. 17.

81. Amnesty International, above n. 79. The 2006 Fafo Institute Survey found that nine of the 16 countries surveyed (Argentina, Australia, Belgium, Canada, Germany the Netherlands, South Africa, Spain and United Kingdom) had fully incorporated the Rome Statutes' three crimes – genocide, crimes against humanity and war crimes – into their domestic legislation: Fafo Institute Survey, above n. 3, 15–16. The Amnesty International 'Summary of implementing legislation', above n. 79, agrees, except with regard to Argentina which is listed as having draft legislation only.

82. Fafo Institute Survey, above n. 3, 15–16.
83. *Ibid.* The United States is included here on the basis of the ATCA and s. 1331, discussed above, which allow actions for grave breaches of international criminal law, despite the United States' refusal to ratify the Rome Convention.
84. Indian Penal Code 1860 s. 4, extension of Code to extra-territorial offences (applies to Indian citizens and '[a]ny person on any ship or aircraft registered in India wherever it may be'.
85. Canada became the first country in the world to incorporate the obligations of the Rome State into its national laws when it adopted the Crimes Against Humanity and War Crimes Act on 24 June 2000.
86. Implementation of the Rome Statute of the International Criminal Court Act 27 of 2002 (18 July 2002) (South Africa).
87. International Crimes and International Criminal Court Act 2000 (effective 1 October 2000) (New Zealand).
88. International Crimes Act 2003 (effective 1 October 2003) (the Netherlands). Discussed in Larissa van den Herek, 'The difficulties of exercising extraterritorial criminal jurisdiction: the acquittal of a Dutch businessman for crimes committed in Liberia' (2009) 9 *International Criminal Law Review* 211.
89. Gómez-Jara Díez and Chiesa, above n. 48, 5.
90. International Criminal Court Act 2001 (c. 17).

6. Bringing the TNC under the jurisdiction of international law: theory and principles

A. INTRODUCTION

This book now turns to the argument that if TNCs are to be allowed the freedom and power to *behave* as global entities, they can and should be expected to bear the responsibilities inherent in global citizenship as well. They need not necessarily be treated as full members of the global community in the same sense that sovereign states are. They should be subject to a lesser number of modified rights and obligations under international law, just as international organizations currently are.[1] I want to argue that the exercise of power on a global scope should give rise to a corresponding duty to exercise that power responsibly and in conformity with globally recognized standards of care. Likewise, the ability to claim rights against other members of the global community should give rise to corresponding duties owed to those other global citizens.

It is time for TNCs to take the rhetoric of globalization and global citizenship seriously in a legal, and not just an economic sense. The distinction is a vital one. While economists have long recognized the modern multi-national corporation as a global economic actor, and political scientists and sociologists have likewise recognized the part that TNCs play in international politics and society, international lawyers have lagged far behind. For the idea of global citizenship to be taken to its logical conclusion, TNCs must be subject to the principles enshrined in international law. One major implication of this would be that in addition to those international instruments they voluntarily sign up to, TNCs should be subject to the same fundamental principles of customary international law recognized universally as binding peremptory norms (*jus cogens* in international law) that states and international organisations are subject to.

In the first years of the twenty-first century, normative expectations as regards corporate duties and responsibilities have shifted from those held previously, and will continue to change.[2] What is now needed is a degree of consensus on uniform global standards that apply to all TNC operations irrespective of location, cultural or national background. Certainly both the growing number of individual corporate and industry-wide codes of conduct, as well as the Global Compact initiative, recognize the *principle* of global good corporate citizenship. In order to turn that principle into a reality, voluntary codes of behaviour need to be given 'teeth' by being made enforceable in the event that they are breached. By enforceable I mean that when TNCs are found to be responsible for breaches of agreed global standards, mechanisms exist to both compensate individuals and communities affected by such breaches, and to bring relevant business operations back into compliance.

Such a suggestion is not as radical as it might seem. First, only the most fundamental principles would be recognized as universally binding. Such principles would draw upon the commonly shared elements in thousands of individual voluntary codes of conduct, including those which have been designed by NGOs and international organizations. Second, any attempt to introduce more effective 'enforcement mechanisms' will inevitably have to be consultative, and take into account the need to attract the voluntary acceptance and participation of a majority of global TNCs. The reality is that just as a significant number of states (including four of the five permanent members of the UN Security Council),[3] have declined to accept the compulsory jurisdiction of the International Court of Justice (ICJ), so also will a number of global business organizations continue to remain outside international efforts to subject them to global standards of behaviour.

The rest of this chapter explores the current legal position of TNCs under international law and the limitations of the principle of international personality when applied to TNCs. While the Special Representative of the Secretary-General (SRSG) has argued that TNCs are, or at least should be, subject to a 'responsibility to respect' human rights, the prevailing view remains that, so far as international law is concerned, they simply are not. There is no binding international law imposing even the most basic of enforceable human rights obligations on TNCs. I then explore how international law might be reformed to bring TNCs under the coverage of binding international legal principles, including principles of international human rights law and environmental law.

B.   CURRENT STATUS OF THE PRIVATE CORPORATION IN INTERNATIONAL LAW

The question of the subjects of international law has been in a state of gradual evolution since the early years of the twentieth century. Over the intervening period, both theory and practice have firmly abandoned the doctrine that states are the exclusive subject of international rights and duties. By the middle of the century, both international organizations and individuals had been brought under the coverage of international law. So far as individuals are concerned, a number of international instruments have expressly recognized the procedural capacity of the individual as a claimant of rights and as the subject of duties imposed by international law. Thus, for example, individuals in those states which are party to the First Optional Protocol to the International Covenant on Civil and Political Rights[4] may lodge complaints relating to breaches of Covenant rights with the UN Human Rights Committee.[5] It is not necessary for the individual lodging the complaint to be a citizen of the state against which the complaint is made.[6] So far as individual responsibilities are concerned, the 1998 Rome Statute of the International Criminal Court,[7] seen as the modern successor to the Nuremburg war crimes tribunal, now provides an avenue for bringing individuals to account for 'the most serious crimes of concern to the international community as a whole'.[8]

For the most part, however, the individual remains an object, not a subject of international law, whose most important characteristic for international law purposes is her nationality. It is this, for example, that determines which state (the national state) may protect her against the extravagances of another[9] and, more ominously, places her within the domestic jurisdiction, and hence the discretionary treatment, of her national state. It is nationality also that most often decides whether an individual can benefit from treaty guarantees that a state secures for and on behalf of its citizens and residents.

Just as is the case with individuals, there is no doubt that international treaties not only provide certain rights for TNCs, but can also impose duties upon private corporate persons. One example of this is the International Convention on Civil Liability for Oil Pollution Damage 1969.[10] Article III of this treaty imposes strict liability for oil pollution on the ship's owner, usually a company. Even this treaty, however, treats the corporate owner as an object, rather than a subject of international law. Moreover, the treaty only applies to the extent that states are willing to ratify its provisions, and thus can only impose liability on owners of ships registered or present in a contracting state and in accordance with the procedures established by the competent authorities of the relevant contracting state.[11]

We have seen (in Chapter 3) that the relationship between the nation-state and the foreign TNC is an unequal one, both economically and legally. Moreover, so far as human rights are concerned, only states are subject to mandatory human rights requirements established by international law. TNCs, at the global level, are subject to nothing stronger than the 'motherhood-statements' contained in aspirational Guidelines. Thus, as recently as 2002, McCorquodale has observed that:

> International human rights law, for all its diversity and size, places direct legal obligations only on states. The international human rights law system is a state-based system, a system in which the law operates in only one area: state action. It ignores actions by non-state actors, such as the United Nations and other intergovernmental organizations, transnational corporations, armed opposition groups, and

terrorists (however defined). Non-state actors are treated as if their actions could not violate human rights, or it is pretended that states can and do control their activities.

International human rights law privileges the state and is silent in relation to the nonstate. International human rights law simply does not hear the voices of those who are being violated by nonstate actors.[12]

McCorquodale, however, overstates his case. Ever since the *Reparations* case,[13] it has been clear that the United Nations is a subject of international law, able to claim rights and bear liabilities under international law. Other international organizations are also subjects of international law; that is, the international legal personality of such organizations is recognized by international law. Moreover, scholarship in relation to the applicability of international law to non-state entities has evolved considerably over the past decades, and continues to do so. Thus, Adam McBeth has recently and persuasively argued 'that private entities, such as corporations, can be said to have obligations under international human rights law, even though those obligations are not readily enforceable under present arrangements'.[14] McBeth goes on to argue that:

> Given the underlying purpose of human rights law as a guarantee of certain inalienable levels of treatment and entitlement for all people, efficacy logically demands that the principles extend beyond obligations on States alone.[15]

This book agrees with McBeth, and further argues that to subject TNCs to mandatory standards of international law comparable to those which states are subject to would be to the benefit of *both* the global community *and* the individual TNC. From the firm's point of view, when TNCs are given a responsible role in both developing and maintaining standards of labour and environmental protection then this could help to free directors from the shackles of the short-term profit motives of shareholders. In making decisions to invest for the long-term future of the firm rather than short-term profit, directors would be able to point to legal requirements imposed by international law. This might not be to the immediate benefit of short-term profits or the individual director's annual bonus if linked to such profits, but would be to the long-term benefit of shareholder value, market stability and business sustainability. The existence of CSR-linked market-based indexes such as the Dow-Jones Sustainability Indexes and the FTSE4Good Index recognizes that profit and independently-verified standards for responsible corporate conduct *can* co-exist.[16]

Clear international requirements in relation to human rights, labour rights and the environment would also provide a basis for governments in host states to legislate at the local level in conformity with those standards, without risk of being accused of breaching obligations imposed by trade and investment treaties. Rather than the continual tension and outright conflict between the interests of labour and the environment on the one hand, and the interests of the corporation on the other, subjecting both states and TNCs to a similar set of obligations arising from global citizenship would unite both in striving for economic development that was both sustainable and respectful of basic human rights.

C.   NATURE AND SOURCES OF INTERNATIONAL LAW

Subjecting TNCs to international mandatory standards of behaviour need not be in conflict with the voluntary nature of international legal relations. Just as sovereign states are free to subscribe or not subscribe to international conventions, so also global corporations should be free to subscribe or not subscribe to global standard-setting instruments. Once a TNC has appropriately indicated its 'consent to be bound' by the terms of a treaty, however, that treaty should be equally as binding on the TNC as it is on states parties to the treaty. The 1969 Vienna Convention on the Law of Treaties outlines the various means by which a state may express its consent to be bound by a treaty. These include signature, ratification, acceptance, approval or accession.[17] Similar processes either exist, or could be included, in the articles of association of TNCs so that the corporation's consent to be bound could likewise be expressed in accordance with its own internal constitutional arrangements. Just as is gradually becoming the case with the Global Compact, the business case for a good reputation would help to motivate TNCs to subscribe to relevant global standards governing their international activities. The only exception to the rule of voluntariness in subscribing to international standards would be for those norms of international law which have been recognized as having the status of peremptory norms or *jus cogens*. Article 53 of the Vienna Convention on the Law of Treaties defines a peremptory norm as 'a norm accepted and recognised by the international community ... as a whole as a norm from which no derogation is permitted'.

In addition to treaties, which are the most widely accepted formal source of international law, article 38(1) of the Statute of the International Court of Justice lists as sources of international law '(b) international custom as evidence of a general practice recognised as law', and '(c) general principles of law recognised by civilised nations'.

In relation to states, the phrase 'international custom as evidence of a general practice accepted as law' requires that a customary practice be broadly followed by a large enough number of states to demonstrate a degree of unanimity in following that practice (state practice).[18] It also requires that the states following the allegedly binding customary practice should do so because they feel bound to do so as a matter of law. This subjective element of customary international law, *opinio juris*, must be proved by satisfactory evidence that the alleged rule 'is of such a nature, and has been so widely and generally accepted, that it can hardly be supposed that any civilised State would repudiate it'.[19] The requirement of *opinio juris* would seem to address itself to the question of motive – something which the International Court of Justice (ICJ) has found harder to investigate in particular cases than almost anything else.[20] As a result, the ICJ has generally taken a pragmatic approach when determining the content of international customary law, recognizing that considerations of political expediency and self-interest will nearly always be found somewhere in the motives behind actions that are taken by states. What is required is such a degree of constant and uniform usage by states generally that a sense of obligation is indicated.[21] A similar inquiry to determine practices and standards that are accepted and followed by TNCs as a matter of *international obligation* is bound to be even more complex and difficult. That does not mean, however, that the attempt should be abandoned. Where international custom is uncertain or silent on a particular matter, an examination of the 'general principles of law recognized by civilised nations' can be used to provide guidance, and could involve, for example, a survey of the standards of behaviour expected of corporations in nations around the world.

D.   NEW INTERNATIONAL PRINCIPLES OF TNC RESPONSIBILITY

1.   TNC Responsibility should be Modelled on State Responsibility

The Draft Articles on Responsibility of States for Internationally Wrongful Acts ('Draft Articles') were adopted by the International Law Commission (ILC) at its 53rd Session in August 2001, bringing to completion one of the ILC's longest running and most controversial studies. On 12 December 2001, the United Nations General Assembly adopted Resolution 56/83, which 'commended [the Draft Articles] to the attention of Governments without prejudice to the question of their future adoption'.[22] The Draft Articles set out simple, straightforward guidelines for attributing behaviour to states without relying on concepts such as 'sphere of influence'.

The rules on attribution of conduct to a state in Chapter II of the Draft Articles are aimed at dealing with the problem that states, like corporations, can only act through the agency of private individuals. Chapter II thus sets out principles reminiscent of corporation law principles found throughout the world. Article 4 provides that the conduct of any state organ is to be considered an act of the relevant state. A state organ is defined to include any person or entity which has the status of a state organ under the internal law of the relevant state. Likewise, the conduct of any person or entity that has the status of an 'organ' of a TNC under the internal rules of that TNC (its articles of association) should be attributed to that TNC. Such entities and persons would include the typically recognized 'agents' of the TNC, including its board of directors, its chairman, secretary, and senior executive officers. While rules for attribution of conduct to a company already exist in domestic law systems, a new set of globally-agreed rules is needed for the purpose of establishing the *international* law responsibilities of TNCs. This new set of rules should reflect general principles of law recognized in different legal systems around the world, and should be allowed to develop and evolve in accordance with those principles.

2. Concept of Complicity

The ILC's 2001 Draft Articles on State Responsibility give expression to principles of complicity which could also usefully be applied to TNCs. Chapter IV of the Draft Articles deals with 'Responsibility of a state in connection with the act of another state'. A state can be held internationally responsible for knowingly aiding and assisting in the commission of an internationally wrongful act by another state (article 16). A state can also be held responsible if it knowingly 'directs and controls another state in the commission of an internationally wrongful act by the latter' (article 17). And finally, a state which coerces another state to commit an act is internationally responsible for that act if the act would, but for the coercion, be an internationally wrongful act of the coerced state; and the coercing state does so with knowledge of the circumstances of the act (article 18).

Each of the three versions of complicity outlined in Chapter IV of the Draft Articles – aiding and assisting; directing and controlling; and coercion – could usefully and appropriately be applied to TNCs. They are useful because of the significant percentage of allegations against TNCs for violations of international law standards that rely on indirect forms of company involvement in such violations.[23] They are appropriate because they rely upon concepts already familiar in domestic legal systems. The concept of directing and controlling is a particularly useful one to apply in the context of corporate groups and supply chains. It could be applied to distinguish those cases where a parent company should be held responsible for the actions of a subsidiary or related entity in a foreign country. It could also be used to identify cases where a TNC should be held responsible for the actions of a supplier or other business partner – although its application in such cases would probably be rare. More relevant to the context of supply chains would be the concept of coercion, as found in article 18 of the Draft Articles. Coercion has been defined to include economic coercion,[24] which could again prove particularly relevant to business contexts.

Owing to the relatively limited case history in relation to companies rather than individuals, and given the variations in definitions of complicity within different legal contexts, it is not possible to specify precise tests for what constitutes complicity within the legal sphere. The SRSG has noted that the clearest guidance comes from international criminal law and the cases there on aiding and abetting.[25] These cases have developed several key principles that provide useful guidance when thinking about corporate complicity. While currently applicable only to individuals and not to legal persons, international criminal law is also relevant because it can and does influence domestic legal systems.

The Statutes for the International Criminal Court (ICC), the International Criminal Tribunal for the former Yugoslavia (ICTY) and the International Criminal Tribunal for Rwanda (ICTR), as well as other international criminal tribunals, provide for individual liability based on aiding and abetting. In the jurisprudence before the ICTY and ICTR, the tribunals have emphasized that such liability will depend on proving both:

(i)   a physical element: an act or omission having a substantial effect on the commission of an international crime; and

(ii)   a mental element: knowledge of contributing to the crime.

(a)   Act or omission having a substantial effect on the commission of an international crime

Cases on aiding and abetting heard in ad hoc international tribunals have found that aiding and abetting consists of 'acts [by individuals] directed to assist, encourage or lend moral support to the perpetration of a crime, and which have a substantial effect upon its perpetration'.[26] The assistance need not cause, or be a necessary contribution to, the commission of the crime. In other words, it does not have to be shown that the crime would not have happened without the contribution. Furthermore, the assistance may occur before, during or after the principal crime has been committed, and it need not occur within geographic proximity to the crime.[27]

The International Law Commission, in commentary on its Draft Code of Crimes Against the Peace and Security of Mankind, indicated that aiding and abetting liability should require that an accomplice:

> must provide the kind of assistance which contributes directly and substantially to the commission of the crime, for example by providing the means which enable the perpetrator to commit the crime. Thus, the form of participation of an accomplice must entail assistance which facilitates the commission of a crime in some significant way.[28]

The sole fact that a company is present in a county where human rights abuses are occurring – even the fact that a company benefits from such abuses – is unlikely to result in legal liability for complicity.[29] Nevertheless, the South African Truth and Reconciliation Commission noted that benefiting from abuse may constitute a relevant factor in determining the responsibility of companies for involvement in abuses. In 1998, the South African Truth and Reconciliation Commission found that there were three levels of business involvement in apartheid: (i) playing a central role in designing and implementing apartheid; (ii) profiting directly from activities that promoted apartheid; and (iii) benefiting indirectly by operating in apartheid society. The Commission said that the first two levels must result in accountability. However, it said that benefiting indirectly from apartheid policies was of a 'different moral order'.[30]

(b)   Knowledge

Cases in international criminal tribunals have required that the accused know the criminal intentions of the principal perpetrator, and also know that their own acts provide substantial assistance to the commission of the crime.[31] However, aiding and abetting has not required that the individual share the same criminal intent as the principal, or even desire that the crime occur.[32] It is also not necessary to show that the accused knew the precise crime that was intended and which was actually committed, but only that one of several possible crimes must be committed.[33] The ICC's Rome Statute provisions on aiding and abetting provide that liability will arise if, 'for the purpose of facilitating' a crime, an individual 'aids, abets or otherwise assists in its commission or its attempted commission, including providing the means for its commission'.[34]

The knowledge requirement can be established through direct and indirect or circumstantial evidence. Therefore, objective facts can be used to infer the subjective mental state of the accused, and constructive knowledge can be inferred even where the accused has not admitted to having, or has denied having, such knowledge.

What would be required to prove knowledge on the part of a company would depend on the context. The international criminal law cases imposing liability on individuals for their role in abuse by companies during the Second World War imputed knowledge by looking to information readily available to the company representative about the perpetrator at the time the company provided the assistance. This included records of meetings,[35] or the context of the business transaction, such as unusually large orders for harmful chemical substances.[36] In some of these cases knowledge was also imputed from the position and experience of the individual in the company, for instance, where the individual occupied a particular position of authority or influence.[37]

3. Corporations and Complicity

The SRSG also looks to domestic criminal laws around the world for further guidance on the concept of complicity.[38] The ways in which domestic legal jurisdictions have struggled to deal with the concept of corporate complicity were discussed above in Chapters 4 and 5. The main difficulty, as in international criminal law, lies in accepting that a legal fiction – the corporation – can be guilty of complicity which, by definition and like most other crimes, requires an element of knowledge or intent: the *mens rea* part of the crime.

Apart from acknowledging the differences between different domestic approaches to the concept of corporate complicity, and the differences between international and domestic law versions of that concept, the SRSG does not reach any conclusions or make any recommendations in his 2008 'clarification' of the concept of complicity. Instead, he goes on to acknowledge the importance of 'social expectations that companies avoid complicity'.[39] To understand the nature and content of these 'social expectations', the SRSG looks to internationally agreed standards (including the Global Compact and the OECD Guidelines), investment policies (e.g., the Ethical Guidelines used by the Norwegian Council on Ethics for the Government Pension Fund) and the principles advocated by NGO human rights groups (e.g., Amnesty International's 'Human Rights Principles for Companies'). Again, the SRSG reaches no conclusions and makes no recommendations arising from his exploration of 'social expectations that companies avoid complicity', except to note the significant differences between legal and social expectations in this area. In particular, he notes that beneficial complicity (being seen to benefit from abuse) and silent complicity (being present in contexts where abuses are taking place) may attract social opprobrium, but are unlikely, by themselves, to lead to legal liability.[40]

4. Avoiding the Criminal Liability of Corporations at International Law

Perhaps the most attractive aspect of the ILC's Draft Articles when applied to TNCs is the way in which those Articles avoid notions of 'criminality' without losing 'teeth' or failing to provide effective remedies. As originally written, the Draft Articles did refer to a category of 'international crime' for which states could be liable.[41] In his first report to the International Law Commission as Special Rapporteur on State Responsibility, however, Professor James Crawford severely criticized the category of 'crime of state', and strongly recommended it be deleted from the Draft Articles, albeit 'without prejudice' to the notion of 'international crimes' of states 'and its possible future development'.[42] The main reason for this rejection was the 'domestic analogy' with criminal law that the term necessarily evokes.[43] The word 'crime' has strong penal implications in domestic law and, especially since the coming into force of the ICC's Rome Statute, in international law as well. Such implications are simply not appropriate when it comes to discussing either state responsibility or corporate responsibility in an international law context.

First, there is the practical reason that fictional legal persons cannot be placed in jail, so penal sanctions in that sense have no meaning. As the International Military Tribunal said in 1946:

> Crimes against international law are committed by men, not by abstract entities, and only by punishing individuals who commit such crimes can the provisions of international law be enforced.[44]

Even where pecuniary sanctions or business sanctions can be imposed on a responsible state or corporation, the impact of such sanctions is nearly always unfairly felt by those who are innocent (e.g., civilians or shareholders), while the effectiveness of such sanctions as a form of deterrent punishment is highly questionable. At international law, it also remains questionable whether the imposition of punitive sanctions on a state is even allowable. While the United Nations' most powerful organ, the Security Council, has powers under Chapter VII of the United Nations Charter to impose diplomatic, economic and/or military sanctions on a state when deemed necessary to 'maintain or restore international peace and security', it is unlikely that this power includes the power to inflict post-compliance sanctions on an aggressor state. Certainly, the ILC appears to have recognized that 'States, by definition, cannot be the subject of criminal sanctions akin to those provided for in national criminal systems'.[45]

The distinction made in the First Reading version of the Draft Articles on State Responsibility (article 19) between 'international delicts' and 'international crimes' does have one important virtue, however. It recognizes the existence in international law of two species of violations of international obligations. There are ordinary violations of international law, and there are those basic substantive norms which are so important to the international community as a whole that their violation involves a difference not merely of degree, but of kind. It was necessary for the ILC to indicate in the Draft Articles 'that there are wrongful acts regarded by the international community as more serious than all others because they affect essential interests of the Community'.[46] The point is, however, that there is not and never was any need to invoke the concept of criminality to achieve this aim. International law has long recognized a concept of obligations *'erga omnes'*; that is, obligations which are so important that they are owed to the international community as a whole. Such obligations arise primarily (although not entirely) from peremptory norms of international law known as *jus cogens*.[47] Peremptory norms of international law are norms that are so important that no derogation from them is permitted. The existence of *jus cogens* has long been recognized in customary international law, and the concept of peremptory norms was expressly recognized and defined in article 53 of the 1969 Vienna Convention on the Law of Treaties. So it was a relief to many when the terminology of 'crime' (and the consequent distinction between 'crimes' and 'delicts') was dropped from the Draft Articles on State Responsibility, and replaced with a new Chapter on 'Serious breaches of obligations under peremptory norms of general international law'.[48]

5. Internationally Wrongful Acts of TNCs and the Need for Remedies: The Concept of Reparation

An equally attractive aspect of the Draft Articles on State Responsibility is the emphasis placed on providing clear and simple rules governing 'Reparation for injury'.[49] A duty to provide 'prompt, effective and adequate' reparation was recognised in paragraph 18 of the Draft UN Norms on Human Rights in terms which reflect the standard set in most bilateral investment treaties for host governments which violate the property rights of a foreign investor corporation. An obligation to provide reparation is thus particularly apt in the context of international harms for which a TNC is responsible. In the context of the Draft Articles, article 34 provides that 'Full reparation for the injury caused by the internationally wrongful act shall take the form of restitution, compensation and satisfaction, either singly or in combination'. Each of these three forms of reparation is well recognized in international law.[50]

Reparation in line with principles set down in the Draft Articles on State Responsibility would mean that the responsible TNC would be 'under an obligation to ... re-establish the situation which existed before the wrongful act was committed'. This is the duty spelt out in article 35 of the Draft Articles, and one which would surely be welcomed by communities affected by TNC mining and other environmentally damaging activities. Nor would it present any major threat of insurmountable or endless liabilities for TNCs. The duty to make restitution would be limited, as it is for states, to those circumstances where it is materially possible to make such restitution, and with the limitation that making restitution should not involve 'a burden out of all proportion to the benefit deriving from restitution instead of compensation'.[51]

To the extent that damage for which it is responsible is not made good by restitution, a state responsible for an internationally wrongful act is under an obligation to compensate for the damage. The compensation 'should cover any financially assessable damage'.[52] Principles governing compensation for wrongful acts are already well established, with a large degree of consistency, in domestic legal systems and the jurisprudence of international tribunals around the world.[53] There should be little difficulty in transferring such principles to the international responsibility of TNCs.

Article 37 of the Draft Articles provides that 'the State responsible for an internationally wrongful act is under an obligation to give satisfaction for the injury caused by the act insofar as it cannot be made good by restitution or compensation. Satisfaction may consist in an acknowledgement of the breach, an expression of regret, a formal apology or another appropriate modality'. Again, protections for the wrongdoer are also present in the requirement that 'Satisfaction shall not be out of proportion to the injury and may not take a form humiliating to the responsible State'. The concept of satisfaction as a remedy is particularly appropriate in the context of TNC activities causing harm. In particular, it recognizes the importance of the 'social' aspects of 'corporate social responsibility', and provides a way for TNCs to repair some of the social harm caused by their wrongful activities.

E.   THE GLOBAL FIRM AND THE INTERNATIONAL CRIMINAL COURT

It has been suggested that the International Criminal Court (ICC) may be ideally placed to take on some significant responsibility for the prevention and punishment of at least some of the most egregious human rights abuses when private commercial operations are involved.[54] This section explores the issues raised by such a proposal. As evident from the discussion above on the potential criminal liability of TNCs at international law, I do not support expanding international criminal law to corporations. Instead, the conclusion is reached below that the Rome Conference which established the Statute of the ICC was right to decide that TNCs should not be rendered directly subject to the jurisdiction of the ICC.

The birth of the ICC in 2002 was undoubtedly a major development in international law. The ICC has jurisdiction over 'the most serious crimes of concern to the international community as a whole'.[55] It is able to try individuals accused of genocide, crimes against humanity or war crimes, whenever the state with domestic criminal jurisdiction is unable or unwilling to carry out a criminal investigation.[56]

The ICC clearly has jurisdiction to try individuals for grievous international crimes committed in the course of business just as for crimes committed in a non-business context. The ICC may, for example, prosecute the individual directors and other officers of a corporation where those individuals were complicit in, or responsible for facilitating or allowing, corporate involvement in serious international crimes.

As Andrew Field has noted, the first such application of the term 'international crime' to individuals was:

> in 1945 at the conclusion of the Second World War, [when] a number of German government and military leaders were put on trial at Nuremburg for crimes against humanity. What is not so well known is that in subsequent trials, other German leaders, including leaders of industry, were also tried and convicted. The manner in which they conducted their business and led their companies was found to be illegal under international law ...
>
> In 1948, officials from the Krupp company were found guilty of 'plunder and spoliation' for their seizure of plant and machinery in conquered France and Holland and sentenced to prison. They were also found guilty of enslavement for Krupp's use of thousands of forced foreign workers, prisoners of war and concentration camp inmates.
>
> Other industrialists experienced a similar fate, including officials from the massive IG Farbenindustrie AG chemical and synthetics business.[57]

The United States Military Tribunal at Nuremburg also famously prosecuted the directors of IG Farben on the basis of acts committed in the name of the company. The allegations levelled against IG Farben included:

> The plunder, spoliation and exploitation of public and private property in occupied territory; the enslavement and deportation to slave labour of large numbers of civilian inhabitants of countries under the belligerent occupation of Germany in the course of which the latter were ill-treated, tortured and killed.[58]

Despite the fact that IG Farben, as a legal person, was not itself on trial, the military tribunal analysed the actions of the company with regard to criminal offences and complicity in pillage and forced labour under the Nazi regime in occupied territories. The tribunal noted that IG Farben profited from Nazi human rights abuses, for example, by using concentration camp forced labour. The tribunal then went on to observe:

> It is appropriate here to mention that the corporate defendant, Farben, is not before the bar of this Tribunal and cannot be subjected to criminal penalties in these proceedings. We have used the term Farben as descriptive of the instrumentality ... in the name of which the enumerated acts of spoliation were committed. But corporations act through individuals and, under the conception of personal individual guilt ... the Prosecution ... must establish ... beyond a reasonable doubt that an individual defendant was either a participant in the illegal act or that, being aware thereof, he authorized or approved it. Responsibility does not automatically attach to an act proved to be criminal merely by virtue of a defendant's membership in the Vorstand [board]. Conversely, one may not utilize the corporate structure to achieve an immunity from criminal responsibility for illegal acts which he directs, counsels, aids or abets.[59]

On the basis of these and other principles spelt out by the Nuremburg tribunals, modern international criminal law has developed mechanisms for prosecuting individuals for their role in a greater criminal enterprise, which are potentially applicable in the context of TNC operations. These are the concepts of command responsibility and joint criminal enterprise.

Command responsibility holds superiors responsible for crimes committed by their subordinates, and was developed with the military chain of command in mind. Under the Rome Statute, however, it expressly applies to civilians in relation to international crimes committed 'by subordinates under his or her effective authority and control'.[60] Command responsibility liability for civilians under the Rome Statute has three elements: knowledge or wilful blindness that a subordinate was about to commit a crime; the crime concerned activities within the scope of the superior's authority; and failure to take all reasonable measures to prevent or repress the commission of the crime. As McBeth has noted:

> International crimes committed in pursuit of a corporate goal, such as systematic and brutal treatment of those who stand in the way of a particular development, could satisfy those criteria, and render the responsible manager or director criminally liable. Indeed, in *Prosecutor v Musema*, the International Criminal Tribunal for Rwanda convicted the director of a tea factory on the basis of command responsibility for the acts of his employees in massacring Tutsis.[61]

An alternative approach is that of joint criminal enterprise or 'common plan' liability. Article 25 of the Rome Statute of the ICC provides that an individual will be criminally responsible, *inter alia*, if he or she 'commits such a crime, whether as an individual, jointly with another or through another person, regardless of whether that other person is criminally responsible',[62] or 'in any way contributes to the commission or attempted commission of such a crime by a group of persons acting with a common purpose'.[63] Whether or not the other 'person' in the context of a joint criminal enterprise includes legal (corporate) persons remains uncertain.[64] Certainly, it would be consistent with the approach of the military tribunal in IG Farben to examine first the culpability of the legal person en route to finding a group of individuals criminally responsible for 'directing, counselling, aiding or abetting' the culpable behaviour. However, article 25(1) of the Rome Statute clearly provides that 'The court shall have jurisdiction over natural persons pursuant to this Statute'. It could be argued that the word 'person' throughout the Statute should be read to include only natural persons, consistently with article 25(1). Alternatively, it can be argued that the use of the term 'person' without the qualifier 'natural' in subsequent paragraphs of article 25 must have been adopted with awareness of its potential to extend to legal persons in the context of joint criminal enterprise liability.[65]

Alternatively, in the context of TNC operations, it may be sufficient to focus upon the common purpose of the natural persons involved in the relevant commercial operations giving rise to international criminal liability. The ICTY has held that a person who intentionally participates in a common plan can be liable not just for the elements of the plan itself, but also for acts that are 'a natural and foreseeable consequence of the effecting of that common purpose'.[66]

What is clear, however, is that there is, as yet, no provision for the court to exercise criminal jurisdiction over corporate persons. This raises the question of whether the jurisdiction of the ICC should be expanded to include TNCs. In 1998 at the Rome Conference that led to the final Statute of the ICC being opened for signature, the French delegate proposed a jurisdictional article that extended to legal persons. The original proposal was to include the following paragraphs:

> The Court shall have jurisdiction over legal persons, with the exception of States, when the crimes committed were committed on behalf of such legal persons or by their agencies or representatives.
> The criminal responsibility of legal persons shall not exclude the criminal responsibility of natural persons who are perpetrators or accomplices in the same crimes.[67]

Additional articles that set out the penalties that would apply to legal persons were also included in the proposal. After insufficient support was received during the Conference, a compromise proposal was also put forward by France, but ultimately omitted from the Rome Statute.[68]

There are many arguments in favour of expanding the jurisdiction of the ICC to cover legal (corporate) persons as well as natural persons.[69] First, it would help to unify the different standards and rules of corporate criminal liability currently found within the diverse jurisprudence of many countries. Such diversity helps perpetuate forum-shopping so that the individuals and states most affected by criminal corporate activity effectively lose control over their own futures when left to seek the assistance of foreign courts. As well as preventing forum shopping, allowing all such actions to be brought before a single tribunal such as the ICC would help to consolidate and unify a shared understanding of the principles of international criminal law. It would also help to promote a shared interpretation of international human rights treaties as applied to TNCs.

I want to argue here, however, that the arguments against an expansion of ICC jurisdiction are even more compelling. First, there are the *real politik* arguments against such a move. The ICC had a difficult birth surrounded by political controversy, and the controversy surrounding its operations continues.[70] Given the political difficulties inherent in gaining acceptance of the ICC in its current form, the politics of extending its jurisdiction is likely to preclude any such expansion for a very long time.

But there are other, more fundamental arguments against subjecting TNCs to international criminal jurisdiction. The first is based on the idea, noted above, that an abstract entity cannot have a guilty *mens rea*, and so cannot, itself, be guilty of criminal intent. Nor can an abstract entity actually commit a crime. It can only do so through its agents – hence the recognition by the Nuremburg tribunal that 'crimes against international law are committed by men, not by abstract entities'.[71]

The second argument against international criminal liability is that if TNCs are to participate in international society on essentially the same basis as states, then they need to be treated according to the same principles of responsibility as states.

As noted earlier in this chapter, international law recognizes that states can be responsible for '[s]erious breaches of obligations under peremptory norms of general international law', but the language of criminality is not used.[72] The officers and agents of a TNC, just like the leaders and other agents of a state, can and should be held criminally liable where appropriate. But it is not appropriate to talk about the criminal liability of a state, and it is equally inappropriate to invoke the penal concept of criminality when it comes to TNCs. That does not mean that TNCs should not be held responsible and accountable for their internationally wrongful actions; just that invoking penal concepts of criminality is not the appropriate way to do it. The next chapter explores international forums for the invocation of TNC responsibility in a more appropriate manner.

NOTES

1. Nigel D. White, *The Law of International Organisations* (2nd edn, Manchester University Press, 2005).
2. Steven R. Ratner, 'Corporations and human rights: a theory of legal responsibility' (2001) 111 *Yale Law Journal* 443, 464–5.
3. Of the five states that are permanent Security Council members, only the United Kingdom (by declaration dated 5 July 2004) has recognized the compulsory jurisdiction of the ICJ. China, France, Russia and the United States have either never recognised or no longer recognize the compulsory jurisdiction of the ICJ under art. 36(2) of the ICJ Statute: 'Declarations Recognizing the Jurisdiction of the Court as Compulsory', available at http://www.icj-cij.org/jurisdiction/index.php?p1=5&p2=1&p3=3.
4. Adopted and opened for signature in New York by GA Res. 2200A (XXI) of 16 December 1966; 999 UNTS 171. (entered into force 23 March 1976 in accordance with art. 9). As at 24 June 2010, there were 113 states parties to the First Optional Protocol (see UN Treaty Collection, http://treaties.un.org/).
5. For an example of such a complaint, see Communication to the UNHRC No. 488/1992. For a discussion of the UNHRC decision in relation to that complaint, see Sarah Joseph, 'Gay rights under the ICCPR: commentary on *Toonen v Australia*' (1994) 13:2 *University of Tasmania Law Review* 392.
6. *A v Australia*, No. 560/1993 (Australia's detention and treatment of refugees found to be in violation of arts 9 (the right to liberty) and 2(3) (the right to an effective remedy) of the ICCPR).

7. Rome Statute of the International Criminal Court, opened for signature 17 July 1998, 2187 UNTS 3 (entered into force 1 July 2002).
8. *Ibid.*, art. 5.
9. *Barcelona Traction Light and Power Co. Ltd (Second Phase) (Belgium v Spain)* [1970] ICJ Rep. 3. See also Draft Articles on Responsibility of States for Internationally Wrongful Acts (adopted by the International Law Commission at its 53rd Session (2001), Official Records of the General Assembly, 56th Sess., Supp. No. 10 (A/56/10), chp IV.E.1, art. 44; which provides that 'The responsibility of a State may not be invoked if (a) the claim is not brought in accordance with any applicable rule relating to the nationality of claims'.
10. (1975) UKTS, Cmnd 6183; 973 UNTS 3; (1970) ILM 45, signed in Brussels, 29 November 1969, in force 1975 with 46 parties, cited in D.J. Harris, *Cases and Materials on International Law* (6th edn, Sweet and Maxwell, 2004) 141; full text of the treaty available at http://sedac.ciesin.org/entri/texts/civil.liability.oil.pollution.damage.1969.html. See also the 1992 Protocol to amend the International Convention on Civil Liability for Oil Pollution Damage, IMO 1992, available at www.jus.uio.no/lm.imo.civil.liability.oil.pollution. damage.protocol.1992/doc.
11. See art. VII of the Convention and see also discussion in Simon Gault, R.G. Marsden, S.J. Hazelwood and A.M. Tettenborn, *Marsden on Collisions at Sea* (Sweet and Maxwell, 2003).
12. Robert McCorquodale, 'Overlegalizing silences: human rights and nonstate actors' (2002) 96 *American Society for International Law Proceedings* 384, as quoted in Adam McBeth, *International Economic Actors and Human Rights* (Routledge, 2010) 59.
13. *Reparation for Injuries Suffered in the Service of the United Nations* (Advisory Opinion) [1949] ICJ Rep. 174. See also *Certain Expenses of the United Nations* (Advisory Opinion) [1962] ICJ Rep. 151.
14. Adam McBeth, *International Economic Actors and Human Rights* (Routledge, 2010) 249.
15. *Ibid.*
16. For discussion see Craig Deegan, 'The legitimising effect of social and environmental disclosures: a theoretical foundation' (2002) 15:3 *Accounting, Auditing and Accountability Journal* 282; and Aly Salama, 'A note on the impact of environmental performance on financial performance' (2005) 16:3 *Structural Change and Economic Dynamics* (September) 413.
17. Vienna Convention on the Law of Treaties, opened for signature 23 May 1969, 1155 UNTS 331 (entered into force 27 January 1980), arts 7–17. For discussion see D.J. Harris, *Cases and Materials on International Law* (6th edn, 2004) 786–820.
18. *North Sea Continental Shelf (FRG v Denmark); (FRG v The Netherlands)* [1969] ICJ Rep. 3; 41 ILR 29.
19. *West Rand Central Gold Mining Co.* [1905] 2 KB 391, 407.
20. See e.g., *Arrest Warrant of 11 April 2000 (Congo v Belgium)* [2001] ICJ Rep. 3, where the majority of the ICJ did not refer to *opinio juris*, confining its analysis of relevant custom to state practice, international instruments and the decisions of international tribunals. Cf. *Legality of the Threat or Use of Nuclear Weapons* (Advisory Opinion) (1996) ICJ Rep. 226, (1997) 35 ILM 809, where the ICJ found that the necessary *opinio juris* was lacking where the policy of deterrence was based on the possible threat or use of nuclear weapons, thereby illustrating that *opinio juris* continues to be a vital element in the search for custom.
21. *Ibid.*
22. Official Records of the General Assembly, 56th Sess. UN Doc. A/56/10.
23. John Ruggie, *Clarifying the Concepts of 'Sphere of Influence' and 'Complicity'*, UN Doc. A/HRC/8/16 (15 May 2008) para. 29, noting that 'Most of the over 40 Alien Tort Claims Act (ATCA) cases brought against companies in the United States ... have concerned alleged complicity, where the actual perpetuators were public or private security forces, other government agents, armed factions in civil conflicts or other such actors. Moreover, a recent study conducted by the Office of the High Commissioner for Human Rights (OHCHR) ... which maps allegations against companies, documents that 41 per cent of the 320 cases (from all regions and sectors) in the sample alleged indirect forms of company involvement in various human rights abuses', citing A/HRC/8/5/Add.2.
24. *Report of the International Law Commission on the Work of its 31st Session*, UN Doc. A/34/10, Supp. No. 10 (1979) para. 29. See also Omer Y. Elagab, 'Coercive economic

measures against developing countries' (1992) 41:3 *International and Comparative Law Quarterly* 682 and James D. Fry, 'Coercion, causation and the fictional elements of indirect state responsibility' (2007) 40:3 *Vanderbilt Journal of Transnational Law* 611.

25. Ruggie, above n. 23, par.a 33.
26. *Ibid.* para. 36. See also *Furundžija*, ICTY Trial Chamber, 10 December 1998; *Simić*, ICTY Appeals Chamber, 28 November 2006, paras 85–6; *Blagojevic and Jokic*, ICTY Appeals Chamber, 9 May 2007, para. 127; *Blaskic*, ICTY Appeals Chamber, 29 July 2005, paras 45–6; *Vasiljevic*, ICTY Appeals Chamber, 25 February 2004, para. 102; and *Ntagerura*, ICTY Appeals Chamber, 7 July 2006, para. 370.
27. Ruggie, above n. 23, paras 36–7.
28. The ILC also noted that this standard is consistent with the other relevant international provisions, including the Nuremburg Charter and the ICTY and ICTR Statutes: (1996) *Yearbook of the International Law Commission, Report of the Commission to the General Assembly on the Work of its Forty-eighth* Session, vol. II, Part 2, UN Doc. A/CN.4/SER.A/1996/Add 1 (Part 2) (A/51/10), 21, para. 11 of the commentary to art. 1.
29. Ruggie, above n. 23, para. 41.
30. South African Truth and Reconciliation Commission, *Final Report 1998*, vol. 4, ch. 2, paras 23, 27, 32 and 148. The full report is available at www.polity.org.za/polity/govdocs/commissions/1998/trc/4chap2.htm.
31. Ruggie, above n. 23, para. 42.
32. *Simić*, ICTY Appeals Chamber, 28 November 2006, para. 86; and *Aleksovski*, ICTY Appeals Chamber, 24 March 2000, para. 162.
33. *Blaskic*, ICTY Appeals Chamber, 29 July 2005, para. 50; and *Simić*, ICTY Appeals Chamber, 28 November 2006, para. 86.
34. Ruggie, above n. 23, para. 42, noting that 'The ICC has yet to interpret the Rome Statute's provision on aiding and abetting, which states that liability will arise if "for the purpose of facilitating" a crime, an individual, "aids, abets or otherwise assists in its commission or its attempted commission, including providing the means for its commission". There is some disagreement whether the words "for the purpose of" imply an additional requirement of proof that the contribution was given *for the purpose of* facilitating a crime. This would be a requirement above and beyond the accepted parameters of aiding and abetting in the ad hoc tribunals and what is now considered customary international law.
35. *Zyklon B, Trial of Bruno Tesch and two others*, Law Reports of Trials of War Criminals, vol. I, 95, available at www.ess.uwe.ac.uk/WCC/zyklonb.htm.
36. *Ibid.*, 101.
37. Ruggie, above n. 23, para. 44, citing *United States v Von Weizsaeker*, Law Reports of Trials of War Criminals, vol. XIV, 622.
38. Ruggie, above n. 23, paras 45–53.
39. *Ibid.*, paras 54–69.
40. *Ibid.*, para. 70.
41. Draft Articles on State Responsibility adopted by the International Law Commission on First Reading (January 1997); full text available in *Report of the International Law Commission on the Work of its Forty-eighth Session*, 6 May–26 July 1996, Official Reports of the General Assembly, 51st Sess., Supp. 10, UN Doc. A/51/10 and Corr. 1, 125–51. See especially art. 19 which defines a distinction between 'international crimes and international delicts'. International crimes are defined to include any 'internationally wrongful act which results from the breach by a state of an international obligation so essential for the protection of the international community that its breach is recognised as a crime'. See also art. 40(3), which provides that if the internationally wrongful act constitutes an international crime, then 'all other states' are defined as 'injured states' for the purposes of the Draft Articles.
42. James Crawford, *First Report on State Responsibility*, ILC 50th Sess., UN Doc. A/CN.4/490/Add.3 (11 May 1998) para. 101.
43. *Ibid.*, para. 81.
44. International Military Tribunal for the Trial of the Major War Criminals, judgment of 1 October 1946, reprinted in (1947) 41 *American Journal of International Law* 172, 221.
45. *Prosecutor v Blaskić*, IT-95-14-AR 108*bis*, (1997) 101 ILR 698, para. 25. See also

Crawford, above n. 42, para. 91 and D.J. Harris, *Cases and Materials on International Law* (6th edn, 2004) 546.
46. Marina Spinedi, 'International crimes of state: the legislative history', in J. Weiler, A. Cassese and M. Spinedi (eds), *International Crimes of States: A Critical Analysis of the ILC's Draft Article 19 on State Responsibility* (Walter de Gruyter, 1989) 52.
47. Crawford, above n. 42, para. 98. Note also that although all *jus cogens* norms necessarily, by their nature, give rise to obligations *erga omnes*, not all *erga omnes* obligations are of a *jus cogens* nature.
48. Draft Articles (2001), Part II, ch. III.
49. Draft Articles (2001), Part II, ch. II.
50. Julie Campagna, 'United Nations Norms on the Responsibilities of Transnational Corporations and Other Business Enterprises with regard to Human Rights: the international community asserts binding law on the global rule makers' (2004) 37:4 *John Marshall Law Review* 1205, 1251–2, noting that the duty of reparation has been a standard duty of international law since Grotius.
51. Draft Articles (2001), art. 35(b).
52. *Ibid.* art. 36.
53. André Nollkaemper, 'Concurrence between individual responsibility and state responsibility in international law' (2003) 52 *International and Comparative Law Quarterly* 615; Dinah Shelton, 'Righting wrongs: reparations in the Articles on State Responsibility' (2002) 96 *American Journal of International Law* 833; John R. Crook, 'The United Nations Compensation Commission: a new structure to enforce state responsibility' (1993) 87:1 *American Journal of International Law* 144.
54. Alice de Jonge, 'Corporate social responsibility: an international law perspective', in Gabriele G.S. Suder (ed.), *International Business under Adversity: A Role in Corporate Responsibility, Conflict Prevention and Peace* (Edward Elgar, 2008) ch. 3. See also Andrew Clapham, 'Extending international criminal law beyond the individual to corporations and armed opposition groups' (2008) 6:5 *Journal of International Criminal Justice* 899.
55. Rome Statute of the International Criminal Court, opened for signature 17 July 1998, 2187 UNTS 3 (entered into force 1 July 2002), art. 5. See also art. 12. For commentary, see Claire de Than and Edwin Shorts, *International Criminal Law and Human Rights* (Sweet & Maxwell, 2003).
56. Rome Statute, art. 25(3).
57. Andrew Field, 'Nuremberg defence doesn't make the grade for suspect corporate citizens', *The Age*, 18 January 2006.
58. *In re Krauch and Others (IG Farben Trial)* (1948) 15 ILR 668.
59. *Ibid.*, 678. The military tribunal ultimately convicted 12 of the 23 accused corporate officers of IG Farben on the basis of their part in the criminal operations of the company.
60. Rome Statute, art. 28(b).
61. Adam McBeth, *International Economic Actors and Human Rights* (Routledge, 2010) 309, citing *Prosecutor v Musema*, Case No. ICTR-96-13-A, ICTR Trial Chamber, Judgment, 27 January 2000. Alfred Musema was convicted of genocide and the crime against humanity of extermination on the basis of command responsibility, and also on the basis of ordering and aiding and abetting.
62. Rome Statute, art. 25(3)(b).
63. *Ibid.*, art. 25(3)(d).
64. McBeth, above n. 61, 309, arguing that 'the term "person" in the context of committing a crime "jointly with another or through another person" is not expressly limited to natural persons, so potentially extends to a person who commits a crime through the instrumentality of a corporation'.
65. *Ibid.*, 309, n. 323.
66. *Prosecutor v Tadic*, Case No. IT-94-1-A, ICTY Appeals Chamber, Judgment, 15 July 1999, para. 204.
67. Draft Text of the Statute of the International Criminal Court, UN Doc. A/CONF.183/2/Add.1, art. 23(5) and (6). The paragraphs extracted here were contained

within square brackets in the draft, indicating that their inclusion was expected to be debated: McBeth, above n. 61, 306.

68. The compromise proposal was circulated as a working paper, UN Doc. A/CONF.183/C.1/WGGP/L5/Rev2. The text of the various proposals and a discussion of the proceedings at the Rome Conference that led to their eventual rejection are contained in Andrew Clapham, 'The question of jurisdiction under international criminal law over legal persons: lessons from the Rome Conference on an International Criminal Court' in Menno Kamminga and Saman Zia-Zarifa (eds), *Liability of Multinational Corporations under International Law* (2000) 143–60.

69. See further Prince Albert Kumwamba N'Sapu, *Why the ICC Should Prosecute Legal Persons*, ICC Coalition (March 2010), available at Global Policy Forum, www.global policy.org/.

70. See e.g., Mary Kimani, 'International Criminal Court: justice or racial double standards?', *Afrik.com*, 16 December 2009; Mary Kimani, 'Pursuit of justice or Western plot?', *Africa Renewal*, October 2009; Phillip Hammond, 'The tyranny of international justice', *Spiked*, 30 March 2009; Mahmood Mamdani, 'Beware of human rights fundamentalism', *Pambazuka*, 26 March 2009; Malif Deen, 'Aren't there war criminals in the US?', *Inter Press Service*, 9 March 2009, all available at Global Policy Forum, www.globalpolicy.org/.

71. Above n. 58.

72. Draft Articles on Responsibility of States for Internationally Wrongful Acts, adopted by the International Law Commission at its Fifty-third Session (2001), Official Records of the General Assembly, 56th Sess., Supp. No. 10 (A/56/10), ch. III, arts 40–1.

7. Bringing the TNC under the jurisdiction of international law: institutional avenues

A. INTRODUCTION

The third pillar of the Special Representative of the Secretary-General (SRSG)'s Framework for business and human rights points to the need for greater access for victims to effective remedies, both judicial and non-judicial. So far, this is the area where recommendations from the SRSG have been most tentative in nature.[1] This is understandable as the issues involved are highly controversial and political in nature. Within the boundaries of principles governing state jurisdiction (discussed above), international law has long recognized that states are free to exercise discretion in determining the scope of their own criminal and civil laws and procedures.[2] While there is a clear state duty to take appropriate steps to investigate, punish and redress corporate abuses of human rights occurring within their jurisdiction, the content of that duty remains unclear. Many states currently lack adequate policies and regulatory arrangements for effectively managing the complex business and human rights relationship. While some are moving in the right direction, overall state practices exhibit substantial legal and policy incoherence and gaps, which often entail significant consequences for victims, companies and states themselves.[3]

So far as judicial mechanisms are concerned, significant barriers to accessing effective remedies persist throughout even the most advanced legal systems – as demonstrated in Chapters 3 to 5. Furthermore, these legal and practical access barriers are often accentuated for 'at risk' or vulnerable groups, particularly in the case of transnational claims. Non-judicial mechanisms thus play an important part in providing more immediate, accessible, affordable and adaptable points of initial recourse. At both national and international level, however, non-judicial grievance mechanisms remain patchy and incomplete.[4] What is needed, therefore, is a more complete and deliberate *international* system that can transcend the deficiencies of company level or national level grievance mechanisms. International mechanisms are needed to overcome the ability of TNCs to move from country to country, and from region to region. Tribunals at all levels are also needed to tackle social and environmental impacts that cross national borders. The increasing mobility of labour, and the increasing tendency of environmental events (bushfires, oil-spills, etc.) to transcend national borders requires that tribunals established to deal with corporate violations of human rights and environmental standards should also transcend national borders. In particular, where breaches of *international* standards have occurred, it should be possible for victims to seek redress at the international level.

Various stakeholders have pressed for a new international institution to improve access to non-judicial remedies. Proposals have included a clearing house to direct those with complaints against a TNC towards mechanisms that might offer a remedy; a capacity-building entity to help disputing parties use those mechanisms effectively; an expert body to aggregate and analyse outcomes, enabling more systemic learning and dispute prevention; and an international grievance mechanism for when local or national mechanisms fail or are inadequate. As the SRSG noted in his April 2009 Report, the first three of these suggestions hold promise of practical, achievable benefits, if done appropriately.[5] The proposition of creating a single, mandatory, non-judicial but adjudicative mechanism at the international level, however, is much more problematic. In handling complex disputes that involve diverse and economically unequal parties in remote locations, the demands of investigating and hearing disputes are likely to raise significant evidentiary, practical, financial and political challenges, while offering only limited prospects of effective remedy.[6]

Local, regional and international mechanisms are all needed, but the focus of this chapter is on the possibility of looking to existing bodies and networks with international standing. While some voluntary codes, multi-stakeholder initiatives and investor-led standards have established grievance mechanisms, most initiatives lack grievance procedures and this erodes their perceived legitimacy.[7] The obvious answer is for them to adopt such mechanisms. Providing for oversight by internationally recognized bodies is a further way of enhancing the legitimacy of existing codes and standards. These internationally recognized oversight bodies could include strengthened National Contact Points (NCPs) established under the OECD Guidelines for Multinational Enterprises, existing regional and UN human rights bodies, the ILO, the World Bank and the IMF and/or the WTO. Each of these institutional possibilities is considered below.

First, however, it needs to be recognized that a major barrier to victims' accessing available mechanisms, at any level, is the sheer lack of information about them. This information deficit also makes it difficult to improve such mechanisms and to learn from past disputes and avoid their replication. With these barriers in mind, the SRSG, in collaboration with the IBA, launched in 2008 a global wiki: Business and Society Exploring Solutions – A Dispute

Resolution Community.[8] BASESwiki (www.baseswiki.org) is an interactive online forum for sharing, accessing and discussing information about non-judicial mechanisms that address disputes between companies and their external stakeholders. It includes information about how and where mechanisms work, solutions they have achieved, experts who can help, and research and case studies. In January 2010, BASESwiki 2.0 was launched with an improved set of community tools to facilitate more communication and collaboration between contributors.[9]

Non-judicial mechanisms to address alleged breaches of international standards should meet certain principles to be credible and effective. A set of six principles which should underlie all non-judicial grievance mechanisms was outlined by the SRSG in his 2008 Report.[10] These are uncontroversial, and provided a useful set of parameters for the IBA Working Group when revising the effectiveness of the grievance procedures established by the OECD Guidelines. They are also useful for evaluating other international mechanisms for dealing with grievances against TNCs. The six principles are:

(a) Legitimacy: a mechanism must have clear, transparent and sufficiently independent governance structures to ensure it remains free from actual or perceived undue influence;

(b) Accessibility: a mechanism must be publicized to those who may wish to access it and provide adequate assistance for aggrieved parties who may face barriers to access, including language, literacy, awareness, finance, distance, or fear of reprisal;

(c) Predictability: a mechanism must provide a clear and known procedure with a timeframe for each stage and clarity on the types of process and outcome it can (and cannot) offer, as well as a means of monitoring the implementation of any outcome;

(d) Equitable: a mechanism must ensure that aggrieved parties have reasonable access to sources of information, advice and expertise necessary to engage in a grievance process on fair and equitable terms;

(e) Rights-compatibility: a mechanism must ensure that its outcomes and remedies accord with internationally recognized human rights standards;

(f) Transparency: a mechanism must provide sufficient transparency of process and outcome to meet the public interest concerns at stake and should presume transparency wherever possible; non-state mechanisms, in particular, should be transparent about the receipt of complaints and the key elements of their outcomes.[11]

So far as company-level mechanisms are concerned, the SRSG also stressed that, as a seventh principle, they should operate through dialogue and mediation rather than the company itself acting as adjudicator. Company level grievance mechanisms should be designed and overseen jointly with representatives of the groups who may need access to it.[12]

B.   AN INTERNATIONAL NETWORK OF NATIONAL CONTACT POINTS

In his 2009 Report, the SRSG recognized that the NCPs of states adhering to the OECD Guidelines are potentially important avenues for remedy.[13] An important part of that usefulness is that the NCPs operate as both national institutions and as part of an international network; that is, they operate at both national and international level. It is the ability of the NCP network to operate as an international mechanism, able to deal with complaints transcending national boundaries, that interests me here.

The current OECD Guideline Procedures require that NCPs should operate 'in accordance with core criteria of visibility, accessibility, transparency, and accountability in order to achieve the objective of functional equivalence'.[14] This is consistent with the SRSG's Framework's principles for grievance mechanisms. At the same time, however, NCPs have in practice stressed the need for operational flexibility that reflects national circumstances, and this has tended to detract from the desire to ensure international minimum standards.[15] It is not surprising, therefore, that the NCP process has not so far enjoyed a great deal of credibility with NGOs that have been involved in specific instances. As OECD Watch has written, 'NGOs increasingly view the process as arbitrary, unfair and unpredictable. The cumbersome and vague manner in which many NCPs have dealt with specific instances is detrimental to the credibility of the Guidelines'.[16] The complaints procedures used by NCPs have not contributed to a meaningful and effective resolution of most of the complaints filed. By the beginning of 2010, only five out of the total of 85 NGO cases raised between 2000 and 2009 had been concluded through a mediated outcome or a satisfactory final statement.[17]

By 2010, over one-half of all NCPs were still based within government departments.[18] This can be a strength to the extent that it provides a strong incentive for parties to a dispute to participate. It can also, however, lead to policy incoherence, particularly where an NCP is staffed and controlled by a government trade and investment agency with no independent oversight and no checks and balances to ensure independence. Policy incoherence is a term used by the SRSG to designate inconsistent action in areas such as human rights or the environment by different government entities; that is, one agency may be charged with assuring the protection of human rights or the environment, while another is charged with promoting trade and investment activities, with little or no communication between the two.[19] Small wonder that TNCs become disconcerted when mixed messages are received from different government areas.

Being convened by government also detracts from the independence of NCPs. It is critical that NCP governance structures be independent, so it is promising that the inclusion of stakeholders into NCP structures has markedly expanded since 2000. By June 2009, the Chair of the Annual Meeting of NCPs could report that 'the number of NCPs with tri- or quadripartite organisations has increased, and advisory committees or permanent consultative bodies involving non-government partners have become widespread in countries with government-based NCP structures'.[20] In 2007, the Dutch NCP became independent from government when it changed from an inter-departmental office to a mixed structure consisting of four independent experts and four advisers from four ministries.[21] The IBA Working Group (IBA WG) response to the 2010 update of the Guidelines recommended the use of multi-stakeholder and independent structures akin to the Dutch model for all NCPs. It also stressed the importance of independent oversight of NCP activities at both national and international levels. A peer review mechanism would be particularly valuable in enabling self-reflection and evaluation amongst NCPs, and to help end the extreme variability in the use of the NCP process from country to country.[22]

The IBA WG also recommended that NCP procedures be rendered more professional by separating the functions of investigation and evaluation from those of mediation and conciliation.[23] Where NCPs are unable to access proper training in alternative dispute resolution techniques, they should consider following the lead of the UK NCP by outsourcing the mediation function to independent alternative dispute resolution professionals.[24]

Procedural improvements are also clearly needed. There are currently no procedural rules or timelines NCPs must follow after a complaint has been filed, and NCPs have a large amount of discretion in how they handle matters placed before them. What is needed, therefore, is a new Procedural Chapter for harmonizing the complaints system. The model could be a hybrid of existing NCP best practice procedures along with the timelines and procedures used by international non-judicial tribunals. Examples of the former include the Australian NCP timelines that recommend 30 days for the initial assessment phase and 90 days for the second (mediation) phase of the complaint process.[25] The UK NCP also has new procedures for handling specific instances within a 12-month timeframe.[26] Examples of international best practice procedures include the procedural rules of the various UN administrative tribunals established to resolve employment disputes between the relevant UN bodies and their staff members. These include the International Labour Organisation Administrative Tribunal,[27] the World Bank and IMF Administrative Tribunals[28] and, until it was abolished as of 31 December 2009, the United Nations

Administrative Tribunal.[29] Another model that might show promise would be the World Bank Inspection Panel's complaint mechanism.[30]

Other important changes to the NCP procedure are also required before the NCP network can begin to play any credible role as an international forum for handling complaints against TNCs. The two most important of these are first, facilitating cooperation between NCPs when specific instances cross national boundaries (as is often the case), and second, giving the NCP procedure 'teeth' by building in consequences for TNC failure to comply with an NCP determination.

Alleged violations of the Guidelines by a company often occur in a country that is remote from the NCP's home state. The NCP is not a court and has no power to compel the production of witnesses and evidence. Geographic distance remains a significant barrier in the way of aggrieved individuals and groups seeking access to a remedy. One way of addressing the problem would be to require governments and TNCs to facilitate site visits and the conduct of hearings in the host country where an alleged violation has occurred.[31] Cooperation between NCPs in both the home state of the accused TNC and the host country where the alleged violation has occurred is another important feature of an effective mechanism. With only 42 states out of 192 UN member states adhering to the Guidelines, there are obviously many cases where there is no local host state NCP for the home state NCP to contact. The obvious solution is for the United Nations to take up (an improved version of) the OECD Guidelines and to encourage all UN member states to establish NCPs.[32] For those countries unwilling to sign up to the OECD Guidelines, it may be possible to nominate local contact officials for cases involving the simultaneous application of two governance systems – the normative system of the Guidelines in the TNC's home state, and a state legal system in the host country.[33]

When cooperation does occur it can be useful but does not necessarily ensure the successful resolution of a complaint. For example, in August 2008 a complaint was lodged simultaneously at the Irish and Dutch NCPs regarding the operation of the Corrib gas project on the west coast of Ireland. The Corrib gas field is controlled by a consortium consisting of Shell E&P Ireland (45 per cent) which is controlled by headquarters in the Netherlands, Statoil Exploration Ireland (36.5 per cent) and Vermilion (18.5 per cent), which bought out Marathon Oil's share in 2009. The Norwegian and US NCPs were also notified. The complaint came from a local Mayo community group, Pobal Chill Chomáin, supported by NGOs,[34] who alleged breaches of the OECD Guidelines, Chapter II (General Policies) and Chapter V (Environment). On 19 February 2009, following close work between the Irish and Dutch NCP, the complaint was deemed to be admissible. However, in an unrelated initiative the Irish government undertook active mediation with the community groups and the concerned consortium. The NCPs suspended their process for fear of compromising the mediation, but in April 2009 the two NCPs resumed their work on the case when Ministerial efforts stalled. The Irish and Dutch NCPs wrote to the parties summarizing their findings in September 2009, and asked the parties to provide their reactions to the findings before the end of November. In their findings, the NCPs estimated that mediation in the case would be extremely difficult given the irreconcilable positions of the parties on the main issue: relocation of the planned processing plant. Shell E&P refused to discuss any relocation, claiming it had received all necessary government permits for the plant. In mid-January 2010, the complainants wrote a letter to the Irish NCP agreeing with the NCPs' assessment that mediation appeared impossible and requesting that the NCP close the procedure with a final statement.[35]

A more successful outcome was reached following a request lodged with the Australian NCP in July 2007. The complaint involved alleged non-observance with several provisions of the Guidelines by mining company BHP Billiton, operating via its 33.33 per cent ownership of Cerrejon Coal mine in Columbia. The Australian NCP consulted with the Swiss and UK NCPs in relation to the complaint, which primarily concerned forced relocation of local communities to make way for mine expansion. In response to the lodging of this complaint and public criticisms issued by dissident shareholders and NGOs, BHP Billiton and the two other TNCs involved in Cerrejon coal (Anglo American and Xstrata) commissioned an Independent Panel of Investigation to look into Cerrejon Coal's social programmes and its general impacts on local communities. NCP investigations were suspended pending release of the Panel's report. The Panel report when issued made a number of recommendations, particularly concerning a just settlement for the people of Tabaco, a small farming village which had been bulldozed in August 2001 to make way for mine activities.[36] The three TNC owners of Cerrejon Coal broadly accepted the Panel's recommendations. An independent facilitator was appointed in August 2008, and by December 2008 an agreement was reached between the company and the residents of Tabaco. Negotiations began with other small farming communities facing relocation as the mine expands.

But conflict continues. There has been strong criticism of the levels of financial compensation in the Tabaco agreement, and the land identified for relocation is insufficient for farming on the scale practised at Tabaco, leaving it unclear how people will make a living. In addition, the Cerrejon Coal mine owners had not, by February 2010, taken steps to fulfil the Panel's recommendations that the company engage in open, transparent negotiations with communities badly affected by the proximity of the mine, leading to collective relocation with community consent. Nor has the company, as recommended by the Panel, taken steps to ensure that people facing relocation are assured of being able to make a living following relocation.[37]

To the extent that any remedy for victims is obtained in cases such as the Cerrejon Coal case, it typically relies on the relevant TNC's desire to be seen as making a goodwill gesture and/or a determination by the TNC that providing such a remedy is otherwise in its own self-interest. What is needed is amendments to the OECD Guidelines so that consequences are attached to an adverse NCP determination. The IBA WG in its January 2010 Response to the OECD consultation recommended that at the very least NCPs should be authorized to recommend, where appropriate, that an adhering state attach formal consequences to a failure by a TNC to bring itself into line with the Guidelines following an adverse NCP finding.[38] These consequences could include:

- ensuring that stakeholders and other interested parties are made aware, if necessary through NCP and/or government websites, that the TNC is the subject of an adverse finding;
- withdrawing public subsidies, export credits or other government benefits from the TNC;
- excluding the TNC from public procurement tendering processes or trade missions; and/or
- actively pursuing more stringent measures, such as seeking disqualification of company directors or seeking delisting of public companies, through established legal avenues, in cases of more egregious and deliberate violations.[39]

C.   ENFORCING THE HUMAN RIGHTS RESPONSIBILITIES OF TNCs THROUGH THE UNITED NATIONS, REGIONAL AND NATIONAL HUMAN RIGHTS BODIES

A growing number of countries have not only signed up to international or regional human rights standards, but have provided their citizens with access to regional or international human rights forums as a means of asserting such rights.[40] National human rights institutions (NHRIs) now exist in many states. Regional human rights courts now operate in Europe, the Americas and Africa. The European Court of Human Rights can examine complaints lodged by individuals against one of the 47 member states of the European Human Rights Convention.[41] In the Americas, the American Convention on Human Rights creates two organs to promote and protect human rights, the Inter-American Commission on Human Rights and the Inter-American Court of Human

Rights. Twenty-one of the 35 members of the Organization of American States (OAS) have accepted the compulsory jurisdiction of the Court.[42] The newest regional human rights court is the African Court of Human and Peoples' Rights, which was inaugurated on 16 July 2006.[43]

In Asia, the ASEAN Charter signed by the ten members of the Association of Southeast Asian Nations in November 2007 provides (in article 14) for the establishment of 'an ASEAN human rights body'. Following the entry into force of the ASEAN Charter on 15 December 2008, a High Level Panel was established to draft terms of reference for the new human rights body, and the ASEAN Intergovernmental Commission on Human Rights (AICHR) was inaugurated on 23 October 2009.[44] Along with other developments, this steady evolution of international human rights institutions and jurisprudence has made the area of human rights law perhaps the most important example of rules which have now obtained the status of universally binding *jus cogens* norms.

So far as the various national-level human rights institutions are concerned, there are some with mandates that preclude them from work on business and human rights, while for others it has been a question of choice, question or capacity. The SRSG in his 2009 Report welcomed the decision of the International Coordinating Committee of NHRIs to establish a working group on business and human rights, and in so doing pointed to the potential of an international network of active NHRIs.[45]

Given their mandate and expertise, the UN and regional human rights bodies appear to be well placed to implement and enforce TNCs' human rights duties. As David Kinley and Junko Tadaki have noted, in addition to avenues for hearing individual petitions, the human rights bodies can and do also undertake the public examination of the human rights records of individual states by way of reporting procedures.[46] While it would be 'both conceptually difficult and practically impossible' to require all TNCs themselves to submit human rights reports, it would be possible for the various human rights bodies to become more insistent on states providing them with details of measures (including private initiatives) taken to improve the human rights behaviour of corporations operating or established within their territory.[47] The problem arises in the case of TNCs which are responsible for human rights infringements in countries other than their own home state of original incorporation. In such cases, the TNC's home state can deny responsibility for what goes on in the territory of another state and rely on the rule of non-interference in another state's affairs. The state where the alleged human rights infringement occurs can similarly refuse to accept responsibility for the actions of a foreign legal person, and similarly try to pass legal and moral responsibility onto the TNC's home state. A slanging match between two different nations may be the result, while the TNC itself escapes responsibility altogether.

The regional human rights bodies, and even more so the UN human rights bodies, have regularly been criticized for being too subject to political influences and/or for a perceived lack of effectiveness.[48] Problems faced by the human rights bodies stem partly from a lack of adequate status and authority, partly from lack of enforcement powers and mechanisms, partly from an ambiguous attitude towards contentious political issues, and partly from lack of adequate financial and human resources. These deficiencies have been recognized, and efforts have been made to improve both the standing and the resourcing of the human rights bodies. Most notably, the UN General Assembly recently (on 15 March 2006) overwhelmingly voted to establish a new Human Rights Council to replace the much criticized Human Rights Commission.[49] While the compromise outcome was recognized as being imperfect, the new Human Rights Council is generally agreed to be an improvement on its predecessor.

First, the Council is established as a subsidiary body of the General Assembly, giving it a higher status than its predecessor, the Commission, which reported to the Economic and Social Council of the UN (ECOSOC). The Resolution establishing the new Council also required an increased number of meetings: 'not fewer than three sessions per year, for a total duration of no less than 10 weeks'.[50] This compares with a single session of only six weeks per year during the life of the Commission. The new Council can also convene 'special sessions' if the need arises at the request of a member of the Council with support from one-third of the Council.[51] The expectation that the new Council will meet more frequently and will 'carry out universal periodic review of States' fulfilment of their human rights obligations'[52] has already attracted extra budget resources from the General Assembly, including the creation of two new posts.[53]

The new 47-member Council is also likely to be seen as having greater legitimacy than did the 53-member Commission. This is, first, because the new Council is more (geographically and demographically) representative in its composition, based as it is upon regional groups, with the largest number of seats going to Africa and Asia.[54] Second, each of the individual Council members must be elected by an absolute majority of the General Assembly; that is, each individual member must obtain more than 96 votes of support in a General Assembly secret ballot.[55] In addition, the General Assembly, by a two-thirds majority of members present and voting, can suspend the rights of membership of a Council member who commits gross and systematic violations of human rights.[56] This power is supported by the fact that all states sitting on the new Council are subject to a 'universal periodic review mechanism' that examines their human rights records.[57] The intention of this provision is to keep states from using the Council to shield their own human rights records from scrutiny or from 'hiding out' when criticizing other states.

The new Human Rights Council, while an improvement on its predecessor, has also been criticized – for example, for its tendency to resort to 'bloc' voting along regional political lines.[58] I remain optimistic, however, that the Council's ability to carry out its mandate successfully will continue to improve. Assuming the political will to resource the Council adequately for the purpose, there is also no reason why the investigative procedures of the Council could not be extended to cover the activities of TNCs. This could be done by expanding relevant UN mandates of special rapporteurs to include both an investigative function and the ability to refer allegations against TNCs to the Human Rights Council. Examples of relevant mandates which could be extended in this way include those of:

- the SRSG on human rights and transnational corporations and other business enterprises;
- the special rapporteur on the right to health;[59]
- special rapporteur on violence against women, its causes and consequences;[60]
- the special rapporteur on the promotion and protection of the right to freedom of opinion and expression;[61] and
- the various special rapporteurs on human rights in specific countries such as Cambodia.[62]

As Adam McBeth points out, the complaints procedure of the Council, based on the old 1503 procedure of the Commission, is intended 'to address consistent patterns of gross and reliably attested violations of all human rights and all fundamental freedoms occurring in any part of the world and under any circumstances'.[63] The complaints procedure is structured on the assumption that complaints are to be made against states, thus making arrangements for engagement with 'the State concerned'.[64] Nonetheless, consideration of violations by non-state entities is not expressly excluded. It is therefore conceivable that these procedures could be used to investigate and address serious human rights violations by TNCs.[65]

An alternative or complementary approach would be to enable the Advisory Committee of the Human Rights Council to investigate and monitor complaints against TNCs, perhaps through a dedicated working group. The Advisory Committee's predecessor, the Sub-Commission on the Promotion and Protection of Human Rights, contemplated such a process for the implementation of the UN Norms:

> The Commission on Human Rights should consider establishing a group of experts, a special rapporteur, or working group of the Commission to receive information and take effective action when enterprises fail to comply with the Norms.

> The Sub-Commission on the Promotion and Protection of Human Rights and its relevant working group should also monitor compliance with the Norms and the developing of best practices by receiving information from non-governmental organisations, unions, individuals and others, and then by allowing transnational corporations or other business enterprises an opportunity to respond.[66]

The Commission, however, made clear its view that such monitoring and enforcement was premature, noting in its 2004 decision on the Norms that the document had 'not been requested by the Commission and, as a draft proposal, has no legal standing, and that the Sub-Commission should not perform any monitoring function in this regard'.[67]

The Commentary to the UN Norms also suggests expanding the role of the UN treaty-monitoring committees, 'through the creation of additional reporting requirements for states and the adoption of general comments and recommendations interpreting treaty obligations'.[68] The treaty-monitoring bodies are currently confined to focussing upon the obligations of states arising from the relevant treaty or treaties, including the duty of states to protect human rights against breaches by non-state entities. TNCs currently cannot be parties to the relevant treaties, and so cannot be directly accused of breaching the terms of those treaties. If, however, it was recognized that TNCs could be party to human rights treaties, then the jurisdiction of the treaty monitoring bodies could be expanded accordingly. TNCs can currently sign up to the Global Compact, which encompasses a non-enforceable commitment to abide by the major human rights instruments. Surely the logical next step is to allow those TNCs able and willing to do so to sign up to a binding (and 'enforceable') form of those same instruments. Global standards monitored by global agencies have a number of advantages. In particular, global monitoring agencies would be able to view the global enterprise (group) as a whole, and would not be constrained by the boundaries of national jurisdiction. The concept of enterprise liability, as elaborated upon by US and Canadian courts, could usefully be adopted by the international tribunals in this regard.[69]

So far as remedies are concerned, the existing international human rights monitoring bodies have never had the power to impose binding remedies on states or any other actors, although specific remedies are often recommended in the non-binding reports and Concluding Observations of these bodies. If the existing system is utilized to give effect to obligations of TNCs, a similar model should be followed, at least in the early stages of the system. TNCs are more likely to accept a system to which entry is voluntary, and which relies on voluntary compliance. The traditional mechanism employed in the context of compliance by sovereign states with human rights-related recommendations, namely the mobilization of shame, should prove just as effective against TNCs with a valuable brand name to preserve, or vulnerable to pressure from civil society groups, consumer boycotts or the threat of withdrawal of government support.

While it is likely to be some time before the UN community is prepared to recognize the existence of a body able to publicly investigate the activities of TNCs, an international law system of responsibilities for TNCs is slowly emerging. Proposals for broadening the monitoring powers and capacities of existing human rights institutions depend, however, on the ability of states to cooperate, and the political willingness of the governments concerned to commit the significant resources required. In the meantime, the process could begin by strengthening the existing network of national human rights monitoring bodies to facilitate the entry of TNCs into the international law enforcement system. Such entry should be on a voluntary basis, as it currently is for states signing up to human rights reporting and submission to jurisdiction obligations; and as it currently is for TNCs signing up to the Global Compact. The state duty to promote human rights would be enough to ensure that states should encourage locally organized TNCs to sign up to human rights treaties, or at least that states should do nothing to deter TNCs from doing so.

It will also be important to ensure that the international law system as it relates to TNCs remains compatible with existing principles governing the relationship between domestic (national) legal systems and the international legal system. For example, access to international law tribunals should be restricted to those cases where existing municipal avenues for bringing TNCs to account do not reasonably exist, or have been exhausted.[70] This is currently the case in respect of individuals lodging complaints against a state with the existing UN and regional human rights tribunals.

D.   THE WORLD BANK AND OTHER GLOBAL FINANCIAL AND AID INSTITUTIONS AS AVENUES FOR REMEDY

David Kinley, Adam McBeth and others have explored the question of whether or not international law does or should impose human rights obligations on the entities of the World Bank group,[71] the IMF, the WTO and other international economic actors. This book will not repeat that examination, but instead will explore the extent to which the World Bank group and other international financial organizations could be utilized in the regulation of TNC activities.

One important reason for turning to international financial institutions (IFIs) is that when compared to the UN Human Rights Council and the regional human rights bodies, IFIs like the World Bank and the Asian

Development Bank have fewer problems in terms of adequate resources, political support and institutional technical expertise to enforce their rules effectively. Given their pivotal role in the process of globalization, and their direct relations with and impact upon corporations, there is logic in seeking to utilize the major IFIs to ensure TNCs' observance of human rights and environmental standards. So far as the World Bank is concerned, its prominent role in facilitating global investment flows, and its close connection with private business, make it a potentially powerful regulator of TNC activities, particularly in developing countries. A key body in this respect is the Bank's private sector arm, the International Finance Corporation (IFC), which provides businesses with loans to implement development projects, usually in partnership with host states. The IFC has a standing policy to carry out all of its operations in an 'environmentally and socially responsible manner' and it requires its business clients to abide by the IFC's environmental, social, and disclosure policies.[72] These policies include some of the existing international human rights standards, such as prohibitions on forced labour and child labour, and the rights of indigenous peoples. They are normally incorporated into the investment agreement between the IFC and the corporate client, and the client's failure to comply with the policies can result in suspension or cancellation of an IFC loan. Further, sensitivity to environmental and social issues in the operations of international finance has also been boosted by the recent development and adoption of the 'Equator Principles' by a number of international banks. The Equator Principles are in fact based on the social and environmental policies of the World Bank and the IFC, and seek to place certain conditions on the provision of development project finance by the signatory banks.

Both the IFC and other financial aid institutions have been accused of violating their own policies, by funding projects that have caused or are implicated in human rights abuses.[73] This indicates the presence of real obstacles to the more meaningful integration of human rights in the strategic thinking, policy-planning and project implementation of the World Bank, the IMF and other major IFIs. Politically, the views of some member states are equivocal, if not hostile in some cases, to the notion of human rights entering the domain of international finance. There is also the obstacle of bureaucratic intransigence. Where there is an 'approvals culture' that emphasizes and rewards getting projects started and completed rather than their substantive merits or efficacy, a lack of relevant expertise and an innate reluctance to take on anything new, then bringing about the lasting incorporation of human rights considerations into the work of an IFI becomes an uphill battle at best.[74]

The desire for economic success often provides a disincentive for IFIs to take non-economic issues (such as human rights or environmental externalities) into account. Moreover, IFIs, even those motivated by aid and development-promotion agendas, do not have a mandate for protecting human rights.

In the absence of explicit mandates to protect human rights, they cannot be expected to act as general enforcement agencies of the relevant human rights norms that TNCs should respect. The extent to which they are currently willing to enforce human rights obligations of TNCs is limited by their economic objectives. For example, while the World Bank supports efforts to abolish child and forced labor and to promote gender equality, it is ambivalent about promoting freedom of association and collective bargaining because the economic effects of those labor standards are apparently unclear. Thus the human rights norms that these institutions are prepared to protect inevitably tend to be selective, based on the 'market friendliness' of the rights rather than on the needs that give rise to the invocation of the rights.[75]

Adam McBeth, on the other hand, argues that the development mandate of the World Bank institutions can and should be interpreted to incorporate human rights concerns. He quotes Ibrahim Shihata, the former General Counsel of the World Bank, who recognized that:

> ... no balanced development can be achieved without the realization of a minimum degree of all human rights, material or otherwise,

and argues that:

> An approach that embraces human rights at the centre of the World Bank's activities is ... not only permitted under the Bank's Articles of Agreement ... but is necessary for its development focus to be meaningful.[76]

E.   THE WTO AND THE INTERNATIONAL HUMAN RIGHTS OBLIGATIONS OF TNCs

A number of writers have explored in depth proposals for linking human rights to trade through the WTO and/or the various trade-promoting treaties that it oversees.[77] This book does not seek to revisit the already well-trodden debate over whether or not the WTO can or should play a role in human rights or environmental protection. Suffice to note that at the heart of the question lies the dilemma of how to bring non-economic considerations (such as human rights or the environment) onto the WTO's agenda given the free-market imperative that drives the organization's culture. There is also the dilemma of the moral double-standards that can appear when trade sanctions are used to promote non-economic objectives. The problem is that human rights abuses and environmental damage are all too often found in the very nations that need greater access to developed country markets if they are to earn the resources needed for addressing environmental and social objectives. Imposing trade sanctions on developing nations where human rights and environmental abuses occur may not only impose greater hardship on societies already under strain, but may also serve to make worse the very problems sought to be addressed.

Given these limitations, and as a number of commentators have shown, the WTO, like the World Bank/IFC, is only able to provide enforcement mechanisms in specific circumstances in a piecemeal manner. Although this does not mean that their potential for upholding human rights should be dismissed altogether, their enforcement devices can apparently only be used so far as upholding environmental or social principles coincides with the economic imperatives that drive their operations.[78]

F. THE GLOBAL FIRM AND THE INTERNATIONAL LABOUR ORGANIZATION

In the area of international labour standards, Virginia Leary has convincingly argued that 'the focus in international law on state action alone fails to address the influence of the activities of non-state actors, such as multinational enterprises (MNEs), on labor and other social issues'.[79] This focus only on state activity is in fact one reason for the increased adoption of voluntary codes of conduct by TNCs (discussed in Chapter 2). Since that time, the ILO Tripartite Declaration and the OECD Guidelines, as discussed above, have purported to 'guide' governments, employers and worker organizations in 'adopting social policies'. As noted above (in Chapter 2), one of the major defects of the ILO Declaration as an instrument purporting to establish global standards is the lack of willingness amongst states to subject themselves to ILO scrutiny, even via the relatively anonymous mechanism of the survey.

If TNCs were given greater access to, and permitted to become part of, the Annual Conference, the Governing Body and the various sub-committees of the ILO, and if they had greater input into the design of ILO documents, they would have greater incentive to subscribe to ILO standards. Individual firms could also be left free to agree to mandatory ILO arbitration in the event of an alleged breach of ILO standards, or could be left to the mercy of adverse publicity in the event of such an allegation.

Once a firm had agreed to abide by the standards established in an ILO instrument, that firm would still be free to invest in countries operating lower standards of protection than those provided for internationally, but in so doing the firm would bring with it the higher standards agreed upon at ILO level. The introduction of the higher standard would provide both an example and a competitive incentive for other firms in that country.

NOTES

1. See e.g., John Ruggie, *Business and Human Rights: Towards Operationalizing the 'Protect, Respect and Remedy' Framework*, UN Doc. A/HRC/11/13 (22 April 2009), Part V 'Access to Remedy', paras 86–115; and John Ruggie, *Business and Human Rights: Further Steps Toward the Operationalization of the 'Protect, Respect and Remedy' Framework*, UN Doc. A/HRC/14/27 (9 April 2010), Part V 'Access to Remedy', paras 88–119.
2. *SS Lotus (France v Turkey)*, PCIJ Rep. Ser. A, No. 10.
3. Ruggie, A/HRC/14/27 (9 April 2010), above n. 1, para. 18.
4. *Ibid.*, paras 96–102, discussing state-based non-judicial mechanisms.
5. Ruggie, A/HRC/11/13 (22 April 2009), above n. 1, paras 109–10.
6. *Ibid.*, para. 111.
7. Ingrid Macdonald, 'The limits of corporate codes of conduct' (2002) 7:3 *Mining Monitor* (September) 9.
8. BASESwiki was launched with support from the Compliance Advisor/Ombudsman of the World Bank Group and the JAMS Foundation: Ruggie, A/HRC/11/13 (22 April 2009), above n. 1, paras 107—8. BASESwiki now also attracts support from the Open Society Institute.
9. Noteworthy additions include a fully searchable database of dispute mechanisms, resources and case stories, and a seek assistance tool to connect users with experienced contributors. BASESwiki 2.0 can be accessed at http://baseswiki.org/en/Main_Page.
10. John Ruggie, *Protect, Respect and Remedy: A Framework for Business and Human Rights*, UN Doc.. A/HRC/8/5 (7 April 2008) para.. 92.
11. *Ibid.*
12. *Ibid.*, para. 95.
13. Ruggie, A/HRC/11/13 (22 April 2009) paras 102–4.
14. *The OECD Guidelines for Multinational Enterprises: Decision of the Council*, DAFFE/IME (2000) (June 2000) 20, Procedural Guidance, '1 National Contact Points' (introductory para.).
15. Ruggie, A/HRC/11/13 (22 April 2009), ABOVE N. 1, para. 104.
16. OECD Watch, *Five Years On: A Review of the OECD Guidelines and National Contact Points* (2005)), available at www.foei.org/en/resources/publications/economic-justice-resisting-neoliberalism/2000-2007/pagesfiveyears.pdf/
17. IBA Working Group on the OECD Guidelines for Multinational Enterprises, *Response to the OECD Consultation on an Update of the OECD Guidelines for Multinational Enterprises* (31 January 2010) para. 60 ('IBA WG Response')..
18. As at June 2009, 17 NCPs were based in a single government department, while 11 were based in multiple government departments: *Annual Meeting of National Contact Points 16–17 June 2009, Report by the Chair*, Section II 'Innovations in NCP structure and procedures', notes 3 and 4.
19. IBA WG Response, above n. 17, para. 65.
20. *Annual Meeting of National Contact Points, Report by the Chair*, above n. 18, noting nine NCPs with a tripartite structure involving governments, business and trade unions (Belgium, Denmark, Estonia, France, Latvia, Lithuania, Luxembourg, Norway and Sweden); and one quadripartite NCP in Finland involving NGOs in addition to government, business and trade union representation.
21. *Ibid.*, note 8.
22. IBA WG Response, above n. 17, paras 75–9.
23. *Ibid.*, para. 63, noting that these functions (neutral conciliator versus authoritative evaluator) have already been separated in the Compliance Ombudsman of the World Bank.
24. *Ibid.*, para. 62.
25. *Ibid.*, paras 81–2.
26. *Ibid.*, para. 82.
27. See www.ilo.org/public/english/tribunal/.

28. World Bank Administrative Tribunal, http://Inweb90.worldbank.org/crn/wbt/wbtwebsite. nsf; International Monetary Fund Administrative Tribunal, www.imf.org/external/imfat/ index.htm.
29. The UN Administrative Tribunal was abolished as a result of the decision of the General Assembly to establish a new system of administration of justice, including a two-tier formal system comprising a first instance, the UN Dispute Tribunal, and an appellate instance, the UN Appeals Tribunal: See Resolutions 61/261 of 4 April 2007; 62/228 of 22 December 2007 and 63/253 of 24 December 2008. See also GA Res. 351 A(IV) (24 November 1949) which established the Tribunal.
30. See http://web.worldbank.org/. See also IBA WG Response, above n. 17, para. 87.
31. IBA WG Response, above n. 17, para. 62.
32. The Investment Committee currently conducts outreach activities in non-adherent countries to elevate the Guidelines' profile and continues to consult with interested non-adherent countries: *Annual Meeting of the National Contact Points 19–20 June 2007, Report by the Chair*, Section III.d; *Annual Meeting of the National Contact Points 16–17 June 2009, Report by the Chair*, Section III.c.
33. For discussion of such a case, see Larry Catá Backer, *Law at the End of the Day*, Part II, *The OECD, Vedanta, and the Indian Supreme Court: Polycentricity, Transnational Corporate Governance and John Ruggie's Protect/Respect Framework* (3 November 2009), available at http://bit.ly/4Jzc8x. Also available at http://lcbackerblog.blogspot.com/2009/11/part-ii-oecd-vedanta-indian-supreme.html.
34. The NGOs supporting the community's efforts were Action from Ireland (Afri) and Sherpa, a French NGO.
35. See *Pobal Chill Chomain Community et al. v Shell*, available at http://oecdwatch.org/cases/Case_146.
36. *Columbian Communities v BHP Billiton*, available at http://oecdwatch.org/cases/Case_121/.
37. For full discussion and analysis, see BHP Billiton Watch, 'Cerrejon Coal mine profile' (21 October 2009), available at http://bhpbillitonwatch.wordpress.com/2009/10/21/cerrejon-coal-mine-profile/.
38. IBA WG Response, above n. 17, para. 67.
39. *Ibid.*
40. Adopted and opened for signature in New York by GA Res. 2200A (XXI) (16 December 1966), 999 UNTS 171 (entered into force 23 March 1976 in accordance with art. 9). As at 24 June 2010, there were 113 states parties to the First Optional Protocol (UN Treaty Collection, http://treaties.un.org/).
41. The European Court of Human Rights based in Strasbourg consists of a number of judges equal to the number of member states of the Council of Europe that have ratified the Convention for the Protection of Human Rights and Fundamental Freedoms and its Protocols. By 2010 there were 47 states parties to the Convention, although not all had joined the various Protocols to the Convention. Judgments delivered by the Court are binding: see further the Court's website at www.echr.coe.int/ECHR/EN/.
42. The American Convention on Human Rights entered into force on 18 July 1978 when the 11th instrument of ratification by an OAS member was deposited. See further Inter-American Court of Human Rights, www.corteidh.or.cr/.
43. The 11 judges of the inaugural African Court on Human and Peoples' Rights were sworn in at the Seventh Session of the Meeting of the African Union Heads of Government in Banjul, Gambia, on 16 July 2006. The Protocol to the African Charter on Human and Peoples' Rights Establishing an African Court of Human and Peoples' Rights entered into force on 25 January 2004 after the Union of Comoros became the 15th state to ratify the Protocol on 26 December 2003. (Amnesty International Press Release, 'Establishing an African Court on Human Rights' (26 January 2004), available at www.scoop.co.nz/; Innocent Anaba, 'African human rights court judges sworn in' (17 July 2006), available at http://vanguardngr.com/).
44. See further AICHR, at ASEAN, www.aseansec.org/22769.htm.
45. Ruggie, A/HRC/11/13 (22 April 2009), above n. 1, paras 102–3.
46. David Kinley and Junko Tadaki, 'From talk to walk: the emergence of human rights respon-

sibilities for corporations at international law' (2004) 44 *Virginia Journal of International Law* 931, 997–8.

47. *Ibid.*
48. Lula Ahrens, 'UN Human Rights Council faces the same criticism as its predecessor', *RNW-Radio Netherlands Worldwide*, 21 May 2010, available at www.rnw.nl/international-justice/article/un-human-rights-council-faces-same-criticism-its-predecessor;   Lauren Vriens, 'Troubles plague UN Human Rights Council', *Council on Foreign Relation Backgrounder*, 13 May 2009, available at www.cfr.org/publication/9991/troubles_plague_un_human_rights_council.html; Robert Evans, 'UN chief tells rights body drop rhetoric, blocs', *Reuters*, 12 December 2008; Linda Mamoun, 'A conversation with Richard Falk', *The Nation*, 30 June 2008; 'The European Court on Human Rights: a body under pressure,' *Deutsche Welle DW-World.de*, 18 February 2010, available at www.dw-world.de/dw/article/0,,5254314,00.html.
49. General Assembly Resolution establishing the Human Rights Council, UN Doc. A/RES/60/251 (15 March 2006). See also 'UN creates new human rights body', BBC News, 15 March 2006, available at http://news.bbc.co.uk/2/hi/europe/4810538.stm. See also Human Rights Council, www2.ohchr.org/english/bodies/hrcouncil.
50. UN Doc. A/RES/60/251 (15 March 2006) para. 10.
51. *Ibid.*
52. *Ibid.*, para. 5(e).
53. General Assembly Department of Public Information, News and Media Division, 'Fifth Committee considers budget implications of proposed Human Rights Council', 60th General Assembly, Fifth Committee, 37th Meeting (AM), UN Doc. GA/AB/3720, available at www.un.org/News/Press/docs/2006/gaab3720.doc.htm.
54. The regional distribution of seats is African Group, 13; Asian Group, 13; Eastern Europe Group, 6; Latin American and Caribbean Group, 8; and Western Europe and other Western Democracies, 7: UN Doc. A/RES/60/251 (15 March 2006) para 7.
55. UN Doc. A/RES/60/251 (15 March 2006) para. 7.
56. *Ibid.*
57. *Ibid.*, para. 9.
58. See above n. 48.
59. Who could, for example, report on the role of TNCs in facilitating or blocking access to essential medicines: see *Report of the Special Rapporteur on the Right to Health*, UN Doc. A/61/338 (13 September 2006) Part III.
60. Resolution establishing the mandate of the Special Rapporteur on Violence against Women, its Causes and Consequences, UN HRC Res. 1994/45 (4 March 1994); HRC 59th Sess., Res. 2003/45; HRC Decision 1/102 (March 2006). See also www2.ohchr.org/english/issues/women/rapporteur/.
61. Mandate established in 1993, extended by HRC Res. 7/36 (March 2008). See also www2.ohchr.org/english/issues/opinion/index.htm.
62. As at June 2010, there were eight country mandates established under the 'special procedures' mechanism adopted by the Human Rights Council to investigate the human rights situation in specific countries. This compares to 31 thematic mandates established to address thematic issues (such as women's rights) in all parts of the world. See further 'Special Procedures of the Human Rights Council', available at www2.ohchr.org/english/bodies/chr/special/index.htm.
63. Adam McBeth, *International Economic Actors and Human Rights* (Routledge, 2010) 318.
64. Institution Building of the Human Rights Council, HRC Res. 5/1, contained in UN Doc. A/HRC/5/21, Annex, para. 85, cited in McBeth, above n. 63.
65. McBeth, above n. 63, 318.
66. United Nations Sub-Commission on the Protection and Promotion of Human Rights, *Commentary to the Norms on the Responsibilities of Transnational Corporations and Other Business Enterprises with regard to Human Rights*, UN Doc. E/CN.4/Sub.2/2003/38/Rev.2 (26 August 2003) para. 16(b)
67. Commission on Human Rights, Decision 2004/116 (20 April 2004) para. (c).
68. *Commentary to the Norms*, above n. 66, para. 16(b).

69. See Chapter 4. See also Aurora Institute, *Submission to the Canadian Democracy and Corporate Accountability Commission* (17 June 2001), available at www.aurora.ca/docs/AccountabilityCommSubmisssion.pdf; and Sarah Joseph, *Corporations and Transnational Human Rights Litigation* (Hart Publishing, 2004) 138–42.

70. Gillian Triggs notes that 'the traditional requirement that a ... claimant in international law must first exhaust local remedies has contemporary vibrancy before recently established bodies such as the regional human rights courts and the UN Human Rights Committee': Gillian D. Triggs, *International Law: Contemporary Principles and Practices* (Butterworths, 2006) 470. The requirement to first exhaust local remedies was recognized in *Elettronica Sicula Spa* [1989] ICJ Rep. 15, 40–2; and is also recognized in the Draft Articles on Responsibility of States for Internationally Wrongful Acts (2001), art. 44(b).

71. McBeth, above n. 63, ch. 5, 165–242 and David Kinley, *Civilising Globalisation: Human Rights and the Global Economy* (Cambridge, 2009) 132–44. See also Galit A. Sarfaty, 'Why culture matters in international institutions: the marginality of human rights at the World Bank' (2009) 103:4 *American Journal of International Law* 647 and Mac Darrow, *Between Light and Shadow: The World Bank, the IMF, and International Human Rights Law* (Hart Publishing, Oxford and Portland, 2003).

72. The IFC adopted its Environmental and Social Safeguard Policies and its Disclosure Policy in 1998. Since 2006, IFC has applied the Policy and Performance Standards on Social and Environmental Sustainability to all investment projects. See further IFC Environmental and Social Standards, www.ifc.org/ifcext/sustainability.nsf/Content/EnvSocStandards.

73. Joseph E. Stiglitz, *Globalization and its Discontents* (W.W. Norton & Co., 2002); Joseph E. Stiglitz, *Making Globalization Work* (W.W. Norton & Co., 2006); Ngaire Woods, *The Globalizers: the IMF, The World Bank and their Borrowers* (Cornell Studies in Money, 2006) and Jeffrey D. Sachs, *The End of Poverty: Economic Possibilities for Our Time* (Penguin Press, 2005).

74. David Kinley, *Civilising Globalisation: Human Rights and the Global Economy* (Cambridge University Press, 2009) 139–40.

75. *Ibid.* See also David Kinley and Justine Nolan, 'Trading and Aiding Human Rights: Corporations in the Global Economy' (2008) 25:4 *Nordic Journal of Human Rights* 353.

76. McBeth, above n. 63, 181.

77. See e.g., David Bodansky, 'What's so bad about unilateral action to protect the environment' (2000) 11:2 *European Journal of International Law* 339; Andrew Field, 'Catching the Tasmanian Salmon Laws: how a decade of changing world trade law has tackled environmental protection' (2000) 19:2 *University of Tasmania Law Review* 237.

78. McBeth, above n. 63, ch. 4, 85–164 and David Kinley, *Civilising Globalisation: Human Rights and the Global Economy* (2009) ch. 2, 37–89. See also Kinley and Tadaki, above n. 46, 1014; and Field, above n. 77.

79. Virginia Leary, '"Form follows function': formulation of international labor standards – treaties, codes, soft law, trade agreements' in James Gross (ed.), *Workers Rights as Human Rights* (Ithaca: NY, Cornell University Press, 2003) 179–206, 194.

8.   The global firm and the environment

Just as corporations should be invited to subscribe to obligations spelt out in the key human rights treaties of the United Nations and its organizations, so also should corporations be invited and permitted to sign up to relevant international treaties in the area of the environment. TNCs should also be bound by, and take their place in the formation of, accepted tenets of customary international law relating to protection of the environment – at least those which have attained the status of *jus cogens* or peremptory norms of behaviour in international law. Customary environmental legal principles which have attained this status have been said to include such concepts as the preventive principle, the principle of sustainable development, the precautionary principle, the polluter pays principle and the concept of intergenerational equity.[1]

A.   THE FRAGMENTED STATE OF INTERNATIONAL ENVIRONMENTAL LAW

1.   A Multiplicity of Instruments

Environmental issues are undoubtedly global in nature. However, most serious attempts made so far to deal with environmental problems have occurred at national or regional level and/or on an ad hoc, specific issue basis. The result has been, as described in the UN Secretary-General's Report *In Larger Freedom*, a proliferation of instruments and agencies dealing with environmental matters:

> There are now more than 400 regional and universal multilateral environmental treaties in force, covering a broad range of environmental issues, including biodiversity, climate change and desertification. The sectoral character of these legal instruments and the fragmented machinery for monitoring their implementation make it harder to mount effective responses across the board.[2]

As the Secretary-General also went on to note:

> There is a clear need to streamline and consolidate our efforts to follow up and implement these treaties. Already in 2002, the World Summit on Sustainable Development, held in Johannesburg, emphasised the need for a more coherent institutional

framework of international environmental governance, with better coordination and monitoring. It is now high time to consider a more integrated structure for environmental standard-setting, scientific discussion and monitoring treaty compliance. This should be built on existing institutions, such as the United Nations Environment Programme, as well as the treaty bodies and specialized agencies.[3]

The other part of the story of how international environmental law jurisprudence has become fragmented relates to the way in which environmental issues have arisen in a variety of different contexts, including in the context of human rights and trade-related disputes.

2.   A Multiplicity of Tribunals

The growth since the Second World War in the number of adjudicative institutions at the international level has generated many positive effects. This is particularly true in the area of human rights law, with human rights commissions and tribunals now established in nearly all regions of the world. Individuals in an increasing number of countries now have the very real possibility of obtaining an international remedy when their rights are violated. Ad hoc and permanent arbitral tribunals have also proliferated in response to growing demand for the orderly resolution of international business disputes. International trade disputes between states are resolved by professional World Trade Organization (WTO) dispute resolution panels,[4] while investment disputes between investor and host state are resolved within ICSID[5] or a similar arbitral tribunal. Private commercial disputes between business partners from different nations are also increasingly resolved under international arbitration rules, such as the UNCITRAL Model Law on International Commercial Arbitration[6] or the ICC's arbitration rules.[7]

Many of the regional human rights bodies and other specific subject matter tribunals have now developed particular expertise in their own areas of international law. It can be argued that international law jurisprudence has grown stronger as the result of the growth of these specialized tribunals. But the parallel operation of multiple adjudicative institutions also poses a range of legal and practical difficulties. It can, and sometimes does, lead to 'forum shopping' by opportunistic litigants. It also creates a variety of sometimes conflicting lines of jurisprudence in relation to the same legal issue. Conflicting decisions from different tribunals create considerable uncertainty, and can have a destabilizing effect on whole areas of law.[8] Tim Stephens argues that this has become particularly the case in the area of environmental law. He points out that the process of decentralization evident in other areas of international law 'has been particularly evident in the environmental context, with detailed regulatory regimes devised to address environmental challenges at national, regional and global scales'.[9]

In his exploration of the way in which the jurisprudence of international environmental law has been fragmented, Stephens examines the way in which environmental claims have been dealt with by specialized forums in the areas of human rights and international trade. He thus explores an expanding body of environmental jurisprudence emanating from some of the most active international adjudicative institutions.[10] Importantly, he finds no evidence that these institutions have preferred inadequate or 'skewed' interpretations of environmental rules and principles.

In relation to the human rights bodies, Stephens finds that attempts to seek redress for environmental damage have been pursued predominately through the language of human rights, such as the right to health and cultural rights, and including the right to life. This has served to relieve the relevant bodies of any need to examine potentially relevant environmental norms.[11] As Stephens also points out, however, the future of human rights petitions raising environmental issues may not be so unproblematic. There are distinct possibilities of normative conflict if complaints are made concerning state environmental policies that, among other things, interfere with social, economic or cultural rights, including the right to development.[12]

Second, in relation to procedural rights, the potential for fragmentation has been lessened by the almost complete overlap between the human rights and environmental agendas to improve access to information, to enhance public participation, and to provide effective remedies for rights infringements. Indeed, the human rights jurisprudence on such matters is likely to be of considerable value as procedural environmental rights receive greater recognition in international environmental law.[13]

The resolution of disputes involving environmental issues in the WTO system involves substantially greater opportunities for environmental norms to be considered in a selective and parochial manner.[14] This is particularly noticeable in relation to those WTO rules that purport to allow member countries to rely upon environmental protection claims to justify measures that would otherwise constitute violations of WTO undertakings.

The two most important rules underpinning the WTO system of 'free trade' in goods are the most favoured nation rule, and the national treatment rule, both contained in the General Agreement on Tariffs and Trade 1994 (GATT). The most favoured nation rule requires that all WTO members provide equality of treatment for like products from any other WTO member country,[15] while the national treatment rule requires that domestic and imported products should be treated equally in terms of the application of internal regulations and taxes.[16]

Crucial to the relationship between the WTO system for trade in goods and protection of the environment is article XX of GATT. Article XX sets out certain exceptions to the GATT's free trade rules for health and environmental measures. It provides that so long as such measures do not constitute a 'disguised restriction on international trade', and so long as they are not applied in a manner which would constitute 'a means of arbitrary or unjustifiable discrimination between countries where the same conditions prevail', WTO members may adopt and enforce measures:

(b)   necessary to protect human, animal or plant life or health; ...
(g)   relating to the conservation of exhaustible natural resources if such measures are made effective in conjunction with restrictions on domestic production or consumption.[17]

The meaning and content of article XX(b) is further elucidated upon by the WTO Agreement on Sanitary and Phytosanitary Measures ('SPS Agreement').[18] Member states are permitted to make their own decisions concerning SPS measures, so long as such measures 'do not arbitrarily or unjustifiably discriminate between [countries] where identical or similar conditions prevail', and are not 'applied in a manner which would constitute a disguised restriction on international trade'.[19] In addition, SPS measures must be applied only to the extent necessary to protect human, animal or plant life or health, as determined through the use of internationally accepted risk assessment procedures, and after taking into account 'the objective of minimizing negative trade effects'.[20]

As Tim Stephens notes, only a small number of the many (well over 100) Panel and Appellate body reports adopted by the WTO since its dispute settlement system commenced operation in 1995 have dealt with environmental issues. Of these, none has dealt with a direct conflict between environmental rules and WTO commitments.[21] Rather, both the nature of the disputes which have been litigated and the careful way in which they have been framed by Panels and the Appellate Body have allowed WTO jurisprudence to develop on its own terms,[22] without, however, ignoring the broader context of international law, including international environmental law.[23] For example, while recognizing the existence of the precautionary principle in international law, WTO jurisprudence has found it unnecessary to make a finding on the status of that principle.[24] In other cases, the decision has been based on a finding that the measure in issue was applied in an arbitrary, discriminatory and unjustifiable manner, and/or that the measure was not 'necessary' within the meaning of article XX(b).[25] Only rarely (as in the *Beef Hormones* and *Shrimp Sea-Turtle* cases for example) has the Panel/ Appellate Body found it necessary to consider arguments beyond the terms of the WTO instrument itself, or to make any reference to environmental instruments potentially having a bearing on the case before it.[26]

In the *Tuna Dolphin* cases, the Panels also adopted a narrow interpretation of article XX, questioning the legality of using domestic measures for an extra-territorial purpose, namely to affect the environmental policies of other states.[27] If this interpretation is upheld, it may create a conflict between the need for global action on climate change, on the one hand, and the liberalization of trade, on the other. In particular, it may create problems for any country attempting to implement climate change measures, such as a carbon tax, in a way that simply sends local industries overseas to a country with less stringent environmental standards.[28] It may also create difficulties for any effort to enforce global action on climate change through trade-related measures, such as trade-related and other economic sanctions.

B. ROLE OF TNCs IN OVERCOMING CONFLICTS BETWEEN TRADE LIBERALIZATION AND ENVIRONMENTAL PROTECTION

Trade liberalization can have positive consequences for the environment by providing poorer nations with the material capacity to implement environmental policies, and by mandating the removal of subsidies to uneconomic and ecologically unsustainable agricultural or fishing industries. However, trade liberalization can also have negative environmental effects by, among other things, creating incentives for industry to move production to states with poor environmental standards (the so-called 'race to the bottom'). In the context of climate change, worldwide action is needed to control climate change to within habitable limits. Following the Copenhagen Conference of late 2009, however, doubts remain as to whether enough of the world's greenhouse gas emitting nations will commit to action so as to achieve the required effect. Even a majority of states committing to action will not work if climate change action simply shifts emissions to those countries which fail to act (carbon leakage). The usual arguments in favour of free trade therefore do not apply when it comes to climate change action. Indeed, the free trade rules of the WTO can even prevent countries from attempting to prevent carbon leakage.[29]

In the absence of a global emissions trading system set up under its own rules and operating independently of the WTO system, the problem arises of how emission abating countries will protect their trade-exposed emission intensive industries in order to prevent them moving offshore. One option is for governments simply to subsidize such industries for the costs of compliance with climate change policies (including the cost of paying carbon taxes if imposed). There are a number of problems with such an approach, including the risk that it could simply neutralize many of the market-adjustment benefits to be gained from, for example, raising the cost of carbon-based energy sources. Direct government subsidies to business can also have implications under GATT.

Article XVI of GATT requires that the details of all government subsidies to local industry (including any form of income or price support) be notified to the WTO. Article VI of GATT then recognizes that importing countries may impose a countervailing duty on imported products equivalent to the value of the estimated bounty or subsidy determined to have been granted directly or indirectly, on the manufacture, production or export of such product in the country of origin. So article VI could conceivably be used to justify imposing an extra tariff burden on imported products, but only if WTO jurisprudence defines 'subsidy' broadly enough to include a country's payments made to local industry for the purpose of defraying the costs of climate change policy compliance measures.

The opposite argument might also be made that governments which *fail* to take climate change action are providing an indirect (hidden) subsidy to local industries through their failure to impose on local industries the costs of adjustment to a carbon-neutral world. It remains unlikely, however, that WTO jurisprudence would ever extend to including within the definition of 'subsidy' a country's failure to impose climate change costs on its local export-oriented industries. For this would require the placing of a monetary and market value on environmental damage in a way not normally recognized by market economists as valid. Likewise, when determining the 'normal value' of a product for the purposes of assessing whether 'dumping' has occurred,[30] it is currently not possible to calculate the cost of production of the product by including 'hidden costs' (externalities) such as environmental costs.

Other government measures aimed at preventing 'carbon leakage' when companies move offshore are also open to a charge of violating WTO rules. For example, a government serious about climate change action might impose a climate tariff (tax) on all imported products at the point of import. The tax would be equivalent to the 'climate costs' of production of the imported product. This measure would, however, be in violation of article I of GATT. Article I requires that most favoured nation status be accorded to like products from all WTO member countries. A climate tariff would inevitably treat like products from different countries differently, according to the different climate costs of the same product from different parts of the world. This would be true even if the climate tariff was waived for imports deemed to have paid carbon taxes in another jurisdiction.

Nor would it work to impose a climate tax on all goods at the point of sale inside the importing country, similar to a GST or VAT. One aim of such a tax would be to adjust the shelf price of carbon-intensive products (whether imported or domestically produced) so that prices reflect the true climate costs of what is being sold. It would not be possible for such a tax to treat all domestic products the same as all imported 'like' products. To impose such a tax is therefore likely to violate the national treatment rule in article III of GATT.

Already governments which have attempted to impose 'green taxes' on, for example, vehicle engine size, have been met with complaints filed under the WTO Disputes Settlement Understanding.[31]

Another protective measure could be to require importers to obtain import permits tied to the climate costs of imported products. Imposing such a measure would, however, violate article XI of GATT. Article XI requires the elimination of all quantitative restrictions on trade, including non-tariff restrictions such as import and export licence requirements. The same rule against quantitative restrictions on trade could also prevent a WTO member state from imposing climate change 'sanctions' on goods from another WTO member that was failing to implement its greenhouse gas reducing obligations.

It can therefore be argued that if the WTO system is to be retained without radical reform, governments alone cannot bring about climate change action on a sufficient scale. Private sector commitment to action is also essential. This increases the need for TNCs in particular to sign up to global-scale environmental standards, and to submit themselves to monitoring and regulatory action in respect of such standards.

C.   TNCs AND ENVIRONMENTAL TREATY-MAKING

Currently TNCs are most notable for their absence in either the creation or binding coverage of international environmental law. It remains true, however, that the vast bulk of environmentally destructive activities are carried out not by states or international organizations subject to international law, but by corporations falling essentially outside of the coverage of that law. Thus, the plaintiffs in the claim against BHP in the *Ok Tedi* case (discussed in Chapter 3) had no avenue for taking their claim to an international forum, despite the undoubtedly international aspects of the dispute, and despite the fact that the International Commission of Jurists expressly condemned the proposed Ok Tedi legislation and BHP's role in drafting that law.[32] Just as with many of the activities of transnational corporations in less developed countries, international law remained blind to the dispute, treating it as an 'invisible' matter of domestic jurisdiction – invisible because it involved non-state parties (the local landowners and the company), and because the United Nations is prohibited from intervening in matters deemed to be 'essentially within the domestic jurisdiction of any state'[33] (as in the dispute between the local landowners and the PNG government).

From a procedural point of view, the key to solving this problem lies in giving TNCs greater access to international processes. In the same way that many NGOs have for several decades now been taking an active part in the activities of UN and other international organizations, so also could TNCs be invited and welcomed as observers, participants and/or members of global environmental forums. If TNCs are to be guided by environmental treaties, it is only fair that they be included within the treaty making process. If private capital is to bear its share of the burden of implementing strategies directed towards environmental protection, then private capital must be brought on board as an essential participant in making development sustainable. The trend towards privatizing more and more state functions and services suggests that governments are likely to rely heavily on private capital for the design, development and marketing of new forms of 'green' technology. In such a context it becomes irresponsible to divorce environmental law, as the concern of government, from environmental practice, the concern of business.

It is a truism to recognize that when government representatives come together to negotiate new environmental treaties, they typically come with a political agenda. It is also stating the obvious to note that political agendas, more often than not, are heavily influenced by lobbyists and pressure groups at home. Corporations, particularly TNCs that boost national income through their trade and investment activities, typically exert more influence than most lobbyists. Bringing TNCs to the international negotiating table would simply help to make the already heavy influence of TNCs much more transparent. No longer would TNCs be able to hide their influence behind government representation. Moreover, with TNCs free to argue their own case at the international negotiating table, national politicians and representatives would be freed from the fear of the political costs of alienating large business interests back at home. They would thus be more able to focus on the interests of their nation as a whole. The final argument in favour of bringing TNCs to the international negotiating table is that many international agreements, particularly environmental and human rights agreements, rely for their effectiveness on the willingness and ability of TNCs to comply with their terms. Surely TNCs themselves are best placed to make clear the limits of such willingness and ability.

There are a number of arguments against allowing TNCs at the international negotiating table. First, there is the lawyer's argument that agreements between states and TNCs are not treaties in a formal, binding sense. In 1952, the International Court of Justice, in *Anglo-Iranian Oil Company*, held that an oil-concession agreement signed between a state and a foreign company was not a treaty.[34] Even when, as sometimes happens, an agreement between a state and a company provides that it shall be interpreted in whole or in part by reference to rules of international law, that does not make it a treaty. Such agreements are informal in the same way that Memorandums of Understanding (MOUs) between states are informal and non-legally binding.[35] In particular, such 'non-legal agreements' are not governed by the rules set out in the Vienna Convention on the Law of Treaties.[36] But treaty-making practice has always proven itself to be very flexible, and the law of treaties 'is by no means incapable of coping with the demands of the twenty-first century'.[37] It may well be that international relations will continue to make excellent use of non-binding yet still meaningful instruments. It may also be the case that the law of international agreements will evolve to impose binding obligations on TNCs that breach the terms of the agreements they sign up to.

A second consideration weighing against allowing TNCs to participate in the making of international agreements is the already unwieldy and cumbersome nature of negotiations between a large number of parties. The December 2009 Copenhagen Climate Conference provided a clear demonstration of the difficulties involved.[38] Adding further parties would simply make the problem worse. Modern communications technology can only go so far in overcoming the difficulties involved. A process of holding local, regional and interest-group series of negotiations first would be one way of getting most of the debate out of the way before higher-level meetings are held to agree on a final text. Holding concurrent series of negotiations between different sub-groups may also work well in some contexts. TNCs could be represented in such negotiations through relevant industry group or other regional/global organization. The International Chamber of Commerce already plays an important role in representing the interests of business in treaty negotiations,[39] and has also been an active participant in talks about promoting corporate social responsibility.[40]

A more serious objection relates to the often highly political nature of international negotiations, particularly in the environmental and human rights area. Allowing the participation of TNCs may not just make their influence more transparent, it may also help to strengthen it. TNCs are, by nature, non-representative and amoral. Giving such organs even more political influence and power than they already possess has inherent dangers. But when those dangers are viewed in a realistic context, it would not be impossible to contain them. For example, there is no reason for TNCs to be involved at all stages and in all aspects of negotiations. Their involvement could be limited to those aspects which directly concern them, and where their input would be valuable. It is at least arguable that bringing TNCs on board when human rights and environmental protection are discussed has greater benefits in terms of generating willing compliance than its risks in terms of undue influence.

There is also the question of TNC access to the key UN organs. So far as the General Assembly and the Security Council are concerned, the often intensely political nature of debates and decision-making within these bodies is a strong argument against giving TNCs access to these forums. But the same arguments do not apply when it comes to giving non-state actors in the international community, including both NGOs and TNCs, limited access to the

ICJ. This involves allowing TNCs (either as of right or on invitation in appropriate cases) to, for example, appear before the specialized Chamber for Environmental Matters established by the ICJ in 1993.[41]

The establishment of a specialized Chamber for Environmental Matters recognized that the special features of environmental law require a specialist body able to accept responsibility both for administrative and judicial functions relating to the environment. The Chamber was periodically reconstituted, consisting of the ICJ president and vice-president, plus five judges elected every three years, from 1993 to 2006. By 2006, however, no state had yet asked for a case to be heard by the Chamber. Cases involving environmental issues, such as *Gabčikova-Nagymaros Project (Hungary/Slovakia)* and *Pulp Mills on the River Uruguay (Argentina v Uruguay)*, were instead submitted to the plenary Bench.[42] So in 2006, the Court decided not to hold elections for a Bench for the Chamber for Environmental Matters, noting that should states parties in future cases request a chamber for a dispute involving environmental law, such a chamber could be constituted under article 26, paragraph 2, of the Statute of the Court.[43] So far as TNCs are concerned, a case could be made for allowing TNCs to present argument before a specialized ICJ Environmental Chamber, at least in those cases where the TNC concerned has been named during proceedings before the plenary Bench and/or where the TNC otherwise has a direct interest in such proceedings.

Non-state access to an internationally recognized forum for resolution of environmental disputes is not a new idea. One recent development in the climate change arena likely to gather momentum following the December 2009 Copenhagen Climate Conference is the establishment of a new International Court for the Environment Coalition ('ICE Coalition'). The ICE Coalition was established by Stephen Hockman QC, former Chairman of the Bar of England and Wales. It aims to 'establish an international adjudicative body for environmental issues that will interpret environmental treaties, sanction both state and non-state actors for violating environmental obligations or causing environmental damage, as well as resolving inter-state environmental disputes'.[44] A similar proposal, for the establishment of a new Climate and Environmental Justice Tribunal, emerged from the World People's Conference on Climate Change and the Rights of Mother Earth, held in Bolivia in April 2010.[45] The proposal was presented to the United Nations by high profile participants at the Conference on 26 April 2010. An important role for such a forum would be to provide a venue for resolving conflicts in the environmental law jurisprudence emerging from other tribunals operating in the international law arena, such as those discussed above. For example, the treaties establishing human rights and trade-related dispute resolution tribunals could be amended to allow for appeals on issues of international environmental law to go to a specialized ICJ chamber or other international environmental law forum.

In early 2010, the ICJ demonstrated that it may be well equipped to take the lead in developing a unified international environmental law jurisprudence. On 20 April 2010, the Court announced its judgment in an environmental dispute between Argentina and Uruguay, concerning Uruguay's authorization for pulp mills on the banks of the Uruguay River forming the border between the two countries. Over strenuous objections from Argentina, Uruguay had authorized construction of one of the largest pulp mills in the world in 2005, which has been converting wood chips into paper pulp on the banks of the Uruguay River since November 2007.[46]

The ICJ ruled that Uruguay was obligated by treaty to notify and consult with Argentina before authorizing the pulp mills and letting construction start; and that Uruguay breached this obligation. The judgment is a significant step forward in the ICJ's jurisprudence on environmental law because the Court recognized environmental impact assessment as a practice that has become an obligation of international law in situations of shared watercourses. The court also fleshed out definitions of 'sustainable development' and 'equitable and reasonable use' in a way which, although confined to the facts of the particular case before it, could potentially be referred to for guidance by future environmental tribunals.[47]

The 2010 *Pulp Mills on the River Uruguay* decision is also important because it represents a break from the ICJ's previously timid approach in the few cases where it has been asked to deal with environmental matters. Examples of this timidity include the following:

- In the 1973 *Nuclear Tests* case brought by New Zealand and Australia to contest the legality of France's atmospheric testing of nuclear weapons in the Pacific, the ICJ refused to deal with the merits of the claim, holding that public statements issued by the French President undertaking to stop the atmospheric weapons testing programme rendered the original complaint redundant.[48] Then in 1995, the Court refused to consider the merits of New Zealand's request for the Court to reconsider the basis for its 1974 dismissal of the claim against France, in light of the resumption by France of underground testing of nuclear weapons in the Pacific.[49]
- In the 1993 *WHO Nuclear Weapons* case, the ICJ refused (by 11 votes to 3) even to attempt an answer to the question put to it : 'In view of the health and environmental effects, would the use of nuclear weapons by a state in war or other armed conflict be a breach of its obligations under international law?'[50]
- More recently, in 2006, the ICJ refused to issue provisional measures requested by Argentina to prevent pollution of the River Uruguay from the pulp mills under construction on the Uruguayan side of the river.

The Court held that Argentina had failed to establish that irreparable damage would be caused to the river environment by the construction of the mills.[51]

The role of the ICJ in the future development of international environmental law remains to be seen. Certainly it can be argued that the role of the Court is not itself to develop international law, but rather to find what the law made by states themselves actually requires. Even accepting this, however, there is surely a great deal of untapped potential for the Court to play a larger role in bringing together a variety of international law decisions and instruments in the environmental arena into a more cohesive jurisprudential whole. The same applies in other areas of international law as well, most notably international human rights law where a similar variety of decisions and instruments exists. Should appeals from the decisions of regional and international human rights tribunals, in appropriate circumstances, lie to the ICJ? What are the arguments for and against creating avenues for the ICJ to act as a global court of appeal, in limited circumstances, from first instance decisions of existing international environmental and human rights forums where no other appeal avenue exists? These questions are explored in Chapter 9.

NOTES

1. Dr Malgosia Fitzmaurice, 'XII. Equipping the court to deal with developing areas of law: environmental law', in C. Peck and R.S. Lee (eds), *Increasing the Effectiveness of the International Court of Justice* (Kluwer Law International, 1997) 410, citing E. Brown Weiss, *In Fairness to Future Generations: International Law, Common Patrimony and International Equity* (1989). See also Tim Stephens, 'Multiple international courts and the "fragmentation" of international environmental law' (2007) 25 *Australian Yearbook of International Law* 227, 234–43.
2. *In Larger Freedom: Towards Development, Security and Human Rights for All, Report of the Secretary-General*, UN GA 59th Sess., UN Doc. A/59/2005 (21 March 2005) para. 212.
3. *Ibid*.
4. Establishment of such Panels is provided for by art. 6 of the Understanding on Rules and Procedures Governing the Settlement of Disputes, Annex II of the Agreement Establishing the World Trade Organization (1994).
5. The International Centre for Settlement of Investment Disputes (ICSID) is an autonomous international institution established under the Convention on the Settlement of Investment Disputes between States and Nationals of Other States, opened for signature 18 March 1965 (entry into force 14 October 1966). ICSID is part of the World Bank group of institutions. By 2010, the ICSID had over 140 states parties. See further http://icsid.worldbank.org/ ICSID.
6. Adopted by the International Commission on International Trade Law on 21 June 1985.
7. Currently under revision by the International Chamber of Commerce. The Task Force on the Revision of the ICC Rules of Arbitration was created in October 2008 with a mandate to determine if amendments to the ICC Rules of Arbitration are useful or necessary, and to make recommendations accordingly. See further Task Force on the Revision of the ICC Rules of Arbitration, www.iccwbo.org/policy/arbitration/index.html?id=28796.
8. International Law Commission, *Report of the Study Group on Fragmentation of*

International Law: Difficulties Arising from the Diversification and Expansion of International Law, UN Doc. A/CN.4/L.676 (2005). See also G. Hafner, 'Pros and cons ensuing from fragmentation of international law' (2004) 25 *Michigan Journal of International Law* 849, and P. Sreenivasa Rao, 'Multiple international judicial forums: a reflection of the growing strength of international law or its fragmentation?' (2004) 25 *Michigan Journal of International Law* 929.

9. Stephens, above n. 1, 228–9.
10. *Ibid.*, especially at 254, noting that 'Since it commenced operation on 1 January 1995, over 335 complaints have been notified to the WTO, with over 100 Panel and Appellate Body reports adopted', making the WTO dispute settlement system 'amongst the most active' worldwide.
11. *Ibid.* 250–2, 270.
12. *Ibid.*
13. *Ibid.*
14. *Ibid.* 270.
15. Article 1 of GATT provides that 'With respect to customs duties and charges of any kind imposed on or in connection with importation or exportation ... any advantage, favour, privilege or immunity granted by any contracting party to any product originating in or destined for any other country shall be accorded immediately and unconditionally to the like product originating in or destined for the territories of all other contracting parties': *The Results of the Uruguay Round of Multilateral Trade Negotiations: The Legal Texts* (GATT Secretariat, Geneva, 1994) 486.
16. Article III of GATT provides, in para. 4, that 'The products of the territory of any contracting party imported into the territory of any other contracting party shall be accorded treatment no less favourable than that accorded to like products of national origin in respect of all laws, regulations, and requirements affecting their internal sale, offering for sale, purchase, transportation, distribution or use': *The Results of the Uruguay Round of Multilateral Trade Negotiations: The Legal Texts* (GATT Secretariat, Geneva, 1994) 490.
17. *Ibid.* 519.
18. Text of SPS Agreement available in *The Results of the Uruguay Round of Multilateral Trade Negotiations: The Legal Texts* (GATT Secretariat, Geneva, 1994) 69–84.
19. WTO Agreement on the Application of Sanitary and Phytosanitary Measures (1994), art. 2(3), available at www.wto.org/english/tratop_e/sps_e/spsagr_e.htm.
20. SPS Agreement, art. 5(5), and see arts 2, 3 and 5 generally.
21. Stephens, above n. 1, 271.
22. For example, in both *Tuna-Dolphin I* and *Tuna Dolphin II*, the United States argued that its import bans on tuna from countries not meeting the fishing regulation requirements of the Marine Mammal Protection Act 1972 were justified under art. XX(b) of GATT as measures necessary to protect animal life. In neither case, however, did the United States seek to make arguments beyond the terms of the GATT itself: *United States – Restrictions on Imports of Tuna*, GATT Doc. DS21/R (1991); *United States – Restrictions on Imports of Tuna*, GATT Doc. DS29/R (1994).
23. Stephens, above n. 1, 270–1.
24. For example, in the *Beef Hormones* case, the EC relied specifically on the precautionary principle as a binding principle of customary international law to justify its import bans imposed on hormone-fed livestock and meat in 1997. The complainant states, United States and Canada, argued that the precautionary principle was only an emerging principle that had not yet crystallized into a binding rule. However, neither the Panels that dealt with the dispute nor the Appellate Body found it necessary to reach a decision on the status of the precautionary principle in international law. Regardless of its status 'under international environmental law', the precautionary principle could not override the express wording of the relevant articles of the SPS Agreement governing assessment of risk. The Appellate Body explained that: 'the Panel itself did not make any definitive finding with regard to the status of the precautionary principle and ... the precautionary principle ... still awaits authoritative formulation ... It is unnecessary, and probably imprudent, for the Appellate Body in this appeal to take a position on this important but abstract question': *European*

Communities – Measures Concerning Meat and Meat Products (Beef Hormones), Report of
the Appellate Body, WTO Doc. WT/DS26/AB/R, WT/DS48/AB/R (1998) para. 123.

25.   For example, in the *Shrimp-Sea Turtles* cases, the Appellate Body found that a US prohibition on the import of shrimp harvested using methods that involved high rates of mortality
for CITES-listed species of sea turtle was 'a means of arbitrary or unjustifiable discrimination' within the meaning of the chapeau of art. XX: *United States – Import Prohibition of
Certain Shrimp and Shrimp Products*, Report of the Appellate Body, WTO Doc.
WT/DS58/AB/R (1998) (*Shrimp-Sea Turtle I*) paras 118–119.

26.   See above nn. 24, 25.

27.   *United States – Restrictions on Imports of Tuna*, GATT Doc. DS21/R (1991); *United States
– Restrictions on Imports of Tuna*, GATT Doc. DS29/R (1994).

28.   Ian Manning, *Complementary Policies for Greenhouse Gas Emission Abatement and their
National and Regional Employment Consequences, A Report for the Australian
Conservation Foundation and Australian Council of Trade Unions*, prepared by the National
Institute of Economic and Industry Research (May 2010) 44–6.

29.   *Ibid.*

30.   Article VI recognizes that dumping, 'by which products of one country are introduced into
the commerce of another country at less than the normal value of the products', is to be
condemned if it 'causes or threatens material injury to an established industry' in the territory of a contracting (GATT member) country. A product is said to be priced at less than
'normal value', *inter alia*, if the price of that product when exported to another country is
less than the cost of production of the product in the country of origin, plus a reasonable
addition for selling cost and profit: GATT, art. VI(1)(b)(ii).

31.   On 21 August 2008, China announced a tax that would classify vehicles by engine size,
taxing larger engine vehicles at a higher rate than vehicles with smaller engines. It was obvious at the time of the announcement that the tax would disproportionately affect imported
vehicles, which have always tended to have larger engines than Chinese-produced vehicles.
The United States and the EU, the two major exporters of large engine vehicles to China,
were therefore expected to file a WTO complaint alleging violation of art. III(2) of GATT in
response to the new tax. For discussion, see Mark Liang, 'Green taxes and the WTO: creating certainty for the future' (2009) 10:1 *Chicago Journal of International Law* 359.

32.   Tony Kaye, 'Jurists condemn Ok Tedi draft bill', *The Age*, 14 September 1995, 5.

33.   Charter of the United Nations, signed on 26 June 1945 (entered into force 24 October 1945),
art. 2(7).

34.   *United Kingdom v Iran (Preliminary Objections)* [1952] ICJ Rep. 89, 112; 19 ILR 507.

35.   Anthony Aust, *Modern Treaty Law and Practice* (2nd edn, CUP, 2007) 18–21.

36.   Vienna Convention on the Law of Treaties, opened for signature on 23 May 1969 (entered
into force on 27 January 1980 in accordance with art. 84(1)) 1155 UNTS 331. By 2007, the
Vienna Convention, which largely codifies the customary law of international treaties, had
108 states parties: Aust, *ibid.*, 6–7.

37.   Aust, above n. 35, 7–8.

38.   Andrew Gilligan, 'Copenhagen climate summit: 1,200 limos, 140 private planes and caviar
wedges', Telegraph.co.uk, 5 December 2009, available at www.telegraph.co.uk/earth/
copenhagen-climate-change-confe/6736517/Copenhagen-climate-summit-1200-limos-140-
private-planes-and-caviar-wedges.html.

39.   See e.g., 'ICC's strategic objectives for multinational trade negotiations to ensure a trade
regime that facilitates competition in telecommunications and e-business', available at
www.iccwbo.org/id504/index.html.

40.   See ICC's Commission on Business in Society, www.iccwbo.org/policy/society/.

41.   Article 26, para. 1 of the ICJ Statute authorizes the Court 'to form one or more chambers,
composed of three or more judges as the Court may determine, for dealing with particular
categories of cases; for example, labour cases and cases relating to transit and communications'. The Chamber for Environmental Matters is the only one to have been established by
the ICJ pursuant to this article: Speech by HE Judge Rosalyn Higgins, President of the
International Court of Justice, to the General Assembly of the United Nations, 26 October
2006, available at www.icj-cij.org/presscom/.

42. Pieter H.F. Bekker, 'Argentina-Uruguay environmental border dispute before the world court', (2006) 10:11 *ASIL Insight* (16 May).
43. Speech by Judge Rosalyn Higgins, 26 October 2006, above n. 41.
44. Debbie Legall, 'Life after Copenhagen: a change of climate' (2010) 64:2 *International Bar News* 41, 42.
45. Laura Guachalla, 'World tribunal would police climate "crimes"', *Science and Development Network* (28 April 2010), available at www.scidev.net/en/news/world-tribunal-would-police-climate-crimes-.html.
46. *Pulp Mills on the River Uruguay (Argentina v Uruguay)*, Judgment of 20 April 2010, available at www.icj-cij.org/docket/files/135/15877.pdf.
47. For further discussion see Cymie R. Payne, *'Pulp Mills on the River Uruguay*: the international court of justice recognizes environmental impact assessment as a duty under international law' (2010) 14:9 *ASIL Insight* (22 April).
48. *Nuclear Tests (New Zealand v France) (Australia v France)*, Judgment of 20 December 1974, available at www.icj-cij.org/docket/files/93/7407.pdf.
49. *Request for an Examination of the Situation in Accordance with the Court's Judgment in the Nuclear Tests Case* [1995] ICJ Rep. 288; ICJ Press Release 541, 'New Zealand's request for examination of issue related to 1974 judgment in Nuclear Tests case is denied by world court' (22 September 1995); both available at www.icj-cij.org/docket/index.
50. *Legality of the Use by a State of Nuclear Weapons in Armed Conflicts*, request for an Advisory Opinion transmitted to the ICJ under a WHO Assembly Resolution of 14 May 1993, available at www.icj-cij.org/dockets/files/93/7648.pdf.
51. *Pulp Mills on the River Uruguay (Argentina v Uruguay)* (2006–2009), documents available at www.icj.cij.org/docket/index, discussed in Peter H.F. Bekker, 'Argentina-Uruguay environmental border dispute before the world court' (2006) 10:11 *ASIL Insight* (16 May).

9. The International Court of Justice as a global court of appeal

In a presentation to the Proceedings of the ICJ/UNITAR Colloquium to Celebrate the 50th Anniversary of the ICJ, Dr Malgosia Fitzmaurice, a prominent international law scholar, identified a need for a system where cases within specialized fields of international law are heard in special courts. Dr Fizmaurice presents a vision of an international legal system where such specialized courts would 'exist within a single, or at least linked, system of international courts, within which the ICJ would maintain an appellate position, enabling it to guide the unified development of general rules of international law'.[1] For example, the Convention establishing the International Centre for Settlement of Investment Disputes (ICSID)[2] – a forum to which TNCs already have access – could be amended so that appeals from ICSID first-instance decisions could be taken to the ICJ in appropriate cases raising questions of unresolved international law.

The benefits of providing for the ICJ to act as a single court of appeal are most obvious in the area of environmental law. It is in this area more than any other that a more unified jurisprudence is needed. Yet similar benefits in the development of other areas of international law jurisprudence are also available. Nor is it a radical new idea to suggest that the ICJ should be able to act as a global court of appeal (in appropriate cases) from decisions made by decentralized international law tribunals. Dr Fitzmaurice, speaking in 1995, envisaged a time when organizations, including non-government organisations and even private organizations could be permitted to access a global system of courts and tribunals, headed by the ICJ. As Dr Fitzmaurice noted, there are a number of ways in which this could readily be achieved with little or no alteration to the existing Statute and Rules of the Court.[3]

A.   ADVISORY OPINIONS AND THE AMICUS CURIAE BRIEF

Dr Fitzmaurice argues that more widespread use of the request for an Advisory Opinion under article 65 of the ICJ Statute, combined with a broadening of the parties who might be entitled to institute such request, is one way of improving the Court's procedures to better deal with increasingly complex issues, including environmental issues, which continue to arise as globalization continues apace.

Article 65 of the Statute of the ICJ provides that the Court may give an Advisory Opinion on any legal question at the request of *whatever body* may be authorized by or in accordance with the United Nations Charter to make such a request. In other words, the advisory jurisdiction of the Court is available to organizations, but not to states. In contrast to judgments in contentious cases, an Advisory Opinion has of itself no binding force – and it is this, perhaps, which has allowed the Advisory Opinion to exert almost unequalled moral and political authority amongst the global community.[4]

At the moment, the right to request an Advisory Opinion is an original right under article 96(1) of the Charter for the UN General Assembly and the Security Council. It is a derivative right (in the sense of being conferred by the General Assembly) for the World Health Organisation (WHO), the Economic and Social Council (ECOSOC), the Trusteeship Council, the International Atomic Energy Agency (IAEA) and other UN organs. I want to argue that access to Advisory Opinion proceedings should be extended to both TNCs and NGOs. This would enable corporations and NGOs to provide evidence in such proceedings, and also allow them to obtain legal guidance on issues of international significance.

The 'floodgates argument' that the ICJ would become overwhelmed should access to it be broadened in this way has to be acknowledged. It can be argued, however, that existing mechanisms already provide sufficient weaponry with which the Court can filter out those requests which are not properly acceded to.

First, there is the rule that the ICJ is never under a duty to give an opinion upon request. It is always open for the Court to refuse on grounds of propriety alone. In fact, the discretionary power to refuse an Advisory Opinion request has only once been utilized, in the *Status of Eastern Carelia* case, when the Permanent Court of International Justice (the ICJ's predecessor) confirmed that an Advisory Opinion should not be given if it would decide the main point of a dispute actually pending between two states.[5] This is because such an approach would violate the important principle of state consent to the Court's jurisdiction.[6] When the World Health Organisation requested an Advisory Opinion on the legality of the use of nuclear weapons, the ICJ declined the request on the basis that it fell outside the WHO's mandate to concern itself with the issues raised by the legal question addressed to the Court.[7] The Court should also refuse to issue an advisory decision whenever the jurisdiction to provide the legal advice requested 'has been allocated elsewhere ... and is not reviewable by the Court'.[8] Thus, in the case of NGOs and/or TNCs, the ICJ would refuse to accede to an

Advisory Opinion request whenever jurisdiction over a matter was more properly exercised by an alternative forum.

The establishment of additional specialized tribunals to which TNCs could have access, and before which TNCs could be brought, would further assist in handling the majority of cases involving the global activities of TNCs without the need for the ICJ to be involved. The ICSID already provides such a forum, and a new tribunal for international environmental law could also play a role. The International Labour Organization (ILO) has a number of mechanisms which could be modified for use in resolving disputes arising from alleged TNC non-compliance with international labour rights standards.

A 'contractual' limitation could be included as part of the relationship agreement between any TNC or international organization and the ICJ to restrict more rigidly the scope of opinions which can be requested. Examples can be found in the form of a fairly standard clause now found in the case of existing UN specialized agencies. For example, a clause in the ILO's relationship agreement with the ICJ allows the organization to request Advisory Opinions only 'on legal questions arising within the scope of its activities other than questions concerning the mutual relationships of the organisation and the United Nations or the specialised agencies'.[9] A similar instrument could be established for NGOs and TNCs that wish to formally accept the jurisdiction of the ICJ as the pre-eminent global juridical organ. Such an instrument could enable signatory organizations and TNCs to access the ICJ Advisory Opinion jurisdiction in return for an undertaking not to seek such access for questions more appropriately decided elsewhere. Requests for advisory assistance from the ICJ could also be precluded (using the discretionary power to refuse advisory requests) where the issue under question has given rise to substantive disputes between sovereign states, or when the political opposition to an opinion is likely to be so severe that the opinion will not be accepted by all or most members of the global community, to the detriment of the Court's reputation and the chances of finding an eventual solution to the problem.[10]

Should the global community not be ready to broaden access to the ICJ's Advisory Opinion jurisdiction in the manner suggested here, a more gradualist approach to allowing NGOs and corporations to be heard could first be trialled under article 66 of the ICJ Statute. Article 66 of the ICJ Statute provides that when a request for an Advisory Opinion is received, all states entitled to appear and 'any international organisation considered likely to be able to furnish information on the question', shall be notified that the Court will be prepared to 'receive ... written statements, or to hear at a public sitting to be held for the purpose, oral statements relating to the question'. A simple amendment to the wording of this article could enable the ICJ to receive information and possibly also arguments from NGOs and private corporations in

Advisory Opinion hearings. Indeed, the Court already has power to permit NGOs to submit information, although early signs of willingness by the Court to receive information from NGOs has not been sustained. For example, in the *International Status of South West Africa* advisory proceedings, the International League for the Rights of Man (ILRM)[11] was accorded permission to make a written statement to the Court, although it failed to do so.[12] Later, however, in the *South West Africa* proceedings of 1970, the ICJ denied permission both to NGOs (including ILRM) and to individuals from the Mandate Territory to submit information. In so doing, the Court effectively denied a voice in the proceedings to those most directly affected.[13]

Again, in the advisory proceedings of the WHO-initiated *Nuclear Weapons* decision, the Court refused, as a matter of discretion, a request to submit information by International Physicians for the Prevention of Nuclear War.[14]

B.   CONTENTIOUS PROCEEDINGS

Public international organizations are even more limited in their ability to access the ICJ in contentious proceedings. This is mainly because of the strict rule, contained in article 34 of the ICJ Statute, that 'Only states may be parties in cases before the Court'. However, article 34 of the Statute does enable the Court to 'request of public international organizations information relevant to cases before it', and also recognizes the right of such organizations to submit such information 'on their own initiative'. The Rules of the ICJ define 'public international organization' as 'an international organization of states'.[15]

Article 43 of the Rules of the ICJ was amended on 29 September 2005 to expressly recognize that public international organizations, and not just states, have the capacity to become, and are in practice, parties to international treaties. Article 43 describes the procedure to be followed in order to implement article 63, paragraph 1 of the Statute of the ICJ. Article 63 of the Statute provides that 'Whenever the construction of a convention to which states other than those concerned in the case are parties is in question, the Registrar shall notify all such states forthwith'. Because article 63 refers only to states, article 43 of the Rules has always, until recently, also referred only to states. Article 43 used to state simply that the Court must consider what directions should be given to the Registrar in cases where the construction of a convention to which states other than those concerned in the case are parties may be in question. Since 29 September 2005, however, paragraph 2 of article 43 now enables, indeed requires, the ICJ to consider whether or not the Registrar should notify any relevant public international organization(s) that is/are party to a convention, the construction of which 'may be in question in a case before the Court'. Paragraph 2 also provides that 'Every public international organization notified by the Registrar may submit its observations on the particular provisions of the convention the construction of which is in question in the case'. The amended paragraph 3 of article 43 then provides that if a public international organiza- tion does furnish observations under paragraph 2, the procedure to be followed is that provided for in article 69, paragraph 2 of the Rules – the procedure used when organizations submit information relevant to a disputed case 'on their own initiative'.

The overall result of the amendment to article 43 of the Rules is to expand the number and kind of cases in which the Registrar will provide notification to public international organizations of disputed cases before the ICJ. Before the amendment, the only situation in which the Registrar was obliged to notify a public international organization of the details of a disputed case was if 'the construction of the constituent instrument of [the] public international organi- zation or of an international convention adopted thereunder' was in question (art. 34(2)). It would seem that public international organizations will now be notified of the details of a disputed case involving the interpretation of a treaty to which the organization is party, even though not adopted under its own constituent instrument. This, in turn, is likely to increase the number and kind of cases in which public international organizations will furnish information relevant to a disputed case before the ICJ *on their own initiative*, as they are entitled to do under article 34(2) of the Court's Statute.[16]

It is precisely the kind of information that can be provided by international organizations and NGOs that is most likely to accurately portray the nature and impact of TNC activities. Submissions from human rights and environ- mental organizations could potentially be of great assistance to the ICJ in this regard, in sharp contrast to the self-interested submissions made by states. For example, Argentina was able to cast considerable doubt upon the integrity and worth of a number of environmental studies relied upon by Uruguay in the Argentina–Uruguay environmental border dispute. In such cases, public inter- est organizations should be permitted to act as 'amicus curiae' and to make independent submissions on questions of relevance before the court. Likewise, in the event that TNCs are named in such submissions, the TNC concerned should be permitted to submit its side of the story. The extra time taken to bring disputed cases to conclusion is a small price to pay for the extra legiti- macy bestowed when all parties concerned feel that they have been properly heard.

In summary, the first important step towards broadening the jurisdiction of the ICJ to include TNCs is for the ICJ to begin to accept more readily the assis- tance of international bodies – something first suggested by Dr Fitzmaurice more than ten years ago.[17] Despite the recent proliferation of international adjudicative tribunals, the ICJ remains the only one competent to decide upon 'any question of international law'. Procedures should therefore be generated to allow it to exercise this competence effectively. The activities of non-state actors are just as likely in today's globalized world to have international legal implications as are the activities of states. What is therefore required is an international court with the procedural powers to hear from, and accord justice to, all actors in the international community – state and non-state alike.

NOTES

1. Malgosia A. Fitzmaurice, 'Equipping the court to deal with developing areas of international law: environmental law' in Connie Peck and Roy S. Lee (eds), *Increasing the Effectiveness of the International Court of Justice, Proceedings of the ICJ/UNITAR Colloquium to Celebrate the 50th Anniversary of the Court* (Kluwer Law International, 1997) 397.
2. Convention on the Settlement of Investment Disputes between States and Nationals of Other States, opened for signature 18 March 1965 (entry into force 14 October 1966).
3. Fitzmaurice, above n. 1.
4. The ICJ judges themselves have spoken of 'the great legal value' and 'moral authority' to be attributed to Advisory Opinions, despite the fact that ordinary Advisory Opinions do not produce the effects of *res judicata*: per Judge Winiarski in his dissenting opinion in *Peace Treaties* [1950] ICJ Rep. 89, 91. See also Judge Azevedo's opinion in the same case, [1950] ICJ Rep. 80. Both cited in Elihu Lauterpacht (ed.), *International Law Reports* (CUP, 1968) vol. 37, 487.
5. Philippe Sands and Pierre Klein (eds), *Bowett's Law of International Institutions* (5th edn, Sweet and Maxwell, 2001) para. 13-050, also noting, however, that 'the effect of this limitation has to be considered in the light of the Court's opinions in the *Peace Treaties* case and the *Namibia* case. In the former the Court emphasised that its opinions are given to the requesting organ, not to the states, that they are not legally binding and that the principle in the *Eastern Carelia* case would not apply where the opinion related to a purely procedural matter and not the substantive issues involved. In the latter case, the Court found that there was no dispute pending between states (as it was bound to do following its decision in 1966 rejecting the *locus standi* of Ethiopa and Liberia) and the *Eastern Carelia* principle could not, therefore, apply to preclude the Court from proceeding to exercise jurisdiction. The phrase used by the Court – that "the reply of the Court, itself an 'organ of the United Nations', represents its participation in the activities of the organisation, and, in principle, should not be refused" – suggests that refusal will come very reluctantly'; para. 13-050 citing [1950] ICJ Rep. 71.
6. *Status of Eastern Carelia* (Advisory Opinion) [1923] PCIJ Ser. B No. 5, 27–9.
7. *Legality of the Use by a State of Nuclear Weapons in Armed Conflict* [1996] ICJ Rep. 66. See, however, the strong dissenting judgment of Judge Weeramantry in that case: available at www.dfat.gov.au/intorgs/icj_nuc/weeram_a.html/.
8. Sands and Klein, above n. 5, para. 13-049.
9. *Ibid.* para. 13-050, citing Relationship Agreement, art. 11.
10. *Ibid.* para. 13-049, noting the unhappy experience of the *Advisory Opinion on Certain Expenses of the UN* [1962] ICJ Rep. 151.
11. Formed in 1941 and known as the International League for Human Rights since 1976, the ILRM was one of the early human rights organizations to be granted UN consultative status. See further Roger S. Clark, 'The International League for Human Rights and South West Africa 1947–1957: The human rights NGO as catalyst in the international legal process' (1981) 3 *Human Rights Quarterly* 101.
12. Prof. Christine Chinken in C. Peck and R.S. Lee (eds), *Increasing the Effectiveness of the International Court of Justice* (Kluwer Law International, 1997) 53, citing Clark, above n. 11.
13. *Legal Consequences for States of the Continued Presence of South Africa in Namibia (South*

West Africa) Notwithstanding Security Council Resolution 276 (Advisory Opinion, 21 June 1970) summary available at www.icj-cij.org/.

14.   *Legality of the Use by a State of Nuclear Weapons in Armed Conflict*, 8 July 1996, General List No. 93 (Advisory Opinion, Preliminary Objections), available at www.icj-cij.org/.

15.   Chinken in Peck and Lee, above n. 12, 53, noting that the Court has continued to restrict the interpretation of 'international organization' to inter-governmental organizations, despite the difference in wording between arts 66(2) and 34(3) of the ICJ Statute. Article 34(3) refers to 'public international organization' while art. 66(2) refers to 'international organization'.

16.   Article 34(2) provides that 'The Court ... may request of public international organizations information relevant to cases before it, *and shall receive such information presented by such organizations on their own initiative'* (emphasis added).

17.   Fitzmaurice, above n. 1, 413–16.

Conclusion

At the Special Representative of the Secretary-General (SSRG)'s regional consultation on the issue of business and human rights held in New Delhi, February 2009,[1] I stood up and asked what would happen if TNCs could sit down at the same table as states when human rights and environmental instruments were negotiated. There were some nods, but many more expressions of doubt and suspicion. There are good reasons for such doubts and suspicions. There are good reasons to remain suspicious of the implications of allowing powerful business a presence at international forums, especially when those forums are debating politically sensitive questions. There is also the whole question of the role and status of NGOs at such forums. Despite the uncertainties, however, working out a role for both TNCs and NGOs in international agreement-making is both necessary and worthwhile.

The main obstacle in the way of bringing TNCs to the same table as other members of the international community is lack of trust. NGOs and smaller, poorer states in particular have become, with good reason, very wary of the influence of TNCs. They would see little benefit in potentially opening up yet another avenue for the exercise of that influence. On the part of TNCs, there is an equally great fear and suspicion of being subjected to further regulation. US firms in particular appear to have a phobia about 'being regulated'.

This book began by examining the nature of the modern corporation both as a legal form and as a social presence. This examination then became the basis for arguing that the increasing global power of multinational firms should bring with it consequent global responsibilities. In a world of global environmental degradation and the increasing international mobility of labour, the problems posed by the activities of global firms need a global solution. International law is the only vehicle currently available for imposing a reasonable and agreed-upon level of responsibility upon TNCs for the consequences of their global-scale activities. The primary focus of this book has thus been on how to overcome the practical and legal obstacles currently in the way of bringing global corporations within the scope of international law. This book has examined the possibility of creating an international framework for recognizing TNCs as both actors in the creation of international law, and as subjects of international law. Making TNCs' actions both visible and accountable under international law will require a collective effort on behalf of all entities, including states, international organizations, NGOs, civil society groups and TNCs themselves.

As Richard Gordon has noted, 'Current trends in international legal scholarship have shifted from a paradigm of state actors working within recognized sources of international law to one that includes networks of domestic regulators that develop and implement best practices or standards on a global basis'.[2] In this book, I have particularly emphasized the role of local courts and local National Contact Points for the OECD Guidelines in developing and implementing best practice for TNC behaviour on a global basis. National unions, business associations and NGOs are also important parts of the 'network of domestic regulators' for implementing such best practice. The work done by this global network of 'domestic regulators' should be reinforced by a global network of international regulators, including national and regional human rights bodies, domestic and regional ILO bodies and possibly also international trade-related dispute resolution bodies. The ICJ should be a final court of appeal from decisions made by these bodies in appropriate circumstances.

Above all, however, what is required in deciding how best to pursue such a vision is what the SRSG has called 'principled pragmatism'.[3] In developing his approach of 'principled pragmatism', the SRSG drew inspiration from the words of Nobel laureate Amartya Sen: 'what moves us', Sen writes, 'is not the realization that the world falls short of being completely just – which few of us expect – but that there are clearly remediable injustices around us which we want to eliminate'.[4] This perspective leads one to inquire how to improve actual lives, Sen continues, rather than to theoretical characterizations of 'perfectly just societies' or institutions, which in any case remain illusory. Accordingly, the United Nations 'Protect, Respect and Remedy' Framework lays the early foundations of a system for better managing the relationship between global business, civil society and the environment. It comprises state duties and corporate responsibilities. It includes preventative and remedial measures. It involves all relevant actors: states, TNCs, affected individuals and communities, civil society and international institutions. It is therefore to be hoped that the early promise and future of such a system is supported by both political will and adequate resources at the highest levels.

NOTES

1. Regional consultation (Asia-Pacific) held by the SRSG on Human Rights and Transnational Corporations and Other Business Enterprises, New Delhi, India, 5–6 February 2009. Summary report available at www.reports-and-materials.org/Report-Ruggie-consultation-Delhi-5-6-Feb-2009.pdf.

2. Richard K. Gordon, 'On the use and abuse of standards for law: global governance and offshore financial centers' (2010) 88 *North Carolina Law Review* 501.
3. John Ruggie, *Business and Human Rights: Further Steps Toward the Operationalization of the 'Protect, Respect and Remedy' Framework*, UN Doc. A/HRC/14/27 (9 April 2010) paras 4-15.
4. Amartya Sen, *The Idea of Justice* (Harvard University Press, 2009) vii, cited in Ruggie, above n. 3, para. 121.

Bibliography

Books and Book Chapters

Alston, Philip (ed.), *Non-State Actors and Human Rights* (Oxford University Press, 2005).

Anderson, Sarah and John Cavanagh, *Top 200: The Rise of Global Corporate Power* (Institute of Policy Studies, Washington, 2000).

Aust, Anthony, *Modern Treaty Law and Practice* (2nd edn, Cambridge University Press, 2007).

Braithwaite, John and Peter Drahos, *Global Business Regulation* (Cambridge University Press, 2000).

Brownlie, Ian (ed.), *Basic Documents in International Law* (4th edn, Oxford University Press, 1995).

Clough, Jonathan and Carmel Mulhern, *The Prosecution of Corporations* (2002).

Crawford, James, *The International Law Commission's Articles on State Responsibility: Introduction, Text and Commentaries* (Cambridge University Press, 2002).

Darrow, Mac, *Between Light and Shadow: The World Bank, the IMF, and International Human Rights* (Hart Publishing, Oxford and Portland, 2003).

Davies, Martin, A.S. Bell and P.L.G. Brereton (eds), *Nygh's Conflict of Laws in Australia* (8th edn, LexisNexis Butterworths, 2010).

de Jonge, Alice, 'Corporate social responsibility: an international law perspective' in Gabriel G.S. Suder (ed.), *International Business under Adversity: A Role in Corporate Responsibility, Conflict Prevention and Peace* (Edward Elgar, 2008).

de Than, Claire and Edwin Shorts, *International Criminal Law and Human Rights* (Sweet and Maxwell, 2003).

Faure, Michael G. and Günter Heine, *Criminal Enforcement of Environmental Law in the European Union* (Kluwer Law International, 2005).

Fawcett, James (ed.), *Declining Jurisdiction in Private International Law* (Clarendon Press, 1995).

Flanagan, Robert J. and William B. Gould, IV (eds), *International Labor Standards: Globalization, Trade, and Public Policy* (Stanford University Press, 2003).

Fukukawa, Kyoko (ed.), *Corporate Social Responsibility in Asia* (Routledge, 2010).

Harris, D.J., *Cases and Materials on International Law* (6th edn, Sweet and Maxwell, 2004).

Heller, Kevin Jon and Markus Dirk Dubber (eds), *The Handbook of Comparative Criminal Law* (Stanford University Press, 2009).

Hepple, Bob A. QC, *Labour Laws and Global Trade* (Hart Publishing, 2005).

Joseph, Sarah, *Corporations and Transnational Human Rights Litigation* (Hart Publishing, 2004).

Kinley, David, *Civilising Globalisation: Human Rights and Global Economy* (Cambridge University Press, 2009).

McBeth, Adam, *International Economic Actors and Human Rights* (Routledge, 2010).

Muchlinkski, Peter T., *Multinational Enterprises and the Law* (2nd edn, Blackwell, 1999).

Muchlinski, Peter T., 'Attempts to extend the accountability of transnational corporations: the role of UNCTAD' in Menno T. Kamminga and Saman Zia-Zarifi (eds), *Liability of Multinational Corporations under International Law* (Kluwer Law International, 2000).

Patel, Raj, *The Value of Nothing: How to Reshape Market Society and Redefine Democracy* (Black Inc., 2009).

Peck, C. and R.S. Lee (eds), *Increasing the Effectiveness of the International Court of Justice*: *Proceedings of the ICJ/UNIITAR Colloquium to Celebrate the 50th Anniversary of the Court* (Kluwer Law International, 1997).

Sachs, Jeffrey D., *The End of Poverty: Economic Possibilities for Our Time* (Penguin Press, 2005).

Sands, Philippe and Pierre Klein (eds), *Bowett's Law of International Institutions* (5th edn, Sweet and Maxwell, 2001).

Sen, Amartya, *The Idea of Justice* (Harvard University Press, 2009).

Stiglitz, Joseph E., *Globalization and its Discontents* (W.W. Norton & Co., 2002).

Stiglitz, Joseph E., *Making Globalization Work* (W.W. Norton & Co., 2006).

Triggs, Gillian, *International Law: Contemporary Principles and Practices* (LexisNexis Butterworths, 2006).

Wei, Yuwa, *Comparative Corporate Governance: A Chinese Perspective* Global Trade and Finance Series, vol. 3 (Kluwer Law International, 2003).

White, Nigel D., *The Law of International Organisations* (2nd edn, Manchester University Press, 2005).

Woods, Ngaire, *The Globalizers: The IMF, the World Bank and their Borrowers* (Cornell Studies in Money, 2006).

Zerk, Jennifer A., *Multinationals and Corporate Social Responsibility* (Cambridge University Press, 2006).

Journals

Acquaah-Gaisie, Gerald, 'Enhancing corporate accountability in Australia' (2000) 11 *Australian Journal of Corporate Law* 139.

Bebchuk, Lucian Arye and Mark J. Roe, 'A theory of path dependence in corporate ownership and governance' (1999) 52 *Stanford Law Review* 127.

Bodansky, David, 'What's so bad about unilateral action to protect the environment' (2000) 11:2 *European Journal of International Law* 339.

Brilmayer, L., 'International law in American courts: a modest proposal' (1991) 100 *Yale Law Journal* 2277.

Bryer, Daniel, 'Liability under the anti-terrorism exception to the Foreign Sovereign Immunity Act: an expanding definition of "Material Support or Resources"' (2007–2008) 11:2 *Gonzaga Journal of International Law* 1.

Burton, Bob, 'PNG law shields BHP from Ok Tedi liabilities' (2002) 6:4 *Mining Monitor* 1.

Campagna, Julie, 'United Nations Norms on the Responsibilities of Transnational Corporations and Other Business Enterprises with regard to Human Rights: the international community asserts binding law on the global rule makers' (2004) 37:4 *John Marshall Law Review* 1205.

Catá-Baker, Larry, 'Multinational corporations, transnational law: the United Nation's Norms on the Responsibilities of Transnational Corporations as harbinger of corporate responsibility in international law' (2005) *Columbia Human Rights Law Review* 287.

Clapham, Andrew, 'Extending international criminal law beyond the individual to corporations and armed opposition groups' (2008) 6:5 *Journal of Criminal Justice* 899.

Clark, Roger S., 'The International League for Human Rights and South West Africa 1947–1957: the human rights NGO as catalyst in the international legal process' (1981) 3 *Human Rights Quarterly* 101.

Clough, Jonathan, 'Not-so innocents abroad: corporate criminal liability for human rights abuses' (2005) 11:1 *Australian Journal of Human Rights* 1.

Clough, Jonathan, 'Punishing the parent: corporate complicity in human rights abuses' (2008) 33:3 *Brooklyn Journal of International Law* 899.

Corbett, Angus, 'Corporate social responsibility: do we have good cause to be sceptical about it?', Michael Whincop Memorial Lecture (2008) 17:1 *Griffith Law Review* 413.

Crook, John R., 'The United Nations Compensation Commission: a new structure to enforce state responsibility' (1993) 87:1 *American Journal of International Law* 144.

Crook, John R. (ed.), 'Contemporary practice of the United States relating to International Law Notes, tentative settlement of ATCA human rights suits against Unocal' (2005) 99 *American Journal of International Law* 497.

Davies, Martin, 'Just (don't) do it: ethics and international trade' (1997) 21 *Melbourne University Law Review* 601.

Davies, Martin, 'Time to change the federal *forum non conveniens* analysis' (2002) 77 *Tulsa Law Review* 309.

Deegan, Craig, 'The legitimising effect of social and environmental disclosures – a theoretical foundation' (2002) 15:3 *Accounting, Auditing and Accountability Journal* 282.

Deva, Surya, 'UN's Human Rights Norms for Transnational Corporations and Other Business Enterprises: an imperfect step in the right direction?' (2004) 10 *ILSA Journal of International and Comparative Law* 493.

Dhooge, Lucien J., 'Due diligence as a defense to corporate liability pursuant to the Alien Tort Statute' (2008) 22:2 *Emory International Law Review* 455.

Duffy, H., 'Towards global responsibility for human rights protection: a sketch of international developments' (2006) 15 *Interights Bulletin* 104.

Egri, Carolyn P. and David A. Ralston, 'Editorial: corporate responsibility: a review of international management research from 1998 to 2007' (2008) 14 *Journal of International Management* 319.

Elagab, Omer Y., 'Coercive economic measures against developing countries' (1992) 41:3 *International and Comparative Law Quarterly* 682.

Field, Andrew, 'Catching the Tasmanian Salmon Laws: how a decade of changing world trade law has tackled environmental protection' (2000) 19:2 *University of Tasmania Law Review* 237.

Florini, Ann, 'Business and global governance: the growing role of corporate codes of conduct' (2003) 21:2 *Brookings Review* 4.

Fortier, L. Yves QC and Stephen L. Drymer, 'Indirect expropriation in the law of international investment: I know it when I see it, or caveat investor' (2005) 13:1 *Asia Pacific Law Review* 79–110.

Fry, James D., 'Coercion, causation and the fictional elements of indirect state responsibility' (2007) 40:3 *Vanderbilt Journal of Transnational Law* 611.

Frynas, Jedrzej George, 'Social and environmental litigation against transnational firms in Africa' (2004) 42:3 *Journal of Modern African Studies* 363.

Gordon, Richard K., 'On the use and abuse of standards for law: global governance and offshore financial centers' (2010) 88 *North Carolina Law Review* 501.

Hafner, G., 'Pros and cons ensuing from fragmentation of international law' (2004) 25 *Michigan Journal of International Law* 849.

Hawke, Neil, 'Corporate environmental crime: why shouldn't directors be liable?' (1997) 13 *London Journal of Canadian Studies* 12.

Henley, Peter, 'Were corporate tsunami donations made legally?' (2005) 30:4 *Alternative Law Journal* 154

Hernstadt, Owen E., 'What's missing from voluntary codes of conduct?' (2000–2001) 16 *The Labor Lawyer* 349.

Horrigan, Bryan, 'Fault lines in the intersection between corporate governance and social responsibility' (2002) 25:2 *UNSW Law Journal* 515.

Joseph, Sarah, 'Gay rights under the ICCPR: Commentary on *Toonen v Australia*' (1994) 13:2 *University of Tasmania Law Review* 392.

Keiserman, Brad J., 'Profits and principles: promoting multinational corporate responsibility by amending the Alien Tort Claims Act' (1998–1999) 48 *Catholic University Law Review* 881.

King, Hugh, 'Corporate accountability under the Alien Tort Claims Act' (2008) 9:2 *Melbourne Journal of International Law* 472.

Kinley, David and Rachel Chambers, 'The UN Human Rights Norms for Corporations: the private implications of public international law' (2006) 6:3 *Human Rights Law Review* 447.

Kinley, David and Justine Nolan, 'Trading and aiding human rights: corporations in the global economy' (2008) 25:4 *Nordic Journal of Human Rights* 353.

Kinley, David, Justine Nolan and Natalie Zerial, 'The politics of corporate social responsibility: reflections on the United Nations Human Rights Norms for Corporations' (2007) 25 *Company and Securities Law Journal* 30.

Kinley, David and Junko Tadaki, 'From talk to walk: the emergence of human rights responsibilities for corporations at international law' (2004) 44 *Virginia Journal of International Law* 931.

Kurtz, Jurgen, 'The Doha Declaration and prospects for investment negotiations in the WTO' (2004) 1:2 *Transnational Dispute Management*.

Kyriakakis, Joanna, 'Corporate criminal liability and the ICC Statute: the comparative law challenge' (2009) 56 *Netherlands International Law Review* 333.

Legall, Debbie, 'Life after Copenhagen: a change of climate' (2010) 64:2 *International Bar News* 41.

Liang, Mark, 'Green taxes and the WTO: creating certainty for the future' (2009) 10:1 *Chicago Journal of International Law* 359.

MacDonald, Ingrid, 'The limits of corporate codes of conduct' (2002) 7:3 *Mining Monitor* 9.

McCorquodale, Robert and P. Simons, 'Responsibility beyond borders: state responsibility for extraterritorial violations by corporations of international human rights law' (2007) 70:4 *Modern Law Review* 598.

Monshipouri, Mahmoud, Claude Welch and Evan Kennedy, 'Multinational corporations and the ethics of global responsibility: problems and possibilities' (2003) 25 *Human Rights Quarterly* 965.

Morvillo, Robert G., and Robert J. Anello, 'Federal RICO Statute: extraterritorial reach and other recent issues', 243:64 *New York Law Journal*, 6 April 2010.

Muchlinkski, Peter, 'Holding multinationals to account: recent developments in English litigation and the company law review' (2002) 23:6 *Company Lawyer* 168.

Murphy, Sean, 'Taking multinational corporate codes of conduct to the next level' (2005) 43 *Columbia Journal of Transnational Law* 389.

Nollkaemper, Andre, 'Concurrence between individual responsibility and state responsibility in international law' (2003) 52 *International and Comparative Law Quarterly* 615.

Noyes, E. and B.D. Smith, 'State responsibility and the principle of joint and several liability' (1988) 13 *Yale Journal of International Law* 225.

O'Neill, Igor, 'Long arm of the law may get longer for companies' (2000) 5:4 *Mining Monitor* 4.

Patten, Dennis M., 'Intra-industry environmental disclosures in response to the Alaskan oil spill: a note on legitimacy theory' (1992) 17:5 *Accounting, Organizations and Society* 471.

Quigley, J., 'Complicity in international law: a new direction in the law of state responsibility' (1986) 57 *British Yearbook of International Law* 77.

Rao, P. Sreenivasa, 'Multiple international judicial forums: a reflection of the growing strength of international law or its fragmentation?' (2004) 25 *Michigan Journal of International Law* 929.

Ratner, Steven R., 'Corporations and human rights: a theory of legal responsibility' (2001) 111 *Yale Law Journal* 443.

Ruggie, John G., 'Business and human rights: the evolving international agenda' (2007) 101:4 *American Journal of International Law* 819.

Sahay, A., 'Environmental reporting by Indian corporations' (2004) 11:1 *Corporate Social Responsibility and Environmental Management* 12.

Sahni, Bindi, 'Limitations of access at the national level: *forum non conveniens*' (2006) 9 *Gonzaga Journal of International Law* 119.

Salama, Aly, 'A note on the impact of environmental performance on financial performance' (2005) 16:3 *Structural Change and Economic Dynamics* 413.

Sarfaty, Galit A., 'Why culture matters in international institutions: the marginality of human rights at the World Bank' (2009) 103:4 *American Journal of International Law* 647.

Schwartz, Juli, '*Saleh v Titan Corporation*: the Alien Tort Claims Act: More Bark than Bite? Procedural limitations and the future of ATCA litigation against corporate contractors' (2006) 37 *Rutgers Law Journal* 867.

Sethi, S. Prakash, 'Standards for corporate conduct in the international arena: challenges and opportunities for multinational corporations' (2002) 107:1 *Business and Society Review* 20.

Shelton, Dinah, 'Righting wrongs: reparations in the Articles on State Responsibility' (2002) 96 *American Journal of International Law* 833.

Sherman, John F. III and Amy K. Lehr, 'Human rights due diligence: is it too risky?' (2010) *CSR Journal* (January) 6.

Spisto, Michael, 'Stakeholder interests in corporate governance: is a new model of governance a change for the better for South Africa? Part 1' (2005) 18 *Australian Journal of Corporate Law* 129.

Spisto, Michael, 'Unitary board or two-tiered board for the new South Africa?' (2005) 1:2 *International Review of Business Research Papers* 84.

Stephens, Beth, 'The amorality of profit: transnational corporations and human rights' (2002) 20 *Berkeley Journal of International Law* 45.

Stephens, Tim, 'Multiple international courts and the "fragmentation" of international environmental law' (2007) 25 *Australian Yearbook of International Law* 227.

Stout, Lynne, 'On the nature of corporations' (2004) 9:2 *Deakin Law Review* 775.

Svantesson, Dan Jerker B., 'In defence of the doctrine of *forum non conveniens*' (2005) 35:2 *Hong Kong Law Journal* 395.

van den Herek, Larissa, 'The difficulties of exercising extraterritorial criminal jurisdiction: the acquittal of a Dutch businessman for crimes committed in Liberia' (2009) 9 *International Criminal Law Review* 211.

Weiler, Todd, '*Metalclad v Mexico* – a play in three parts' (2001) 2 *Journal of World Investment* 685.

Weisbrodt, David and Maria Kruger, 'Norms on the Responsibilities of Transnational Corporations and Other Business Enterprises with regard to Human Rights' (2003) 97 *American Journal of International Law* 901.

Wilder, Martijn and Michael Ahrens, 'Australia's implementation of the OECD Convention on Combating Bribery of Foreign Public Officials in International Business Transactions' (2001) *Melbourne Journal of International Law* 22.

Wilson, Therese, 'The pursuit of profit at all costs: corporate law as a barrier to corporate social responsibility' (2005) 30:6 *Alternative Law Journal* 278.

Young, I.M., 'Responsibility and global labor justice' (2004) 12 *Journal of Political Philosophy* 365.

Court Cases and Tribunal Decisions

A v Australia No 560/1993 (UN Human Rights Committee).

Abdullah v Pfizer 562 F 3d 163 (2nd Cir 2009).

Aldana & Ors v Del Monte Fresh Produce Na Inc & Ors 416 F 3d 1242; 2005 US App LEXIS 13504.

Aleksovski (ICTY Appeals Chamber) 24 March 2000.

Alfred Dunhill of London Inc v Republic of Cuba 425 US 682 (Sup Ct 1976).

American Isuzu Motors Inc v Ntsebeza (No 07-919, affirmed 2008 WL 117862, 76 USLW 3405 (12 May 2008).

Aronson v Lewis 473 A 2d 805 (Del 1984).

Arrest Warrant of 11 April 2000 case *(Congo v Belgium)* (2001) ICJ Reports 3.

AWB Limited v Cole (No 5) [2006] FCA 1234.

Banco Nacional de Cuba v Sabbatino 193 F Supp 375; affirmed 307 F 2d 845.

Banco Nacional de Cuba v Sabbatino 376 US 398 (1964).

Barcelona Traction, Light and Power Co. (Belgium v Spain) (1970) ICJ Reports.

Bayer Polymers Co Ltd v Industrial and Commercial Bank of China, Hong Kong Branch [2000] 1 HKC 805.

Bigio v Coca Cola 239 F 3d 440 (2d Cir 2000).

Bigio v Coca Cola 2005 US Dist LEXIS 1587 (SD NY 3 February 2005).

Bigio v Coca Cola Docket No 05-2426 (2nd Cir 2006).

Blagojevic and Jokic (ICTY Appeals Chamber) 9 May 2007.

Blaskic (ICTY Appeals Chamber) 29 July 2005.

Bodner v Banque Paribas 114 F Supp 2d 117 (FD NY 2000).

Bowoto v Chevron Corp 557 F Supp 2d 1080 (ND Cal 2008).

Bowoto v Chevron Texaco 312 F Supp 2d 1229 (ND Cal 23 March 2004).

Bowoto v Chevron Texaco 2007 WL 2349536 (ND Cal 2007).

Briggs v James Hardie & Co (1989) 16 NSWLR 549.

British American Tobacco (Investments) Ltd v United States, Petition for Writ of Certiorari 08-980 (February 2010).

Burnett v Al Baraka Inv & Dev Corp 349 F Supp 2d 765 (DC SD NY, 18 January 2005).

Canadian Dredge & Dock Co v The Queen [1985] 1 SCR 662 (SCC).

Carlos Abad et al v Bayer Corporation et al No 08-2146 (1 May 2009).

Certain Expenses of the United Nations (Advisory Opinion) (1962) ICJ Reports 151.

Columbian Communities v BHP Billiton, available at http://oecdwatch.org/cases/Case_121.

Connelly v RTZ [1998] AC 854 (HL).

Credit Suisse v United States District Court for the Central Dist of Calif 130 F 3d 1342 (9th Cir, 1997).

Doe v Unocal 963 F Supp 880 (CD Cal 1997).

Doe III v Unocal Corp 70 F Supp 2d 1073 (CD Cal 1999).

Dole Food Co v Patrickson (01-593) 538 US 468 (2003), affirmed No 01-594, 251 F 3d 795.

Dow Jones & Company Inc v Gutnick [2002] HCA 56.

EEOC v Arabian Am Oil 499 US 244 (1991).

European Communities: Measures Concerning Meat and Meat Products, WTO Doc WT/DS26/AB/R, WT/DS48/AB/R (Report of the Appellate Body, 1998).

Filartiga v Peña-Irala 630 F 2d 876 (2d Circuit 1980).
Filler v Hanvit Bank (US Ct of App 2d Cir, 6 August 2004).
Flores v Southern Peru Copper 253 F Supp 2d 510 (FD NY 2002).
Flores v Southern Peru Copper 343 F 3d 140 (2d Cir 2003).
Forti v Suarez-Mason 672 F Supp 1531 (ND Cal 1987).
Furundžija (ICTY Trial Chamber) 10 December 1998.
Gargarimabu v BHP Ok Tedi [2001] VSC 304 (27 August 2001).
Gagarimabu v Broken Hill Proprietary Co. Ltd & Anor [2001] VSC 517 (21 December 2001).
Greenhalgh v Ardene Cinemas [1945] 2 All ER 719.
Grobow v Perot 539 A 2d 180 (Del 1988).
Gulf Oil Corp v Gilbert 330 US 501, 67 S Ct 839 (1947).
Henry v Henry (1996) 185 CLR 571.
Hilton v Guyot 159 US 113 (1895).
Holder v Humanitarian Law Project No 08-1498, US Sup Ct (decided 21 June 2010).
In re Holocaust Victim Assets Litigation 105 F Supp 2d 139 (ED NY 2000).
In re Krauch and Others (IG Farben Trial) (1948) 15 ILR 668.
In re South African Apartheid 617 F Supp 2d 228.
In re South African Apartheid Litigation 633 F Supp 2d 117 (SD NY 2009).
Indonesia-Autos case, Report of the Panel, WTO Doc WT/DS54/R, WT/DS64/R, adopted 23 July 1998.
Industrial Equity v Blackman (1977) CLR 567.
Industrial Pioneer Concrete Services Ltd v Yelnah Pty Ltd (1987) 5 ACLC 467.
International Military Tribunal for the Trial of Major War Criminals, judgment of 1 October 1946, reprinted in (1947) 41 *American Journal of International Law* 172.
Iwanowa v Ford Motor Co F Supp 2d 424 (DNJ 1999).
John Doe et al v Exxon Mobil Corp et al 573 Supp 2d 16 (DDC 2008).
John Doe 1 v Unocal Corp 2002 US App LEXIS 19263 (9th Cir 2002).
Jones v Lipman [1962] 1 All ER 442.
Kadic v Karadzic 70 F 3d 232 (2d Cir 1995).
Khulumani et. al. v Barclay National Bank et. al., filed as Case CV 25952 (ED NY 2002).
Khulumani et al v Barclay National Bank et al, 504 F. 3d 254 (2nd Cir 2007). US Court of Appeals 12 October 2007; available at http://www.ca2.uscourts.gov/.
Khulumani, 2009 WL 960078.
King v Cessna Aircraft (CA 11th Cir, 27 March 2009).
Kinsela v Russel Kinsela Pty Ltd (in Liq) (1986) 4 NSWLR 722.
Koster v American Lumbermens Mutual Casualty Co 330 US 518, 67 S Ct 828 (1947).

Laker Airways v Sabena, Belgian World Airlines 731 F 2d 909 (DC Cir 1984).

Legal Consequences for States of the Continued Presence of South Africa in Namibia (South West Africa) Notwithstanding Security Council Resolution 276 (Advisory Opinion) (1971) ICJ Reports 16.

Legality of the Threat or Use of Nuclear Weapons (Advisory Opinion) (1996) ICJ 226; (1997) 35 ILM 809.

Legality of the Use by a State of Nuclear Weapons in Armed Conflict (Advisory Opinion) (1996) ICJ Reports 66.

Lotus Case, The (France v Turkey) (1927) PCIJ Reports, Series A, No 10.

Lubbe v Cape Plc (No 2) [2000] 4 All ER 268 (HL).

Metalclad Corporation v United Mexican States, ICSID Case No. ARB (AF)/97/1, Award (30 August 2000), reprinted in (2001) ICSID Rev 1 (Arbitrators: Sir Elihu Lauterpacht, Benjamen R. Civilette & Jose Luis Siqueiros), available at http://www.worldbank.org/icsid/cases/mm-award-e.pdf.

North Sea Continental Shelf cases *(FRG v Denmark)*; *(FRG v The Netherlands)* (1969) ICJ Reports 3; 41 ILR 29.

Ntagerura (ICTY Appeals Chamber) 7 July 2006.

Nuclear Tests case (Australia v France) (New Zealand v France) (Judgment of 20 December 1974).

Oceanic Sun Line Special Shipping Co v Fay (1988) 165 CLR 197.

Oppenheimer v Cattermole [1976] AC 249 (HL).

Peoples Department Stores Inc (Trustee of) v Wise (2004) 3 SCR 461, 2004 SCC 68.

Piper Aircraft Co v Reyno 454 US 235 (1981).

Pobal Chill Chomain Community et al vs Shell, available at http://oecdwatch.org/cases/Case_146.

Poller v Columbia Broad Sys Inc (1960) 284 F 2d 599 (DC Circuit).

Presbyterian Church of Sudan v Talisman Energy 244 F Supp 2d 289 (SD NY 2003).

Presbyterian Church of Sudan v Talisman Energy 374 F Supp 2d 331 (SD NY 2005).

Presbyterian Church of Sudan v Talisman Energy 453 F Supp 2d 633 (SD NY 2006).

Presbyterian Church of Sudan v Talisman Energy 582 F 3d 244 (2d Cir 2009).

Prosecutor v Blaskic Case IT-95-14-AR (1997) 101 ILR 698.

Prosecutor v Musema (Judgment) Case No ICTR-96-13-A (27 January 2000).

Prosecutor v Tadic (Judgment) Case No IT-94-1-A (15 July 1999) ICTY Appeals Chamber).

Pulp Mills on the River Uruguay (Argentina v Uruguay) (Judgment of 20 April 2010).

Puttick v Tenon Ltd (2008) 250 ALR 482.

Regie Nationale de Usines Renault SA v Zhang (2002) 210 CLR 491.

Reparations for Injuries Suffered in the Service of the United Nations (Advisory Opinion) (1949) ICJ Reports 174.

Request for an Examination of the Situation in Accordance with the Court's Judgment in the Nuclear Tests case (1995) ICJ Reports 288.

Rodolfo Flores & Ors v Southern Peru Copper Corporation F 2d (2d Circuit 29 August 2003).

Saleh v Titan Corporation 361 F Supp 2d 1152 (SD Cal 2005).

Saleh v Titan Corporation, Case 08-7008, Document 1205678 (11 September 2009).

Salomon v A Salomon & Co Ltd [1897] AC 22.

Sarei & Ors v Rio Tinto plc & Rio Tinto Ltd 221 F Supp 2d 1116 (CD Cal 9 July 2002); 2002 US Dist LEXIS 16235.

Sarei v Rio Tinto 487 F 3d 1193 (9th Cir 2007).

Sarei v Rio Tinto 550 F 3d 822 (9th Cir 2008).

Simić (ICTY Appeals Chamber) 28 November 2006.

Sinaltrainal v Coca Cola 256 F Supp 2d 1345 (SD Fla 2003).

Sosa v Alvarez-Machain 542 US 692 (2004).

Spiliada Maritime Corporation v Cansulex Ltd [1987] AC 460.

Status of Eastern Carelia (Advisory Opinion) (1923) PCIJ Ser B, No 5.

United Kingdom v Iran (Preliminary Objections) (1952) ICJ Reports 89; 19 ILR 507.

United States v Philip Morris 566 F 3d 1095 (DC Cir 2009).

United States: Import Prohibition of Certain Shrimp and Shrimp Products WTO Doc WT/DS58/AB/R (Appellate Body Report, 1998).

United States: Restrictions on Imports of Tuna, GATT Doc DS21/R (1991).

United States: Restrictions on Imports of Tuna, GATT Doc DS29/R (1994).

Vasiljevic (ICTY Appeals Chamber) 25 February 2004.

Vietnam Association for Victims of Agent Orange/ Dioxin v Dow Chemical et. al., United States Court of Appeals, 2nd Circuit, 22 February 2008, available at http://www.ca2.uscourts.gov/.

West Rand Central Gold Mining Co [1905] 2 KB 391.

Wiwa v Shell No 96 Civ 8386, US Dist LEXIS 3293 (SD NY) 22 February 2002.

Wiwa & Ors v Shell Petroleum Development Company of Nigeria Limited, United States Court of Appeals, 2nd Circuit, 3 June 2009; No. 08-1803-cv.

WS Kirkpatrick & Co v Environmental Tectonics Corp International 493 US 400 (1990).

Xuncax v Gramajo 886 F Supp 162 (D Mass 1995).

Zyklon B case Trial of Bruno Tesch and two others, The, Law Reports of Trials of War Criminals, vol 1, 95.

Legislation and Guidelines

Age Discrimination in Employment Act, 29 USC.

Alien Tort Claims Act (1789) 28 USC 1350.

American Restatement (Third) of the Law of Agency.

Australian Securities Commission, Corporate Governance Council, *Principles of Good Corporate Governance and Best Practice Recommendations* (31 March 2003). The Principles were revised in 2006–2007 and on 2 August 2007 the Australian Securities Commission released the *Corporate Governance Principles and Recommendations* (2nd ed, August 2007). Available at the ASX website http://www.asx.com.au/.

Bribery Act (2010) (UK).

Canada Business Corporations Act RSC (1985) c C-44.

Canadian Criminal Code RSC (1985) c-46.

Companies Act 2006 (UK).

Corporations Act 2001 (Cth) (Australia).

Corporations Law (Companies Act) (Japan) enacted in 2005, entered into effect on 1 May 2006; translation available at http://www.japanlaw.info/law/contents.htm.

Criminal Code Act 1995 (Cth) (Australia).

Crimes Against Humanity and War Crimes Act (24 June 2000) (Canada).

Directive 2005/60/EC of the European Parliament and of the Council of 26 October 2005 on the prevention of the use of the financial system for the purpose of money laundering and terrorist financing, as amended by Directive 2008/20/EC of the European Parliament and of the Council of 11 March 2008.

EU, Council Framework Decision 2003/568/JHA of 22 July 2003 on combating corruption in the private sector.

EU, Council Framework Decision 2004/68/JHA of 22 December 2003 on combating the sexual exploitation of children and child pornography.

EU, Council Framework Decision 2005/222/JHA of 24 February 2005 on attacks against information systems.

European Corporate Governance Institute, Index of codes, available at http://www.ecgi.org/codes/all_codes.php.

§1331 Federal question, US Code Title 28, Part IV, Chapter 85.

Foreign Corrupt Practices Act 1977 15 USC §§ 78dd-1 et seq.

Foreign Sovereign Immunities Act 1976 USC Title 28 §§ 1330, 1332, 1391(f), 1441(d) and 1602–1611.

Foreign States Immunities Act 1985 (Cth) (Australia).

Implementation of the Rome Statute of the International Criminal Court Act No 27 of 2002 (18 July 2002) (South Africa).

Indian Penal Code 1860.

International Anti-Bribery and Fair Competition Act 1998 Pub L No 105-366, 112 Stat 3302.

International Crimes Act 2003 (effective 1 October 2003) (The Netherlands).

International Crimes and International Criminal Court Act (2000) (commenced 1 October 2000) (New Zealand).

International Criminal Court Act 2001 (c 17) (United Kingdom).

International Money Laundering Abatement and Financial Anti-Terrorism Act, Title III of the *US Patriot Act* of 2001, Pub L 107-56 (26 October 2001).

Law Concerning Environmental Management (Law No 23 of 1997); as amended by *Law on Environmental Protection and Management* (Law No 32 of 2010) (Indonesia).

Ministry of Corporate Affairs, Government of India, *Corporate Governance Voluntary Guidelines 2009*, available at http://www.mca.gov.in/Ministry/latestnews/CG_Voluntary_Guidelines_24dec2009.pdf.

Ministry of Corporate Affairs, Government of India, *Corporate Social Responsibility Voluntary Guidelines 2009*, available at http://www.mca.gov.in/Ministry/latestnews/CSR_Voluntary_Guidelines_24dec2009.pdf.

Ministry of Enterprise, Energy and Communications (Sweden), *Guidelines for external reporting by state-owned companies* (11 December 2007).

Ministry of Finance Norway, 'Ethical Guidelines for the Government Pension Fund – Global', available at http://www.regjeringen.no/en/dep/fin/Selected-topics/the-government-pension-fund.html?id=1441.

OECD Guidelines for Multinational Enterprises, DAFFE/IME/WPG (2000)15/FINAL (31 October 2001).

OECD, *Implementation Procedures of the OECD Guidelines for Multinational Enterprises* (June 2000).

OECD, *Risk Awareness Tool for Multinational Enterprises in Weak Governance Zones* (2006).

OECD, *2009 Annual Meeting of the National Contact Points, Report by the Chair*, 16–17 June 2009.

OECD Council, *Revised Recommendations of the Council on Bribery in International Business Transactions*, adopted on 23 May 1997 as [C(97)123/FINAL].

OECD Council, *Recommendation of the Council for Further Combating Bribery of Foreign Public Officials in International Business Transactions*, adopted by the Council on 26 November 2009, as amended in 2010 to reflect the inclusion of Annex II, *Good Practice Guidance on Internal Controls, Ethics and Compliance*.

Organized Crime Control Act, Pub L 91-452, 84 Stat 922 (15 October 1970).

PRC Company Law (Amended) [2330/05.10.27] PRC President's Order No 42. Promulgated on 27 October 2005 and effective as of 1 January 2006. Translated in Dec 2005/ Jan 2006 19:10 *China Law and Practice* 21–71.

Racketeer Influenced and Corrupt Organizations Act (RICO) US Code Title 18 Chapter 96 §§ 1961–1968.

Restatement (Third) of the Foreign Relations Law of the United States (2005) §403(1).

South African Truth and Reconciliation Commission, *Final Report 1998 Vol 4*.

Spanish Penal Code.

State Immunity Act RSC 1985, c S-18 (Canada).

Terrorism exception to the jurisdictional immunity of a foreign state USC Title 28 §1605A.

Torture Victim Protection Act of 1991, Pub L 102-256, 12 March 1992, 106 Stat 73. USC Title 28, Part IV, Chapter 85, §1350.

Trans-Tasman Proceedings Act 2010 (Cth) (Australia).

Uniting and Strengthening America by Providing Appropriate Tools Required to Intercept and Obstruct Terrorism Act (US Patriot Act) of 2001.

UN Documents

Crawford, James, *First Report on State Responsibility*, ILC 50th Sess., UN Doc. A/CN.4/490/Add.3 (11 May 1998).

Independent Inquiry Committee, *Final Report of the Independent Inquiry Committee into the United Nations Oil-for-Food Programme* (27 October 2005), available at http://www.iic-offp.org/story27oct05.htm.

International Labour Organization, *Eighth Survey on the Effect given to the Tripartite Declaration of Principles concerning Multinational Enterprises and Social Policy*, '(a) Introduction' and '(b) Summary of reports submitted by governments and by employers' and workers' organizations (Part II)', ILO Governing Body Subcommittee on Multinational Enterprises, 294th Sess. GB. 294/MNE/1/1 (November 2005) and GB. 294/MNE/1/2 (November 2005).

International Labour Organization, *Follow-up to and Promotion of the Tripartite Declaration of Principles concerning Multinational Enterprises and Social Policy*, '(a) Eighth Survey on the effect given to the Tripartite Declaration of Principles concerning Multinational Enterprises and Social Policy: analytical reports of the Working Group on the Reports submitted by governments and by employers' and workers' organizations (Part I)', ILO Governing Body Subcommittee on Multinational Enterprises, 295th Sess., GB. 295/MNE/1/1 (March 2006).

International Law Commission, *Report of the International Law Commission on the Work of its 31st Session*, UN Doc. A/34/10, Supp. No. 10 (1979).

International Law Commission, *Report of the International Law Commission on the Work of its 48th Session*, UN Doc. A/CN.4/SER.A/1996/Add 1 (Part 2) (A/51/10) 1996.

International Law Commission, *Report of the Study Group on Fragmentation of International Law: Difficulties Arising from the Diversification and Expansion of International Law*, UN Doc. A/CN.4/L676 (2005).

Ruggie, John G., *Interim Report of the Secretary-General's Special Representative on the Issue of Human Rights and Transnational Corporations and Other Business Enterprises*, UN Doc. E/CN.4/2006/97 (22 February 2006), available at www2.ohchr.org/english/issues/trans_ corporations/reports.htm.

Ruggie, John G., *Report of the Special Representative of the Secretary-General on the Issue of Human Rights and Transnational Corporations and Other Business Enterprises: Business and Human Rights: Mapping International Standards of Responsibility and Accountability for Corporate Acts*, UN Doc. A/HRC/4/035 (9 February 2007), available at www. business-humanrights.org/Documents/SRSG-report-Human-Rights-Council-19Feb-2007.pdf.

Ruggie, John G., *Protect, Respect and Remedy: A Framework for Business and Human Rights*: *United Nations Human Rights Council Report of the Special Representative of the Secretary-General on the Issue of Human Rights and Transnational Corporations and Other Business Enterprises*, UN Doc. A/HRC/8/5 (7 April 2008).

Ruggie, John G., *Clarifying the Concepts of 'Sphere of Influence' and 'Complicity', Report of the SSRG to the Human Rights Council*, UN Doc. A/HRC/8/16 (15 May 2008).

Ruggie, John G., *Protect, Respect and Remedy: A Framework for Business and Human Rights: Addendum 2: Survey of Scope and Patterns of Alleged Corporate-related Human Rights Abuses, United Nations Human Rights Council Report of the Special Representative of the Secretary-General on the Issue of Human Rights and Transnational Corporations and Other Business Enterprises*, UN Doc. A/HRC/8/5/Add.2 (23 May 2008).

Ruggie, John G., *Business and Human Rights: Towards Operationalizing the "Protect, Respect and Remedy" Framework: Report of the Special Representative of the Secretary-General on the Issue of Human Rights and Transnational Corporations and Other Business Enterprises*, UN Doc. A/HRC/11/13 (22 April 2009).

Ruggie, John G., *Business and Human Rights: Further Steps Towards the Operationalization of the 'Protect, Respect and Remedy' Framework, Report of the Special Representative of the Secretary-General on the Issue of Human Rights and Transnational Corporations and Other Business Enterprises*, GA HRC 14th Sess., UN Doc. A/HRC/14/27 (9 April 2010).

Ruggie, John G., *Report of the Special Representative of the Secretary-General on the Issue of Human Rights and Transnational Corporations and Other Business Enerprises*, UN Doc. A/65/310 (19 August 2010), available at http://www.business-humanrights.org/media/documents/ ruggie-report-to-un-gen-assembly-19-aug-2010.pdf.

Ruggie, John G. and OHCHR, *State Responsibilities to Regulate and Adjudicate Corporate Activities under the United Nations' Core Human Rights Treaties: Individual Report on the International Covenant on Economic, Social and Cultural Rights* (Report No 2, May 2007), available at www.reports-and-materials.org/Ruggie-report-ICESCR-May-2007.pdf.

Ruggie, John G. and OHCRC, *State Responsibilities to Regulate and Adjudicate Corporate Activities under the United Nations' Core Human Rights Treaties: Individual Report on the International Covenant on Civil and Political Rights* (Report No. 3, June 2007), available at www.reports-and-materials.org/Ruggie-report-ICCPR-Jun-2007.pdf.

United Nations Conference on Trade and Development, *World Investment Report 2009*, vol. I, *Transnational Corporations, Agricultural Production and Development*, available at www.unctad.org/en/docs/wir2009_en. pdf).

UNHCR, *Report of the United Nations High Commissioner on Human Rights on the Responsibilities of Transnational Corporations and Related Business Enterprises with regard to Human Rights*, E/CN.4/2005/91 (15 February 2005).

UN Secretary-General, *In Larger Freedom: Towards Development, Security and Human Rights for All, Report of the Secretary-General*, UN GA 59th Sess., UN Doc. A/59/2005 (21 March 2005).

Other Treaties and Declarations

African Charter on Human and Peoples' Rights establishing an African Court of Human and Peoples' Rights, entry into force 25 January 2004, available at http://www.achpr.org/english/_info/court_en.html.

American Convention on Human Rights, entry into force 18 July 1978, available at http://www1.umn.edu/humanrts/iachr/iachr.html.

Australia–New Zealand Agreement on Trans-Tasman Court Proceedings and Regulatory Enforcement, signed on 24 July 2008.

Australia–United States Free Trade Agreement, entry into force 1 January 2005, available at http://www.austrade.gov.au/AUSFTA8310/default.aspx.

Charter of the United Nations, signed on 26 June 1945 at San Francisco, entered into force on 24 October 1945. The *Statute of the International Court of Justice* is an integral part of the *Charter*.

Civil Law Convention on Corruption, CETS No 174, open for signature Strasbourg 4 November 1999 (entered into force 1 November 2003).

Convention Establishing the Multilateral Investment Guarantee Agency, opened for signature 11 October 1985, 1508 UNTS 99 (entered into force 12 April 1988).

Convention concerning Indigenous and Tribal Peoples in Independent Countries, General Conference of the ILO 76th Session, adopted 27 June 1989 (entered into force 5 September 1991).

Convention on the Settlement of Investment Disputes between States and Nationals of Other States, opened for signature 18 March 1965, 575 UNTS 159 (entered into force 14 October 1966).

EU, *Criminal Law Convention on Corruption* CETS No 173.

European Convention for the Protection of Human Rights and Fundamental Freedoms, entry into force 21 September 1970, as amended by various protocols, available at http://www.echr.coe.int/ECHR/en.

International Convention on Civil Liability for Oil Pollution Damage (1969), (1975) UKTS, Cmnd 6183; 973 UNTS 3; (1970) *International Legal Materials* 45. Signed in Brussels 29 November 1969. In force 1975 with 46 parties. Available at http://sedac.ciesin.org/entri/texts/civil.liability.oil. pollution.damage.1969.html. 1992 Protocol available at http://www.jus.uio. no/lm.imo.civil.liability.oil.pollution.damage.protocol.1992/doc.

International Covenant on Civil and Political Rights, opened for signature 16 December 1966, 999 UNTS 171 (entered into force 23 March 1976).

International Covenant on Civil and Political Rights, First Optional Protocol, adopted and opened for signature in New York by GA Res 2200A (XXI) of 16 December 1966; UNTS Vol 999, 171 (entered into force on 23 March 1976).

International Covenant on Economic, Social and Cultural Rights, opened for signature 16 December 1966, UNTS 3 (entered into force 3 January 1976).

North American Agreement on Environmental Cooperation (USA, Canada and Mexico). Entry into force 1 January 1994.

North American Agreement on Labor Cooperation (USA, Canada and Mexico). Entry into force 1 January 1994.

North American Free Trade Agreement (USA, Canada and Mexico). Entry into force 1 January 1994, available at http://www.nafta-sec-alena.org/ en/view.aspx?x=343.

OECD *Convention on Combating Bribery of Foreign Public Officials in International Business Transactions*, opened for signature 17 December 1997 (entered into force 15 February 1999).

Rio Declaration on Environment and Development (UN Conference on Environment and Development, Rio de Janeiro, Brazil, 3–14 June 1992) (1992) ILM 874.

Rome Convention of the International Criminal Court, opened for signature 17 July 1998. UN Doc A/CONF 183/9 (entered into force on 1 July 2002). Available at http://www.icc-cpi.int/Menus/ICC.

UNCITRAL Model Law on International Commercial Arbitration, adopted by the International Commission on International Trade Law on 21 June 1985.

United Nations (1948), The *Universal Declaration of Human Rights*, adopted by the General Assembly on 10 December 1948: UN Doc. A/811.

United Nations (1992), *Rio Declaration on Environment and Development* (1992) *International Legal Materials* 874. Results of the United Nations Conference on Environment and Development, Rio de Janeiro, Brazil, 3–14 June 1992.

United Nations Convention against Corruption, UN Doc A/58/422, GA Res 58/4 (31 October 2003), entered into force 14 December 2005, available at http://www.unodc.org/unodc/en/treaties/CAC/index.html.

United Nations Convention Against Corruption UN Doc A/58/422 (31 October 2003), entered into force 14 December 2005.

United Nations Convention against Transnational Organized Crime, opened for signature on 15 December 2000, UN Doc A/Res/55/25 (entered into force 8 January 2001).

United Nations Convention on the Law of the Sea UN Doc A/Conf 62/122; (1982) 21 ILM 1261 (entered into force 16 November 1994).

United Nations Convention on the Rights of the Child, adopted by the General Assembly and opened for signature on 20 November 1989; entry into force on 2 September 1990. Two optional protocols were adopted on 25 May 2000. The first restricts the involvement of children in military conflicts, and the second prohibits the sale of children, child prostitution and child pornography.

United Nations Convention on the Rights of Persons with Disabilities, adopted by the UN General Assembly on 13 December 2006 and opened for signature on 30 March 2007 (entry into force on 3 May 2008).

United Nations General Assembly, *Charter of the Economic Rights and Duties of States* (GA Res 3281, 29 UN GAOR Supp No 31).

United Nations General Assembly (1969), *Declaration on Social Progress and Development*, GA Res. 2542 (XXIV), 11 December 1969.

United Nations General Assembly, *Declaration on Permanent Sovereignty over Natural Resources*, GA Res 1803 (XVII) GAOR 17th Sess, Supp 17.

United Nations General Assembly, *Declaration against Corruption and Bribery in International Commercial Transactions* GA Res 51/191, UN GAOR, 86th plen mtg, UN Doc A/Res/51/191 (16 December 1996).

United States-Singapore Free Trade Agreement, entry into force 1 January 2004, available at http://www.ustr.gov/trade-agreements/free-trade-agreements/singapore-fta/final-text.

Universal Declaration of Human Rights, adopted by the UN GA 10 December 1948 UN Doc A/811.

Vienna Convention on the Law of Treaties, opened for signature 23 May 1969, 1155 UNTS 331 (entered into force 27 January 1980).

WTO, Agreement on the Application of Sanitary and Phytosanitary Measures

1994, in *The Results of the Uruguay Round of Multilateral Trade Negotiations: The Legal Texts* (GATT Secretariat, 1994).

WTO, *General Agreement on Tariffs and Trade* 1994, in *The Results of the Uruguay Round of Multilateral Trade Negotiations: The Legal Texts* (GATT Secretariat, 1994).

Government Reports and Records

Aurora Institute, *Submission to the Canadian Democracy and Corporate Accountability Commission* (17 June 2001), available at www.aurora.ca/docs/AccountabilityCommSubmission.pdf.

Australian Royal Commission (Cole Commission), *Inquiry into Certain Australian Companies in relation to the UN Oil-for-Food Program* (24 November 2006), available at www.ag.gov.au/agd/www/UNoilforfoodinquiry.nsf.

Corporate Governance Committee, Corporate Governance Forum of Japan, *Corporate Governance Principles: A Japanese View* (30 October 1997).

Corporations and Markets Advisory Committee (Australia), *Report: Social Responsibility of Corporations* (December 2006), available at www.camac.gov.au/camac/camac.nsf/byHeadline/PDFFinal+Reports+2006/$file/CSR_Report.pdf/..

Department of Trade and Industry (United Kingdom), *Modern Company Law for a Competitive Economy: Final Report* (London, 2001).

Filatotchev, Igor , Howard Gospel and Gregory Jackson, *Key Drivers of Good Corporate Governance and the Appropriateness of UK Policy Responses: Final Report to the Department of Trade and Industry* (January 2007).

Jackson, D., *Report of the Special Commission of Inquiry into the Medical Research Fund and Compensation Foundation* (The Cabinet Office, Sydney, 2004).

Joint Committee on Corporations and Financial Services (Parliament of Australia), *Corporate Responsibility: Managing Risk and Creating Value* (21 June 2006).

US Senate Permanent Subcommittee on Investigations, Committee on Governmental Affairs, *Money Laundering and Foreign Corruption: Enforcement and Effectiveness of the PATRIOT Act: Case Study involving Riggs Bank* (released in conjunction with the Permanent Subcommittee on Investigations hearing on 15 July 2004).

Industry and Corporate Documents

IOE, ICC and BIAC, 'Joint views of the International Organisation of Employers, the International Chamber of Commerce and the Business and Industry Advisory Committee to the OECD to the Special Representative of the UN Secretary-General on business and human rights', available at www.reports-and-materials.org/Joint-views-of-IOE-ICC-BIAC-to-Ruggie-Mar-2009.pdf.

International Bar Association, IBA Working Group on the OECD Guidelines, *Response to the OECD Consultation on an Update of the OECD Guidelines for Multinational Enterprises* (31 January 2010).

Minerals Council of Australia, *Enduring Value: The Australian Minerals Energy Framework for Sustainable Development*, available at http://minerals.org.au/environment/code/.

Newmont Mining Corporation, *Annual Report 2008*.

UNOCAL, 'Human rights and Unocal: our position', available at www.unocal.com/responsibility/humanrights/hrl.htm.

News and Press Releases

Amnesty International Press Release, 'Establishing an African Court on Human Rights' (26 January 2004), available at www.scoop.co.nz/.

Anaba, Innocent, 'African Human Rights Court judges sworn in' (17 July 2006), available at http://vanguardngr.com/.

AP DIGITAL, 'ASEAN members finalising rights charter', *The Age* (Melbourne) 19 November 2007, available at www.theage.com.au/news/WORLD/ASEAN-members-finalising-rights-charter/2007/11/19/1195321688151.html.

Bhopal Medical Appeal and Sambhavna Trust, 'What happened in Bhopal', available at www.bhopal.org/whathappened.html.

Boyle, Catherine, 'Portrait: Ken Saro-Wiwa', *The Sunday Times*, 26 May 2009.

Field, Andrew, 'Nuremburg defence doesn't make the grade for suspect corporate citizens', *The Age* (Melbourne), 18 January 2006.

Gilligan, Andrew, 'Copenhagen climate summit: 1,200 limos, 140 private planes and caviar wedges', Telegraph.co.uk, 5 December 2009.

ICJ Press Release 541, 'New Zealand's request for examination of issue related to 1974 judgment in Nuclear Tests case is denied by World Court' (22 September 1995).

Kandar, Fadjar and Deny Sidharta, 'New environmental law: better protection or more legal hurdles for industry', *ALB Legal News*, 31 May 2010.

Kaye, Tony, 'Jurists condemn OK Tedi draft bill', *The Age*, 14 September 1995.

O'Hara, Terence, 'Allbrittons, Riggs to pay victims of Pinochet', *Washington Post*, 26 February 2005.

United Nations Press Release, 'Global leadership group to advise on business and human rights' (22 September 2008).

Other Materials

Bekker, Pieter H.F., 'Argentina-Uruguay environmental border dispute before the World Court' (2006), 10:11 *ASIL Insight* (16 May).

Catá Backer, Larry, *Law at the End of the Day*, Part II, *The OECD, Vedanta, and the Indian Supreme Court: Polycentricity, Transnational Corporate Governance and John Ruggie's Protect/Respect Framework* (3 November 2009), available at http://bit.ly/4Jzc8x.

Cobb, John B. Jr, 'What is free about free trade?' (August 1991), available at www.religion-online.org/showarticle.asp?title=102.

de Schutter, Olivier, 'Extraterritorial jurisdiction as a tool for improving the human rights accountability of transnational corporations' (December 2006), available at www.reports-and-materials.org/Olivier-de-Schutter-report-for-SRSG-re-extraterritorial-jurisdiction-Dec-2006.pdf.

eStandardsForum, *Anti-Money Laundering/ Combating Terrorist Financing Standard: Spain, Report of the Financial Action Task Force* (September 2008).

Fafo Institute and International Peace Academy, *Business and International Crimes: Assessing the Liability of Business Entities for Grave Violations of International Law* (2003), available at www.fafo.no/liabilities/467.pdf.

Global Reporting Initiative, *The 9 UN Global Compact Principles and Selected 2002 GRI Sustainability Reporting Guidelines Core Performance Indicators* (19 January 2004), available at http://commdev.org/content/document/detail/768/.

Global Reporting Initiative, *Synergies between the OECD Guidelines for Multinational Enterprises and the GRI 2002 Sustainability Reporting Guidelines* (June 2004), available at www.oecd.org/dataoecd/25/26/35150230.pdf.

Global Witness, *Undue Diligence: How Banks Do Business with Corrupt Regimes* (March 2009).

Guachalla, Laura, 'World tribunal would police climate "crimes"', *Science and Development Network* (28 April 2010).

Gumley, Wayne, 'Can corporations law reform save the planet: seeking a missing link between environmental and economic policies' in Gerald Acquaah-Gaisie and Val Clulow (eds), *Enhancing Corporate Accountability: Prospects and Challenges Conference Proceedings, 8–9 February 2006, Melbourne* (Monash University, 2006), 239.

Higgins, Judge Rosalyn, *President of the International Court of Justice, Speech to the General Assembly of the United Nations*, 26 October 2006.

International Finance Corporation, *Gaining Ground: Sustainability Investment Rising in Emerging Markets* (March 2009), available at www.ifc.org/ifcext/sustainability.nsf/AttachmentsByTitle/p_SI_Gaining Ground_Mercer/$FILE/270309MIC9080_IFC+rEPORT_web+secured.pdf.

International Finance Corporation, *Sustainable Investment in India 2009* (May 2009), available at www.ifc.org/ifcext/sustainability.nsf/Content/ Publications_Report_SIinIndia.

International Finance Corporation, *Sustainable Investing in Emerging Markets: Unscathed by the Financial Crisis* (July 2009), available at www.ifc.org/ifcext/sustainability.nsf/Content/Publications_Report_SIEmer gingMarkets.

International Finance Corporation and World Resources Institute, *Undisclosed Risk: Corporate Environmental and Social Responsibility in Emerging Asia* (April 2009), available at http://www.ifc.org/ifcext/sustainability.nsf/ Content/Publications_Report_UndisclosedRisk.

International Standards Organisation, *ISO 26000 (CSR Guidance)* (May 2010), available at http://iisd.org/standards/csr.asp.

Jarron, Christine, 'The Social Control of Business' in Gerald Acquaah-Gaisie and Val Clulow (eds), *Enhancing Corporate Accountability: Prospects and Challenges, Conference Proceedings, 8–9 February 2006* (Monash University, 2006), 168.

Kinley, David and Justine Nolan, *Trading and Aiding Human Rights: Corporations in the Global Economy*, Sydney Law School Legal Studies Research Paper No. 08/13 (January 2008), available at http://ssrn.com/abstract=1080427.

Lang, Andrew, *Trade Agreements, Business and Human Rights: The Case of Export Processing Zones*, Working Paper No. 57 of the Corporate Social Responsibility Initiative (April 2010).

Mendes, E.P. and J.A. Clark, 'The five generations of corporate codes of conduct and their impact on corporate social responsibility' (18 September 1996), available at www.uottawa.ca/hrrec/publicat/five.html.

Menéndez, Uria, *Criminal Liability of Companies Survey: Spain* (Lex Mundi, 2008).

Nolan, Justine, 'Corporate accountability and triple bottom line reporting: determining the material issues for disclosure' in Gerald Acquaah-Gaisie and Val Clulow (eds), *Enhancing Corporate Accountability: Prospects and Challenges, Conference Proceedings, 8–9 February 2006* (Monash University, 2006), 196.

Nowak, Manfred, 'A World Court of Human Rights: how would it work?', Speech delivered at the Sydney Ideas Series, University of Sydney, 13 May 2010.

OECD Watch, *Five Years On: A Review of the OECD Guidelines and National Contact Points* (2005).

Payne, Cymie R., 'Pulp Mills on the River Uruguay: the International Court of

Justice recognizes environmental impact assessment as a duty under international law' (2010)14:9 *ASIL Insight* (22 April).

Prince of Wales Business Leaders Forum and Amnesty International, *Human Rights: Is It Any of Your Business?* (2000).

Ramasastry, Anita and Robert C. Thompson, *Commerce, Crime and Conflict: Legal Remedies for Private Sector Liability for Grave Breaches of International Law*: A Survey of Sixteen Countries, Fafo Report 536 (September 2006), available at www.fafo.no/pub/rapp/536/536.pdf.

Richter, Judith, *Holding Corporations Accountable: Corporate Conduct, International Codes and Citizen Action* (UNICEF, 2001).

Sadat, Leila Nadya, 'The International Criminal Court Treaty enters into force' (2002) 86 *ASIL Insight* (April), available at www.asil.org/insights/insigh86.htm.

Social Investment Forum, *Sustainability Reporting in Emerging Markets: An Analysis of the Sustainability Reporting in Selected Sectors of the Seven Emerging Market Countries* (January 2008), available at www.social invest.org/resources/research/documents/SIF-SIRAN-KLDReportfor EMTransparency2008.pdf.

South African Institute for Advanced Constitutional, Public, Human Rights and International Law, *The State Duty to Protect, Corporate Obligations and Extra-territorial Application in the African Regional Human Rights System* (17 February 2010).

Strine, Leo. Lawrence Hamermesh, R. Franklin Balotti and Jeffrey Gorris, *Loyalty's Core Demand: The Defining Role of Good Faith in Corporation Law*, Harvard Joh M. Olin Discussion Paper No. 630, Harvard Law School 3/2009 (26 February 2009), available at http://ssrn.com/abstract=1349971.

Taylor, Phil,'UK Bribery Bill: The long arm of the Crown' February 2010) *China Law and Practice*.

Weiler, Joseph, Antonio Cassese and Marina Spinedi (eds), *International Crimes of States: A Critical Analysis of the ILC's Draft Article 19 on State Responsibility* (Walter de Gruyter, 1989).

Wuerth, Ingrid, 'Wiwa v Shell: the $15.5 Million Settlement' (2009) 13:14 *ASIL Insight* (9 September).

Zerk, Jennifer A., *Extraterritorial Jurisdiction: Lessons for the Business and Human Rights Sphere from Six Regulatory Areas*, Working Paper No. 59 of the Corporate Social Responsibility Initiative (June 2010).

Index